Dying, Death, and Grief in an Online Universe

Carla J. Sofka, PhD, MSW, is an Associate Professor of Social Work at Siena College in Loudonville, NY. She received her PhD degree in 1992 and her Master's in Social Work in 1987 from Washington University in St. Louis. In addition to teaching practice, research, and introductory courses in the Social Work Program at Siena, she offers an elective entitled "Death: The Final Taboo." She has also taught online courses (Palliative Care; Popular Culture and Death) for the Thanatology Program at King's University College at the University of Western Ontario. Her research interests and publications have focused on thanatechnology in death education and grief counseling, "cultural reincarnation," and museums as healing spaces. Working with her local public library, she and her daughter will be creating a blog for young adult readers and their parents that highlights thanatology issues in young adult literature. She has served as an associate editor for *Death Studies* since 1994 and served as president of the Association for Death Education and Counseling from 2011 to 2012.

Illene Noppe Cupit, PhD, received her PhD in 1979 from the Educational Psychology Department of Temple University. Dr. Cupit came to University of Wisconsin Green Bay in January of 1984, where she currently teaches courses in Dying, Death, and Loss; Infancy & Early Childhood; Gender Development; and Developmental Research Methodology. Her research and publications have focused on college student bereavement, adolescent grief, gender issues in death and dying, and death in child care centers. She is an active member of the Association for Death Education and Counseling, where she was editor of *The Forum,* its quarterly publication, and is the president-elect for 2012–2013. At her university, she founded the Institute of Dying, Death, and Bereavement. In addition, she founded and directs Camp Lloyd, a week-long summer day camp for grieving children.

Kathleen R. Gilbert, PhD, CFLE, FT, is a Professor of Family Studies in the Department of Applied Health Science; Executive Associate Dean in the School of Health, Physical Education and Recreation; and is affiliated faculty in the Workshop in Political Theory and Policy Analysis at Indiana University-Bloomington, where she has been on faculty since 1988. She received her PhD in family studies from Purdue University in 1987. Kathleen has taught a variety of graduate and undergraduate courses on the family and family process, including Grief in a Family Context, an online course offered at the graduate and undergraduate level. She has published and spoken on the topics of loss and bereavement within the family, the use of the Internet as a tool for coping with loss, and online modalities for teaching emotionally charged topics. Among her many publications is the edited volume, *The Emotional Nature of Qualitative Research.* She was president of the Association for Death Education and Counseling from 2010 to 2011.

Dying, Death, AND Grief IN AN Online Universe

For Counselors and Educators

Carla J. Sofka, PhD, MSW
Illene Noppe Cupit, PhD
Kathleen R. Gilbert, PhD, CFLE, FT
Editors

SPRINGER PUBLISHING COMPANY
NEW YORK

Springer Publishing Company, LLC
11 West 42nd Street
New York, NY 10036
www.springerpub.com

Acquisitions Editor: Sheri W. Sussman
Composition: The Manila Typesetting Company

ISBN: 978-0-8261-0732-9
E-book ISBN: 978-0-8261-0733-6

12 13 14 15/ 5 4 3 2 1

The author and the publisher of this Work have made every effort to use sources believed to be reliable to provide information that is accurate and compatible with the standards generally accepted at the time of publication. Because medical science is continually advancing, our knowledge base continues to expand. Therefore, as new information becomes available, changes in procedures become necessary. We recommend that the reader always consult current research and specific institutional policies before performing any clinical procedure. The author and publisher shall not be liable for any special, consequential, or exemplary damages resulting, in whole or in part, from the readers' use of, or reliance on, the information contained in this book. The publisher has no responsibility for the persistence or accuracy of URLs for external or third-party Internet websites referred to in this publication and does not guarantee that any content on such websites is, or will remain, accurate or appropriate.

Library of Congress Cataloging-in-Publication Data
Sofka, Carla.
  Dying, death, and grief in an online universe / Carla J. Sofka, Illene Noppe Cupit, Kathleen R. Gilbert. — 1st ed.
    p. cm.
  ISBN 978-0-8261-0732-9
  1. Deat—Psychological aspects. 2. Grief. 3. Virtual reality—Social aspects. 4. Internet—Social aspects. I. Cupit, Illene Noppe. II. Gilbert, Kathleen R. III. Title.
  BF789.D4S66 2012
  155.9'370285—dc23

                                                                    2011050668

Special discounts on bulk quantities of our books are available to corporations, professional associations, pharmaceutical companies, health care organizations, and other qualifying groups.

If you are interested in a custom book, including chapters from more than one of our titles, we can provide that service as well.

For details, please contact:
Special Sales Department, Springer Publishing Company, LLC
11 West 42nd Street, 15th Floor, New York, NY 10036-8002s
Phone: 877-687-7476 or 212-431-4370; Fax: 212-941-7842
Email: sales@springerpub.com

Printed in the United States of America by Gasch Printing

Contents

Contributors

Gail Noppe-Brandon, LMSW, Find Your Voice, New York, New York

Illene Noppe Cupit, PhD, Professor of Human Development, University of Wisconsin, Green Bay, Wisconsin

Joyce Rasdall Dennison, PhD, Clinical Psychologist, Certified Thanatologist, Pointe Claire, Quebec, Canada

Brian de Vries, PhD, Professor of Gerontology, San Francisco State University, San Francisco, California

Louis A. Gamino, PhD, ABPP, FT, Professor of Psychiatry and Behavioral Science, Texas A&M Health Science Center, College of Medicine, Temple, Texas

Eunice Gorman, RN, BSW, MSW, PhD, RSW, Assistant Professor, Department of Interdisciplinary Programs (Thanatology), King's University College at the University of Western Ontario, London, Ontario, Canada

Kathleen R. Gilbert, PhD, CFLE, FT, Professor of Family Studies and Executive Associate Dean in the School of Health, Physical Education and Recreation, Indiana University, Bloomington, Indiana

Lisa D. Hensley, PhD, Associate Professor of Psychology, Texas Wesleyan University, Fort Worth, Texas

Kimberly Hieftje, PhD, Associate Research Scientist, Yale University School of Medicine, Milford, Connecticut

Gloria Horsley, MFC, CHS, PhD, President, Open to Hope Foundation, Palo Alto, California

Heidi Horsley, PsyD, MSW, Executive Director, Open to Hope Foundation and Adjunct Professor, Columbia University, New York, New York

Cendra Lynn, PhD, Director of GriefNet, Ann Arbor, Michigan

Michael Massimi, MSc, BSc, Department of Computer Science, University of Toronto, Toronto, Ontario, Canada

Susan Moldaw, Gerontology Program, San Francisco State University, San Francisco, California

Jane Moore, EdD, FT, Associate Professor, National College of Education, National Louis University, Des Plaines, Illinois

Robert A. Neimeyer, PhD, Professor of Psychology, University of Memphis, Memphis, Tennessee

Antje Rath, MA, LPC, GriefNet, Moab, Utah

Carla J. Sofka, PhD, Associate Professor of Social Work, Siena College, Loudonville, New York

Foreword

Eons ago, Paleolithic men and women would create, using the best of their limited arts and crude tools, drawings on the walls of caves. These drawings told stories of their deceased relatives and friends—the hunts, their experiences, their lives—lest they be forgotten. Later, the pyramids, the richly adorned tombs, the carefully embalmed mummies, and the hieroglyphics would assure that pharaohs were not forgotten, that their memories live long after they died.

Historically, we have always used our foremost technology in the service of the dead. We have used whatever we had at our disposal to mourn, to support, to share memories, and to tell stories. Carla J. Sofka, Illene Noppe Cupit, and Kathleen R. Gilbert, in this new edited work, *Dying, Death, and Grief in an Online Universe*, reaffirm that principle reminding us that this new digital world offers dramatic technologies and creates considerable opportunities to deal with dying, death, and grief.

I have been deeply involved in one such example. For the past near 20 years, the Hospice Foundation of America (HFA) has sponsored an annual program originally by satellite, now via Internet. The origins of the program began when HFA's founding president, Jack Gordon, attended a Hospice Conference. Gordon was deeply impressed with the Conference but was disappointed that fewer than 500 participants shared the benefits. He thought that an educational event organized by satellite television could attract 10 times that number. He was mistaken—nearly 100,000 people participated from all over North America and the Caribbean. Since that first conference, the HFA has now expanded its offerings to not only two national conferences but also web-based broadcasts—including an offering on the effects of technology.

Years ago, authors such as John Gunther or Norman Cousins might later share their experience of an illness, their own or another's, in their writings. Now anyone with access to a computer can share daily blogs on the daily trials and travails experienced. In many ways such as this, the new technology has democratized the process, though the authors are very sensitive to the digital divides that still limit access.

The editors are extraordinarily sensitive to the multiple ways that this new technology has impacted upon the *death system* or the ways that a society organizes behavior around dying and death. Chapters in this book consider a range of topics exploring the effects of the technological revolution.

This includes the ways we mourn. Social networking sites have become particularly important opportunities, especially for adolescents and young adults, to acknowledge grief. Blogs may document journeys with grief. Moreover, there are both private individuals and businesses creating web-based memorial sites. In fact, as the chapters here demonstrate, this gives new meaning to the idea of continuing bonds, as individuals even have opportunities to continue a relationship within the virtual world.

Moreover, it adds a new dimension to funeral rituals where video tributes and online guest books are now common. In addition, many families now stream funerals online, allowing a sense of presence to those who cannot be there in person.

It also affects who we mourn. The Internet offers opportunities to create communities in online relationships, chat rooms, social network sites, and even massively multiplayer online role-playing games. Should death or other forms of loss occur, grief would be a natural result. The Internet cuts both ways.

In addition, the new technologies have potentially therapeutic applications. Beyond the therapeutic value of online memorials, there are other sources of grief support. Information—some accurate, some dated—about grief is readily available online. Other chapters explore the proliferation of online support groups and possibilities for grief counseling online.

Although both can have great value especially in areas where access to qualified counselors or support groups is limited, they also illustrate cultural lag. Cultural lag refers to the fact that certain aspects of the culture such as technology can advance faster than the norms and laws that regulate the use of technology. Online counseling offers such examples. As noted in this book, online counseling creates a variety of ethical and legal issues. Can a counselor licensed in one state offer services to a client in another state? Should issues arise that mandate reporting, to which state should the counselor report?

Issues in counseling are bound to become even more complex as generational divides compound the digital revolution. My informed consent statement now includes issues of texting and other forms of multitasking during sessions, as well as my policies that prohibit befriending clients on Facebook. In both grief groups and with individual clients, I have more extended conversations about confidentiality to generations steeped in the openness and transparency of the web.

Interestingly, the term *brave new world* appears a number of times in the text. The term reminds us that we have entered a new age—there is no going back. Yet, *brave new world* offers a sense of foreboding of the dystopia Huxley once described.

Dying, Death, and Grief in an Online Universe explores all of these issues and others, such as the implications for death education and research offered by the new technologies. *Dying, Death, and Grief in an Online Universe* is bound to be a classic—a fresh look at the ways that technology has already changed the relatively new field of thanatology. And will change it still. The technological revolution is not only irreversible but also fuels itself. The new technology quickens the very pace of change. Each new technological innovation yields others. *Dying, Death, and Grief in an Online Universe* offers an in-depth review that itself will be updated as technology continues to change.

Despite the challenges technology presents to thanatology, we can acknowledge not only its inevitability but also its beauty. Technology now offers opportunities to set up memorials for the person we mourn, free from the constraints of cost, of space, of any rules or regulations. It transcends the limits of space and time. It gives us immediate access. We can visit the site whenever we want or need to, alone or together. We can remember, share, and pass on the stories, even to generations we have not yet met. Although it is a new technology, it fulfills an ancient need.

Kenneth J. Doka, PhD
Professor, The College of New Rochelle
Senior Consultant, The Hospice Foundation of America

Preface

The dynamic field of thanatology encompasses rapidly changing societal practices and views about dying, death, and loss that are increasingly influenced by modern communication technology. This book, written primarily for death educators, clinicians, researchers, students of thanatology, and those interested in how technology interacts with thanatology-related issues, will provide cutting-edge information about thanatechnology, defined as communication technology used in the provision of death education, grief counseling, and thanatology research.

In addition to a broad overview of how the communication technology revolution is impacting individuals who are coping with end-of-life issues, death-related and non-death loss, and grief, implications of the "digital divide," the unequal access to information and communication technologies and one's capacity to make use of the Internet, will be explored. To assist those interested in the use of thanatechnology as a tool for service provision and death education, the book describes online opportunities for social support (online counseling and informal bereavement support as well as the use of social networking sites to cope with loss) and mechanisms for the memorialization and commemoration of loss (virtual funerals, memorials, and cemeteries). The unique issue of disenfranchised grief experienced by online community members will also be explored. The book highlights the use of blogging as a mechanism for storytelling and the use of Skype as a tool for communication during times of crisis and grief. Strategies for providing death education online are described, including lessons learned while teaching college-based online thanatology courses, as well as the use of Internet radio as a resource for providing education and support to the lay public. To assist anyone considering the use of thanatechnology in grief counseling, death education, or research, additional content addresses ethical issues related to the availability and use of this technology and how technology has shaped and changed the ways in which research in thanatology is being conducted. Implications for future consideration regarding the role of thanatechnology in death education, grief counseling, and research will also be presented. Appendices provide guidance regarding the availability of the following resources online: types of informational support, tools to evaluate the integrity of online resources, and ethical standards to guide the provision of online services.

Acknowledgments

Creating this resource about thanatechnology has been a labor of love that would not have been possible without the involvement of many talented and dedicated individuals and the investment of time, energy, and resources by those who have supported our work on this book.

Sheri W. Sussman, our Executive Editor from Springer Publishing, championed this book from her initial conversation with Dr. Sofka about the feasibility of a book on this topic to the completion of the project. We thank her for providing steadfast support, guidance, and patience through the process, including the unanticipated challenges that life placed in each of our paths. Thanks to Katie Corasaniti, our associate editor, for helping us to keep track of all the pieces of the puzzle.

It was a joy to work with our contributing authors. These talented death educators, clinicians, and thanatology researchers (many of whom hold more than one of these roles) have shared their gifts as death professionals and authors, contributing their knowledge and wisdom to this book. Special thanks to Pat Enborg, a freelance writer and Montreal journalist, for her contributions to the appendix on ethics resources and to Katie Berthold and Alexandra Melendez for sharing their technological prowess with Dr. Sofka and helping to identify examples of thanatology-related blogs. Gratitude to Dr. Kristin Vespia, Dr. Regan Gurung, and Dr. Melissa Schnurr for their valuable input on thanatechnological issues to Dr. Cupit.

We are each blessed to work for a college or university that has provided support for this project in many ways. Dr. Sofka would like to thank Siena College, Dean Ralph Blasting, and the Committee on Teaching and Faculty Development for support in the form of release time and financial support (a summer stipend and conference travel support). Dr. Cupit would like to thank her colleagues at the University of Wisconsin-Green Bay for fostering a creative and intellectually demanding environment that has enabled her to grow as a scholar. Thanks go out from Dr. Gilbert to Dr. Mohammad Torabi, who was the Chair of her department and, later, Dean of her school, who provided travel support that facilitated her work on this project.

We are also deeply indebted to our students over the years who have ac-companied us on our shared journey of learning about thanatechnology and kept us on our computer-mediated toes. Students who have participated in our online courses or have helped us to appreciate the ways that technology can be used ef-fectively in death education have truly been some of our greatest teachers.

And last but certainly not least, thanks to our families for their support and patience throughout this project. Dr. Sofka is grateful to her husband, Mike, for sending links to interesting examples of thanatechnology in cyberspace, and her daughter, Gwyn, for assistance with checking references and proofreading. Dr. Cupit wants to thank her children, Alex and Laura, for putting up with a thana-technological mom. Dr. Gilbert would like to thank her husband, Steven, for the help he provided in chapter editing so we could come in as close to our page limit as we did!

Part I

The Communication Technology Revolution and Implications for Thanatology

1

Thanatechnology as a Conduit for Living, Dying, and Grieving in Contemporary Society

*Carla J. Sofka, Illene Noppe Cupit, and
Kathleen R. Gilbert*

In the mid to late 1990s, thanatologists were observing the technological revolution with mixed emotions. On the positive side, it was exciting that thanatology-oriented information was becoming highly visible in this new frontier called *cyberspace*. The popularity of the World Wide Web provided us with new hope that dying-, death-, and grief-related topics could become more widely accessible and perhaps much less "taboo." Because it is always wise to balance optimism with caution, it was equally important for thanatologists to consider the potential challenges and risks that increased exposure to sensitive issues such as suicide and homicide could create. In an attempt to capture the synergy between the topic and the technology that was giving it new exposure, one thanatologist coined the term *thanatechnology*, defined at that time as "technological mechanisms such as interactive videodiscs and computer programs that are used to access information or aid in learning about thanatology topics" (Sofka, 1997, p. 553). In the past 15 years, technology has changed in ways that once were unimaginable. Therefore, the definition of thanatechnology is being broadened in this book to include all types of communication technology that can be used in the provision of death education, grief counseling, and thanatology research.

Technology has expanded the ways that we as a society think about dying, death, and grief. This chapter will explore how the social construction of these concepts and the way that we interact with those around us are currently changing as computer-mediated communication technology evolves. Brief summaries of the chapters in this book will be presented to preview various ways that thanatechnology is being used by death professionals and laypeople alike.

THE IMPACT OF THANATECHNOLOGY ON THE EXPERIENCE OF ILLNESS, DYING, AND GRIEF

It is a universal truth that at some point in each person's life, he or she will experience the death of a significant other. Although dealing with illness, death, and grief is common to all individuals, the emotional, cognitive, and physical reactions that accompany these experiences are now known to be affected by individual differences, culture, and historical period, causing each person's experience to be unique.

In many respects, grief reflects a *social construction of reality* referring to the meanings of death, dying, and grief that evolve from people who share time, place, and culture (Berger & Luckmann, 1966). Although individuals may develop their own unique viewpoint with respect to what death means, sharing that meaning with others helps to validate that perspective and consolidate their concepts about death. For example, in some cultures, the spirit of the deceased continues to be socially active and be a member of the community even after corporeal death (Sweeting & Gilhooly, 1991–1992). Contemporary societies that primarily adhere to a medical model posit that social interaction between the deceased and the living community ends with physical death. However, are these views about death and grief changing as a result of the current technological revolution?

Consider the following examples: In the not too distant past, dying individuals quietly "passed away," often hidden from view in a hospital bed. It is not uncommon, as illustrated by Sofka in Chapter 5, for terminally ill patients to describe their journey in intimate detail to family and friends—perhaps even millions of "strangers"—on a blog. As described in detail by Moore in Chapter 6, patients can interact with friends and family "in person" with the help of thanatechnology. Does an increased level of communication and "openness" about illness, dying, and death have an impact on the dying person and their dying? Does increased access to information lead to a greater understanding of the disease process? Do we seek different treatment options after we (and friends and family) "surf the net" for hopeful solutions? For the survivors, does it change how they cope with the death?

In the virtual world, if you have an online presence in life, you have the issue of your "digital legacy" to consider as you prepare for your eventual death. Hans-Peter Brondmo, the head of social software and services at Nokia in San Francisco, describes one's accumulation of websites, blogs, and personal profiles on various social networking sites (SNSs) and other online records of our existence as one's "digital soul" (Paul-Choudhury, 2011a).

After acknowledging that "We are the first people in history to create vast online records of our lives" (n.p.), Paul-Choudhury (2011a) poses a question worth considering: "How much of it will endure when we are gone?" (n.p.). An individual can preserve the way he or she was prior to illness using images, video, or voiceprint. This can be done with the assistance of a tech-savvy loved one (e.g., see http://kathrynoates.org/, a website created to preserve her memory by her husband, Sumit Paul-Choudhury) or by purchasing the services of a company such as Deathswitch, Digital Legacy, or Virtual Eternity (see Walker, 2011, for detailed information about these companies).

In the new world of thanatechnology, individuals want their "online soul" preserved to create a "technology heirloom" or even to continue to communicate after death (posthumous messaging via e-mails; see http://www.letterfrom beyond.com/). A new cottage industry has evolved to help with the tasks of digital estate planning (e.g., http://www.digitalestateservices.com/), or you can "do it yourself." To learn more, consider consulting *Your Digital Afterlife* by Carroll and Romano (2011), a book that answers the fundamental philosophical (and dare we say thanatechnological) question: "What happens to my digital stuff when I die?" (p. 2). In the contemporary digitized world, getting one's affairs in order may need to include preparing a "digital will."

On the other hand, Mayer-Schonberger (as cited in Walker, 2011) encourages us to consider the possibility that "our tools for recording what we see, experience, and think have become so easy to use, inexpensive and effective that it is easier to let information accumulate in our 'digital external memories' than it is to bother deleting it. Forgetting has become costly and difficult, while remembering is inexpensive and easy" (n.p.). Perhaps, as Walker (2011) notes, "a great deal of our digital expression is simple communication about the present, 'intentionally ephemeral'" (n.p.). Should we bother to preserve it?

With the rising popularity of SNSs came the challenging problems faced by administrators of these sites when deciding upon a policy to handle the death of a member. Boddy (2004) aptly titled his article "Ghosts in the Machines" and described the reactions of family, friends, and even strangers to one deceased social media user's continued online presence as ranging from comfort to unease. Depending upon the policies in place on a particular site and the decisions made by family and friends, the digital legacy of an individual could be removed quickly following an individual's death or may remain indefinitely in cyberspace. Facebook calls this process "memorializing" a deceased user's site, one which allows only confirmed friends to see the profile or locate it during a search.

In addition to that continuing online presence, thanatechnology makes it possible for your digital presence to be experienced in other places affiliated with dying, death, and grief. The *Internet Patrol* (2010) describes the "Serenity Panel," a solar-powered video headstone that allows visitors to the cemetery to celebrate the life of the deceased. Japanese gravestones use two-dimensional bar codes (QR codes), which when scanned by a visitor's cellphone allows the visitor to view photos, videos, and other information about the deceased (Novak, 2008). Family members are able to view a log of who visits with a special device that keeps a record each time the code is scanned. VirtualEternity.com, a company whose motto is "forever made possible," helps a customer to convert the personal data that you provide into an avatar. Walker (2011) describes this "intellitar" as the company calls it "sort of like one of those chatbots that some online companies use for automated but more humanish customer service" (Walker, 2011, n.p.). It is designed to give users the gift of immortality.

With the profiles of the deceased remaining indefinitely on SNSs and sophisticated digital programming that can cause the deceased to once again "come alive at particular places and times through video images or voiceprint," is thanatechnology creating a type of digital immortality? The impact of these decisions and dilemmas regarding "digital ghosts" (Pescovitz, 2011) remain largely unstudied.

The availability of technology has inspired us to create ways to modulate the pain of loss through the use of computers and handheld devices. Mourning rituals now occur online, including virtual funerals and memorial services (see Chapter 10), Facebook tributes (see Chapter 3), and in online communities of bereavement (see Chapters 4, 5, 7, 10, and 11). Although thanatechnology has clearly changed how, when, and where we grieve, has it changed our grief?

The virtual world has truly opened up new issues and questions for the thanatologist. If the shared meanings of death, dying, and grief are culturally defined, would the globalization of technology ultimately create a uniform sense of the meaning of death and the ensuing grieving process? As de Vries and Moldaw argue (see Chapter 10), the World Wide Web has democratized the grief process, challenging who is entitled to grieve and how they should grieve. New online rituals may evolve within the global community, transcending distance, time, reality, diverse beliefs about death, and traditional expectations for the "proper" way to mourn.

THE DEATH SYSTEM AND THANATECHNOLOGY

One way to understand the above-mentioned issues is by reflecting on how societal structures affect and are affected by death. The social construction of death, dying, and grief is intimately tied to *the death system* or the "sociophysical network by which we mediate and express our relationship to mortality" (Kastenbaum, 1972, p. 310). Kastenbaum posited that all societies have a death system that organizes how its citizens think, behave, and structure their death experiences. Death systems vary across culture and historical period, but all have common elements (people, places, times, objects, and symbols) and functions (warning and predictions, prevention of death, care for the dying, disposal of the dead, social consolidation, making sense of the death, and socially approved killing; see Figure 1.1 for definition of the elements and functions of the death system).

With the advent of thanatechnology comes new ways of conceptualizing the elements and functions of the death system. Figure 1.2 presents examples of thanatechnology within the framework of the death system. In a nontechnological world, for example, grief was publically expressed within a proximal community. Death frequently came fast, but communications about the death were slow. Perhaps the ringing of a community bell or the beating of a drum signaled the death. For the most part, the mourner had a personal relationship with the deceased or his or her loved ones and may have directly participated in the care of the deceased when he or she was dying. Many traditional societies have specific roles for the mourner in the funeral process (see, for example,

Figure 1.1 The Death System With "Traditional" Examples

Elements

Element	Description	Example
People	People either directly or indirectly involved with death.	Funeral directors, clergy, florists.
Places	Locations of death.	Cemeteries, funeral homes, battlefields.
Times	The "when" of death.	Anniversaries, periods of mourning and remembrance, times associated with rituals.
Objects	Items associated with death.	Caskets, obituaries, grave markers, guns.
Symbols	Representations of death.	The color black (U.S.), flag at half mast.

Functions

Warnings and predictions	Alerting a citizenry of impending death or factors that could hasten death.	Sirens, labels on smoking materials.
Prevention of death	Social structures and institutions designed to protect its citizenry.	Innoculations, public sanitation, military forces.
Care of the dying	Ways in which a culture treats and ministers to the dying.	Providing comfort measures by family and medical personnel, religious rituals.
Disposal of the dead	Ways in which a society dictates the removal of the body from the living.	Burial, cremation, desiccation.
Social consolidation	The means by which the social group can provide support and remain functional after a death.	Family coming together for the funeral, rules of inheritance, lines of succession.
Making sense of death	Social construction of what death means—finding coherence.	Religious and philosophical views, shared interpretations of the death by families and social groups.
Socially approved killing	Killing that is legal and approved by a society.	Capital punishment, military actions.

Note. Based on Corr, Nabe, and Corr (2009) and Kastenbaum (1972).

Bliatout's 1993 description of a Hmong funeral). In addition, the continuing bond with the deceased was based upon a static representation of that person, even if the survivor's emotions and cognitions regarding the death changed over time

Figure 1.2   A Thanatechnological Death System*

Elements

Element	Description
People	People who are memorialized or use technology to express grief and seek social support. Virtual mourners at a virtual funeral in Second Life or in online gaming communities; participants in an online support group. Virtual grief counselor.
Places	Virtual locations of death, such as online chat rooms; virtual funeral chapel.
Times	Cyberspace is not time bound—communication is instant and may confers digital immortality. Standardized time across multiple time zones for a virtual ritual (Monday Pet Loss Candle Ceremony); "real time" versus "asynchronous" time for chats and meetings.
Objects	Technological platforms (websites, blogs). The paraphernalia associated with technology that can be used to communicate and cope with death, such as cell phones, computers, handheld devices. Virtual candles, virtual flowers left at virtual cemetery plots; memorial or tribute websites.
Symbols	Virtual reality is inherently symbolic as it involves the translation of tangible objects and people into computerized renditions. Emoticons; Txtease / Chatspeak.

Functions

Warnings and predictions	Security options on social network sites that memorialize the deceased; text messages and e-mails warning of potential disasters. Death Clock (predicts date/time of death) Informational support (physical indicators of impending death on hospice sites).
Prevention of death	Suicidal individuals reaching out to friends on Facebook; digital immortality so that in the virtual world one does not die; online medical advice
Care of the dying	Online support groups for the dying and their caregivers. Webinars for hospice workers; posts on sites such as "The Caring Bridge."
Disposal of the dead	Virtual cemeteries; retail websites for funeral goods such as caskets and urns. Internet Memorial Societies.
Social consolidation	Online communication via SNSs such as Facebook and e-mail; virtual funerals, cyberfunerals—actual funerals broadcast by webcams for survivors who cannot come to the funeral (e.g., military personnel); virtual guest books.
Making sense of death	Sharing grief through SNSs (e.g., Facebook); finding coherence through Internet support groups; experiencing online therapy sessions through such venues as Skype; thanatologists conducting Internet-based research. Niche blogs or websites that discuss the meaning of life and death, the afterlife, or spirituality and death.
Socially approved killing	Online games that involve military actions or killing; advocacy sites for the right-to-die, pro-abortion/pro-choice, and the death penalty.

*Note. Elements based on Kastenbaum (1972). Thanatechnological examples generated by the authors.

(Klass, Silverman, & Nickman, 1996). With the advent of technology, this all has changed. "Waiting time" has become irrelevant because of instant computer-mediated communications. Distance can be erased by using thanatechnology and the World Wide Web. Visitors to online memorials and virtual cemeteries do not necessarily know the deceased or the survivors. They may participate in online discussions or leave flowers at a virtual memorial. Survivors may find such communications comforting and seek refuge in a cloak of anonymity. Those who formerly may not have received social support (e.g., grievers of companion animals) may find support in cyberspace from similarly minded others, who, like themselves, are no longer disenfranchised.

Although a great deal of information in this book supports the potential benefits of thanatechnology, there also may be negative consequences. Although it is important to recognize that people have a choice about what they do and do not read online or to what degree they choose to participate in various online activities, it may not always be possible to predict the outcome of these decisions in advance. Pell (2011) describes a powerful example of the joy and pain that results from the "connected life" (and the unpredictability thereof) found in a bereaved father's blog:

"Someday I want to be able to sit and look at her pictures, even watch the videos, and remember how great it was when she was here. For now, accidentally seeing a thumbnail image in a directory on my computer or on my phone or on Flickr or on Facebook is enough to spawn an hours-long cycle of anxiety and depression." (as stated by Daniel Miller, 2010, n.p., capturing his reactions to the links to his deceased daughter via technology).

Unfortunately, the Internet may also attract individuals who seek to inflict psychological harm on others. Two such cases are described in Chapter 4 (the case of Megan Meier, a teenager who committed suicide following incidents of cyberbullying that involved public humiliation) and Chapter 5 (the case of Kaysee, which involves the assumption of a false identity when blogging and the large-scale deception of readers).

In addition, having a virtual presence may complicate the grieving process by rendering the loss as ambiguous. According to Boss (2006), ambiguity occurs when there is no "validation or clarification" (p. 144) to the loss, and the form of ambiguous loss varies dependent upon whether psychological or physical presence is available or absent. In a technological world, might the dead remain both psychologically present and physically (i.e., virtually) present? One possibility arising from such a scenario is that the computer-mediated communications and interactions with a physically deceased but virtually alive loved one may present significant challenges to the formation of a coherent narrative of the loss.

Finally, new rules appear to be evolving that guide how to appropriately and sensitively manage SNSs when someone dies. New culturally appropriate guidelines for proper online behavior when providing social support during times of illness, loss, and grief or when participating in online bereavement rituals are needed. In an article in the *Huffington Post* describing a soon-to-be published book called the *Rules of Netiquette* (in press at the time of the writing of this chapter), Spira (2011) provides some examples of the "social media obituary" that describe the pros and cons of using SNSs to convey information about illness or impending death, to notify others that a death has indeed occurred, or to inform about plans for a funeral or memorial service. One fascinating example described below illustrates how changes in one type of technology, photography, used within the death system at two points in history (19th century as compared with the early 21st century) can be perceived in a totally opposite manner.

In the 1800s, only the wealthy could afford to sit for a session with a photographer. Unlike today when photographs of infants are taken and posted online within hours of birth, it was not common for most families to have portraits of family members, particularly infants and children. The invention of daguerreotypes and carte de visites (types of photographs) made photography more affordable. During times of high infant and child mortality rates, a postmortem photograph taken after the death—may have been the only photograph a family had (Ruby, 1995; *Wikipedia*, 2011). Some families also had a photograph taken of a deceased adult in a coffin surrounded by memorial bouquets, laid out in his or her parlor (ironically now called the *living room*). Examples are posted online at Wikipedia (2011) and can easily be found on YouTube by doing a search on *memento mori* or *post mortem photo*.

Fast forward to modern times of digital photography, cell phones with cameras, and technology that allow us to post photos within seconds of them being snapped. Because postmortem photographs are not common in the 21st century (except perhaps in the case of stillbirth, Brotman, 2010; Saflund, Sjogren, & Wredling, 2004), Spira (2011) raises this question: "What is appropriate to post at the time of death?" She describes the following:

"When I saw a photo of a newly deceased man on his wife's Facebook page, I thought it was disgraceful. It wasn't a photo honoring his memory and life. It was a photograph taken while still in his bed, moments before the ambulance took his body to the mortuary. The visual was not appealing, nor appropriate" (n.p.).

In this case, visitors to a Facebook page are not likely to be expecting (or necessarily desiring) to see a postmortem photograph. Based on the person's age, life circumstances, and loss history, being exposed to such a photograph without preparation may be traumatic. However, are there circumstances under which a photo like this might be requested? Consider someone who is unable to attend the viewing or funeral and has a coping style that benefits from visual confirmation of a death. A postmortem photograph may be a valuable solution; the question remains whether access to that photo should be provided in a very public space. Becoming "thanatosensitive" in how these technologies are used is crucial (Massimi & Charise, 2009).

This Internet-based etiquette of mourning—*mourning netiquette* if you will—has the potential to impact the online community across diverse ethnicities/cultures and religions, presenting a more homogenized social construction of death and grief than what we presently see. Depending upon one's point of view, this can be either a positive or a negative consequence of thanatechnology.

Although the concept of the "death system" as originally described by Kastenbaum (1972) suggests that it is linked to a specific cultural group, a thanatechnological death system, as described in Figure 1.2, may truly be a global one cutting across a number of world views. The meaning making associated with death and grief may take on several new dimensions beyond the traditional individual, family, and cultural/national perspective. In addition to a global perspective, to this we might have to consider a virtual perspective as we modify our social construction of death, dying, and bereavement to encompass another dimension that involves digitized representations and virtual mourning practices that stretch the limits of our imagination.

This book will provide a mere glimpse into the use of thanatechnology by grief counselors, death educators, researchers, and laypeople from a variety of perspectives. Reflective of the field of thanatology, the authors represent a range of disciplinary affiliations: psychology, social work, human development and family relations, nursing, education, and human–computer interaction. Chapters are written in different styles, ranging from the traditional academic style to a more personal or narrative style. To fully understand the implications of thanatechnology, we believe that the issues must be explored through empirical, systematic study using qualitative and quantitative data (Cupit, Chapter 13) and through the "practice wisdom" of those who have been using thanatechnology and observing the impact. Therefore, as described below, research and practice are both represented among the chapters in this book.

SUMMARY OF THE CHAPTERS

Chapter 2 by Kathleen R. Gilbert and Michael Massimi addresses the evolution of the "digital divide" from a division between those who are online and those who are not to several interconnected divides that are associated with the capacity to use technology. Various existing, emergent, and potential future technologies with thanatological applications are discussed. SNSs such as Facebook and MySpace are serving in innovative ways as communities of support. Kimberly Hieftje explores the ways in which SNSs are being used as mechanisms for social support during times of crisis and grief (Chapter 3). Biographic narrative inquiry is used to describe ways in which college students have used SNSs to maintain an ongoing relationship (a continuing bond) with a deceased friend.

A wide range of communication technologies provide opportunities for adolescents and emerging adults to connect in ways that are not possible without the use of this technology. Carla J. Sofka explores the significant benefits and the risks associated with the use of thanatechnology among the net generation (Chapter 4).

Telling one's story is often considered an integral part of coping with crisis and loss. Following a brief history of blogging, Carla J. Sofka (Chapter 5) describes the purposes that blogs serve for individuals dealing with dying, death, and grief.

Computer-mediated communication technology now provides mechanisms for individuals with life-threatening and terminal illness to communicate "in person" using webcams and Skype. A case study by Jane Moore tells one family's story and provides suggestions for incorporating this type of thanatechnology into the services provided by hospice (Chapter 6).

GriefNet.org has served as an Internet community of support for persons dealing with death, grief, and major loss for almost two decades. Cendra Lynn and Antje Rath describe the process of creating and maintaining online support groups for children and adults (Chapter 7). The goals, benefits, and potential drawbacks of these groups are discussed.

Traditional pychotherapeutic sessions involve face-to-contact between a clinician and client. With the advent of online videoconferencing (e.g., Skype) and e-mails, it is now possible to conduct grief therapy online. Robert A. Neimeyer and Gail Noppe-Brandon present a unique account of this "brave new world" as they describe their experiences as therapist (Neimeyer) and client (Noppe-Brandon) who reached across a thousand miles to conduct in-depth grief therapy. This is a personal and professional narrative that highlights the implications of grief therapy in cyberspace (Chapter 8).

As relationships within online communities develop more meaningful roles in the lives of those who participate in them, the potential to experience the loss of these relationships also grows. Following a brief discussion of the relevance of disenfranchised grief in online communities, Lisa D. Hensley presents findings from a survey of individuals who have experienced bereavement in online communities. Suggestions for assisting individuals who are grieving the loss of a relationship from an online community will be provided (Chapter 9).

In the 21st century, one can log on and attend a funeral in cyberspace. Website memorials and virtual cemeteries are some of the ways in which individuals are commemorating the loss of their loved ones. Brian de Vries and Susan Moldaw explore the emerging literature on memorialization on the World Wide Web and the communities that have formed around these memorials. Included is a discussion of the extent to which the funeral industry has used virtual memorialization as well as the consideration of the potential benefits and drawbacks of coping with real-world loss in a virtual environment (Chapter 10).

The availability of the Internet has revolutionized the way that people seek information, and individuals dealing with death, dying, and grief will find a plethora of resources for use in dealing with these life events and challenges. Open to Hope is an online resource center dedicated to helping people find hope again after loss. Gloria and Heidi Horsley describe the Open to Hope Foundation's use of web-based resources and Internet radio as tools for providing education and support to the lay public (Chapter 11).

Chapters 12 and 13 address how death education may be effectively implemented online. In Chapter 12, Illene Noppe Cupit, Carla J. Sofka, and Kathleen R. Gilbert juxtapose what they have learned about death education with the evolving evidence-based strategies of online instruction. From reading this chapter, death educators considering entering thanatechnological pedagogy can benefit from the experiences of colleagues who have worked hard at best course design for students in cyberspace. One of the central concerns for death educators who teach online is creating a safe environment for students to discuss sensitive death-related topics. Eunice Gorman (Chapter 13) describes strategies for building community and safety in the online classroom, including course "netiquette," that is, rules for appropriate behavior in the virtual classroom. Also discussed are ways of building community in the class and facilitating interaction that is appropriately sensitive to the unique mix of students enrolled in each class.

Technology is also being used to conduct thanatology research. Illene Noppe Cupit explores the similarities and differences in conducting thanatological research via computer-mediated communications. To guide researchers in the translation of thanatological research into a technological environment, flowcharts representing decision-making processes for quantitative and qualitative research are presented. Also considered are strategies for collecting online data and aspects of research ethics that are unique to thanatechnological research (Chapter 14).

With new applications of technology come new responsibilities to anticipate and manage any consequences that may arise. The concluding chapters will identify the ethical implications of using communication technologies in the field of thanatology and will summarize the major themes that have emerged out of this examination of thanatechnology.

The provision of grief counseling services online involves a range of ethical issues and challenges. Louis A. Gamino summarizes the types of technology being used to provide Internet counseling, outlines the advantages and disadvantages of online service delivery, and describes the unique ethical challenges inherent in Internet counseling (Chapter 15).

The final chapter (Chapter 16) is intended to summarize and digest what we have learned in this book about our contemporary thanatechnological death system. Upon review of the diverse writings of our contributors, several overarching themes were discerned. We conclude by presenting the implications of thanatechnology for practitioners, researchers, and educators and speculate as to what the future holds for dying, death, and grief in an online universe.

Two appendices have also been included. Appendix A, prepared by Carla J. Sofka, presents a typology of thanatology-related websites. Because of the importance of critically evaluating the reliability and validity of information on these sites, resources to facilitate information literacy and the evaluation of thanatology-related websites are included.

Appendix B, prepared by Carla J. Sofka, Joyce Rasdall Dennison, and Louis A. Gamino, provides material to support the content on ethical issues in online service provision discussed in Chapter 15. Professional organizations and associations are beginning to develop technology-related guidelines to facilitate ethical practice when providing online services. This appendix provides a summary of the content addressed in these ethical codes, steering a reader to the appropriate resources of six organizations and associations. Tools to evaluate website compliance with ethical guidelines and ethical online practice are included.

In 2006, *Time Magazine* announced an unusual choice for their "person of the year." Although encouraging readers to reflect upon the year from an atypical point of view (considering someone other than a famous leader, entertainer, or business mogul), they stated:

. . . look at 2006 through a different lens and you'll see another story, one that isn't about conflict or great men. It's a story about community and collaboration on a scale never seen before. It's about the cosmic compendium of knowledge Wikipedia and the million-channel people's network YouTube and the online metropolis MySpace. It's about wresting power from the few and helping one another for nothing and how that will not only change the world, but also change the way the world changes (Grossman, 2006, n.p.).

We believe that thanatechnology is changing the way the world deals with dying, death, and grief, creating a thanatechnological death system that is, most likely, evolving as we write (and while you subsequently read) this book. We hope that the information in this book will contribute to the ability of death educators, grief counselors, and thanatology researchers to use the wealth of thanatechnology resources that are available to the fullest potential in an informed, responsible, and ethical manner.

We are excited that you are reading this book because that means that you may already be doing fascinating work with thanatechnology and can also contribute to the knowledge base that is evolving about this subject. We look forward to learning from you and would love to hear your stories and observations about thanatology in an online universe.

REFERENCES

Berger, P. L., & Luckmann, T. (1966). *The social construction of reality*. Garden City: NY: Doubleday.

Bliatout, B. T. (1993). Hmong death customs: Traditional and acculturated. In D. P. Irish, K. F. Lundquist, & V. J. Nelsen (Eds.), *Variations in dying, death, and grief* (pp. 79–100). Washington, DC: Taylor & Francis.

Boddy, R. (2004, June 30). Ghosts in the machines. What happens to your online self when you die? *Baltimore City Paper* (online). Retrieved August 5, 2011, from http://www2.city paper.com/news/story.asp?id=8182

Boss, P. (2006). *Loss, trauma, and resilience. Therapeutic worth with ambiguous loss*. New York, NY: W.W. Norton & Company.

Brotman, B. (2010, April 11). Bereavement photographer offers grieving parents a priceless gift. Chicago Tribune. Retrieved from http://articles.chicagotribune.com/2010-04-11/news/ct-news-bereavement-photographer-20100411_1_priceless-gift-baby-shop-life-support

Carroll, E., & Romano, J. (2011). *Your digital afterlife: When Facebook, Flckr, and Twitter are your estate, what's your legacy?* Berkeley, CA: New Riders.

Corr, C. A., Nabe, C. M., & Corr, D. M. (2009). *Death & dying, life & living* (6th ed.). Belmont, CA: Wadsworth.

Grossman, L. (2006, December 25). You—yes, you—are *Time's* person of the year. *Time* (online archive). Retrieved August 1, 2011, from http://www.time.com/time/magazine/article/0,9171,1570810,00.html

Internet Patrol. (2010, July 29). Video headstone – Vidstone's serenity panel celebrates life, after death. Retrieved August 5, 2011, from http://www.theinternetpatrol.com/video-headstone-vidstones-serenity-panel-celebrates-life-after-death/

Kastenbaum, R. (1972). On the future of death: Some images and options. *Omega, 3,* 306–318.

Klass, D., Silverman, P. R., & Nickman, S. L. (Eds.). (1996). *Continuing bonds: New understandings of grief.* Washington, DC: Taylor & Francis.

Massimi, M., & Charise, A. (2009). Dying, death, and mortality: Towards thanatosensitivity in HCI. In *Proceedings of the CHI 2009 Extended Abstracts* (pp. 2459–2468). Retrieved August 10, 2011, from http://www.dgp.toronto.edu/~mikem/pubs/MassimiCharise-CHI2009.pdf

Miller, D. (2010, November 29). The infinitely connected triggers of her memory and the dumb machines of the technopathocracy. Retrieved August 5, 2011, from http://2010.danielsjourney.com/2010/11/29/connected.html

Novak, A. (2008, March 23). Japanese gravestones memorialize the dead with QR codes. *Underwire* (online). Retrieved August 5, 2011, from http://www.wired.com/underwire/2008/03/japanese-graves/

Paul-Choudhury, S. (2011a, May 2). Digital legacy: The fate of your online soul. *New Scientist,* Issue 2809. Retrieved August 1, 2011, from http://www.newscientist.com/article/mg21028091.400-digital-legacy-the-fate-of-your-online-soul.html

Paul-Choudhury, S. (2011b, May 6). Digital legacy: Respecting the digital dead. *New Scientist.* Retrieved August 1, 2011, from http://www.newscientist.com/article/dn20445-digital-legacy-respecting-the-digital-dead.html

Pell, D. (2011, January 7). *Haunted by real life on the Internet. All tech considered commentary.* Retrieved August 5, 2011, from http://www.npr.org/blogs/alltechconsidered/2011/01/07/132715065/haunted-by-real-life-on-the-internet?

Pescovitz, D. (2011, January 12). *Death and digital ghosts.* Retrieved August, 2011 from http://boingboing.net/2011/01/12/death-and-digital-gh.html

Ruby, J. (1995). *Secure the shadow: Death and photography in America.* Boston, MA: MIT Press.

Saflund, K., Sjogren, B., & Wredling, R. (2004). The role of caregivers after a stillbirth: Views and experiences of parents. *Birth, 31*(2), 132–137.

Sofka, C. J. (1997). Social support "internetworks," caskets for sale, and more: Thanatology and the information superhighway. *Death Studies, 21*(6), 553–574.

Spira, J. (2011, August 23). The social media obituary. *The Huffington Post,* Retrieved December 19, 2011 from http://www.huffingtonpost.com/julie-spira/the-social-media-obituary_b_859659.html

Sweeting, H. N., & Gilhooly, M. L. M. (1991–1992). Doctor, am I dead? A review of social death in modern societies. *Omega, 24,* 251–269.

Walker, R. (2011, January 5). Cyberspace when you're dead. *New York Times Magazine,* Retrieved August, 2011 from http://www.nytimes.com/2011/01/09/magazine/09Immortality-t.html?pagewanted=all

Wandel, T. L. (2008). Colleges and universities want to be your friend: Communicating via online social networking. *Planning for Higher Education, 37*(1), 35–48.

Wikipedia. (2011). Post-mortem photography. Retrieved August 1, 2011, from http://en.wikipedia.org/wiki/Post-mortem_photography

2

From Digital Divide to Digital Immortality: Thanatechnology at the Turn of the 21st Century

Kathleen R. Gilbert and Michael Massimi

Technology is rapidly becoming a mainstay of much of what we do in modern life, and we often are not aware of how pervasive our use of technology is and how rapidly things change on the technological front. As the prevalence of digital technologies continues to increase in the industrialized world, there are more opportunities than ever before for information and communication technologies (ICTs) to support the dying and bereaved. Capacity for communication across boundaries and borders is expanding, with the potential for a comingling of public and private, as well as physical reality with virtual. We are seeing increasing use of the Internet for a variety of thanatology-related purposes, many of which are addressed in later chapters in this text. Technology can bring people together for social support (Oliveri, 2003), provide information, and offer a venue for conducting grief work such as telling stories or building digital memorials (Brubaker & Vertesi, 2010; Foong & Kera, 2008). Even in the absence of a desktop or a laptop computer, third-generation mobile phones, like the iPhone, can help people connect with and draw on their social networks, create and share content, and achieve a sense of connection and safety. Technology can also provide a venue for maintaining continuing relationships with the deceased through a variety of resources, such as memorial websites and such social networking sites as Facebook.

Although the promises of technology are certainly reason for excitement, we must bear in mind that access to these resources is not evenly available throughout the world, or even throughout industrialized nations. Norris describes the *digital divide*, a concept we will explore in more depth later in this chapter, as consisting of three parts:

> The *global divide* refers to the divergence of Internet access between industrialized and developing societies. The *social divide* concerns the gap between

information rich and poor in each nation. And finally within the online community, the *democratic divide* signifies the difference between those who do, and do not, use the panoply of digital resources to engage, mobilize, and participate in public life (Norris, 2001, p. 4).

This view of the digital divide addresses access to ICT and its many resources. Individuals with the capacity to access the Internet knowledgeably and regularly have the opportunity to find information and social support in abundance on websites, discussion groups, and e-mail lists. They are able to enjoy these resources consistently and over long periods. Of particular note, it may be possible to derive benefit from normalizing one's grief through continued communication with peer support groups or mental health professionals.

At the same time, progress in hardware and software development results in new and emerging forms of technology. The appearance of smaller, faster, and more powerful devices on the consumer marketplace challenges conventional notions of what "being online" means. For example, third-generation mobile phones have made some individuals "always on" and introduced a new level of access to the Internet that did not exist a decade earlier. In addition, "information appliances" such as digital picture frames or web-based television devices are changing how information is presented and accessed in the home (Norman, 1998).

In this chapter, we describe how a variety of factors affect access to digital resources such as the Internet and how this impacts the dying and the bereaved. We begin by tracing the emergence of the digital divide, including its evolution from a dichotomy between the "haves" and "have-nots" to a more nuanced view of several interconnected divides, all of which result in differential use of technology. We also discuss how this affects the use of technology tools in the context of loss. We then explore emergent "ubiquitous computing" technologies, which may lead to even greater disparity among users, but may also provide opportunities for communication and remembrance. We show how people inherit computers from others, and how inheriting older computers is emblematic of a form of divide. Finally, we conclude with some ideas about possible directions of future technologies.

THE EMERGENCE OF THE DIGITAL DIVIDE

Although the promises of technology are certainly reason for excitement, we must bear in mind that access to these resources is not evenly available throughout the world, or even between households, a phenomenon often conceptualized as the digital divide. Its initial conceptualization focused on differences in access— essentially, the distinction between those who were connected versus those who were not online at all (Hargittai, 2010; Steyaert & Gould, 2009). In early studies, correlations were found between basic demographic and geographic factors like age, gender, race/ethnicity, education, income, employment status, and place of residence and access to ICT (DiMaggio, Hartittai, Celeste, & Shafer, 2004; Epstein, Nisbet & Gillespie, 2010). In a recent review of the literature, Steyaert and Gould (2009) found that variables that had been strong indicators of differential access to technology, such as gender, levels of income, and education, are now less successful in predicting overall differences in access; they found that age, however, continues to predict differences in usage.

An intriguing age-related concept associated with the digital divide is that of "digital natives versus digital immigrants." In his seminal discussion of these two demographic groups, Prensky (2001) proposed that young people, having been born into a digital age, have been exposed to digital media since birth and, as a result, have a higher level of comfort with technology than their elders, the digital immigrants. As a result, digital natives are more connected and more comfortable with the use of technology as an everyday, integrated component of their everyday lives. More recent research has led some to question this assumption and to suggest that there is a diversity of comfort with a digital world among the young, just as there is with members of the digital immigrant generations (Hargittai, 2010). Prensky, however, contends that the physical differences seen in the brains of the young are the result of the omnipresence of technology in their lives, with a natural and an organic higher general level of access and use of technology among the young.

MOVING ON TO DIGITAL DIVIDES

The bimodal view of the digital divide (connected vs. not) comes with an underlying assumption that once limits to access are overcome, issues of inequality are no longer a concern (Hargittai, 2010), yet this has been shown not to be the case (Epstein et al., 2010, Hargittai, 2010). Work done over the past decade has presented us with a more nuanced view, one that involves multiple, sometimes competing, sometimes interconnected, divides (Tsatsou, 2011). There is a "growing emphasis on quality and levels of technology use as well as on the attitudes to and usage of digital technologies, thus going beyond the numbers of people who use such technologies" (Tsatsou, 2011, p. 319).

Steyaert and Gould (2009) recommend changes in what is looked at when considering the divide. Rather than simple access, the definition of access should be broadened to include the quality of access and the quality and extent of Internet usage. Simple time online is not sufficient to determine how the Internet is being used; content preference is important. They suggest that the digital divide is "evolving into a divide on who uses the internet for what" (Steyaert & Gould, 2009, p. 747).

Taking the perspective that a more complex view is needed, Hargittai (2003, p. 822) identified four factors that contribute to digital inequality, "a refined understanding of the 'digital divide' that emphasizes a spectrum of inequality across segments of the population depending on differences along several dimensions of technology access and use." These four factors are the following: (a) technical means, the quality of the equipment used; (b) autonomy of use, that is, access to equipment and the capacity to use the equipment for preferred purposes; (c) a social support network made up of people who can facilitate their use; and (d) the quality and breadth of their experience in using the technology. These four factors combine to contribute to the individual's skill level, the ability to use new technology efficiently and effectively.

Wei, Teo, Chan, and Tan (2011) also considered inequality in identifying three levels of information technology (IT) digital divides. The first-level IT digital divide, the digital access divide, refers to the inequality of access to IT. The digital capability divide, the second-level IT digital divide, is a combination of the first-level digital divide and other contextual factors, such as computer skills. The digital outcome divide, the third-level digital divide, is a combination of the second-level divide and other contextual factors that results in variable outcomes and success rates at achieving the intended goal of one's engagement with technology (Wei et al., 2011).

Interestingly, the first author has encountered the evolution of the digital divide in her online class, Grief in a Family Context, which she has taught since 1996. During the first semester, the class was taught with the simplest view of the digital divide, as the difference between have's and have-not's, was apparent. Some students were located on campuses with excellent computer systems, and others were on unreliable home dial-up connections, in one case using dial-up and a 2400 BAUD modem (i.e., very slow—it was possible to watch as individual letters appeared on the screen, eventually forming words, sentences, and paragraphs. If the student lost connectivity, she would lose the text on the screen and would have to begin her download again); two students were "absent from class" for a period because their servers were destroyed and had to be replaced—in one case, by a flood in Pennsylvania, and in the other, by a sandstorm in Israel. Another student experienced several blizzards in her rural Ontario home, and with each, lost connectivity, in some instances, for days on end. Ultimately, simple access was a principle factor in students succeeding in the class that semester.

Over time, the divides in the class have reflected those seen in the literature. Younger students seem to have an almost intuitive comfort with technology and have requested more and more advanced and complex use of high-bandwidth technology. Digital immigrants, who continue to make up the majority of students in the class, initially had less comfort with anything beyond "point and click," over time have also shown increasing levels of comfort with advanced technology; however, in comparing the two groups, they continue to be more cautious, in general, in adoption of newer technologies. Overall, students have demonstrated a wide range of quality and levels of technology use, as well as attitudes toward using these technologies and motivation toward using them. We have gone from having a student who had never sent an e-mail without her husband's help, to students who now suggest new approaches to interacting across time and space.

THANATECHNOLOGY RESOURCES FOR THE DYING AND BEREAVED

The range of thanatechnology resources is large and growing; they are used by the bereaved for a number of purposes: to deal with loss and with one's grief, to connect with others also bereaved, to maintain a connection with the deceased, and to find informational resources and support from professionals (see Chapters 3–5, 7, 11, and Appendix A). Although limited, research has begun on the use of nonnetworked technologies. In their study of the use of technologies by the bereaved, Massimi and Baecker (2010) identified only one nonnetworked technology, framed digital pictures in the home.

A number of digital technologies are now being used in the funeral industry (McIlwain, 2005); some of these are networked and some not. Videos are now common, ranging from a montage of pictures accompanied by music, through others that are meant to be mini documentaries of the lives of the deceased (McIlwain, 2005). In some cases, video productions begin while the subject is still alive; these videos can then be stored for later showing. Although videos may be created simply for showing at a funeral, they can also be broadcast over distance in the event that the bereaved wish to share them with others who are unable to attend. Webcams may be used in online funerals, which may be broadcast in real time, or they can also be archived so that they can be played back later. Online "guest books" are common, with friends and family members both far and near sharing their thoughts.

In addition to resources associated with funeral services, commemorative websites serve narrative, commemorative, expressive, and experiential functions. These provide opportunities to describe personal stories, express thoughts and emotions, create memorials, and, occasionally, conduct rituals in a supportive environment. These sites may be set up by bereaved loved ones and can be very idiosyncratic to the relationship. They may be larger, institutionalized cybercemetery sites, incorporating obituaries, photos, poetry, prose, and other digital artifacts from the life of the deceased (see Chapter 10).

Thanatechnology resources are increasingly appealing to the bereaved, looking for unique attributes that may not be available in their immediate vicinity. In a study of social support and technological connectedness for the bereaved, Vanderwerker and Prigerson (2004) studied the use of technologies, specifically the Internet, e-mail, and cell phones. They found that almost 60% of their respondents used the Internet, and almost half reported communicating by e-mail as a type of social support. Indeed, the Internet has the potential to provide a community of supporters who legitimize the griever, the loss, or both. The Internet serves as "a kind of refuge from the larger social order where grieving was perceived as unwelcome" (Hollander, 2001, p. 140).

Hollander's (2001) findings are echoed by those of Fiegelman, Gorman, Beal, and Jordan (2008). In a comparison of face-to-face and Internet-based support groups, Fiegelman et al. found that those who chose Internet-based groups did so because of uniquely appealing factors associated with the Internet: the group's "24/7" (i.e., 24 hours each day, 7 days each week) availability and the ability to spend extensive amounts of time participating on the site. In addition, a study of telephone support groups, conducted in Australia, found that the telephone support may provide benefits not present in face-to-face support (Nair, Goodenough, & Cohn, 2006).

As computer skills and the speed of development of different technologies expand, newer technologies are being used in ways for which they were not originally intended. Chapter 12 of this text addresses the use of social networking as a communication mechanism for college students separated from their friendship network.

Grief counseling via the Internet has also been explored (Dominick et al., 2009). Online grief counseling joins existing communities on the Internet dedicated to mutual support for the bereaved (Roberts, 2007). Online counseling and peer support could potentially allow the bereaved to find a more supportive counselor or community than they would otherwise be able to discover.

Newer technologies are used to commemorate lost loved ones and ritualize grief. Second Life, an online, three-dimensional virtual world, allows users to interact with each other using avatars, a graphic representation they choose as depictions of themselves. Multiple users interact with each other electronically and may form close relationships, even if they do not know each other outside the virtual world. In his blog, Pearse (2007) described his experience of attending a funeral for a Second Life friend who had died and for whom he and other friends of the deceased had held a Victorian funeral.

Many social networking and gaming resources were not designed with commemoration in mind. Unfortunately, using media not typically used for this purpose to stage a commemorative event can result in added pain for the bereaved (see Chapter 9). A relatively famous case of this was carried out in *World of Warcraft*, a multiplayer fantasy strategy game in which groups band together to compete with others. In this case, a young woman who played the game as a member of one guild died suddenly in real life, and her guild members decided to hold a virtual funeral in *World of Warcraft*. They announced the funeral and asked other guilds not to play the game (i.e., attack them) while they were holding the ritual. Another guild violated the request and attacked, slaughtering the virtual characters, potentially adding to the pain her guild members felt at the loss of their friend (Nagata, 2010).

EMERGENT UBICOMP/MOBILE RESOURCES

As we have discussed earlier, computers are becoming more widely available to larger sections of the population. As more and more activities become suffused with computational components, computer scientists have begun to posit what the future of computing might be like. With computing devices becoming smaller, less expensive to manufacture, and more powerful, one emerging paradigm is that of *ubiquitous computing* (Weiser, 1991). Also known as *pervasive computing*, this paradigm suggests a future where computing devices augment everyday objects and environments, respond intelligently to changing situations, and support activities "invisibly" by fading into the background. Prominent examples include Georgia Tech's Aware Home (Kidd et al., 1999)—this prototype "house of the future" is fitted to sense where occupants are physically located; it projects user interfaces and information onto walls, tables, or furniture; and it offers connectivity to the Internet and numerous other resources throughout.

Although projects like the Aware Home are grand-scale research prototypes and envisionments of the future, many of the tenets of ubiquitous computing are already here. The burgeoning use of mobile data networks is one example of an "always-connected" lifestyle. Similarly, we capture more information about our lives than ever before, be it through Twitter, camera phones, or e-mail (Truong & Hayes, 2009). Indeed, Weiser's (1991) vision of "pads, tabs, and boards"—interactive devices varying in size from handheld to wall sized—has been realized in the form of iPads and other tablet computers, smart phones, and smart boards (Weiser, 1991).

With this in mind, we now turn to emerging technologies in the ubiquitous computing domain and highlight examples of research prototypes that embody ideas about how technology could, in the future, play a role in the lives of the bereaved. These kinds of technologies push boundaries in both the social and technical dimensions—they use modern cutting-edge hardware systems to create novel interactive situations in unexpected or unusual places.

COMMUNICATION

Compared with even 10 years ago, the tools we use to communicate are very different. Mobile devices, in particular, have emerged as a dominant platform, even in some cases replacing landline telephones for consumers. In addition, text message usage has risen, particularly among younger people. Building on this changing communication landscape, web-based services such as Twitter and Facebook allow people to stay in touch in a one-to-many kind of way that was not previously possible with the traditional telephone.

This changing technological landscape—from private and one-to-one to public and many-to-many—has implications for the ways in which people mourn, communicate about their grief, and seek professional resources. Mourning, that is, outward actions that indicate grief, can occur in a limitless number of ways. One common example, mentioned above, is the creation of a memorial site—traditionally a graveyard or other special place relevant to the death. With technologies such as mobile phones and location sensing, cemeteries can be augmented to tell the "story" of the deceased through a variety of means; for example, some companies have begun to offer a service whereby mobile phones can be used to scan a tombstone and visit an online memorial (Pailthorp, 2011). Furthermore, access to the requisite sentimental materials may be possible through digital means; for example, remote relatives could visit a grave virtually through a webcam. These kinds of technologies are becoming less expensive and more accessible to a broader group of people; as such, they are applied in new ways that technologists are only beginning to recognize as profoundly different from previous use cases (Massimi & Baecker, 2010).

The changing communication landscape also impacts the way that the bereaved receive and provide social support. In the human computer interaction community, for example, design work has focused on developing novel technologies that indicate emotions "at a distance" through haptic feedback (e.g., a key chain that vibrates when a paired key chain is squeezed;Smith & MacLean, 2007) or "ambient displays" that sit in the background and change color or move to indicate a similar sentiment (Chang, Resner, Koermer, Wang & Ishi, 2001). These kinds of more ambiguous forms of communication have the ability to change the way that social support is delivered to, and received by, the bereaved. The communicational requirements and loads placed on the user are smaller and do not demand immediate reciprocation as with a telephone call (Massimi & Baecker, 2011). Rather, the bereaved may be able to see that someone is thinking about them without having to go through the effort of carrying on a potentially uncomfortable conversation.

Finally, we can consider how these new technologies will be taken up by professional service providers to extend the work they may already have been doing using telephones, e-mail, chat, and discussion boards. The webcam cemetery example above is one way in which cemetery managers can potentially improve the experience of visiting a gravesite (or at least make it easier to do).

REMEMBRANCE, INHERITANCE, AND LEGACY

Using technology to remember the deceased is a common practice in modern settings. From Facebook to personalized DVDs, people use their computers to make sense of their loss and meet their grief-related needs (Brubaker & Hayes, 2011; Getty et al., 2011; Massimi & Baecker, 2010). In coming years, the opportunities available to integrate technology into the grieving process will become more pronounced and nuanced. In particular, current computing research is investigating how technology plays a role in remembering the dead through digitally mediated storytelling, reviewing digital possessions, and so on. New devices and scenarios of use that are uniquely positioned to play a role during the grieving process are being developed.

One trend in computing that may be of value to the bereaved is that of home archiving. Concerned with how to store, curate, and review a family's collective history in a way that respects both physical and digital artifacts, this research direction may offer the bereaved opportunities to reminisce about their deceased loved ones in new ways. Microsoft Research's Family Archive, for example, allows users to store photos of physical mementoes alongside existing digital assets such as photo, video, or sound files (Kirk et al., 2010). This kind of design juxtaposes a lifetime's worth of digital materials with the collected digital and physical artifacts of an entire family, thus representing the deceased as a member of a family (rather than an individual "user") and treating digital items with the same kind of respect and sentimentality afforded traditionally to physical mementoes. This type of technology also demonstrates how non-traditional form factors for devices can be augmented to create new experiences. Another compelling example is "ThanatoFesnestra," a design project inspired by domestic altars in Japanese homes that displays a flickering virtual candle on a digital picture frame as photos of a deceased loved one pass by (Uriu & Okude, 2010).

Problematically, these kinds of installations require significant technical and social infrastructure to maintain. They often rely on Internet access through a wireless home network and an underlying personal computer that may need maintenance and upkeep. Professionals are needed to conduct these repairs, or significant expertise on the part of nonprofessional end users. Indeed, making home infrastructure "work" is a serious problem that still remains to be addressed systematically in the ubiquitous computing literature and one that can be shaken by life disruptions such as death (Dimond, Poole, & Yardi, 2010).

Other work has examined how technology plays a role in inheritance. Odom, Harper, Sellen, Kirk, and Banks (2010) interviewed bereaved individuals and conducted home tours to understand how technical artifacts were used to symbolize and maintain the relationship between the living and the dead. They find that some technologies—and in particular communications technologies such as mobile phones—are used by the bereaved to maintain relationships. They share an anecdote of a woman who buried her loved one with his mobile phone so that she could continue to text message him whenever his favorite football team won. The authors also describe the burden the bereaved may sometimes feel as they question why they were chosen to receive particular items. In a landscape where the number of digital "items" we possess continues to grow and grow, these questions of persistence and burden will become more pronounced.

FUTURE DIRECTIONS

In roughly a decade and a half since the digital divide was identified, we have seen a dramatic, one might even say exponential, growth in the range and capacity of equipment, access to communication systems, as well as in the comfort level and enthusiasm for integrating technology into everyday lives. For many, the idea of being disconnected from one's technology induces anxiety.

The use of technology in relation to dying, death, and bereavement has also expanded, and as machines become smaller and faster, potentially implantable technology likely will be incorporated even more. We are already using technology to connect people over distances, and creative uses of as yet unknown technology may reduce the psychological distance even further. Current, primarily text-based communication on the Internet likely will give way to more use of multimedia tools. Already, families are using Skype (one-to-one communication) interdependently with blog sites (see Chapter 6 for an example), and the technology is on the horizon for multiple users to be on Skype video simultaneously. Virtual worlds, like Second Life, already provide an opportunity to interact with others at a distance.

As the use of virtual worlds becomes easier and more intuitive and the images more lifelike, it will be possible to create a virtual world that mirrors real life, or an idealized version of real life that may provide an opportunity to interact with a loved one who is deceased. This would be an extension of the increasingly common practice of the bereaved using the Facebook site of a deceased person as a venue for interacting with him or her (see Chapter 3), with the added value of being able to interact with the avatar of the deceased.

With improved three-dimensional imaging, the visual representation of a loved one will become more lifelike, and the holographic images of science fiction may become fact. Images of three-dimensional avatars that move and speak identically to the person on whom the image is based may be possible. However, will the avatar know how to act? What will the source of the avatar's "personality" be?

Anyone using ICT leaves a digital legacy behind. The digital artifacts of this legacy are surprisingly large. It include, but is not limited to, Facebook and Twitter posts, YouTube videos, blog posts, and a record of where that person has visited. Indeed, anything that was seen (or even clicked on) or posted, anywhere where it was archived, along with any nonnetworked, yet archived digital records may all be part of the legacy. As ICT advances, it will be possible to create a lifelike avatar by harvesting all digital information on a person and compiling a personality, with a history, from the collected information. According to Bell and Gray (2000), both one-way and two-way immortality will be possible. One-way immortality involves preserving and transmitting one's ideas. Two-way immortality allows the digital immortal to grow and learn and be capable of interacting with others. They believe that two-way immortality will be possible within the next century. Kurzweil (2005) takes this a large step further to propose that technological advancements will allow us to move past the creation of lifelike virtual avatars with whom to have conversations to true digital immortality. He has proposed that "singularity" is the point at which rapidly developing technology and biology will combine into a new life form. This combined technobiological life form would be as much a sentient being as humans, and he further proposes that human consciousness could be transferred into it. Perhaps, the ultimate expression of death anxiety, this futuristic view of the role of technology in addressing death, is intriguing yet troubling. It would be a safe guess to suggest that it would not be available to all, creating a new digital divide that was certainly unheard of when the term was first proposed.

REFERENCES

Bell, G., & Gray, J. (2000, October). Digital immortality. *Microsoft Research*. Retrieved from http://research.microsoft.com/apps/pubs/default.aspx?id=69927

Bonfadelli, H. (2002). The Internet and knowledge gaps. *European Journal of Community, 17,* 65–84.

Brubaker, J. R., & Hayes, G. R. (2011). "We will never forget you [online]": An empirical investigation of post-mortem MySpace comments. In *Proceedings of the CSCW 2011* (pp. 123–132). Hangzhou, China: ACM.

Brubaker, J., & Vertesi, J. (2010, April 10–15). Death and the social network. In *Workshop on death and the digital*. Presented at the CHI 2010, Atlanta, Georgia.

Chang, A., Resner, B., Koerner, B., Wang, X., & Ishii, H. (2001). LumiTouch: An emotional communication device. In *CHI '01 Extended abstracts on human factors in computing systems* (pp. 313–314). Seattle, Washington: ACM.

DiMaggio, P., Hargittai, E., Celeste, C., & Shafer, S. (2004). Digital inequality: From unequal access to differentiated use. In K. Neckerman (Ed.), *Social inequality* (pp. 355–400). New York, NY: Russell Sage Foundation.

Dimond, J. P., Poole, E. S., & Yardi, S. (2010). The effects of life disruptions on home technology routines. In *Proceedings of GROUP 2010* (pp. 85–88). Sanibel Island, FL: ACM.

Dominick, S. A., Irvine, B. A., Beauchamp, N., Seeley, J. R., Nolen-Hoeksema, S., Doka, K. J., & Bonnano, G. A. (2009). An Internet tool to normalize grief. *Omega, 60*(1), 71–87.

Epstein, D., Nisbet, E. C., & Gillsespie, T. (2010). Who's responsible for the digital divide? Public perceptions and policy implications. *The Information Society, 27,* 92–104.

Feigelman, W., Gorman, B. S., Beal, K. C., & Jordan, J. R. (2008). Internet support groups for suicide survivors: A new mode for gaining bereavement assistance. *Journal of Death and Dying, 57*(3), 217–24.

Foong, P. S., & Kera, D. (2008). *Applying reflective design to digital memorials*. Presented at the International Workshop on Social Interaction and Mundane Technologies 2008, Cambridge, United Kingdom.

Getty, E., Cobb, J., Gabeler, M., Nelson, C., Weng, E., & Hancock, J. (2011). I said your name in an empty room: Grieving and continuing bonds on Facebook. In *Proceedings of CHI 2011* (pp. 997–1000). Vancouver, BC, Canada: ACM.

Hargittai, E. (2003). The digital divide and what to do about it. In D. C. Jones (Ed.), *New Economy Handbook* (pp. 821–839). San Diego, CA: Academic Press.

Hargittai, E. (2010). Digital na(t)ives? Variations on Internet skills and uses among members of the "Net generation". *Sociological Inquiry, 80,* 92–113.

Hollander, E. M. (2001). Cyber community in the valley of the shadow of death. *Journal of Loss and Trauma 6*(2), 135–146.

Kidd, C. D., Orr, R., Abowd, G. D., Atkeson, C. G., Essa, I. A., MacIntyre, B., . . ., Newsetter, W. (1999). The aware home: A living laboratory for ubiquitous computing research. In *Proceedings of the Second International Workshop on Cooperative Buildings, Integrating Information, Organization, and Architecture* (pp. 191–198). New York, NY: Springer-Verlag.

Kirk, D. S., Izadi, S., Sellen, A., Taylor, S., Banks, R., & Hilliges, O. (2010). Opening up the family archive. In *Proceedings of CSCW 2010* (pp. 261–270). Savannah, GA: ACM.

Kurzweil, R. (2005). *The singularity is near: When humans transcend biology*. New York, NY: Penguin Books.

Massimi, M., & Baecker, R. M. (2010). A death in the family: Opportunities for designing technologies for the bereaved. In *Proceedings of CHI 2010* (pp. 1821–1830). Atlanta, GA: ACM.

Massimi, M., & Baecker, R. M. (2011). Dealing with death in design: Developing systems for the bereaved. In *Proceedings of the 2011 Annual Conference on Human Factors in Computing Systems, CHI '11* (pp. 1001–1010). Vancouver, BC, Canada: ACM.

McIlwain, C. D. (2005). When death goes pop: Death, media & the remaking of community. New York, NY: Peter Lang.

Nagata, T. (2010). *The WoW funeral raid—Four years later.* Retrieved from http://www.games radar.com/pc/world-of-warcraft-the-burning-crusade/news/the-wow-funeral-raid-four-years-later/a-2010030510656885018/g-20060403131624956087

Nair, K., Goodenough, B., & Cohn, R. (2006). Telephone support groups for isolated bereaved parents: A review of the literature and an example of Australian paediatric oncology. *Illness, Crisis, and Loss 14*(4), 319–336.

Norman, D. (1998). *The invisible computer: Why good products can fail, the personal computer is so complex, and information appliances are the solution.* Cambridge, MA: MIT Press.

Norris, P. (2001). Digital divide? Civic engagement, information poverty and the Internet in democratic societies. New York: Cambridge University Press.

Odom, W., Harper, R., Sellen, A., Kirk, D., & Banks, R. (2010). Passing on & putting to rest: Understanding bereavement in the context of interactive technologies. In *Proceedings of CHI 2010* (pp. 1831–1840). Atlanta, GA: ACM.

Oliveri, T. (2003). Grief groups on the Internet. *Bereavement Care, 22*(3), 39. doi:10.1080/02682620308657581

Pailthorp, B. (2011, May 30). Technology brings digital memories to grave sites. *KPLU: National Public Radio.* Retrieved from http://www.npr.org/2011/05/30/136676964/technology-brings-digital-memories-to-grave-sites

Pearse, E. (2007, February 13). A second life funeral. Retrieved from http://victorianaesthetic.blogspot.com/2007/02/secondlife-funeral.html

Prensky, M. (2001). Digital natives, digital immigrants. *On the Horizon, 9*(5), 1–6.

Roberts, P. (2004). Here today and cyberspace tomorrow: Memorials and bereavement support on the Web. *Generations, 28*(2), 41–46.

Smith, J., & MacLean, K. (2007). Communicating emotion through a haptic link: Design space and methodology. *International Journal of Human–Computer Studies, 65*(4), 376–387.

Steyaert, J., & Gould, N. (2009). Social work and the changing face of the digital divide. *British Journal of Social Work, 39*, 740–753.

Truong, K. N., & Hayes, G. R. (2009). Ubiquitous computing for capture and access. *Foundation and Trends in Human–Computer Interaction, 2*(2), 95–171.

Tsatsou, P. (2011). Digital divides revisited: What is new about divides and their research? *Media, Culture, & Society, 33*, 317–331.

Uriu, D., & Okude, N. (2010). ThanatoFenestra: Photographic family altar supporting a ritual to pray for the deceased. In *Proceedings of DIS 2010* (pp. 422–425). Aarhus, Denmark: ACM.

Vanderwerker, L. C. & Prigerson, H. G. (2004). Social support and social connectedness as protective factors in bereavement. *Traumatic Loss, 9*, 45-57.

Wei, K. -K., Teo, H. -H., Chan, H. C., & Tan, B. C. Y. (2011). Conceptualizing and testing a social cognitive model of the digital divide. *Information Systems Research, 22*, 170–187.

Weiser, M. (1991). The computer for the twenty-first century. *Scientific American, 265*(3), 94–104.

Part II

Building Online Communities of Support

3

The Role of Social Networking Sites in Memorialization of College Students

Kimberly Hieftje

S tudies suggest that approximately 25% to 50% of college students have lost a significant family member or friend within the past 2 years (Balk, 2001; Hardison, Neimeyer, & Lichstein, 2005). Often regarded as a "silent epidemic" on campus, bereavement can have adverse consequences for how students engage in the academic, social, and developmental challenges of college (Neimeyer, Laurie, Mehta, Hardison, & Currier, 2008). More so, college campuses may not be supportive environments for the bereaved (Taub & Servaty-Seib, 2008), who feel isolated from peers who frequently do not understand their grief.

For most emerging adults—bereaved or not—college presents a unique opportunity for personal growth and discovery, including forming a stable, focused identity (Balk, 1996). Identity formation, one of the most important developmental challenges of adolescence, is the cultivation of a conception of values, abilities, and hopes for the future (Arnett, 1995) and involves trying out various life possibilities and gradually moving toward making enduring decisions. For the bereaved college student, the experience of loss may disrupt one's developing sense of self and worldview, thus challenging the normative developmental process of self-discovery and identity formation.

Finding meaning following a loss is central to the grieving process. From this perspective, meaning making can be viewed as the process by which individuals reassess and revise their sense of how the world works after their worldviews have been challenged by loss (Neimeyer, 2002). Identity reconstruction, described by Neimeyer and Anderson (2002) as one of the major processes of meaning making after the death of a loved one, may become a difficult task for college students who do not yet have a well-formed identity to "reconstruct." Many college students are turning to social networking sites (SNSs) such as Facebook and MySpace to feel connected to their deceased friends and family during their grief.

Students may be hundreds of miles away from their homes and may lack access to a deceased friend's gravesite. Participation in an SNS during a time of grief may facilitate the meaning-making process in bereaved students by alleviating some of the "disconnect" experienced as a result of unsupportive peers while creating a valuable connection to significant others—including the deceased. This may also pave the way for the development of a coherent sense of self and personal identity that incorporates a continued bond with the deceased.

This exploratory qualitative study examines this interesting psychosocial phenomenon. Following a brief overview of SNSs, the research design, methodology, and findings of the study are described. Implications for grief counselors, death educators, parents, and thanatology researchers are presented.

SOCIAL NETWORKING SITES

An SNS is a website that uses specialized software to enable people to connect or collaborate to form online communities (Goodstein, 2007) that incorporate three commonalities: profiles, friends, and comments. They are individual home pages that incorporate a profile, or description, of each member. This description may include demographics (e.g., age, gender) but most often includes information of a more personal nature (e.g., pictures, videos, personal weblogs, or blogs).

Most emerging adults use online SNSs as a means to connect with and interact with peers. College students, who are often on their own for the first time, use SNSs as a way to stay connected with family and high school friends and connect with new friends and colleagues. Emerging adults report that browsing other people's profiles, also known as "walls," helps users keep track of their friends, the events in their life, and their friend's interactions with others (Subrahmanyam, Reich, Waechter, & Espinoza, 2008). Posting comments on another person's profile can help deepen an association between individuals, thereby making relationships feel more intimate (Manago, Graham, Greenfield, & Salimkhan, 2008). This aspect of social networking is particularly relevant to this study because self-disclosure is an important component of emerging adults' feelings of intimacy and intimate behavior in friendships. This includes emotional support, trust and loyalty, sharing activities, and offers of instrumental support (Radmacher & Azmitia, 2006).

According to Lenhart, Purcell, Smith, and Zickuhr (2010), going online is a central and indispensable element in the lives of American teens and young adults, with use of online SNSs being reported by 73% of teens aged 12 to 17 years and 72% of young adults aged 18 to 29 years. Emerging adults make up the majority of online social network users and mainly have profiles on MySpace and Facebook.

Some SNSs have message boards that are focused on a particular experience or interest (a.k.a. groups or "forums" such as the bereavement group on MySpace). Magid and Collier (2007) describe message boards as resources for holding discussions and for asking questions or seeking help or advice. Although "conversations" are generally more in-depth, "real-time" personal interactions do not occur because the postings are asynchronous (they are not necessarily posted one immediately after the other—significant time can pass in between the posting and a response). Because message boards may not be monitored and postings may not be screened, users are also reminded of the need to "be careful that you don't say anything inappropriate and have a thick skin in case someone else forgets to mind their manners" (Magid & Collier, 2007, p. 98). Message boards have been used in very creative ways during times of tragedy, such as posting updates about a person's condition following an accident (e.g., St. George, 1999), or being used first as a missing persons site that changed to a condolence site, and then monitoring the resulting court case and soliciting donations to a foundation established in the victim's name (www.findingjackie-hartman.blogspot.com).

Some SNSs have chat rooms or online spaces often "organized by categories and topics where people have a conversation by typing and sending short messages to people on the same page in real time" (Magid & Collier, 2007, p. 95). Therefore, what a user types is instantly visible to everyone. These authors note that in-depth conversations are rare and may or may not be moderated, so a user should be prepared to "leave the room" if a concern arises. Mechanisms are often available to report a user who is being inappropriate or causing a disturbance.

Other SNSs provide users with the opportunity to create a weblog, commonly known as a blog—a public diary that is posted online, and the author or blogger provides updates on a more or less regular basis (Levine, Young Levine, & Baroudi, 2007). Posts are typically listed in reverse chronological order, and the creator of the blog usually has the option to allow readers to post responses. Boyd (as quoted in Goodstein, 2007) describes blogging as an extension of normal adolescent communication. "Teens go through a period where they express themselves loudly in order to attract others like them. It's a flocking ritual" (p. 33). Keeping a personal blog was reported by bereaved teens to be useful for "getting emotions out" and "sharing thoughts," and reading someone else's blog was helpful because the teens could "see what they have gone through" and to "know others are going through what I am" (Sofka, 2009).

Goodstein (2007) notes that the most popular blogging applications among teens are LiveJournal, Xanga, and Blogger, with many teens also using a blog as a feature on their MySpace or Facebook accounts. Huffaker and Calvert (2005) describe the possibility that teens experience a sense of empowerment in revealing thoughts and feelings without hiding behind a public mask. However, it is crucial that teens understand the impact of their decision about whether the blog will be public (readable by anyone) or private (the owner of the blog must grant access to other users).

In addition to using SNSs for documenting their experiences, thoughts, and feelings, participants can use their personal page to commemorate someone who has died. If the personal page of the deceased is maintained after death, it is also possible to add material if the page is public (open to anyone to post) or if they have been given access to private material on a site (being "friended"). Over a decade ago, Niebuhr and Wilgoren (1999) reported that exposure to violent deaths has grown among teenagers. Perhaps, this is one reason why adolescents are using these SNSs in fascinating and creative ways following the loss of a friend. Within hours (sometimes minutes) of a tragedy, messages are posted, often including condolence messages to the family. SNSs are being used by grieving teenagers all over the world, including England (e.g., West, 2007), Ireland (e.g., O'Brien, 2008), and Australia (e.g., Blaxland, 2007). For example, following the shooting of ninth-grader Jordan Manners of Toronto, Canada, a candlelight vigil was quickly organized using Facebook technology, and 26 groups with more than 1,500 members were formed in a single day in memory of the victim (Siad, 2007). Even after a SNS user's death, the deceased's site "beams with life" (Belenkaya, 2006). A friend may ask the deceased to watch over them (Natekar, 2007). Anytime, day or night, if a teenager feels alone, he or she can log in and not feel isolated (Horsley, as quoted in Belenkaya, 2006). Goodstein (2007) notes that profiles once filled with light-hearted comments from friends just stopping by to say hello become filled with comments from grieving friends. For this generation, the newspaper obituary is being replaced by online shrines where friends, family, and strangers can all remember the deceased together.

Empirical research exploring the use of SNSs after the loss of a peer is extremely limited. Williams and Merten (2009) studied 20 online social networking profiles authored by adolescents in the United States who died suddenly between the years of 2005 and 2007. The researchers examined the comments on the deceased individual's SNS web page posted by users who had known the deceased to gain insight into how the Internet facilitated coping, expression, and interaction after the death of a peer. Perhaps, the most interesting finding included one-sided dialogue between the friends and their deceased peers. Williams and Merten (2009) noted that the main purpose for visiting the profile was to "talk" to the deceased adolescent. The researchers also suggested that talking to the deceased indicated that the adolescents were attempting to maintain the same relationship they had prior to their peer's death.

In addition to the use of SNSs, web memorials provide a mechanism for online communication with the deceased (see Chapter 10 by de Vries and Moldaw). More evidence that the use of the Internet does provide an outlet for grief in the form of web memorialization and through online communication with other bereaved individuals is becoming available. Continuing bonds with the deceased appeared to be salient themes through the use of thanatechnology. Disenfranchised grievers are also often mentioned in existing research, as they are often drawn to the Internet, where their grief can be recognized and legitimatized. The current research that examined how the use of SNSs might contribute to meaning making after death, continuing bonds with the deceased, and the grief process in college students will now be described.

METHODOLOGY

Participants

This exploratory research study used a biographic–narrative–inquiry method (BNIM) interview approach, described below, for the purpose of data collection. This approach, combined with the use of a purposive nonrandomized sampling system, results in detailed, information-rich transcripts (Patton, 1990, p. 169). From an initial eight participants, six interviews were determined to be richly detailed, descriptive narratives and served as the sample for this study.

Participants were all undergraduate college students enrolled at a large, 4-year residential university. Four of the participants were women and two were men, with age range from 19 to 23 years and average age of 21 years. Time elapsed from death to time of the interviews ranged from 2 to 20 months. Five of the participants experienced the death of a single friend; in one case, there were two deaths. Interestingly, the resulting story was not substantially different than those who had lost one friend. Deaths were sudden, unanticipated, and in most cases, traumatic. Of the seven deaths, four were the result of suicide, one friend had been killed in the war in Iraq, and two deaths were accident related.

As predicted by Wengraf (2001), the narratives of those who had lost a friend during the previous year were similarly detailed to those who had lost a friend between a year and 2 years prior to the time of the interview.

Participants who had experienced a more recent loss did differ in one particular way, in that those whose losses were more "fresh" visited their friends' social networking web pages more frequently than those whose losses were less recent.

Data Collection

As noted above, the BNIM interviewing method (as described by Wengraf, 2001) was used to provide rich, in-depth narratives. The BNIM is designed to explore the lived experience of participants, in which they are guided through the telling of an autobiographical narrative. According to Wengraf (2001), BNIM, if done correctly, will result in a relatively coherent personal narrative, with a large number of detailed, incident-specific stories.

Narrative Analysis

All narrative inquiry is concerned with content—what is said, written, or shown (Riessman, 2008). Narrative analysts strive to preserve sequence and the wealth of detail contained in long sequences while attending to time and place of narration. In thematic analysis, which we used here, prior theory also serves as a resource for interpretation, with most narrative investigators rejecting the idea of generic explanations (Riessman, p. 74).

During analysis, each participant's transcripts were read and reread, with a focus on identifying themes, first for individual participants and then across cases. This reading was interactive with and contextualized by researcher journal entries, field notes, and the literature. A useful analytic tool used in BNIM is the microanalysis panel, which involves detailed analysis of verbatim transcript segments or of developing themes (Wengraf, 2006). This approach was used to refine case-by-case themes and then across-case themes.

FINDINGS

Social networking sites such as Facebook and MySpace served several functions, both personally and socially, for bereaved friends after the death of their loved ones. Upon reading the individual narratives and comparing across cases, responses could be grouped into four main categories: connection, communication, commemoration, and continuation of the relationship.

Connection

The recurrence of grief suggests that the bereaved continue to stay connected to the deceased (Rosenblatt, 1996). Grief may be linked to the remembrance of happy memories, love, and a time of laughter. Looking through photographs or visiting a cherished place connected with the deceased may evoke grief but also provides the person with a reminder of how important that person was in his or her life. People often welcome grief recurrence, and even if there is a sad or bitter side to it, there may also be a sweet, affirming side to be cherished (Rosenblatt, 1996). Similar to visiting a loved one's gravesite, browsing through a deceased friend's web page might bring with it fresh pangs of grief for the bereaved. However, looking through old pictures and reading conversations between the bereaved and the deceased may also rekindle fond memories of the relationship. Social networking web pages left behind by the deceased may provide a venue for the bereaved to feel connected to their deceased friend and important others in their lives.

Being away at college for many participants made visiting their deceased friends' gravesites difficult, if not impossible. Social networking sites provided a way for the participants to feel connected to their deceased friends even when they could not access the gravesite. For instance, after Iris's best friend died in Iraq, she would often drive several hours home from college on the weekends so that she could visit his gravesite or his family. Much like the gravesite, Ben's Facebook page also provided Iris with a personal connection with her friend: "I go to his grave as often as I can and talk to him there but his grave is in (another city) and I'm (200 miles away). And so sometimes I feel it's really nice to have his Facebook still there." (Iris).

Several participants relied completely on the social networking web page as a way to feel a personal connection with their deceased friend. Michelle, for instance, did not have a gravesite or memorial to visit at all because her friend was cremated after his suicide and his ashes are kept at his parents' home: "And he was, uh, cremated, it's not like we can go to his grave or anything either, so." (Michelle).

For three participants, the web pages provided a place to go because attending the funeral was not an option because of school commitments. Having two friends commit suicide within 2 weeks of each other, Brian struggled with not being able to go home to attend either funeral, keeping him secluded from other grieving friends and classmates:

> The horrible thing was that it was—the day of—I had two midterms on the day of his funeral so I couldn't go to his funeral . . . I e-mailed one professor and uh, he wouldn't let me, uh, reschedule it. So I, you know, it was either get two F's basically or, you know, go back to the funeral. That—that was, you know, that really hurt. I hated not being able to go there. (Brian)

Like most of the participants, Brian used his deceased friends' web pages as a way to feel connected to others during his grief, especially when he felt disconnected from others after their deaths:

> And to see a bunch of people talk to him like he's there . . . this is how people are dealing with their grief. Like, this is, you know, it was good to see, you know, 'cause it's good to see people that are comfortable with grieving, you know . . . everyone had the same, you know, everyone from our high school and like out of all our extended friends, you know, we all—it was good to see that we all felt the same thing. (Brian)

One participant, however, did not find comfort in using the web page as a way to connect to her deceased friend. After Carrie's friend died in a car crash while she was away at college, she avoided going to his web page for weeks after his death. When she finally did visit his site, she was only able to browse through it for a few minutes, briefly looking at his pictures and reading comments posted by others. To her, visiting the web page was like confronting a ghost:

> It's—it's like your heart stops a little second . . . he's staring right at you from that picture . . . And it's just—eerie. And–and–and it's almost like you're facing, um, a ghost. That's what it's like. It's like you are seeing something that's not supposed to be there. It should be gone—he's gone. So, why is this still here? . . . it's something that shouldn't be there. It's like a living memory. Um, if a ghost came back to haunt you. (Carrie)

Communication

Literature on continuing bonds with the deceased has described the need to communicate with deceased loves ones through writing (Lattanzi & Hall, 1984;

Rosenblatt, 2000) and talking to the deceased (Klass, 1988; Rosenblatt, 2000; Shuchter & Zisook, 1993; Silverman & Nickman, 1996). Bereaved individuals might write letters to the deceased, talk to them at their gravesite, or even speak out loud to the person in hopes that their message will reach them posthumously. With the advent of the Internet, bereaved individuals are finding new ways to continue relationships with the deceased, including sending personal e-mails to the deceased or posting comments on their friend's SNS or other web memorial.

For almost all of the participants, the social networking web pages provided a way to personally communicate with the deceased. For Iris, her friend's web page seemed to be, to her, the only way she could communicate directly with him aside from talking to his picture or at his grave:

> Just I don't have any other place to send him anything. I can't send a letter in the mail to God. Can't call him up. Not going to send letters to his house and upset his family. And I can't call his phone and leave him a message or anything because his brother—he gave his brother his new phone before he went to war, so. Uh. Just like the only place to leave him a message. (Iris)

Without a gravesite or memorial at all to visit, Jacob's web page created an important way for Michelle to communicate with her deceased friend:

> Um, so it's sort of this way that we could see him and um, just like talk to him as we would if we were visiting, like, his grave, you know. It was just this really, um, it was as close to him as we could get at that point. (Michelle)

Aside from the personal benefits of writing to the bereaved, individuals may write with the hope of having others find comfort or benefit from reading their experience (Lattanzi & Hall, 1984). Although messages posted on social networking web pages are often directed to the deceased and not the public, a sense of community may be created through the sharing of the bereaved friends' grief. In some ways, the SNSs may be similar to a support group in providing a place for persons with similar losses to interact and find comfort and understanding (Moss, 2004). For instance, Michelle used her deceased friend's web page as a way to communicate with others, especially during moments of intense grief and the search for understanding following Jacob's suicide:

> Just seeing them post something that they're just like so, like, depressed or sad or missing him a lot. And kind of just—sending them something is a like a gesture, like, you know, "I'm—I'm right there with you." (Michelle)

The web pages also provided a place for participants to express their grief openly without fear of ridicule or rejection by their peers. After experiencing two close friends' suicides one right after the other, Brian appreciated being able to visit his friend's Facebook page as a way to work through his grief and express his feelings in a supportive environment with others who had also experienced the same loss:

So like, if you see guys, you know, expressing their feelings and girls like, just, you know, seeing that as alright and just everybody just seeing that as okay, like I think that really helps. Like, not so much the individual but the group, the—the effectiveness of his suicide as a whole, you know. So I think–I think Facebook actually is, is more of an outlet, you know, just like, your need to express your grief. (Brian)

One participant used the web page as a way to keep in touch with her deceased friend's social network, even 2 years after her friend's accidental death. For Melissa, keeping everyone aware of events and activities involving Jessica helped to keep her memory alive:

I think I just like going on, it helps everyone keep it touch, really. I mean, that, um, I mean, it's hard for everybody to keep in touch since there's so many people that cared about her and want to be involved with different things. Um. Just uh, you know, make her more alive, I guess. (Melissa)

Commemoration

For many participants, as the pain of grief subsided, the web pages became personal memorials, celebrating their deceased friends' lives. For Brian, who had been in a band with his two friends before their death, he used the web pages as a way to remember the good memories they shared together without focusing as much on the pain of their deaths:

Their (social networking web page) is more of uh, celebrating their life instead of grieving about their death. That's what I think the most important part is. You remember the good times, and you forget the horrible tragedy event. (Brian)

Writing about the deceased provided an intimate account of a loved one's life for others to read, including shared stories or memories that may provide a sense of who the person was when he or she was alive. For many participants, the social networking web pages provided a way to keep their deceased friends' memories alive and to feel their ongoing presence, even years later. For instance, Melissa used Facebook's ability to upload videos and picture slideshows as a way to preserve her friend's memory and share it with others who visited the site:

But I feel that's the way that I keep her alive, but many people keep her alive by, you know, going on her Facebook, and that's a really good way to, you know, keep her presence there. Um. I mean even though she's not there, there are many things that are there that like remind people of her and make them feel that she's with them, especially her Facebook, I think. (Melissa)

For Carrie, however, having numerous photos and videos "constantly" appearing on their friend's personal web page each time she visited felt overwhelming and uncomfortable:

So, his wall was just bombarded with photo albums that friends had made and— and videos that they had on their computers that they wanted to post for people to see. So, all of the sudden it was this exhausting amount of "We miss you (John)" photo album. And "John: My best friend" photo album. And, you know, things of that nature. And it's just bam, bam, bam, bam! And then you are like, wow, that is exhausting. (Carrie)

For several participants, looking through pictures and videos of their deceased friends created meaningful insight into their own lives, which included cherished memories of their loved ones:

I think having that, having that ease of access to it is just . . . makes you remember just every little time that you could have had with them. And then it makes . . . me wish every time that I look at them that I would cherish that moment just that little much more, you know, that little bit more cause, you know, you never expect anything like that to happen . . . at first it's just, every picture is a new tear. But I think now every picture is a new smile and a new laughter because you remember and you just celebrate their life instead of grieving over it. (Brian)

Continuation of the Relationship

Continuing bonds with the deceased can be described as a dynamic, ever-changing process that includes constructing an inner representation of the deceased into the lives of the living. Phenomena that indicate interaction with the inner representation of a deceased person have been described as a sense of presence, hallucinations in any of the senses, belief in the person's continuing active influence on thoughts or events, or a conscious incorporation of the characteristics or virtues of the dead into the self (Marwitt & Klass, 1996). The inner representation of the deceased may change over time and can include an active or a passive role in the lives of the bereaved. At times, the deceased may play a central, leading role in their lives, whereas at other times, the role may be that of a supporting one. The connection, however, remains intact.

Most participants used the personal web pages as a way to continue their relationship with their deceased loved ones. Alex, who left for college a month after his best friend took his own life continued to remain close to their high school friends and even made several other close friends while at college. However, he still considered Michael his best friend, even in death. He noted: "He's always going to be my best friend whether he's alive or dead" (Alex).

For Brian, the web page provided a way to contact his friends even beyond death, even though he knew he would not be receiving a response in return:

But, I did, you know, talk to him like he's there, you know, like, I'm just like it is on Facebook. It's like he's there. So you talk to him, you know, you talk to him like—like he's living, you know, but somewhere else, you know. It's—not even like really he died. It's like he moved really far away. 'Cause you can still contact, you can still contact him. (Brian)

Although most participants left messages for others to see on the web page, Iris would sometimes use the site as a way to send very personal, private messages to her best friend that could not be read by others:

> When I'm really emotional and upset about it, I will get on it and send him a private message just about, basically just going on about how sad I am and how much of disbelief I am in that's he's really gone. And how I hate that he's gone and I hate the war and just hate it all. But other times when I just have something little to say I'll leave, like, just on the wall where anyone can see. (Iris)

Most participants felt that the web page was an important link to maintaining their relationship with the deceased. Without a place to go to talk to her deceased friend, Jacob's MySpace page represented a much needed ongoing connection for Michelle to maintain their relationship: "Just like whenever we are thinking of him, that's kind of our way to, like, let him know or get a hold of him." (Michelle)

Although Iris was not sure how Anthony was receiving her e-mail messages posthumously, she felt confident that her messages were being received by her friend, no matter how they were directed toward him:

> I definitely just trying to feel like, I mean, I don't know if he can, you know, get on a computer up in heaven and get on Facebook, see what people are saying. But I kind of—I hope that wherever he is, that like he can look down on the world, you know, and that like when I direct something towards him that way, that it gets to him. (Iris)

For all but one participant, the social networking web pages of their deceased friends provided an important way to connect, communicate, commemorate, and continue a relationship with their deceased friends after death. The pages also provided a connection to others in their lives, creating a sense of community and belonging during their grief.

DISCUSSION

After the death of a loved one, SNSs may provide several important functions for college students, including the ability to feel connected to important others— including the deceased—during their grief. Logistically, because SNSs can be accessed at any time of the day from anywhere in the world, bereaved individuals are able to connect with their social network whenever the desire arises. This may be especially important to college students who may be hundreds of miles away from their family and friends and may lack access to their deceased friends' gravesites. Feeling connected to others during grief might also provide a much needed sense of comfort and community for the bereaved, something that may not be readily available away from home.

For most emerging adults, college presents a unique opportunity for self-growth and discovery. Finding meaning after the loss of a loved one may become an overwhelming task, especially when confronted with the normative developmental task of establishing a personal identity or sense of self. More so, bereaved students may be far away from the support of valuable friends and family during their grief.

College campuses, like most ecological niches, do not necessarily support or acknowledge grief expressions, much less ongoing attachments to the deceased. A survivor's inner representation of the deceased is in many ways dependent upon the survivor's social support. The living can influence the individual's desire and ability to remain involved with the deceased (Silverman & Nickman, 1996). Survivors may look to their social support network for help in keeping their continued relationships alive. Emerging adults who are enrolled at a residential university hundreds of miles away from those they would typically turn to in times of stress may use web pages on SNSs as a way to continue a bond with the deceased within the supportive presence of their online social network.

Based upon these case studies, the SNS Facebook, with its own unique social structure and social interactions, appears to be openly accepting of the expression of grief and continuing relationships with the deceased. In essence, the members of this SNS created their own definitions of certain roles such as "bereaved friend" and "grieving member." In modern society, public expression of the emotions of grief may be looked down upon, especially if the loss occurred many months earlier. Alternatively, the same expression of grief on a deceased person's social networking web page appeared to be accepted, even months after the death. Although an individual who disclosed in an everyday conversation that he or she spoke to a deceased friend might be viewed as "odd," talking to a deceased friend on an SNS seemed commonplace. Within the social networking realm, discussing grief emotions and talking to a deceased friend appeared to be accepted and supported by other social network members.

Participation in these SNSs, because of their unique nature and definitions of particular roles, may assist in the formation of identity and self as emerging adults learn to incorporate such newly defined roles as bereaved friend and "friend of a deceased person" into their identities. Specifically, visiting a deceased person's social networking web page might provide the opportunity for role taking, where bereaved individuals may attempt to imagine themselves in the place of others who are experiencing the same grief—and hence, the same roles. Although grief is a private venture, it yearns for public validation. Social networking sites may provide this opportunity.

Social networking sites have essentially created their own unique culture through the social interactions of their members. Although this "online culture" is important and worthy of discussion, it is also important to consider the many other cultural variations that exist outside of the "cyberworld" that was the focus of this study. The participants in this study were reflective of a White, middle-class, Midwestern college population who have frequent—if not continuous—Internet and technology access. The online culture described in this study was undoubtedly shaped by these social determinants. It is important to recognize that different cultural variations and social determinants might influence online culture and interaction among its members. In addition, the purpose or meaning of the sites for individuals of different cultures might be notably different than what was represented here.

Another important topic to discuss is the idea of a "digital divide" or the division between those who do and those who do not, or cannot, use certain technologies such as SNSs because of financial, disability, or economic, reasons. It is essential to recognize the limits to this research in relation to its ability to explain or take into account other cultural variations outside of the ones represented by these six participants, especially to those who may be considered a part of the digital divide. Some important questions to consider include the following: Are those who are grieving and do not, or cannot, access the Internet at a disadvantage compared with those who can? What role, if any, does the Internet play for those with limited Internet access during grief?

Aside from the inability to truly understand how cultural variations might have played a part in this study, it is still important to acknowledge the unique online culture that was represented in the participants' narratives. For instance, it was apparent that the use of technology was a vital component of their relationships with their friends. Aside from the use of SNSs, they also talked about using text messages, online instant messages, and e-mails as a way to develop and maintain friendships. Online and offline communication appeared to be equally intertwined and important in their relationships. This might have translated into the ease and comfort that the participants felt in turning to SNSs, both as a form of communication with the deceased and for their social support. The use of the social networking web pages of their deceased friends was a way for the participants to feel connected to their dead loved ones and social support network, just as it had helped them to stay connected with each other before the death occurred. As one participant explained, it was "just what you do" because everyone else also seemed to be doing it.

CONCLUSIONS

Web memorials established on SNSs often remain active indefinitely, providing an ongoing place for friends and loved ones to feel a personal connection to the deceased and significant others during grief. Social networking sites are very popular among emerging adults and appear to provide a unique venue for grief in a space that feels familiar and comfortable to them. As the use of the Internet and SNSs continues to increase, those working with emerging adults may benefit from recognizing and appreciating the significance of these social networking web pages as a venue for both the expression of grief and the continuation of bonds with the deceased, especially for those who are physically separated from their social support network or friend's gravesite during times of grief. Because this study describes the experiences of a limited sample of college-age individuals, further research is warranted to document the narratives of individuals within this age group whose circumstances are different. For instance, what meanings might these sites provide for individuals who *do* have ongoing access to their social support network and to a friend's gravesite or memorial during grief, such as college students who live at home or those who do not attend a traditional residential college campus?

Research also suggests that writing during times of grief may be a helpful and healing experience. Most research has been on the personal benefits of writing as a means of self-support (Lattanzi & Hale, 1985), where writing during grief is seen as a personal, reflective process. With the advent of the Internet, researchers now have seemingly endless access to personal writings during grief that can be found in personal blogs, e-mail listserves, chat rooms, online guestbooks and virtual memorials, and the social networking web pages of deceased loved ones. However, unlike the writings found in personal diaries or journals, postings on the Internet are written with the knowledge that others might—or will—read what they write. The idea of a "watchful other" during grief writing is both an exciting and warranted topic of continued research.

Messages left to the deceased in a public forum may also benefit other bereaved friends who may be visiting the personal web page. Visits to both the traditional cemetery and the web memorial are post death rituals symbolizing private mourning in a public place (Moss, 2004). Although messages posted on a personal web page are often directed to the deceased and not the public, a sense of community may be created through the sharing of the bereaved friends' grief. In some ways, the SNSs may be similar to a support group in providing a place for persons with similar losses to interact and find comfort and understanding (Moss, 2004). It is therefore important to appreciate the significance of not only writing messages to the deceased but also the act of reading messages to the deceased.

However, as was the case for one participant in this study, visiting a friend's personal web page soon after the death may feel too overwhelming and not necessarily comforting. For Carrie, visiting the web page was like confronting a ghost, creating a sense of uneasiness and discomfort. Therefore, although visiting and writing upon personal web pages as a way to feel connected to the deceased and others may be of great benefit for many during the grief process, it is not necessarily for everyone.

Family members, particularly parents and perhaps siblings, may be placed in the position of deciding whether to maintain an individual's SNSs. Funeral directors, lawyers, or perhaps grief counselors may need to facilitate conversations about an individual's "digital legacy," providing an opportunity to discuss the potential benefits and disadvantages of keeping these online resources active.

Research to document the factors that influence these decisions and the dynamics involved would provide useful guidance to professionals who may be in a position to assist during times of loss.

The use of technology in our lives continues to increase. Emerging adults are living in a time when communication is instantaneous, information and answers to questions are at their fingertips, and video games are becoming so lifelike that it is difficult to differentiate between reality and virtuality. It is imperative that researchers, practitioners, teachers, and even parents recognize and appreciate the powerful role that technology can play in the lives of emerging adults—even after death.

REFERENCES

Arnett, J. J. (1995). Adolescents' uses of media for self-socialization. *Journal of Youth and Adolescence, 24*(5), 519–533.

Balk, D. (1996). Attachment and the reactions of bereaved college students: A longitudinal study. In D. Klass, P. Silverman, & S. L. Nickman (Eds.), *Continuing bonds: New understandings of grief* (pp. 311–328). Philadelphia, PA: Taylor & Francis.

Balk, D. (2001). College student bereavement, scholarship, and the university: A call for university engagement. *Death Studies, 25*(1), 67–84.

Belenkaya, V. (2006). Lost pals stay alive on Web. *Daily News*, p. 28.

Blaxland, M. (2007, April 29). Grieving 4 u Amy: Teenagers share memories of friend on the Net. *Sun Herald*, p. 1.

Gilbert, K. R. (2002). Taking a narrative approach to grief research: Finding meaning in stories. *Death Studies, 26*(3), 223–239.

Goodstein, A. (2007). *Totally wired: What teens and tweens are really doing online.* New York, NY: St. Martin's Press.

Hardison, H. G., Neimeyer, R. A., & Lichstein, K. L. (2005). Insomnia and complicated grief symptoms in bereaved college students. *Behavioral Sleep Medicine, 3*(2), 99–111.

Huffaker, D. A., & Calvert, S. L. (2005). Gender, identity, and language use in teenage blogs. *Journal of Computer-Mediated Communication, 10*(2). Retrieved June 18, 2008, from http://jcmc.indiana.edu/vol10/issue2/huffaker.html

Klass, D. (1988). *Parental grief: Resolution and solace.* New York, NY: Springer Publishing.

Lattanzi, M., & Hall, M. E. (1984). Giving grief words: Writing during bereavement. *Omega: Journal of Death and Dying, 15*(1), 45–52.

Lenhart, A., Purcell, K., Smith, A., & Zickuhr, K. (2010, February 3). *Social media and mobile Internet use among teens and young adults.* Retrieved June 14, 2011, from http://www.pewinternet.org/Reports/2010/Social-Media-and-Young-Adults.aspx

Levine, J. R., Young Levine M., & Baroudi, C. (2007). The Internet for dummies. Hoboken, NJ: Wiley.

Magid, L., & Collier, A. (2007). *MySpace unraveled: A parents guide to teen social networking.* Berkeley, CA: Peachpit Press.

Manago, A. M., Graham, M. B., Greenfield, P. M., & Salimkhan, G. (2008). Self-presentation and gender on MySpace. *Journal of Applied Developmental Psychology, 29*(6), 446–458.

Marwit, S. J., & Klass, D. (1996). Grief and the role of the inner representation of the deceased. In D. Klass, P. R. Silverman, & S. Nickman (Eds.), *Continuing bonds: New understandings of grief.* Washington, DC: Taylor & Francis.

Moss, M. (2004). Grief on the web. *Omega: Journal of Death and Dying, 49*(1), 77–81.

Neimeyer, R. A. (2002). *Lessons of Loss: A Guide to Coping* (2nd ed.). New York, NY: Brunner-Routledge.

Neimeyer, R. A., & Anderson, A. (2002). Meaning reconstruction theory. In N. Thompson (Ed.), *Loss and grief* (pp. 45–64). London, England: Palgrave.

Neimeyer, R. A., Laurie, A., Mehta, T., Hardison, H., & Currier, J. M. (2008). Lessons of loss: Meaning-making in bereaved college students. *New Directions for Student Services, 2008*(121), 27–39.

Niebuhr, G., & Wilgoren, J. (1999, April 28). Terror in Littleton. *New York Times.* Retrieved May 22, 2008, from www.nytimes.com

O'Brien, B. (2008, March 1). Suicide and what it means to the Bebo generation. *Irish Times,* p. 16.

Owuegbuzie, A., & Leech, N. (2007). Sampling design in qualitative research: Making the sampling size more public. *The Qualitative Report, 12*(2), 238–254.

Patton, M. (1990). *Qualitative research & evaluation methods.* Thousand Oaks, CA: Sage.

Radmacher, K., & Azmitia, M. (2006). Are there gendered pathways to intimacy in early adolescents' and emerging adults' friendships? *Journal of Adolescent Research, 21*(4), 415–448.

Riessman, F. (1965). The "helper" therapy principle. *Social Work, 10*(2), 27–32.

Rosenblatt, P. C. (1996). Grief that does not end. In D. Klass, P. Silverman, & S. Nickman (Eds.), *Continuing bonds* (pp. 45–58). Philadelphia, PA: Taylor & Francis.

Rosenblatt, P. C. (2000). *Parent grief: Narratives of loss and relationship.* Philadelphia, PA: Brunner/Mazel.

Shuchter, S. R., & Zisook, S. (1993). The course of normal grief. In M. Stroebe, W. Stroebe, & R. Hansson (Eds.), *Handbook of bereavement: Theory, research, and intervention* (pp. 23–43). New York, NY: Cambridge University Press.

Siad, S. (2007, May 25). Teens cope with grief online. *The Toronto Star,* p. A01.

Silverman, P., & Nickman, S. (1996). Concluding thoughts. In D. Klass, P. Silverman, & S. Nickman (Eds.), *Continuing bonds: New understanding of grief* (pp. 349–355). Bristol, UK: Taylor & Francis.

Sofka, C. J. (2009). Adolescents, technology, and the Internet: Coping with loss in the digital world. In D. Balk & C. Corr (Eds.), *Adolescent encounters with death, bereavement, and coping* (pp. 155–173). New York, NY: Springer Publishing.

St. George, D. (1999, November 26). On the Web, a world of hope is spun for teen. *The Washington Post,* p. A, 1:3.

Subrahmanyam, K., Reich, S. M., Waechter, N., & Espinoza, G. (2008). Online and offline social networks: Use of social networking sites by emerging adults. *Journal of Applied Developmental Psychology, 29*(6), 420–433.

Taub, D. J., & Servaty-Seib, H. L. (2008). Developmental and contextual perspectives on bereaved college students. *New Directions for Student Services, 121,* 15–26.

Wengraf, T. (2001). *Qualitative research interviewing: Biographic narrative and semi-structured methods.* London: Sage.

West, E. (2007, May 8). How the Web is helping us deal with death. *Daily Telegraph, News,* p. 21.

Williams, A. L., & Merten, M. J. (2009). Adolescents' online social networking following the death of a peer. *Journal of Adolescent Research, 24*(1), 67–90.

4

The Net Generation: The Special Case of Youth

Carla J. Sofka

Ongoing data gathered by the Pew Internet and American Life Project confirms that teenagers use technology at high rates, with 93% of teens using the Internet and mobile Internet technology (Lenhart, Purcell, Smith, & Zickuhr 2011). The current generation of adolescents have been described in some fascinating ways over the past decade, such as the "young Turks of technology" (Bunn, 2000), "coming of age online" (Harris, 2005), and "growing up online" (PBS, 2008). They have also been nicknamed *Generation MySpace* (Kelsey, 2007), *digiteens* (Davis, 2009), *webheads, keyboard kids, cyberchildren*, and *Digital Generation* (Montgomery, 2007). Blais, Craig, Pepler, and Connolly (2008) noted that the Internet is a "significant aspect of the educational, social, and recreational experiences of adolescents" (p. 535). Since current teenagers have never known a world where the Internet did not exist in some form (Whitaker, 2002), parents whose children have experienced loss as well as professionals providing services to bereaved adolescents would be wise to recognize the roles that the Internet and other forms of technology may have in their process of coping with loss.

In what ways are adolescents using thanatechnology to help them deal with death and grief? This chapter will describe the appeal of digital technology among teenagers, summarize how various types of technology are being used by adolescents to cope with loss, identify the potential benefits and risks of these resources, and discuss implications for parents, grief counselors, death educators, and researchers.

This chapter is an update of a previously published chapter: Sofka, C. (2009). Adolescents, technology, and the Internet: Coping with loss in the digital world. In C. Corr & D. Balk (Eds.), *Adolescents and death* (pp. 155–173). New York, NY: Springer Publishing Company. Used with permission.

THE APPEAL OF TECHNOLOGY AND THE INTERNET AMONG TEENAGERS

Why have teenagers been captivated by resources in the digital world? What is not to like about technologies that combine access to digital information with technologies for communicating with others—also referred to as information and communication technologies (ICTs; Harris, 2005). Mesch and Talmud (2010) note that ICTs facilitate access to opportunities, knowledge, resources, and social capital, which might be otherwise difficult for teenagers to acquire. According to Rideout, Foehr, and Roberts (2010), the mobile and online revolutions have arrived in the lives of American youth, who consume an average of 7 hours and 38 minutes of media each day of the week.

A growing body of literature is available to describe the study of *cyberculture*, an area of research concerned with "questions about who we are and the world we live in as affected by digital technologies" (Whitaker, 2002, p. 131). This literature describes a multitude of reasons for the widespread use of technology among adolescents. First, more than ever before, teens are treating the Internet as a venue for social interaction (Lenhart, Madden, Macgill, & Smith, 2007). According to Pascoe (2007), social networking sites (SNSs) are extremely popular because teen culture is a social culture. The digital world is a perfect example of a *participatory culture*, defined by Jenkins, Clinton, Purushotma, Robison, and Weigel (2006) as a culture with relatively low barriers to civic engagement and artistic expression, strong support for creating and sharing one's creations with others, and a process whereby the most experienced members share what is known through some type of informal mentorship. Members of participatory cultures also believe that their contributions matter even if they do not actively contribute—"but all must believe they are free to contribute when ready and that what they contribute will be appropriately valued" (p. 7). Members also feel some degree of social connection with one another.

Second, the Internet provides adolescents with a great deal of independence, a "private space even while they're still at home" (Pascoe, 2007, p. 3). Teenagers are also attracted to the "immediacy" of the process of posting and receiving responses (Keller, as quoted in Natekar, 2007; Brett, as quoted in Siad, 2007), as well as having a sense of control over what little discretionary time they have available (Harris, 2005).

Third, adolescence is a time of exploration regarding one's own values and identity, and many young adults are using resources online to express and explore their forming identities (Schmitt, Dayanim, & Matthias, 2008). Although struggling with issues that may not be easy to discuss with parents or peers, Hellenga (2002) notes that Internet communication can provide a relatively safe and anonymous way to gain information and support. According to Whitaker (2002), a great deal of thought on how the Internet is impacting our identity revolves around whether access to and use of technology influences our perceptions of ourselves and how we are perceived by others. Dretzin (2008) ponders the interplay between online identity and actual identity, wondering how this plays out during adolescence, a time when identity is profoundly in flux.

Fourth, an adolescent who experiences marginalization in everyday life can find a sense of community online (Pascoe, 2007). Because traditionally oppressed or voiceless groups are speaking out online, Internet-savvy teenagers can be connected with others, gaining a sense of empowerment that may not otherwise be achievable (Hellenga, 2002). Servaty and Hayslip (2001) note that loss among adolescents may alter their perception of interpersonal relationships, resulting in social isolation and the lack of social support at a time when these relationships are a crucial part of identity development and well-being. Bereaved teens can experience a heightened sense of vulnerability and a sense of difference or stigma (McCarthy, 2007). It seems logical that identifying oneself as a bereaved adolescent in an online environment where being a grieving teenager is the "norm" has the potential to create a sense of "sameness."

Finally, technology is dramatically changing the speed at which teenagers gain tragic news and the way that they mourn (Burrell, 2007). Therefore, thanatologists would be wise to learn as much as possible about the topic referred to by Natekar (2007) as *e-grieving*.

ONLINE COMMUNITIES OF BEREAVEMENT

Following the events at Columbine High School in April of 1999, Linenthal (as quoted in Niehbuhr & Wilgoren, 1999) noted that the creation of shrines following tragic deaths might indicate the desire to overcome feelings of powerlessness and to experience a sense of unity as a "community of bereavement." Because this generation has been reared on technology, Atfield, Chalmers, and Lion (2006) note that it seems only logical that teenagers turn to cyberspace during times of grief, sometimes immediately following the news of a tragedy (e.g., Siad, 2007). A variety of online "communities of bereavement" exist, and those designed specifically to assist adolescents will be described in this chapter.

Although many virtual memorial sites commemorate individuals of all ages (see de Vries and Moldaw, Chapter 10), some virtual memorial sites are designed specifically to memorialize teenagers. For example, the National Teen Research Center and the Joshua Brown Foundation have partnered to sponsor the www.teensremembered.org website to honor the memories of teens who died in vehicular crashes and to provide a form of survivor advocacy for the victims' families ("an opportunity to prevent other families from experiencing the unspeakable pain they have suffered"). One bereaved mother has created a website in memory of victims of child suicide (http://www.childsuicide.com/memorialsites.html).

Although grief-specific memorial sites are available, teenagers are much more likely to use SNSs such as MySpace or Facebook (previously described by Hieftje in Chapter 3). Additional information about issues related to virtual communities will be addressed in Chapters 7, 9, and 11 of this book. Although online communities have the potential to be of great benefit to grieving teenagers, some websites create concern about the safety of or appropriateness of the use of some SNSs by this population. One controversial website that may be popular among some teens is www.MyDeathSpace.com. Visitor beware: the content on this website's home page tends to change and formerly contained the following disclaimer: "MyDeathSpace.com is an archival site, containing news articles, online obituaries, and other publicly available information. We have given you the opportunity to pay your respects and tributes to the recently deceased MySpace.com members via our comment system. Please be respectful." As this author was verifying the URLs in this chapter, the home page flashed provocative photos of adults from my local area in the "AdultFriendFinder." The entry for this website on Wikipedia reports that the site receives between 15,000 and 20,000 unique visitors each day, with the creator of the site receiving 75% hate mail and 25% fan mail. In addition, consent from surviving family members or friends to post information is not required to post information on this site, and a visitor may react to the skull logo.

Goodstein (2007) notes that although the content posted by teens on SNSs can be as simple as recording the events of the day or venting feelings out of frustration or anger, some content may appropriately be interpreted as a red flag or a cry for help. Consider postings that involve suicidal ideation or suicide that was linked to being a victim of cyberbullying. Because postings on SNSs have been linked with incidences of suicide (e.g., Megan Meier as discussed in Pokin, 2007; Joshua Ballard as discussed in Gagnon, 2005), there is intense debate about the monitoring of SNS postings versus banning the use of these sites by teenagers.

Does the Internet contribute to suicide among teens? Lee (2008) states: "Some say it's all due to the Internet, to the SNSs so beloved of teenagers which are quickly filled with glowing tributes to the dead, providing them with a brief, if dark, moment of fame. I don't buy that. If this were 30 years ago, we'd be blaming the telephone. The net may be a conduit for grief, but not its primary cause" (p. 8). Sadly one can find isolated reports of a teenager committing suicide online (e.g., Madkour, 2008) or reports of a suicide influenced by individuals participating in an online suicide group (Scheeres, 2003). Proposed legislation would make it a federal crime for someone to use the Internet to promote or advocate and encourage others to take their own life (http://suzyslaw.com/).

Malone (as quoted in O'Brien, 2008) notes that adolescents may have a notion of "virtual life after death," divorced from the reality and finality of death and its consequences. O'Brien (2008) observes that communities and schools attempting to deal with the aftermath of suicides do so with trepidation. They have to maintain a balance between expressing respect and compassion for the deceased, and sensitivity to the grief and sadness of the bereaved, but without glorifying the action of suicide itself.

Although these debates continue, it is reassuring to know that Internet resources exist to provide support to teens dealing with issues related to suicide. One site designed to commemorate those who have taken their own lives also provides links to suicide prevention information (e.g., the Wall of Angels Suicide Memorial at http://www.suicide.org/wall-of-angels-suicidememorials. html). The parents of a teenager who committed suicide after being bullied on an SNS created a foundation in her memory that has advocated for stronger legislation related to cyberbullying, with Megan Meiers' story and the outcome of these efforts documented online (http://www.meganmeierfoundation.org/ story/). Draper and Le (as quoted in Magid & Collier, 2007) of the National Suicide Prevention Lifeline report that kids are, at times, using their online profiles to convey suicidal intent. They also note the strong potential for saving lives when there are postings online because "the first people to hear about kids at risk are other kids" (p. 174). Suicide prevention profiles have been set up on MySpace, Xanga, and Facebook to provide easy access to this information to anyone who should need it, and links to this information are highly visible on other relevant pages (e.g., on the MySpace link to the Good Charlotte song "Hold On"). Because of easily available links, these SNSs are a large source of referrals to the suicide prevention hotline. Draper and Le "don't know how many lives can be saved as a result of referrals through social networks, but it's certainly something that should be thought about by policy makers seeking to restrict teens' access to these sites. This is just one powerful example of how monitoring teen social networking can be much more beneficial to teens than banning it" (p. 174–175).

SUPER-COMMUNICATION: E-MAIL, TEXT MESSAGING, INSTANT MESSAGING, AND TWEETING

Lenhart, Madden, Macgill, and Smith (2007) described a subset of teens—about 28% of the entire teen population—as "super-communicators": teens with multiple technology options to contact friends, family, and other people with roles in their busy lives. In addition to the SNSs previously described, teens potentially have access to traditional landline telephones, cell phones for verbal communication and text messaging (TM), and computers that can be used for instant messaging (IM) and e-mail.

E-mail is reported by some adolescents to be "too formal" to use with friends (Pascoe, 2007) and by others as something used to talk to "old people" or institutions or to send complex instructions to large groups (Lenhart, Madden, & Hitlin, 2005, p. ii). They do, however, report using e-mail with teachers and employers (Pascoe, 2007). It is extremely important to note that the published research about the use of digital technology among adolescents that informed the writing of this chapter did not specifically inquire about the use of various forms of technology to cope with loss. According to data gathered by this author to inform the writing of this chapter from a convenience sample of teenagers seeking assistance from a bereavement support organization, some teenagers do use e-mail to seek support from friends while coping with loss. It should also be noted that a professionally moderated support group sponsored by Griefnet.org that uses e-mail as the sole method of communication between group members (k-2-k-teens at http://kid said.com/k2k_support.html) has been active and successfully supporting teens aged 13 to 18 years since 1995 (see Chapter 7 in this book). E-mail can also be used to provide "e-therapy" or online counseling (see Oravec, 2000, as an excellent resource). The use of e-mail as a resource for coping with loss among bereaved teens merits further investigation. Although adults often prefer e-mail when using technology to communicate with others, research conducted through the Digital Youth Project has documented that some teenagers may prefer to use TM to communicate with one another (Pascoe, 2007), with e-mail "losing its luster" (Lenhart et al., 2007, p. iv).

Although texting messages to a cell phone or other handheld device may be perceived as lacking intimacy, Pascoe (2007) notes that teens are not rendered vulnerable the same way they are in other person-to-person interactions. Initially contacting someone via TM to begin a conversation may lead to increased intimacy in subsequent communications. No data are currently available to describe the use of these modes of communication by teens seeking support during times of impending loss or grief.

Instant messaging may be used by teens who do not have access to a cell phone with TM privileges. This type of computer-mediated communication occurs in real time and therefore is always interactive as opposed to TM, which potentially involves a delayed response if the recipient cannot respond immediately. Instant messaging also has the advantage of being able to communicate with more than one person at a time. Research by Blais et al. (2008) found that using IM to communicate with best friends had a positive effect on the quality of these friendships. Pascoe (2007) also notes that some teens use IM to have important conversations that cannot be done via a traditional telephone or cell phone without the risk of being overheard by a parent.

Prior to 2006, the word *twitter* was typically used to describe the vocalization of a bird, chattering among a group of people, or a fluttering movement (www.m-w.com). Although only a mere 8% of teenagers between ages 12 and 17 years report using Twitter and other microblogging services (also known as "tweeting"; Lenhart et al., 2010), it would be wise to note that thanatology-related issues are likely to be described by some teenagers in 140 characters or less. Because of the rapid evolution of technology, it is tricky to know what new types of technology for communication will evolve and capture the attention of teens during the next few years.

THE "GOOGLE" STAGE OF GRIEF

While posting to a blog on March 20, 2005, Laura at 11D noted that "maniacal googling is a new stage of grief. After denial and before resignation comes the google stage" (McKenna, 2005). Following the diagnosis of a life-threatening illness or during the grieving process, "informational support" or factual information about topics involving illness, death, or grief may be useful during the process of coping with these events (Sofka, 1997).

How frequently do adolescents use the Internet to gain information about thanatology-related topics? Surveys estimate that between 31% and 49% of adolescents "cybersurf" for health-related information, including mental health issues, cancer, and other diseases (Borzekowski & Rickert, 2001; Lenhart, Madden, & Hitlin, 2005). Following the death of a loved one because of illness, teenagers may need information to alleviate fears that the illness was contagious (Fitzgerald, 2000). Although research documenting the use of thanatology-specific sites among this age cohort is not currently available, it is important to be familiar with content related to death and grief that is targeted specifically for teens should they seek it out.

Some websites are designed for teens (http://teenadvice.about.com/od/deathgrieving/Death_Loss_Grieving.htm) or for teens and adults who have a need for information about this age group (parents, teachers, and helping professionals). For example, Teen Health and Wellness (www.teenhealthandwellness.com) has detailed information on death and grief that can be easily located using a keyword search. Beliefnet has an advice column specifically for grieving teens that is written by Helen Fitzgerald (http://www.beliefnet.com/Health/Health-Support/Grief-and-Loss/2001/02/Resources-The-Grieving-Child-And-Teen.aspx). To identify additional resources, simply Google keywords such as *teen grief* or other combinations or *teen/adolescent* and the topic of interest and this search engine will provide links to sites that contain resources to help adults provide support to grieving teens (e.g., http://www.hospicenet.org/html/teenager.html or http://www.dougy.org/grief-resources/help-for-teens/). Be aware that keyword searches will also locate potentially inappropriate content unrelated to coping with loss. Because of the possibility that misinformation can easily be posted online, it is also important to review content before referring individuals to material posted online (see Appendix A).

In addition to sites for informational support, the World Wide Web also contains narrative sites that provide opportunities for grieving teens to read the personal stories of others or post their own story (www.teencentral.net—type *grief* into the "Search-O-Matic" or http://www.webhealing.com/honor.html). Adolescents may find it reassuring to discover that the thoughts and reactions of other teens are very similar to their own.

Expressive sites exist that contain young adults' artwork (e.g., http://www.kidsaid.com/stories.html) and poetry (e.g., http://newhope.provisiondata.net/teengrief/Poetry/tabid/88/Default.aspx). Tech-savvy teenagers are probably creating amazing things with technology without our awareness. Lenhart et al. (2010) report that 38% of teens share self-created content online (e.g., photos, videos, artwork, or stories), some of which may be used to share information about a deceased family member or friend. Twenty-one percent of teens report sharing material that they have found online and "remixed" into their own artistic creation, whether the original content consisted of songs, text, or images. Parents and grief counselors would be wise to ask teenagers about their innovative uses of technology as a coping strategy.

POTENTIAL RISKS AND CHALLENGES IN CYBERSPACE

It is a reality that teenagers are using digital technology in their everyday lives. In addition to providing a comfortable environment within which teenagers prefer to interact, there are no barriers regarding transportation and no conflicts between parents' schedules and the timing of an adolescent's desire to interact with friends. Although these advantages and other benefits are important, it is crucial to recognize the potential risks and challenges that teenagers may face while using this technology.

The literature documents a wide range of "double-edged" swords. Hellenga (2002) acknowledges that online communication can provide adolescents who are typically shy or uncomfortable with peers with an alternative socialization ground. Stanfield (as quoted in Natekar, 2007) notes that being online may provide an excuse to avoid face-to-face interactions, which is not always healthy. Is it possible that adolescents who spend most of their time online will never develop the skills to be successful in face-to-face social interactions (e.g., reading nonverbal social cues, confidently using verbal skills)? Is the quality of social support received online as effective as that provided in-person?

Although adolescents may find other like-minded teens online that are not easy to find in person, Pascoe (2007) notes that there are also subcultures online that are a little bit more dangerous. "Kids who are marginalized can find community online . . . but for kids who are engaging in pathological behaviors . . . (the Internet) can be incredibly dangerous, because they can find other people who support that kind of behavior" (p. 8). While considering the impact of Internet use on mental health, Hellenga (2002) notes the importance of investigating whether individuals who spend a great deal of time in online activities may be doing so specifically because they are lonely, maladjusted, or unhappy and may require professional help.

"Safety" online can be defined in a variety of ways. As previously noted, it is important for adolescents to be educated about the differences between "public" and "private" in online environments and the potential risks of posting personal information in a public forum. An adolescent's physical safety can be compromised by sharing one's address or making arrangements to meet someone face-to-face who is a "virtual stranger" because it is not uncommon for children to pretend to be older and for some adults to pretend to be younger.

Trust is a key component of safety in online environments, and one must be aware of potential ways that trust can be violated. Joinson and Dietz-Uhler (2002) note that the anonymity inherent in some Internet-based communities provides ample opportunity for participants to engage in deception. If the deception were to involve the creation and subsequent demise of a member of an online community of bereaved participants already dealing with loss, reactions to the loss of a community member could create additional challenges for people who may already be in a vulnerable emotional state. Administrators of grief-specific sites and moderators of support groups should be familiar with strategies to detect a fabricated crisis or fictitious illness (Feldman, 2000).

One's emotional safety can also be impacted by cyberbullying, which can include flaming, harassment, denigration, impersonation, outing and trickery, and exclusion (Kelsey, 2007). Knobel (2003) notes that a "rant" (simply venting) can be easily misinterpreted as a "flame," and it can often be difficult to provide a "fair" account or interpretation of the exchanges that have occurred. A response to a question about the absence of message boards on GriefNet notes that this site does not use them because sometimes people post nasty or hurtful things, and administrators or moderators do not find them before they cause some damage. Although data regarding the incidence of cyberbullying within thanatology-related groups are not readily available, the reality of these inappropriate behaviors is widely documented as a risk of participating in all types of resources in the digital world (Goodstein, 2007). Raw emotions may also be shared in postings, and although they may not be intended to be offensive, it is possible that they may have a negative impact on some participants. User agreements should clearly describe the policies that exist regarding the screening or withholding of potentially objectionable postings, and moderators have a responsibility to all members to communicate in a timely manner with the author of any posting that is deemed questionable or inappropriate. Adolescents should be reminded to inform a trusted adult if they perceive or experience a threat to their safety as a result of online activities.

Those responsible for the oversight of these online resources must also consider the impact on a person seeking support or guidance if no one in the group responds to a member's posting. When members join a group, should they be prepared for the possibility that there are times when "traffic" on the site is slow, meaning that they may not get an immediate response to their posting (or perhaps no posting at all)? Should members also be reminded that others are depending upon them for support even when they themselves may not be actively needing it and be asked to check the site at least once during a prescribed period? When someone has decided to stop participating in an online community of bereavement, should they be asked to inform the group and say goodbye? These questions merit consideration.

IMPLICATIONS FOR CLINICIANS, DEATH EDUCATORS, AND PARENTS

In the past, the "digital divide" referred to differences in one's access to technology because of the lack of physical access to a computer or the inability to afford online services (see Chapter 2 by Gilbert and Massimi for additional information about how the meaning of this concept is changing.) According to Dretzin (2008), "the digital divide is less about having access than it is about using the access that's available" (p. 9), with parents being in particular need of learning about the technology that is available to and being used by their teenagers. Many grief counselors and death educators may find themselves in the good but uninformed company of these parents.

Prensky (2001) has described members of the D-gen [for digital generation] as "digital natives," meaning that adolescents are "native speakers of the digital language of computers, video games and the Internet" (p. 1). Those of us who were not born into the digital world but have, at some later point in our lives, begun to use some or most aspects of technology will always be "digital immigrants." One important distinction between digital natives and digital immigrants is that all immigrants, regardless of how well they adapt to their new environment, retain their "accent" or tendency to do things in the way that they were initially socialized (e.g., calling to ask if someone received your e-mail). Although Prensky's comments are written in relation to students and educators in a school setting, it is not difficult to translate the implications of this distinction to the context of bereaved adolescents working with grief counselors or death educators who are unfamiliar with digital technology. Prensky states: ". . . the single biggest problem facing education today is that our Digital Immigrant instructors, who speak an outdated language (that of the pre-digital age), are struggling to teach a population that speaks an entirely new language. This is obvious to the Digital Natives—school often feels pretty much as if we've brought in a population of heavily accented, unintelligible foreigners to lecture them; they often can't understand what the immigrants are saying. What does 'dial' a number mean, anyway?" (p. 2).

Bridging the differences in knowledge about and familiarity with thanatechnology involves a need for "digital literacy" for not only the digital immigrants but also the digital natives. Parents, grief counselors, death educators, and researchers must spend time learning about digital technology with the goal of developing a common language that can be spoken with the adolescents with whom they interact. To reassure parents and thanatologists that adolescents will not be harmed by use of these digital resources, adolescents also have a need for digital literacy. Pascoe (2007) describes digital literacy as including the need to know how to keep themselves safe online (e.g., www.blogsafety or http://wiredsafety.org/), to think about the information they are putting out there, and to be able to have discussions with their parents about it.

In addition to being digitally literate, parents and thanatologists must consider the best way to have open discussions with adolescents about these resources (resources to assist include Goodstein, 2007; Kelsey, 2007; Magid & Collier, 2007). As Pascoe (2007) notes, forbidding the use of technology just shuts down communication, and the teenagers will definitely find a way. Goodstein (2007) provides similar advice for parents about monitoring blogs: "Beginning a dialogue sounds a lot better than breaking and entering, online or off" (p. 50). Inviting adolescents to share tales of their adventures in the digital world, whether the genre of the tale turns out to be a drama, a comedy, or a horror story, is a useful way to help them process these experiences and to alleviate one's own worries or fears about the impact of digital technology on their social and emotional well-being.

IMPLICATIONS FOR RESEARCH

Montgomery (2007) notes the need for a conversation, informed by research, on how digital technologies can best meet the needs of children and youth. It would be wise for thanatologists to have a role in this dialogue, as well as facilitating the collection of data from bereaved youth, thereby ensuring that their voices are heard. Empirical studies must be conducted to understand the potential risks and benefits of the use of digital technology in the lives of bereaved adolescents. It would be valuable to document adolescents' access to and usage of thanatology-related informational resources as well as the usage and impact (effectiveness and any potential risks or harm) of computer-mediated communications to specifically cope with loss-related events. How is "virtual grief" similar or different from grief that is expressed without the use of thanatechnology? These and other questions posed in this chapter merit attention.

However, the process of conducting research with bereaved adolescents about their use of the Internet in combination with conducting research on-line involves a challenging set of ethical issues that will be discussed by Cupit in Chapter 13.

CONCLUSIONS

Noting the need to understand that adolescents live in a new, massive, and complex virtual universe, Greenfield and Yan (2006) encourage us to see the Internet as a "new cultural tool kit" that provides us with an infinite series of applications (p. 392). In 2002, Hellenga noted that the rapid growth of computer-mediated communication in all forms made it difficult to imagine all future uses of this technology. In 2012, it is amazing to recognize that iPads and iPhones will all too soon be replaced with a new generation of iGadgets. Oltjenbruns and James (2006) encouraged thanatologists to become familiar with online resources because talking about them could create opportunities for positive dialogue with teens on how to use the Internet in a safe and positive manner. Doing this will require efforts to gather data informally from the adolescents whom we serve and to formally conduct empirical research in a manner that honors and respects the challenges of data collection in cyberspace. Perhaps, with the assistance of a few bereaved adolescents who are savvy with the technical aspects of web design and computer programming, thanatologists will be able to develop new resources that merge the latest in technology with content specific to the experiences of bereaved teenagers (e.g., how to respond to friends when they are not being helpful during times of grief). When working with current and future members of the "digital generation," implementing that tried and true counselor's directive to "meet the clients where they are at" will require gaining a level of comfort being in cyberspace, a place where today's teenagers appear to be very comfortable. However, when learning about and using ICT and spending time in an SNS to assist grieving adolescents, it will be important to remember to use some good old fashioned TLC.

REFERENCES

Atfield, C., Chalmers, E., & Lion, P. (2006, November 21). Safety net for grief—Anguished teens reach out across cyberspace. *The Courier Mail*, p. 9.

Blais, J. J., Craig, W. M., Pepler, D., & Connolly, J. (2008). Adolescents online: The importance of Internet activity choices to salient relationships. *Journal of Youth and Adolescence, 37*(5), 522–536.

Borzekowski, D. L. G., & Rickert, V. I. (2001). Adolescent cybersurfing for health information: A new resource that crosses barriers. *Archives of Pediatric Adolescent Medicine, 155*, 813–817.

Bunn, A. (2000, August). The rise of the teen guru. *Brill's Content*. Retrieved June 18, 2008, from http://www.austinbunn.com/articles.php?target=teenguru.html

Burrell, J. (2007, January 18). Electronic age changes face of grief: IMs, Facebook allow youths to connect without having to be face to face. *Contra Costa Times*, p. A1.

Davis, V. (2009, December 9). *Digiteens: Digital citizenship by digital teenagers.* K12 Online Conference 2010. Retrieved July 21, 2011, from http://k12onlineconference.org/?p=431

Dretzin, R. (2008). *What we learned.* Retrieved June 12, 2008, from www.pbs.org/sgbh/pages/frontline/kidsonline/etc/notebook.html

Feldman, M. D. (2000). Munchausen by Internet: Detecting factitious illness and crisis on the Internet. *Southern Medical Journal, 93*, 669–672.

Fitzgerald, H. (2000). *The grieving teen: A guide for teenagers and their friends.* New York, NY: Fireside.

Gagnon, M. (2005, December 1). *Teenager posts suicide note on MySpace.com.* Retrieved June 5, 2008, from http://news.newamericamedia.org/news/view_article.html?article_id=6d81 34fbbe964d76f864b3b9682dcb19

Goodstein, A. (2007). *Totally wired: What teens and tweens are really doing online.* NY: St. Martin's Press.

Greenfield, P., & Yan, Z. (2006). Children, adolescents, and the Internet: A new field of inquiry in developmental psychology. *Developmental Psychology, 42*(3), 391–394.

Harris, F. J. (2005). *I found it on the Internet: Coming of age online.* Chicago, IL: American Library Association.

Hellenga, K. (2002). Social space, the final frontier: Adolescents on the Internet. In J. T. Mortimer & R. W. Larson (Eds.), *The changing adolescent experience: Societal trends and the transition to adulthood* (pp. 208–249). Cambridge, UK: Cambridge University Press.

Huffaker, D. A., & Calvert, S. L. (2005). Gender, identity, and language use in teenage blogs. *Journal of Computer-Mediated Communication, 10*(2). Retrieved June 18, 2008, from http://jcmc.indiana.edu/vol10/issue2/huffaker.html

Jenkins, H., Clinton, K., Purushotma, R., Robinson, A. J., & Weigel, M. (2006, October 16). *Confronting the challenges of participatory culture: Media education for the 21st century* (white paper). Chicago, IL: MacArthur Foundation. Retrieved May 21, 2008, from http://www.digitallearning.macfound.org/atf/cf/%7BE45C7E0-A3E0-4B89-AC9C-E807E1B0AE4E%7D/JENKINS_WHITE_PAPER.PDF

Joinson, A. N., & Dietz-Uhler, B. (2002). Explanations for the perpetration of and reactions to deception in a virtual community. *Social Science Computer Review, 20*(3), 275–289.

Kelsey, C. M. (2007). *Generation MySpace: Helping your teen survive online adolescence.* New York, NY: Marlowe & Company.

Knobel, M. (2003). Rants, ratings, and representations: Issues of validity, reliability and ethics in researching online social practices. *Education, Communication and Information, 3*(2), 187–210.

Lee, S. (2008). Lack of hope for kids that leads to despair. *Liverpool Daily Echo*, p. 8.

Lenhart, A., Madden, M., & Hitlin, P. (2005, July 27). *Teens and Technology: Youth are leading the transition to a fully wired and mobile nation*. Pew Internet & American Life Project. Retrieved July 25, 2011, from http://pewinternet.org/~/media/Files/Reports/2005/PIP_Teens_Tech_July2005web.pdf.pdf

Lenhart, A., Madden, M., Macgill, A. R., & Smith. A. (2007). *Teens and social media*. Retrieved July 21, 2011, from http://www.pewinternet.org/~/media//Files/Reports/2007/PIP_Teens_Social_Media_Final.pdf.pdf

Lenhart, A., Purcell, K., Smith, A., & Zickuhr, K. (2010, February 3). Social media and mobile Internet use among teens and young adults. Retrieved June 14, 2011, from http://www.pewinternet.org/Reports/2010/Social-Media-and-Young-Adults.aspx

Madkour, R. (2008, November 21). Teen commits suicide online. Retrieved July 21, 2011, from http://www.msnbc.msn.com/id/27841948/ns/technology_and_science-tech_and_gadgets/t/report-teen-commits-suicide-online/

Magid, L., & Collier, A. (2007). *MySpace unraveled: A parents guide to teen social networking*. Berkeley, CA: Peachpit Press.

McCarthy, J. R. (2007). "They all look as if they're coping, but I'm not": The relational power/lessness of "youth" in responding to experiences of bereavement. *Journal of Youth Studies, 10*(3), 285–303.

McKenna, L. (2005, March 17). The Google Stage. 11D. Retrieved June 11, 2008, from http://11d.typepad.com/blog/2005/03/the_google_stag.html

Mesch, G. S., & Talmud, I. (2010). *Wired youth: The social work of adolescence in the information age*. New York, NY: Routledge.

Montgomery, K. C. (2007). *Generation digital: Politics, commerce, and childhood in the age of the Internet*. Cambridge, MA: MIT Press.

Natekar, A. (2007, November 12). *Egrieving: Teens turning to their Web pages to mourn friends, family*. Retrieved March 19, 2008, at http://www.redorbit.com/news/technology/1140749/egrieving_teens_turning_to_their_web_pages_to_mourn_friends/index.html

Niebuhr, G., & Wilgoren, J. (1999, April 28). Terror in Littleton. *The New York Times*. Retrieved May 22, 2008, from www.nytimes.com

O'Brien, B. (2008, March 1). Suicide and what it means to the Bebo generation. *Irish Times*, p. 16.

Oltjenbruns, K. A., & James, L. (2006). Adolescents' use of the Internet as a modality of grief support. *The Forum, 32*(4), 5–6.

Pascoe, C. J. (2007). Interview conducted on July 17. Retrieved June 11, 2008, from www.pbs.org/wgbh/pages/frontline/kidsonline/interviews/pascoe.html

PBS. (2008). *Growing up online*. Documentary originally aired on January 22. Retrieved March 12, 2008, from http://www.pbs.org/wgbh/pages/frontline/kidsonline/

Pokin, S. (2007, November 10). A real person, a real death. *St. Charles Journal*. Retrieved June 10, 2008, http://www.meganmeierfoundation.org/story/

Prensky, M. (2001). Digital natives, digital immigrants. *On the Horizon, 9*(5), 1–6. Retrieved June 19, 2008, from http://www.marcprensky.com/writing/Prensky%20-%20Digital%20Natives,%20Digital%20Immigrants%20-%20Part1.pdf

Rideout, V. J., Foehr, U. G., & Roberts, D. F. (2010, January). Generation M^2: Media in the lives of 8- to 18-year olds. Retrieved July 23, 2011, from http://www.kff.org/entmedia/upload/8010.pdf

Scheeres, J. (2003, June 8). A virtual path to suicide: Depressed student killed herself with help from online discussion group. *San Francisco Chronicle*. Retrieved July 23, 2011, from http://articles.sfgate.com/2003-06-08/news/17493615_1_suicide-rat-poison-monoxide

Schmitt, K. L., Dayanim, S., & Matthias, S. (2008). Personal homepage construction as an expression of social development. *Developmental Psychology, 44*(2), 496–506.

Servaty, H. L., & Hayslip, B. (2001). Adjustment to loss among adolescents. *Omega: Journal of Death and Dying, 43*(4), 311–330.

Siad, S. (2007, May 25). Teens cope with grief online. *The Toronto Star*, p. A01.

Sofka, C. J. (1997). Social support "internetworks", caskets for sale, and more: Thanatology and the information superhighway. *Death Studies, 21*(6), 553–574.

Whitaker, J. (2002). *The Internet: The basics*. New York, NY: Routledge.

5

Blogging: New Age Narratives of Dying, Death, and Grief

Carla J. Sofka

Bloggers have become the curators of our collective experience.
- Scott Rosenberg

This fascinating statement from the front-inside dustcover of Rosenberg's (2009) "biography" of blogging encourages us to consider the potential impact of a communication medium that puts the power of personal publishing into the hands of anyone with access to software designed to create what is commonly known as a weblog or blog. According to the Merriam-Webster (2011) online dictionary, a blog is a "web site that contains an online personal journal with reflections, comments, and often hyperlinks provided by the writer" (n.p.). Rosenberg (2009) notes that "efforts to identify the first web log are comical and ultimately futile" because "blogging was not invented; it evolved" (p. 81). Prior to the advent of blogging, *Wikipedia* (2011a), a source that this author trusts to accurately document the origins of computer-mediated communication modalities, reminds us that individuals shared their thoughts via e-mail lists and threaded discussions on electronic bulletin boards.

The term *WebLog* was introduced in 1997 by Jorn Barger, who "capitalised the L because the syllable 'blog' seemed so hideous" (p. 79), to describe the new phenomenon of personal sites with links and commentary in reverse chronological order (Rosenberg, 2009). Blogs sometimes contain lists of the author's favorite blogs (known as a *blogroll*) and often provide readers with the opportunity to post comments, adding an interactive element (Yang, 2006). However, Gunnelius (2009) wisely reminds us that some people are merely passive readers.

All of these elements combined are currently referred to as the *blogosphere*, a name proposed by William Quick in 2002 for the intellectual cyberspace occupied by bloggers (Rosenberg, 2009) and described by Badger (2004) as the web environment in which bloggers "form connections with others while progressing along their own paths" (n.p.). *Microblogs* (originally labeled *tumblelogs* in 2005) were made popular by services such as Twitter and Tumblr and incorporated into social networking sites (Facebook, MySpace) as "status updates"/wall postings (*Wikipedia*, 2011a) and have added a new dimension to the blogosphere in the last several years. They provide a platform for very brief postings (e.g., Twitter is 140 characters or less) and/or the sharing of a video or photo with minimal text.

Over the past few decades, the telling of personal stories regarding illness, death, and grief has occupied a prominent place within contemporary culture (Bingley, McDermott, Payne, Seymour, and Clark, 2006). This chapter will describe how web-based thanatechnology resources have facilitated the sharing of these personal narratives. The various types of blogs, the motives for blogging, and the potential benefits of blogging will be described. The traits and characteristics of bloggers will be summarized, and factors that influence blogging behavior will be discussed. Factors that influence the roles that people take on within this component of cyberspace will also be considered. Following a guided tour of a small subset of thanatology-related sites in the blogosphere, the chapter will conclude with implications of the availability of this type of thanatechnology for grief counselors, death educators, and researchers.

Types of Blogs

Information about the types of blogs is available from a wide range of sources in the popular press and the scholarly literature. Blogs are incredibly diverse, and the need to describe blogs within popular culture and to understand them from a scholarly perspective has resulted in a variety of ways to categorize them. For example, *Wikipedia* (2011a) states that "there are many different types of blogs, differing not only in the type of content, but also in the way that content is delivered or written" (n.p.) and uses the following characteristics to categorize blogs: (a) is the "owner" of the blog an individual (a personal or private blog), a corporation or business, or an organization; (b) what subject does the blog typically address (sorting blogs by "genre" such as travel, fashion, music, art, politics, project blogs, education blogs, or specialized subjects—"niche blogs"); (c) what media type is used (video or vlogs, linklogs, sketchlogs, photoblogs, or tumblelogs that combine short posts and mixed media types); and (d) what type of device is used to compose it (a mobile device such as a smart phone, wearable wireless webcam, etc.).

Gunnelius (2010) mentions a rarely discussed type of blog "event" known as a blog carnival, describing it as a promotional event considered to be a component of a blogger's marketing plan. The FAQ site of *Blog Carnival* (http://blogcarnival.com/bc/p_about.html) states that a blog carnival is a particular type of "blog community" that functions somewhat like a magazine with a title, a topic, editors, contributors, and an audience. "Editions" of the carnival come out on a regular basis, and each edition is a special blog with links to all the contributions that have been submitted. According to Gunnelius (2010), "blog carnivals work well for focused, niche topics where readers are actively looking for more information or varied opinions on a specific subject" and "provide an excellent way to help participating bloggers build relationships with each other and with the other participating blogs' audiences" (p. 494). This concept is reminiscent of the memorial webrings described in Sofka (1997). *Wikipedia* (2011c) describes a webring (or web ring) as "a collection of websites linked together in a circular structure, and usually organized around a specific theme, often educational or social. They were popular in the 1990s and early 2000s, particularly among amateur websites, but have since become quite rare" (n.p.).

The scholarly literature also contains ways to categorize blogs. Blood (2002) describes a classic form of weblog called a "filter blog"—blogs that focus on links to interesting places on the web and add commentary by a blogger. BoingBoing is a personal favorite because this site often publishes quirky thanatology-related blurbs with links that my husband forwards to me for use in my death and dying class. Krishnamurthy (2002) classified blogs into four basic types according to two dimensions (focus of the content and authorship/interactivity): topical versus personal and individual versus community. Miura and Yamashita (2007) also acknowledge the important distinction between tools that facilitate self-description (personal/individual) versus those that facilitate interaction with others (dialogue among members of a "community").

Hearst and Dumais (2009) recognize that multiauthored blogs (also known as group, collaborative, collective, community, company, team, or project blogs [Plogs]) are a growing phenomenon. Content-oriented group blogs can also be wisely used to assist those dealing with illness/dying, death, and grief. For an example of this type of blog, see Chapter 11 for a description of the rich range of resources developed by the Open to Hope Foundation.

Motives for Blogging/Benefits of Blogging

What motivates someone to blog? Gunnelius (2009), in *Google Blogger for Dummies*, describes the following reasons: (a) for fun; (b) to help people or make a difference—educating people or changing the way people think about a topic; (c) sharing tips or influencing views or politics or to establish yourself as an expert in a specific field (for exposure); (d) to build a business; and (e) to make money (from advertising and other blog monetization efforts). It is important to remember that many thanatology-related blogs do have a commercial element, either selling a product (often books about grief and loss) or a service (counseling or public speaking).

Empirical research has also investigated what motivates a person to blog. Nardi, Schiano, Gumbrecht, and Swartz (2004) identified 5 major motivations for blogging that are frequently cited: 1) to document one's life; 2) to provide commentary and opinions; 3) to express deeply felt emotions; 4) to articulate one's ideas through writing; and 5) to form and maintain community forums. According to Nardi, Schiano, and Gumbrecht (2004), blogs serve as a social activity – "a form of social communication in which blogger and audience are intimately related through the writing and reading of blogs" (p. 224) and object-oriented activity – "the inscriptions in the blog communicate specific social purposes to others" (p. 225).

Another way to approach the question of motive is to consider the possible benefits of blogging. According to Yang (2006), "the need to express life's frustrations and joys on the page is an age-old tradition harkening back to the earliest days of quill and ink" (p. 111). There is a longstanding belief that writing can be therapeutic and that writing about personal experiences can help us to understand ourselves more deeply and mitigate major problems or conflicts (Frank, 1995; Bolton, 1999; Miura & Yamashita, 2007; Neimeyer, Smythe, & Pennebaker, 2008; Smyth & Pennebaker, 2008). A case study published by Tan (2008) provides evidence that blogging can serve as a form of self-therapy.

In addition to these "benefits to self," Miura and Yamashita (2007) note benefits that stem from connections with others when the writing occurs within a blogging community, such as creating relationships through the dialogue that occurs, the sense of "belonging" to an interactive community that one gains, gaining "acceptance" from others as evidenced by positive comments in their postings, and receiving social support, sympathy, and encouragement. Yang (2006) agrees that a circle of readers can form and revolve around the blog, creating sprawling but interlinked communities that connect and support people.

Formal research about participation in thanatology-related blogging activities (individual and community oriented) is needed to determine if there are unique motives for individuals who are dealing with illness, impending death, or grief. Based on the blogs and articles that were read during the literature review for this chapter, participation in blogging communities appears to be mutually beneficial for bloggers and readers alike, which supports the tried and true "helper" therapy principle described by Riessman (1965). This principle postulates that by helping others, an individual also gains some type of personal benefit. Within the blogosphere, by talking about one's experiences, you might in some way prepare others in a similar situation for what is ahead, making their journey less stressful or less uncertain. Confirmation that one's experience is a shared one not only reassures a person that he or she is "normal" but also reminds everyone who participates in the exchange of comments that he or she is not alone. Moore and Serva (2007) also note the relevance of altruistic versus egoistic motives for participation in virtual communities.

Bob Meyer, a bereaved spouse who participated in a listserve while his wife battled multiple myeloma, eloquently states: "The cliché is, of course, that misery loves company. But what misery really loves is understanding" (as quoted in DeMarco, 2004, p. E1). Although some people have never met face to face, the members of these online communities become important to each other. "Even though I don't know them, they were friends in a certain way, and I wanted them to know" (Steve Weissburg, as quoted in DeMarco, 2004, p. E1). According to

Stefanone and Jang (2007), computer-mediated communication creates opportunities for relationship maintenance and support beyond those that are accomplished through telephone calls and face-to-face visits. Self-disclosure may have a positive impact on "social capital" (Ko & Kuo, 2009).

Last but certainly not least, there may be benefits of participation that do not relate to emotional well-being. Miura and Yamashita (2007) note that blogging may improve one's information-handling skills. In addition, there may be physiological benefits from blogging (Wapner, 2008).

Traits of Bloggers and Factors Influencing Blogging Behavior

What are the traits and characteristics of bloggers? Interpreting the data about blogging from the Pew Internet and American Life Project is a challenging task. Lee Rainie, director of this project, cautions against interpreting decreases in reported percentages of individuals who are blogging incorrectly, because he believes that blogging is not so much dying as shifting with the times; "The act of telling your story and sharing part of your life with somebody is alive and well—even more so than at the dawn of blogging. It's just morphing onto other platforms" (Rainie, as quoted in Kopytoff, 2011).

There are clear generational differences in blogging behavior as described in two reports from the Pew Internet and American Life Project. According to Zickuhr (2010), only half as many teens aged 12 to 17 years (14%) worked on their own blog in 2009 as did in 2006. Lenhart, Purcell, Smith, and Zickuhr (2010) note that rather than using a platform solely for blogging, 73% of online teens are communicating about their lives on social networking sites. These studies also report a modest decline in blogging among millennial generation adults with ages 18 to 33 years, also likely because of the growing popularity of social networking sites among this age group. Zickuhr (2010) reports that blogging among members of Gen X increased from 10% in December 2008 to 16% in May 2010, and 11% of younger and older boomers currently blog as well. Overall, this results in a slight increase in blogging for adults overall, from 11% in late 2008 to 14% in 2010. Blogging's popularity increased among most older generations, and as a result, the rate of blogging for all online adults rose slightly overall from 11% in late 2008 to 14% in 2010. "Yet while the act formally known as blogging seems to have peaked, internet users are doing blog-like things in other online spaces as they post updates about their lives, musings about the world, jokes, and links on social networking sites and micro-blogging sites such as Twitter" (Zickuhr, 2010).

What factors influence a person's decision to blog, the style of blogging that is selected, and the content that a blogger shares? The empirical literature, although not specific to thanatology-related blogs, is beginning to generate a list of traits and characteristics that are worthy of consideration. Although it is beyond the scope of this chapter to describe this literature in detail, readers can consult prior research (e.g., Nowson, Oberlander and Gill, 2005; Miura & Yamashita, 2007; Stefanone & Jang, 2007) to learn about how factors such as gender, education, self-disclosure traits, personality traits such as extroversion versus introversion, neuroticism, openness, "reassurance seeking" and "agreeableness," and social factors such as the type of feedback (sympathy, support, and encouragement vs. criticism or complaints) relate to blogging behavior. There is tremendous potential for thanatology researchers to add to this growing body of literature, and death professionals should explore the motives behind blogging and factors that influence this behavior among clients who have selected to use this type of thanatechnology as a coping strategy.

THANATOLOGY IN THE BLOGOSPHERE: A GUIDED TOUR

Although bloggers have written about every topic imaginable (and some that are hard to fathom), this chapter will focus on how blogs (perhaps we should call them *thanablogs* written by *thanabloggers*) have been used as a type of thanatechnology. In other words, what role does the blogosphere play in bringing thanatology-related topics into the public eye?

Thanatourism/Dark Tourism

Because I have referred to this overview of thanatology-related blogs as a guided tour and have penned "Adventures of a Thanatologist" in the News and Notes column of *Death Studies* for years, it seems appropriate to begin with a link between the ever-popular "travel blogs" and thanatology. Thanatourism or dark tourism involves visiting places that are associated with death, typically cemeteries or sites affiliated with genocide, war, homicide, or other tragedies/horrors. One example of a thanatourism blog is written by "I am Thanorak," who was blogging about two new sites for thanatourism at the time that this chapter was being completed: the shrine outside of Amy Winehouse's home in Camden (UK) and a proposed (but perhaps wisely cancelled) tour of sites affiliated with the Casey Anthony murder trial in Orlando, Florida. This thanablogger describes the appeal: "These fascinating places teach us about the nature of our existence—the fleeting reality of life, the failings of civilizations. And yet in them we find reminders of the essential need for compassion in our every waking action." (I am Thanorak, 2011). Blogs such as this one take advantage of the natural fascination that can occur when popular culture and death collide.

Journal Thanablogs/Personal Thanablogs by Online Diarists

Next on our guided tour of thanablogging sites are those that fall into the category of "journal blogs" or "personal blogs." Although there has been no research to empirically document the distribution among types of thanatology-related blogs, it is this author's observation that blogs serving as online diaries are the most common type. Sharing personal information is the hallmark of journal bloggers, also known as online diarists. Rosenberg (2009) describes one of the earliest recorded bloggers, Justin Hall, as the person who invented "oversharing" in 1994. "Of course, we didn't have a name yet for the compulsion to tell the online world too much about yourself. Back then, Hall was just an eccentric nineteen-year-old college student who recorded minutiae of his life on his personal website; no one knew that the self-revelation he found so addictive would one day become a temptation for millions" (Rosenberg, 2009, p. 17). When gathering information about the factors that influenced Hall's calling to public autobiography, Rosenberg discovered that it was driven in part by the trauma of a parental suicide. Yang (2006) notes this new type of blogging emerged in the late 1990s with blogs being written by people who were primarily interested in expressing himself or herself in his or her own words.

What influences a blogger's choice of topic? How does one decide to become a thanablogger (a "digital diarist" with a thanatology-related topic)? One label used to describe blogging that focuses on a particular topic is "niche blogging," and thanablogger Harriet Hodgsen (2010) states: "I didn't choose my niche—my niche chose me" (n.p.). Hodgsen began blogging about grief resources after experiencing the deaths of four loved ones within 1 year. Experiencing illness or loss (both anticipated or sudden/tragic) seems to prompt people to share their stories with anyone who happens to locate their blog if it is posted on a public site or for private audiences if the blog is password protected.

Using websites to gain health-related information has evolved into the field of e-health, with health consumers who use the Internet to gather information about a medical condition and who use electronic communication tools (including Web 2.0 tools) in coping with these medical conditions being referred to as *e-patients*, *Internet patients*, or *Internet-savvy patients* (*Wikipedia*, 2011b). It is becoming increasingly common for people to use blogs to document a personal journey with illness, referred to by Meares (2011) as *patient bloggers*.

Well-known examples of patient bloggers include Randy Pausch and Leroy Sievers. Randy Pausch's story became famous overnight following the broadcast of his "Last Lecture" as he prepared to "retire" from a career as a professor of computer science and human–computer interaction at Carnegie Mellon because of his battle with pancreatic cancer. His blog site (http://thelastlecture.com/blog/) remains active several years after his death, providing an opportunity for his surviving family members and friends to learn about the continued impact of his journey with illness and preparing for his own death. The postings by thousands of individuals who have read Pausch's book serve as a continuing source of inspiration for patients with pancreatic cancer and their loved ones.

Leroy Sievers was an award-winning journalist and commentator for NPR who kept a blog and a podcast called *My Cancer* (http://www.npr.org/blogs/mycancer/), which documented his struggle with metastatic colon cancer. His blog evolved into a large community of patients with cancer and survivors and significant others of these individuals who regularly contributed to the blog, frequently offering Sievers and his wife Laurie messages of support and gratitude for sharing his story. Following his death, Laurie continued to blog about her grief journey until a decision was made to shift the *My Cancer* blog to a blog hosted by Johns Hopkins called *Our Cancer* (http://our-cancer.blogs.hopkinsmedicine.org), which allowed other members of this community to also post their stories. The new blog continues to thrive and touts the following motto: A community of people living and fighting everyday (with "the beast").

Rosenberg (2009) describes "lifeloggers" who "record personal data—photos, videos, text documents, anything that can be reduced to bits—for their own personal use, and sometimes as a legacy for descendants" (p. 347). Creating a digital legacy for surviving loved ones can be done through the use of a private blog. "Lifecasters" are those who do the same thing but "also open up the feeds of their experience for others on the Web to follow" (p. 347). Perhaps, a specialized niche will develop for hospice thanatechnologists who can assist individuals in preparing this type of digital legacy.

Although individuals have created blogs on personal websites to document their journeys, there are also well-established and widely used "community" websites available for patient bloggers and their families/friends. Some are disease specific (e.g., http://www.blogforacure.com/, a community of cancer survivors supporting each other) or available for use by anyone dealing with illness or tragedy (e.g., CarePages at http://www.carepages.com/ and CaringBridge at http://www.caringbridge.org/). For detailed information about this type of thanatechnology resource, readers are encouraged to read the detailed case study by Jane Moore describing how a CarePages site (in conjunction with another type of thanatechnology—Skype) was used to cope with the impending death of her mother (see Chapter 6).

In addition to being commonly used in situations involving illness, the use of journal blogs and microblogs in times of crisis and tragedy gained momentum in the immediate aftermath of the events on the morning of September 11, 2001. Because of the shock and devastation that resulted from the terrorist attacks, there was a demand for immediate and continuous information (Yang, 2006; Rosenberg, 2009). According to Yang (2006), "even with the traditional media working overtime, it wasn't enough for many people. Hundreds of thousands of readers flocked to person weblogs to get the human perspective from the foot of the WTC [World Trade Center]. Some blogs even posted minute-by-minute accounts of the tragedy as it happened, making for harrowing and intense reading" (p. 12). When the high volume of traffic on the websites of mainstream news operations clogged the Internet's "arteries," people communicated through blogs—the Internet's capillaries (Rosenberg, 2009). Archival sites documenting this day and the aftermath of this event still remain (e.g., http://www.nycbloggers.com/911.asp; http://lcweb2.loc.gov/diglib/lcwa/html/sept11/sept11-overview.html). Gopal (2007) has also studied the types of blogging that occurred after the Katrina disaster in 2005, noting blogs from media channels and citizen journalists. Because most individuals personally impacted by this natural disaster had no Internet access, personal stories were somewhat minimal. The circumstances surrounding a large-scale tragedy certainly impact the nature of the blogs and blogging that evolves.

Blogs and microblogs, particularly Twitter, Tumblr, and postings on Facebook, are often the first places where news of breaking tragedy will appear. Rather than learning of a tragedy or a death in person, death notifications are being more commonly made via a "tweet," a status update, or a text message on a smart phone. Individuals should think carefully about the timing of posting news of a tragedy or death online to guarantee that those who deserve to be notified in person have definitely been informed. Grief counselors will also need to update their assessment repertoire to include questions about the role of thanatechnology when asking "How did you find out?" or "What information do you have?" and take this into account when evaluating the accuracy of the information.

Personal thanabloggers are also documenting the grief journeys that have resulted from an incredibly wide range of loss events, including but not limited to widowhood; the death of a child, parent, or sibling; pet bereavement; adoption-related losses; nondeath physical trauma; and war-related losses (including the impact of posttraumatic stress disorder/the loss of mental health).

Describing all of the grief-related thanablogs would fill volumes. Therefore, readers are encouraged to use blog search engines and two thanatology-specific search engines (e.g., http://www.blogcatalog.com/category/personal/death/ and http://en.wordpress.com/tag/death-and-dying/) to explore the wealth of examples available. This section will conclude with a brief description of one of the more unique thanablogs that was discovered during my travels through the blogosphere.

Imagine spending your life in a shadow cast by the death of someone you never met and a quest to find this person's physical remains that were never recovered. Sharon Estill Taylor, a war baby whose father never came home from World War II, has used a website and blog to document her quest to know her father and to locate her father's missing remains and the remains of his plane. Taylor's website/blog (2010-2005), entitled *My Phantom Father: A Daughter's Quest for Elegy*, describes her journey that culminated with the repatriation of her father's remains and the creation of a documentary film telling the story (also see Taylor, 2006). Taylor's words taken from the "About" section of the website/blog capture its essence: "This project is about honor and sacrifice, another way to be a daughter, and a tribute to the eternal spirit of father-love across time and reality." (n.p.).

Expressive/Creative Thanablogs

One need only visit the nearest art gallery or museum to see examples of how grief and pain have inspired creativity throughout history. The blogosphere also contains examples of how this type of thanatechnology not only helps the blogger to cope with loss but also hopefully inspires a visitor to nurture his or her creative spirit. Two examples of this type of thanablog will be presented.

Thanatology professionals have created resources for individuals to use. A Registered Nurse (RN) named Jennie serves as editor and webmaster for Recover from Grief/*The Grief Loss Blog* (http://www.recover-from-grief.com/grief-loss-blog.html). The website describes the concept of "healing through creative grieving":

> We present in our website a variety of creative mourning techniques; talking, writing, creating art, music or poetry, or memorializing are all good ways to express your bereavement. Explore our site to find the expressive techniques that feel "just right" for you. (n.p.)

This website and blog serves as a "workshop" where a visitor can pick and choose topics to explore and post submissions to the blog in different sections: Yourspace ("tell your story of grief"), Theirspace ("Post a simple but beautiful memoriam to your lost one"), Petspace ("Tell us about a beloved pet you have lost"), or Grief Poetry ("Write a comforting poem about your loss"). The section on the "Creativity of Grief" guides visitors in therapeutic activities that include how to "draw out" one's emotions, craft a grief mask, and build an alter or memory box to name a few of the options (http://recover.from-grief.com/creativity-grief.html).

Bereaved individuals have also created amazing resources to assist others in using creative outlets to cope with loss. One such example is the *Good Grief Blog* developed by Amanda Probst (http://www.goodgriefblog.com). Following the sudden, accidental death of her father, Amanda was unable to participate in her tried and true creative outlet of scrapbooking. When she returned to her hobby and began scrapbooking about her dad, she realized that this process provided a therapeutic outlet to work through "things I especially miss, things I wish could be different, and things I want to remember" (n.p.). She felt compelled to start her blog on the second anniversary of her father's death because the structure of creating the blog helped her by providing her with deadlines. Creating the "scrapbooking challenges" for her readers (scrapbooking activities with elements of memorialization) allowed her to share her own journey and to be inspired by the submissions from her readers. She also notes:

> My second reason for starting this blog is that I truly believe that this is what my dad would want. He'd want me to live my life and remember him in this way, not dwell on what could have been. I feel like this is his message that he wants me to share, and I've always trusted my dad. (n.p.)

Along with the help of additional bereaved contributors, Amanda continued the blog for a year. She wrote a message that began "Parting is such sweet sorrow" and reported that she felt it was fitting to draw the blog to a close on the 3-year anniversary of her father's death. She issues her readers the final challenge to simply "continue. Whether that means continuing to scrapbook about your loved one or continuing to think about the challenges posted here or merely continuing to get through each day . . . just continue" (n.p.).

Political/Advocacy Thanablogs

It is not difficult to find debates about political issues on blogs, with Drezner and Farrell (2004) noting that "weblogs occupy an increasingly important place in American politics" (p. 2). It is also not difficult to find thanablogs that focus on politically charged issues regarding dying and death. For example, Derek Humphry, one of the founders of the assisted dying movement, has been documenting his views and opinions about the right to seek assistance in dying for many years. His blog can be found at http://assisted-dying.org/blog. A second example involves a blog related to the death penalty, which can be found at http://civilliberty.about.com/od/capitalpunishment/tp/blogs_capital.htm.

Survivor advocacy is also represented within the blogosphere, with blogs dealing with fundraising for medical research and programs to provide support for individuals coping with loss. One example is a blog for a group called "Cures Rock!" (http://curesrock.blogspot.com/). They are a grassroots organization:

> that advocates and fund raises for cancer charities to fight to find a cure for cancer. The group works to break down global silos and stigmas around cancer, creates awareness about the disease in young adults, and inspires those impacted by the cancer through endurance sports, music and online social media. (n.p.)

Death professionals working with individuals or groups who are looking for "something to do" to make a difference may want to consider the possibility of locating existing blogs that provide these individuals with an opportunity to "do something" or to encourage them to investigate the possibility of creating a thanablog of their own.

It is absolutely fascinating to explore the range of thanablogs that are available. Readers are encouraged to use any of the following blog search engines and portals to explore the blogosphere: http://technorati.com/; http://www.blogsearchengine.com/; www.blogpulse.com (for trends in blogging topics); http://www.blogtopsites.com/; www.portal.eatonweb.com; www.blogcatalog.com; and www.icerocket.com.

IMPLICATIONS FOR DEATH EDUCATORS, GRIEF COUNSELORS, AND RESEARCHERS

In addition to figuring out a strategy to simply keep up with the constant technological changes in the blogosphere, death educators, grief counselors, and thanatology researchers must figure out the potentially daunting task of appropriately weaving this type of thanatechnology into their teaching, clinical work, and/or research initiatives.

Thanatologists must first accept the reality that the sheer volume of information available about dying, death, and grief within the blogosphere is overwhelming. Death educators (and grief counselors) would be wise to consider ways in which the information available on the wide variety of thanablogs can be used as teaching tools and resources for informational support for those whom they serve. Taking into account the need to evaluate the accuracy and other aspects of these sources carefully (see the evaluation tools provided in Appendix A), blogs and blogging communities provide a wealth of "case study" material to learn about personal experiences with illness, dying, death, and grief. These resources create a "living laboratory" that allows students to "witness" interactions between the bloggers and those who have chosen to read the blogs and respond. Imagine the enthusiasm and energy in the classroom during the discussions that would evolve and the teachable moments that would arise during analysis of these fascinating sociocultural interchanges. The blogosphere serves as an incredibly rich teaching aid. Reading about others' experiences can also provide a bereaved individual with a "reflective mirror" in which he or she can compare his or her own experiences, perhaps with the support of a counselor.

Formally documenting the presence of thanatology-related issues within the blogosphere and learning about the impact of blogs as a type of thanatechnology on individual and collective journeys with illness and grief are empirical tasks ripe with the potential to generate exciting research projects. It is important to begin conducting research that will answer some basic questions about thanablogging: What influenced this person's decision to share his or her story? What personal traits and characteristics as well as situational factors not only influence when a person blogs and about what he or she blogs but also differentiate between those who blog and those who do not? What is the thanablogger hoping will happen as a result of sharing this story—for not only the reader but also the writer? What impact does participation in the blogosphere, whether blogging or "visiting," reading, and commenting, have on the individual's bereavement process, his or her social support network, and his or her ability to cope with loss and change?

The role of "anonymity" in cyberspace is intriguing. Is it possible that one's identity "changes" in the blogosphere? Pitts (2004) describes the fascinating concept of "cyberagency" or "cyberliberation," the idea that in the absence of a corporeal body in cyberspace, individuals represent themselves through words, images, codes, and symbols. Is our "virtual self" in cyberspace different from our "real self"? Does this play a role adaptation to illness or loss?

In addition to studying the impact on individuals, it is absolutely fascinating to think about the types of connections that are formed between bloggers and those who read their blogs, as well as the impact of all interactions within blogging communities on each of the participants. Researchers are already proposing models that can be used to analyze these interactions, such as the one described by Cardon, Delaunay-Teterel, Fluckiger, and Prieur (2007), which includes factors such as the type of interaction that is shared (mutual revelation of inner feelings vs. mutual activities done in real life vs. sharing a similar interest vs. debate and discussion of views on a public issue), the degree to which the identity of the blogger is known (anonymous vs. one's true identity), and the size of the blogging community. Gopal (2007) describes the importance of the cultural geography of the blogosphere, including "cybergeography" (the spatial structuring of computer networks, including blogs), and the social networking aspects of communities in the blogosphere. Adding in factors already known to thanatologists to impact reactions to loss (demographic characteristics, circumstances of the loss, etc.) and investigating the role of grieving styles in relation to blogging behavior would truly open up the possibility for some fascinating research collaborations between thanatologists (academics and clinicians) and scholars from other fields of study who are already conducting computer–human interaction research and developing models and scales to measure components of blogging and virtual communities (e.g., Baker & Moore, 2011; Moore & Serva, 2007).

Hearst and Dumais (2009) note that "group blogs are inherently interesting from a social media viewpoint as a hybrid way for people to interact with one another and with ideas" (p. 229). As previously described in this chapter (and by Moore in Chapter 6), community-oriented personal thanablogs such as CarePages and CaringBridge that allow for documentation of life journeys involving life-threatening or terminal illness and the posting of supportive comments by significant others are important thanatechnological resources. Nurturing the development of "social support internetworks" (Sofka, 1997) is a potentially valuable intervention that death professionals can implement, provided that empirical research verifies a positive impact of participation in these communities that can result in the receipt of informational, emotional, and material support. Because the sense of "community" that can be gained by finding other bloggers who are dealing with a similar illness or loss event may be beneficial, a tech-savvy grief counselor might want to consider hosting a blog carnival that creates an "event" for individuals dealing with a similar life challenge or loss, such as one that celebrates survivorship of an illness or honors the memories of deceased loved ones. Although the label *carnival* seems a bit incongruent with the somber nature of thanatology-related topics, the desired goal has merit.

Perhaps thanatologists should become more involved in blogging about life as a death educator or grief counselor, or the challenges and joys of conducting thanatology research. This author has included the occasional feature "Adventures of a Thanatologist" (including her not-so-secret life as a thanatourist) in the News and Notes column of *Death Studies* for many years; perhaps, it is time to go more "public" with a thanablog? Or perhaps, it is time to create a blog carnival for thanatologists to come together to compare and contrast our adventures?

As a death educator, I have been working in conjunction with the youth librarians at my local public library to develop a new thanablog that we anticipate will be launched in the summer of 2012. Each entry will identify young adult books that include thanatology-related issues, provide two reviews of each book (my review that will represent a "joint" thanatologist/parental point of view and one from a teen's point of view, most likely written by my teenage daughter or one of the other teen library volunteers), and invite readers of the blog (young adults and their parents) to participate in the discussion. Links to reliable online information about the topic(s) in each book and local resources for assistance will also be included. Death education in conjunction with the public library via thanatechnology—pretty cool!

Perhaps at this point you are excited about the possibilities but are thinking "I have never used these types of technology before" and are reluctant about learning new technology skills; you are encouraged to visit the "Blogging for Dummies" section (no offense intended) of your local public library because there are a wealth of resources available. If you are thinking "I'm not a technogeek—I don't have a tech-savvy bone in my body," consider approaching a techie that you know who would be willing to take on a project for you, or contact the computer science department at a local college or university and ask to be connected with a professor who may be looking for a service learning project for one of his or her classes. Tech-savvy teenagers may also need community service hours to qualify for the National Honor Society and would love to assist with a manageable and well-defined project (contact your local high school and ask to be connected with the "tech" instructor).

It is this author's belief that the possibilities to enrich our work as death educators, grief counselors, and researchers through the use of thanablogs are endless. However, there are also cautions and concerns that merit recognition.

Some of the challenges and concerns identified by Louis A. Gamino in Chapter 15 are relevant within the blogosphere. Issues of identity and the related issue of trust may be challenging in an environment where it is common for bloggers to use screen names and for many "about" pages to be devoid of identifying or contact information. Stories of deception and the use of a false identity within an online community sometimes occur (e.g., the case of "Kaycee" as described by Geitgey, 2002, and Jordan, 2005), confirming the need for caution when forming connections with others in the blogosphere.

Throughout this chapter, evidence of the formation of significant relationships and a sense of community has been noted as potential benefits of involvement in the blogosphere. Once these bonds have been developed, there is a possibility that these relationships could end for a variety of reasons (e.g., one's death, discontinuation of one's blogging activities). It is important for grief counselors to recognize the potential for disenfranchised grief if a blogger does not openly discuss his or her online relationships. (For an in-depth discussion of the relevance of disenfranchised grief in online communities, see Chapter 9 by Lisa Hensley.) Heilferty (2009) noted the possibility of negative consequences that accompany illness blogging, including hurt feelings (for readers, the author, or both), isolation, skewed perception, time away from loved ones to blog, and strained relationships.

Blogging during times of illness or grief means exposing oneself during a time of intense vulnerability. Grief counselors should "check in" with consumers who participate in blogging activities and help them consider the implications of the self-disclosure that is occurring online (particularly if the person is blogging in "public" space) and possible boundary issues that may develop depending upon the circumstances of the blogging community that is involved. Death professionals have a responsibility to remind clients to be mindful of safety issues when grief and distress may cloud a person's judgment.

CONCLUSION

The blogosphere is an amazing place to explore thanatology-related issues. Be prepared for an emotional roller coaster ride when perusing the range of resources, because a reader is likely to experience joy and sadness, laughter and tears within a single entry. Let me conclude with an illustration from one of my favorite discoveries, wonderfully titled "Death and dying and other messy stuff" by a thanablogger identified as "roadplug" (2011):

> For anyone who has ever had a dying friend or relative but are not the primary caregiver, there are, or should be some basic rules about visiting at all, and rules to follow during the visit.
>
> Acknowledging to oneself that who they are visiting is going to die—would be a good thing. During a visit, we should not pretend or talk like in a day or two the patient is going to be 'fine'. Actually the patient will be fine, dead but fine. It is a normal 'fine' end of life.
>
> Embrace it. Consider yourself fortunate that your dying friend is giving you the gift of witnessing the death experience. It could be very beneficial. It is okay to not feel completely miserable during this time too. I wished relatives a good trip back home and the aunt took offence. "How can it be a good trip? We just saw her to say goodbye!"
>
> I backed up a little, "Okay well then Just don't get in a wreck." (n.p.)

Almost a decade prior to the publication of this book, Blood (2002) wrote the following in the introduction to a collection of essays describing how weblogs were changing our culture: "Weblogs bring the Web—in theory a leveler, a democratic medium—to the People. To anyone with an Internet connection, the Web is now a two-way medium" (p. x). Numerous writers have highlighted the fact that bloggers have the opportunity to speak to the masses or to only a few. Regardless of the sphere of influence of any one blogger's message, thanatologists would be wise to pay attention to the impact that the various forms of thanablogging will have on society's collective experiences with dying, death, and grief.

REFERENCES

Badger, M. (2004). Visual blogs. In L. J. Gurak, S. Antonijevic, L. Johnson, C. Ratliff, & J. Reyman (Eds.), *Into the blogosphere: Rhetoric, community, and culture of weblogs*. Minneapolis, MN: University of Minnesota. Retrieved from http://blog.lib.umn.edu/blogosphere/visual_blogs.html

Baker, J. R., & Moore, S. M. (2011). Creation and validation of the personal blogging style scale. *Cyberpsychology, Behavior, and Social Networking, 14*(6), 379–390.

Bingley, A. F., McDermott, E., Thomas, C., Payne, S., Seymour, J. E., & Clark, D. (2006). Narratives about dying: A review of narratives written since 1950 by people facing death from cancer and other diseases. *Palliative Medicine, 20*, 183–195.

Blog Carnival. (2011). Blog carnival FAQs. Retrieved August 1, 2011, from http://blogcarnival. com/bc/p_about.html

Blood, R. (2002). Weblogs: A history and perspective. In J. Rodzvilla (Ed.), *We've got blog: How weblogs are changing our culture* (pp. 7–16). Cambridge, MA: Perseus Publishing.

Bolton, G. (1999). *The therapeutic potential of creative writing: Writing myself.* Philadelphia, PA: Jessica Kingsley.

Cardon, D., Delaunay-Teterel, H., Fluckiger, C., & Prieur, C. (2007, March 26–28). *Sociological typology of personal blogs.* Paper presented at the International AAAI Conference on Weblogs and Social Media, Boulder, CO. Retrieved July 12, 2011, from http://icwsm.org/ papers/4--Cardon--Delaunay-Teterel--Fluckiger--Prieur.pdf

DeMarco, P. (2004, November 9). Diary of a death: Families form online bonds as they share medical struggles. *Boston Globe,* p. E1.

Drezner, D. W., & Farrell, H. (2004, September 2–5). *The power and politics of blogs.* Paper presented at the 2004 Conference of the American Political Science Association, Chicago, IL. Retrieved August 1, 2011, from http://www.cs.duke.edu/courses/spring05/cps182s/ readings/blogpowerpolitics.pdf

Frank, A. W. (1995). *The wounded storyteller: Body, illness, and ethics.* Chicago, IL: The University of Chicago Press.

Geitgey, A. (2002). The Kaysee Nicole (Swenson) FAQ. In J. Rodzvilla (Ed.), *We've got blog: How weblogs are changing our culture* (pp. 89–98). Cambridge, MA: Perseus Publishing.

Gopal, S. (2007). The evolving social geography of blogs. In H. J. Miller (Ed.), *Societies and cities in the age of instant access* (pp. 275–293). New York, NY: Springer Publishing.

Gunnelius, S. (2009). *Google blogger for dummies.* Hoboken, NJ: Wiley.

Gunnelius, S. (2010). *Blogging all-in-one for dummies.* Hoboken, NJ: Wiley.

Hearst, M. A., & Dumais, S. T. (2009). Blogging together: An examination of group blogs. *Proceedings of the 3rd International ICWSM Conference* (pp. 226–229). Retrieved August 5, 2011, from http://citeseerx.ist.psu.edu/viewdoc/summary?doi=10.1.1.153.3139&rank=1

Heilferty, C. M. (2009). Toward a theory of online communication in illness: Concept analysis of illness blogs. *Journal of Advanced Nursing, 65*(7), 1539–1547.

Hodgson, H. (2010, June 8). *Author's defined niche promotes book sales—What is yours?* Retrieved July 8, 2011, from http://publishingguru.blogspot.com/2010/06/authors-defined-niche-promotes-book.html

I am Thanorak. (2011). About thanatourism. Retrieved July 31, 2011, from http://thanatourism. wordpress.com/about-2/

Jordan, J. W. (2005). A virtual death and a real dilemma: Identity, trust, and community in cyberspace. *Southern Communication Journal, 70*(3), 200–218.

Ko, H. -C., & Kuo, F. -Y. (2009). Can blogging enhance subjective well-being through self-disclosure? *CyberPsychology & Behavior, 12*(1), 75–79.

Kopytoff, V. G. (2011, February 20). Blogs wane as the young drift to sites like Twitter. *New York Times.* Retrieved August 4, 2011, from http://www.pewinternet.org/Media-Mentions/2011/ Blogs-Wane-as-the-Young-Drift-to-Sites-Like-Twitter.aspx

Krishnamurthy, S. (2002, October). *The multidimensionality of blog conversations: The virtual enactment of September 11th.* Paper presented at Internet Research 3.0, Maastricht, the Netherlands.

Lenhart, A., Purcell, K., Smith, A., & Zickuhr, K. (2010, February 3). *Social media and mobile Internet use among teens and young adults.* Retrieved July 14, 2011, from http:// pewinternet.org/Reports/2010/Social-Media-and-Young-Adults.aspx

Meares, J. (2011). The cancer report. *Columbia Journalism Review, March/April.* Retrieved July 6, 2011, from http://www.cjr.org/feature/the_cancer_report.php?page=all&pring=true

Merriam-Webster. (2011). Blog. Retrieved July 3, 2011, from http://www.merriam-webster. com/dictionary/blog

Miura, A., & Yamashita, K. (2007). Psychological and social influences on blog writing: An online survey of blog authors in Japan. *Journal of Computer-Mediated Communication, 12*(4), article 15. Retrieved from http://jcmc.indiana.edu/vol12/Issue4/miura.html

Moore, T. D., & Serva, M. A. (2007). Understanding member motivation for contributing to different types of virtual communities: A proposed framework. In *Proceedings of the 2007 ACM SIGMIS CPR Conference on Computer Personnel Research* (pp. 153–158).

Nardi, B. A., Schiano, D. J., & Gumbrecht, M. (2004). Blogging as a social activity, or would you let 900 million people read your diary? *Proceedings of the 2004 ACM conference on Computer Supported Cooperative Work, 6*(3), 222–231. Retrieved July 31, 2011, from http://citeseerx.ist.psu.edu/viewdoc/download?doi=10.1.1.102.3591&rep=rep1&type=pdf

Nardi, B. A., Schiano, D. J., Gumbrecht, M., & Swartz, L. (2004). Why we blog. *Communications of the ACM, 47*(12), 41–46.

Neimeyer, R. A., van Dyke, J. G., & Pennebaker, J. W. (2008). Narrative medicine: Writing through bereavement. In H. Chochinov & W. Breitbart (Eds.), *Handbook of psychiatry in palliative medicine* (pp. 454–469). New York, NY: Oxford University Press.

Nowson, S., Oberlander, J., & Gill, A. J. (2005). Weblogs, genres, and individual differences. In *Proceedings of the 27th Annual Conference of the Cognitive Science Society* (pp. 1666–1671). Hillsdale, NJ: Lawrence Erlbaum Associates. Retrieved July 30, 2011, from http://nowson.com/papers/NowOberGilCogsci05.pdf

Pennebaker, J. W., & Beall, S. K. (1986). Confronting a traumatic event: Toward an understanding of inhibition and disease. *Journal of Abnormal Psychology, 95*(3), 274–281.

Pitts, V. (2004). Illness and empowerment: Writing and reading breast cancer in cyberspace. *Health: An Indisciplinary Journal for the Social Study of Health, Illness, and Medicine, 8*(1), 33–59.

Riessman, F. (1965). The "helper" therapy principle. *Social Work, 10*(2), 27–32.

Roadplug. (2011, June 18). Death and dying and other messy stuff. Retrieved July 5, 2011, from http://roadplug.wordpress.com/2011/06/18/death-and-dying-and-other-messy-stuff/

Rosenberg, S. (2009). *Say everything: How blogging began, what it's becoming, and why it matters.* New York, NY: Crown.

Smyth, J. M., & Pennebaker, J. W. (2008). Exploring the boundary conditions of expressive writing: In search of the right recipe. *British Journal of Health Psychology, 13*, 1–7.

Sofka, C. J. (1997). Social support "internetworks," caskets for sale, and more: Thanatology and the information superhighway. *Death Studies, 21*(6), 553–574.

Stefanone, M. A., & Jang, C. -Y. (2007). Writing for friends and family: The interpersonal nature of blogs. *Journal of Computer-Mediated Communication, 13*(1), article 7. Retrieved July 14, 2011, from http://jcmc.indiana.edu/vol13/issue1/stefanone.html

Tan, L. (2008). Psychotherapy 2.0: MySpace® blogging as self-therapy. *American Journal of Psychotherapy, 62*(2), 143–163.

Taylor, S. E. (2010–2005). *My phantom father.* Retrieved July 5, 2011, from http://myphantom-father.com/blog/

Taylor, S. E. (2006, March). A daughter's search for her phantom father. *Lost Magazine,* Issue 4, Retrieved July 5, 2011, from http://www.lostmag.com/issue4/father.php

Wapner, J. (2008, May 22). Blogging—It's good for you. *Scientific American.* Retrieved July 23, 2011, from http://www.scientificamerican.com/article.cfm?id=the-healthy-type

Wikipedia. (2011a). Blog. Retrieved June 5, 2011, from http://en.wikipedia.org/wiki/Blog

Wikipedia. (2011b). E-Patient. Retrieved July 8, 2011, from http://en.wikipedia.org/wiki/E-Patient

Wikipedia. (2011c). Webring. Retrieved June 5, 2011, from http://en.wikipedia.org/wiki/Webring

Yang, J. (2006). *The rough guide to blogging.* New York, NY: Rough Guides Ltd.

Zickuhr, K. (2010, December 16). *Generations online in 2010.* Retrieved July 15, 2011, from http://www.pewinternet.org/Reports/2010/Generations-2010.aspx

6

Being There: Technology at the End of Life

Jane Moore

The story is not unusual. An 89-year-old woman falls and breaks her hip on a Tuesday. The woman is on Coumadin and is unable to have surgery until Friday. She has one daughter, Susan, in Houston, with whom she lives; one in New Orleans (about a 5-hour drive away), Nancy; and another in Chicago, Jane. The patient, Blanche, had been displaced from her lifelong home in New Orleans and lost all of her possessions as a result of Katrina. She had been living in Houston with Susan, who had also lost her home because of Katrina. Blanche had five grandchildren residing in New Orleans; Mt. Sterling, Kentucky; Chicago, Illinois, and Houston, Texas; four great-grandchildren in Houston and Kentucky; and one great-grandchild on the way in Chicago.

The youngest daughter, Nancy, a librarian at a private school in New Orleans, immediately drove to Houston. The middle sister, Susan, who lived with her mother, left her work at an oil and gas company and met the ambulance at the hospital. The oldest daughter, Jane, a professor in Chicago who teaches on a per quarter system, had classes on Tuesdays, Wednesdays, and Thursdays. The accident occurred on the seventh week of a 10-week term. She booked the first flight she could on Friday morning and put her classes online.

Families all over the country are separated by great distances and by commitments to work, children, and spouses. When a loved one is in the dying process, what do family members need? For this family, the first need was information— How is she? Is she in pain? Can this be corrected? Will she be able to be on her own again? Another great need was the sense that Blanche was being cared for— Did she get into a room? Have they given her pain medication? Then, there was the need to be with her. Nancy, the daughter in New Orleans, spoke with her principal and got a substitute for the coming week. Jane, the oldest daughter, found a flight out of Chicago leaving early Friday morning. The sisters kept in touch by telephone, by e-mail, and by text every few hours. Because Jane was separated by over a thousand miles, she set up a CarePages account (www.CarePages.com/) and made all three sisters editors so that everyone could update information as it was received. As it turned out, only Jane (J) and Nancy (N) posted.

The CarePages entries tell the story.

10/30/08 – 8:00 a.m.

Blanche fell down yesterday and fractured her hip. Fortunately Ronnie (a close family friend) got to her and called 911 only an hour after the fall. At first the ER doc thought that the hip might be repaired with a pin, but as of this morning, the thought is that the hip needs replacement.

Mama's condition is compromised by her heart condition, including the issue of making sure that her blood thinner is as out of her system as they need it to be before she can go to surgery.

We are waiting to hear from her cardiologist as to when they might schedule the surgery. At this point we are guessing Friday or Monday. Susan (the Houston sister) told us that they plan to put her in traction to ease the pain today. Please keep Blanche in your thoughts and prayers. Nancy and I plan to be in Houston for the surgery if at all possible. – J

10/31/08 – 1:37 p.m.

I just arrived here in Houston. Mama is in recovery and pretty incoherent, but has stable blood pressure, is off the breathing tube and the face mask and now on a nasal cannula. They are cleaning her up and she should be in her room in the next hour or so. She doesn't seem to be aware of the fact that Nancy and I are here, but we're glad to be here. – J

11/05/08 – 3:35 p.m.

I arrived at the hospital about a half hour ago. Mama not only recognized me, but was alert and happy to see me. Chris (Jane's son) and Nola (his daughter, just over a year old) came to visit her Nonnie. Blanche was smiling and laughing at Nola as she yelled, 'Obama,' and walked for us.

Mama ate some applesauce and is dozing. Sue said that she had a CT scan on her belly because they were checking for any gall bladder problems since it was tender.

Today is the first day I'm seeing my mom in the bed, which is a happy, happy circumstance. – J

11/06/08 – 9:55 a.m.

It is certainly discouraging to be in a catch-22 where it seems to be a choice between lucidity (eating, taking medication, moving) and pain. – J

11/08/08 – 9:13 a.m.

We're all here in the ICU. When we came in, she said, 'I want all my children here' and we told her that her wish came true. – J

11/10/08 – 8:57 a.m.

When we arrived this morning, Mama was sitting up, but not looking especially good. She said she hadn't seen us in days and we reminded her that it was hours. – J

11/11/08 – 9:55 a.m.

We are meeting with the social worker soon to talk about palliative care for Mama. The TPN (nutrition) is a short-term solution and she is still unable to eat without vomiting. We'll know more after our conversation. – J

11/11/08 – 6:01 p.m.

We are all settled at Odyssey Hospice in Houston. Mama is in Rm. 108. The people are absolutely lovely and Mama is on oxygen, nausea meds and pain meds. She is chatting a bit, laughing sometime and sleeping some. Ronnie, Sue, Nan and I are here. – J

11/12/08 – 8:21 a.m.

Mama had a very restless night. Nancy stayed with her—we've decided that one of us will stay every night until the pain meds have been figured out. Understandably it takes time to get the right dosage. She was agitated and Nancy said she talked all night long. She was packing china and silver and other household goods. (The symbolism does not go unnoted.)

Nan and Sue went to get some breakfast and she's dozing now. The people here are wonderful. – J

11/12/08 – 10:22 p.m.

Sicily (Chris' wife) brought Nola and Eliza to visit. Eliza (4) was a little afraid, even though she assured me in the lobby that her mama had told her about the hospital bed and the oxygen cannula. I'm wondering now if the sound of the oxygen machine was a bit scary—late at night in the room alone I might think so too. ☺

Luckily Emma and John in Kentucky (Nancy's grandchildren) were on Skype [an Internet-based free videoconferencing tool] with Nancy and so Eliza got to visit with her cousins and hear Emma play 'Jingle Bells' on her violin. – J

[11/16/08 – Jane returns home to Chicago to teach the final week of her classes.]

11/17/08 – 5:15 p.m.

Sue and I went for a walk and realized when we passed the same place twice that we were walking in circles literally and figuratively. When we were passing the hospital, we saw Kathy (the director of Odyssey) and she asked how we were doing. We told her it was a tough day and why. She suggested we go get a coffee and she would look at Mama's file and at Mama and come talk to us.

What she told us is that she thinks that Mama has declined appreciably since Friday. She said that the next 24 hours would be telling. She also assured us that no one was "giving us our hat." She thought also that Mama's decline may preclude her moving anywhere. Sue and Ronnie really want her to come home if there needs to be a move. I'm comfortable with that if we can arrange round the clock sitters so that Ronnie and Sue give meds and support and nothing else. Two different people told us that if we get sitters rather than RN's it would be in the same ball park as a nursing home.

I think it is fairly remote that Mama will get home. She is not responding at all today. We thought it might be because of the increase in her meds, but Kathy said that if it were the meds she would react when you shook her. She's not doing that. They were even hammering in the hall this morning and it didn't seem to affect her. She grimaced when they put the methadone in her cheek. (Meaghan, her nurse, said it's real bitter.)

The bottom line from Kathy (and she said she's the one that makes the decision) is that no one is forcing us out. If she is in "active" period, no one is going to make us move her. Once home, hospice would follow her and when she gets within 72 hours, someone could be there 24 a day if needed. I don't anticipate that we're a great deal more than that at this point. I think I'm going to reassess tomorrow—that would be the 24 hours that Kathy was talking about. I may take the rest of the week off knowing that there are no more extensions—this is it. – N

11/18/08 – 9:45 a.m.

I called to Odyssey when I woke up and they told me Mama needed break-through pain meds during the night, but by and large had rested well. When we left there at ten last night, Stella was on duty and she said she was going to do her charting in Mama's room so Mama would "have some company."

This morning when I called I spoke to Kathy (the director) and she said Mama was comfortable but there were some new signs of decline. Sue and Ronnie feel better than if we need to move Mama that she can come home, but I don't think that is going to happen.

For those of you that know Ethel S, who is very close to Mama's age now, we got the sweetest voicemail from her when we got home last night. She said that she was thinking and praying for Mama and hoped she didn't have to struggle since her life had been difficult. Then she said, "You know, I think I love your Mama." It was the sweetest thing. – N

11/18/08 – 12:05 p.m.

Mama's breathing is labored. Sue, Nan, Ronnie, and Chris are with her at Odyssey House. I'm on Skype sitting vigil with them and Jennie (Jane's pregnant daughter) is on the way to keep me company. Mama seems very peaceful. – J

11/18/08 – 3:32 p.m.

Blanche died peacefully in her sleep, surrounded by her family, both in person and on Skype at 1:50 p.m. She just suddenly stopped breathing. – J

What the CarePages do not tell is the sense of really being there that all the grandchildren in New Orleans, Kentucky, and Chicago felt when they used Skype to connect with their Memére (their name for Blanche). Jennie, Jane's daughter, who was due to deliver in 3 weeks' time, showed Blanche her belly, and they laughed about how big it was. The grandchildren told her stories about their days; Emma, the oldest great-granddaughter at 6 years old, played her violin for Blanche and received the generous comments that only a great-grandmother could provide. Skype provided a real sense of "being there" among the family members, who were reading the CarePages daily as well.

While sitting vigil on the 18th, there was a lot of small talk among the family members in Houston and Jane, her husband, and daughter in Chicago. Blanche's breathing was very labored and the "death rattle" was loud. Suddenly, Susan said, "She's stopped breathing." They used the call button to get a nurse, who came in and checked her vitals. "She's gone," the nurse said, and then turning to the computer, said to Jane and her family, "I'm so glad you were here with her."

IMPLICATIONS FOR END-OF-LIFE CARE

The story is not unusual. The mortality risk for older adults who break a hip is significantly greater than those who do not. In today's society, families are spread out and especially in difficult economic times, have fewer and fewer opportunities to meet in person. When faced with a serious illness or the impending death of a loved one, communication and connection are complex problems that families must face. What is unusual about this story is that it is mine. Blanche is my mother and I sat with her using Skype to be present at her death.

Videoconferencing can be a powerful tool to assist families who live thousands of miles apart to "be there," to say those important words, and to feel connected at the end of life. The granddaughter who was pregnant and unable to travel felt that the videoconferencing allowed her to share important news with her much beloved

Figure 6.1: Instructions for Videoconferencing with Skype

* If you want to see and talk to your relatives or friends who are unable to be with you, click on the blue SKYPE icon on the computer. The program is set up automatically with the onscreen name xxxxxxx and the password xxxxxxxxx.
* If your relatives/friends do not have a Skype account, they will need to set one up by going to Skype.com, clicking on downloads, and following the prompt. Then they should let you know what their username is.
* Once you have the username, you type it in, and they will add you to their list. You will now be able to see when they are online and call them. You will not need extra headphones or speakers and there is a built-in camera so that they can see you. You can move the computer around so they can see others who are with you at the Ark if you'd like.
* Jane Moore is added to the list of callers if you want to practice with me. The icon will be colored when I am online.
* To turn on the computer, press the top right button. It will light up.
* If you are uncomfortable using the touch pad, plug in the mouse on the right side of the computer (there is a rectangular plug attached to the mouse and a matching slot in the computer).
* It takes a few moments for the computer to start and then you will see a blue icon with a white S on it. That is Skype.
* Click on it using the left side of the mouse and you're ready to call.
* When you are finished using the computer, click on START on the lower left side of the computer. Then click TURN OFF COMPUTER twice and the computer will do the rest.

grandmother. However, technology is dependent on so many outside influences that it may not always work in the way it is intended. One of Blanche's grandchildren felt that using videoconferencing was very difficult: "We could never get it right . . . it never failed that either someone's microphone or video wasn't working right!"

Rainbow Hospice, a Chicago-based hospice for whom I volunteer, has implemented a videoconferencing option for families and patients in their inpatient facility, The Ark. I provided a netbook with Skype installed on it and detailed directions to families as to how to use the computer, what to tell distant relatives, and how to use the videoconferencing program (see Figure 1 for a copy of the instructions).

Some of the issues that arose among the staff were concerns about privacy and security, worries that the program would take time away from their other duties or provide additional work for them. There was also some apprehension as to whether "nontechie" families would struggle with using the computer. None of these fears were realized. I provided antivirus software for the netbook. Staff found that the written directions were understandable to families and that many families already had experience with videoconferencing. In fact, the hospice put videoconferencing on its menu of services offered to patients and families.

The inaugural use of the system provided a mobility-challenged sister the opportunity to communicate with a developmentally disabled brother who was a patient in the hospice. They were able to see each other, and a nurse took the computer around to the common areas of the hospice so that she could see the environment, and they were able to communicate easily. They planned another call for the next day, but by that time, the brother had slipped into a coma and died the next evening. Perhaps that call gave the siblings the opportunity to say what they needed to say to each other before his death.

Some challenges with current technology are unavoidable. There may be bandwidth problems, or Internet access may be unreliable. As technology advances, these issues are rapidly disappearing. However, the staff at the Ark believe that the opportunities for families and patients outweigh the problems. They noted that patience, staff buy-in, and stories like the case study and their own experiences in which technology made a difference are key to having such a program succeed.

Another hospice in Indiana has requested the handouts and information (which I had provided to the Chicago hospice) and plans to implement the use of Skype in their inpatient facility.

During the time that this manuscript was in process, a friend of the author (a clergyperson) began a death vigil for her father on Facebook. It was interesting that the posts were of a similar nature to those in the case study. Shawn noted, "I have been a little concerned that it might bother some people but figured they could [choose] not [to] read it. I have written because it helps me, is an easy way to keep people informed and I think it is good to let people see where I . . . am."

Her initial post came in late summer when she reported that she had "turned off the light in my dad's apartment for the last time after 34 yrs. He is up and down." As the posts continued, interspersed with news about her church, her cats, and her nieces and nephews, she chronicled the medical information, sharing that her father had cataract surgery: "Why? He wants to see better for the time he has." She then goes on to describe his downward spiral: "Dad started on morphine last week. Really struggling to breathe and has infection. Still has some humor." As with the sisters in the case study, Shawn, the owner of the Facebook page, requests support both tangible and intangible. At one point she posted that friends from Facebook had provided her with a chili supper. She requested prayers from her Facebook friends: "For the first time that I can think of my father asked me to pray for him. So you all can also," and then, she writes his name.

At times, she just posted a picture of her dad or of herself keeping vigil. She described day-to-day events, like reading Westerns to her father and the visit of her siblings who do not live nearby but have traveled to spend time with their father in his last days. She shared the photos that her father has with him under the bedcovers of his mother and his son who died 12 years ago. She also shared the decision to do palliative care: "We are still keeping Vigil. It took a few days to get him comfortable enough to relax in to dying. Like his life his dying is filled with great courage, pain, love and very much his way."

At one point, Shawn asked her Facebook friends what music they would listen to as they were dying. Fifteen people responded with selections, some even sending links to songs.

Another friend writes a tribute to Shawn and her Facebook postings: "I just want you to know that I think you are extraordinary in the way that you invite all of us to walk this part of the journey with you and your dad and family. Thank you for your openness and vulnerability, for your honesty and communication - when you feel inspired, when you need a prayer, and when you . . . are tired too. Know that you all are in our prayers, and that none of us is alone. Love to you all."

Shawn's father died peacefully surrounded by family. Fortunately, they were all able to be physically present, but Shawn felt that her Facebook "family" was present with them as well, carrying them through a difficult time.

CONCLUSION

The use of technology allowed my family to connect with loved ones in other areas of the country. We were able to use a blog to communicate with family and friends and videoconferencing to allow distant family to speak with and see the patient. As her condition deteriorated, her declining health became evident in both her communication and the visuals. Those far away could be prepared for her eventual death.

Throughout the blog, information was disseminated to family and friends. The technology allowed readers to be assured that the patient was well cared for and that choices were being made to support her comfort and well-being. Although my sisters and I were able to be present in-person for much of our mother's hospitalization and hospice residency, at the end of life, I was "there" virtually.

Members of the family were able to connect, to have important conversations, and to share themselves with the patient via videoconferencing. The patient watched her great-granddaughter play the violin, learned the name of her great-grandson-to-be from her pregnant granddaughter, and said prayers with her son-in-law, a clergyman.

In the Facebook example, the daughter was able to share the burden of her death vigil with friends across the country. She uploaded pictures of her family for those who were not able to be present as her father grew weaker and weaker. The sharing of her story facilitated the receipt of emotional and tangible support (a meal) from her Facebook friends.

As professionals working with patients and families at the end of life, or simply as caring persons who have some knowledge of technology, we can help local hospitals and hospices use thanatechnology to facilitate this kind of communication among families. Most hospitals (even intensive care units) and in-patient hospices do have Internet connections. If you are familiar with videoconferencing, you can arrange to meet with a development staff member or with a social worker and explain the process for providing videoconferencing to families. The cost of this thanatechnology is minimal—netbooks with webcams can be purchased for a few hundred dollars, and many donors are looking for something tangible to provide to an organization. Communication among family members at the end of life certainly seems like a worthy "cause." Some institutions will provide their own security software, and among volunteers there is likely to be at least one (probably several) who can provide assistance should families need a "techie" to help with the first call. Providing the hospital or hospice with a copy of this chapter should help them to see the value in this type of communication for families who are separated by distance at difficult times.

Technology is not always easy or perfect, yet it allows connections to be made, life events to be shared, and support to be given, even when families are thousands of miles apart and when friends are unable to "be there" for those they care about. What is even more helpful is that the software required to facilitate videoconferencing is cost free. Readers can secure a free account with a video-conferencing site (Skype, OoVoo, SightSpeed, etc.) or set up a free Facebook account, CarePages, or CaringBridge blog; become familiar with the technology; and then work with a family, hospital, or local hospice to implement a similar approach to being there at the end of life.

Author's note: Further information can be obtained by contacting the author at jmoore@nl.edu.

REFERENCES

CarePages.com. (2010). CarePages: About us. Retrieved from http://www.carepages.com/
CaringBridge. (n. d.). CaringBridge: About us. Retrieved from http://www.caringbridge.org/about
Facebook.com. (2011). Facebook. Retrieved from http://www.facebook.com

7

GriefNet: Creating and Maintaining an Internet Bereavement Community

Cendra Lynn and Antje Rath

TECHNOLOGY + THANATOLOGY = SERENDIPITY

GriefNet is an online grief support community run by the bereaved for the bereaved. It began in 1994 as a simple list of grief support services in Michigan and in 2011 has grown to include 50 e-mail support groups, a separate section for kids, links to resources and memorials, a bookstore with reviews, a library of personal and professional articles, and a gift store with products to comfort the bereaved. The creation and the growth of GriefNet are excellent examples of how thanatology and technology merged organically and how the growth of each stimulated the growth of the other.

The prequel to GriefNet's founding began in 1985 in the Michigan chapter of the Association for Death Education and Counseling, which I founded in 1983. One of our projects was publishing a bimonthly bulletin of grief resources in Michigan. This bulletin was widely used, so when the chapter dissolved in the early 1990s, I took it over. I formed a nonprofit corporation, Rivendell Resources, Inc., and continued publication under that aegis.

The *Bereavement Bulletin* grew in size and drew subscribers because it filled the need of caregiving professionals who focused on grief. I repeatedly suggested to the Association for Death Education and Counseling that we take on publication of the Bulletin but that was declined. Then at an informal moment of the 1993 Annual Meeting, outgoing President David Meagher suggested that I consider putting the publication up "on one of those electronic bulletin boards."

I live in Ann Arbor where much of the development of the Internet happened. While learning to send and receive e-mail, I read the then-bible, *Zen and the Art of the Internet* (Kehoe, 1992), to learn how Internet sites connect with each other. I sought advice from Edward Vielmetti, who had been involved with Internet development since 1985. He was excited at the thought of making grief resources more public and spent several months putting Bulletin data into a gopher server, a text-only forerunner of the World Wide Web. We went live in February 1994.

Ed set me up with ic.net, a local Internet service provider. One result of stepping into Internet usage at such an early stage is that I inadvertently learned the basics of its structure and its ongoing development. This knowledge enabled GriefNet's growth and development.

Although the Internet then had relatively few users, people who wanted to talk about grief found our site and sent me e-mails. I began to correspond with six, then several dozen people eager to talk about a topic that was still largely taboo. Ed created a discussion group using a program called Majordomo, whereby we could all talk with each other. We called it grief-chat, and it became the first e-mail-based grief group on the Internet in May 1994.

People in this group wrote intensely about all aspects of grief. More people found us, and by August 1994, we had over four dozen people in the group. Then members who had lost a child asked if they could have their own group. They felt no one understood what it was like to have a child die unless they had personally experienced this loss. The group "grieving-parents" was created. Those who were widowed then requested "grief-widowed." Adding groups in response to expressed need became an integral part of GriefNet, making us dynamic and organic.

Management of these three groups was easy. There were two to three dozen members in each, and I could easily read the 8 to 10 messages generated every day. Our members were polite and caring. People could join and unsubscribe just by sending a request to Majordomo. Instructions were on our gopher site. The groups pretty much ran themselves.

Although our gopher server was small, it required continuous maintenance and updating. Simultaneously, we had to make certain that e-mail was flowing through our groups properly, which was not a sure thing. My 26 years of computer use did not include programming, so I sought local people to help us, including a second programmer and an entrepreneur. We met for an hour or two on Friday afternoons. We did business under our corporate name, Rivendell Resources, and our name on line was rivendel. It was during one of these Friday meetings in the summer of 1995 that we spontaneously came up with our permanent Internet name: GriefNet. It popped out of a discussion, seemed perfect, and became our registered business name and our site name.

During 1994–1995 technology was changing rapidly. At regular Friday night geek sessions at ic.net, I learned about new developments, including the nascent World Wide Web. In late 1994, after spending an hour to connect to the right site, we finally saw a video of a programmer walking out the back door of his office to a fountain in his courtyard. We were greatly underwhelmed. However, by mid-1995, technology had taken the World Wide Web from that video to websites with graphics and links to other websites. An early designer of the web, Lou Rosenfeld, designed a web-based home page for us.

In addition, in 1995 my daughter, Elyzabeth, then 9 years old, observed that it was not just adults who were dealing with grief but kids as well. She founded KIDSAID—a deliberate pun: kids aid or kid said. This was a site especially for kids, giving them a place to have fun and also to discuss their feelings through a support group, through art, and through their stories. She had the help of Ian, an 11-year-old boy in England, in creating the site.

THE PRIDES AND PERILS OF A VERTICAL GROWTH CURVE

During the second half of 1995, we were in double states of growth: the growth of technology and the growth of our support groups and resources. The growth of our groups made us eager for better technology. The growth of technology allowed our site to be more available, which increased our exposure and membership.

Reading the e-mail and dealing with members was not difficult at first. My training and experience enabled me to handle just about anything interpersonal. A few of the members had either experience working with people or personal grief experience. They began to be the people I could turn to when problems arose, and we few were the GriefNet staff.

One of these was an experienced web author based in the UK, Tony Novak. In January 1996, he began to convert our whole site from gopher to web server. This allowed us to create multiple links to other Internet sites, which then linked back to us, increasing our rates of access once again. In 1996, GriefNet was a finalist for an award by the National Information Infrastructure, which recognized excellence and innovation in the use of the Internet. This prestige increased our exposure and growth exponentially and quickly overwhelmed our ability to respond to those seeking our help. Suddenly, it became imperative to increase our staff size. Requests for help in our support groups and those posted on our website began drawing individuals who were willing to volunteer their time, expertise, and services to help GriefNet.

A widow, Sue Bennett, whose husband had been killed in the bombing over Lockerbie, volunteered to continue the web programming. One of the founders of grieving-parents, Janet Mann, offered to oversee that group. She had lost her daughter and granddaughter in 1990. Both of these volunteers, bereaved for a number of years, saw how our groups were lifelines for those in anguish. We began turning into a community of the bereaved for the bereaved and developing a sense of mission.

We added new groups as fast as we were able: several groups for bereaved parents, several for widowed people, and new groups for adults who had lost parents or siblings. A number of unique losses were also given groups: one for mothers who had put their children up for adoption (birth-mothers), one for women who had had abortions (grief-choice), a group for those who had lost a loved one to AIDS (grief-aids), and a group for parents who lost a child to miscarriage or neonatal death (griefparents-neonate). By the spring of 1997, we were sponsoring 25 support groups.

By now, the growth of technology approached vertical, and we were able to keep pace only because of amazing and talented people who found their way to us and dedicated themselves to our work. Michael Fenimore joined GriefNet in 1997 when his brother died from exposure to Agent Orange while serving in Vietnam. Within a year, Michael offered to become our webmaster and has been ever since. He kept us connected to the Internet during the era when sites went down frequently. He stepped us through each advance, donating his knowledge, time, and often his own hardware and software. Just keeping us connected to the Internet took many hours per week, and almost from the start, Michael did not have time to update the website. Sheri Huffman, who joined GriefNet after her brother was murdered, took over that job in 1998. She made our site easy to read and navigate, including being accessible by the blind. The number of pages on our website grew and needed to be kept up to date with current technology.

People who visited our site were often looking for more than only joining a group, such as seeking out books about grief. In autumn, 1994, we had been approached by a publisher who wanted us to sell her books on line. With no Internet models to use, we created our own online bookstore with an annotated bibliography that I had compiled. Quickly, other authors and publishers found us, and the bookstore, like the mailing lists, grew with increasing rapidity.

Stocking and selling books were more than we could manage, and recouping a percentage of sales on authors' websites was technically difficult and unreliable. Technology got us out of this bind when Amazon began and offered the Amazon Associates program in 1998 for marketing through them. We began generating an income stream and making books easily available for review or purchase.

Our members also wanted to put up memorials for their loved ones. Michael Fenimore created a template on our website with which to create a personalized memorial. This was cumbersome, but in the late 1990s, it was the best we could manage. As the number of memorials grew, they became harder to organize. Tom Stidham managed the memorials, keeping them orderly and helping confused members, but he was not able to develop memorials using new technology. It was not until 2007 that I stumbled onto Virtual Memorials, created and run by Sharon Mnich. We formed an affiliation; her site directs users to our groups, and ours directs our members to her memorial site.

In the beginning, I could manage all the finances. We had no payroll, just overhead expenses, and they were minimal. With expansion, expenses grew, and we began asking members for donations. Those became our only regular source of income and were insufficient.

In February 1997, Jacqueline Hamilton, a bereaved mother, become our Development Director. She enhanced and increased acquisition and organization of staff. She helped us identify our different departments, such as programming, monitoring, and accounting. She convinced her mother, an accountant, to handle our bookkeeping and file our papers with the IRS. Jacqueline also developed a plan for fundraising. She helped us begin classified advertising, which did not work well in the long run, and got volunteers to upgrade our bookstore. She began learning who was funding grief resources online and off. She helped us develop a relationship with Last Acts, a Robert Wood Johnson Foundation national program to increase communication between national health and consumer groups that were working to change end-of-life culture, attitudes, and care. She was hoping this would lead to a grant or at least advice on finding grants. However, we could neither provide bang-for-the-buck nor pass the requirement that charities should spend less than 10% of their income on overhead, the rest directly on clients. Our virtual nonprofit has 100% overhead. No one yet understood that virtual charities delivered services, knowledge, and communication, spending money only on overhead.

I handled our subscribe and unsubscribe requests in the beginning and then passed this task to Steven Cox, whose partner had died of AIDS and who found GriefNet to be a refuge. He took over tracking membership and donations. When he began, Excel was the best tracking software. As we grew, so did our main spreadsheet, until in 2000, it was an 11,000 row, 10 column bedsheet-sized spread sheet. In early 2003, Steve had to retire. Along came David Roach, who built us a relational database in Access. By this time, we had one person in charge of subscription-related issues, another in charge of bookkeeping and tracking donations, and all staff needed access to the database. David used his own computer with network server technology that allows each of us to synchronize our copies to his hub.

Technological challenges and changes shaped the inception and the direction of GriefNet. Our choices have been influenced by available technology, and by adopting emerging technology, we have been able to offer our wide array of groups. Although it is easy to create and run one e-mail support group, when there are many, an enormous amount of back-end technology and human work are required.

TECHNOLOGY TRAINS THANATOLOGIST

In the early days of GriefNet, the dynamics of e-mail groups were brand new. Because of the absence of books or manuals for guidance, learning how to run e-mail support groups was entirely experiential. Over the years, we have learned that online groups have both benefits and dangers.

E-mail offers instant communication and anonymity, lending itself to intimacy in a group formed for people to share their deepest feelings. People who join often feel alone and isolated because of their grief. Assuaging that loneliness through talking to others with similar feelings brings great relief and comfort. People will tell things to group members that they cannot say to their own families. A sense of community with high trust is fostered, and members begin to rely on the group messages to bolster them.

The words of several of our members capture the benefits of these groups. A widowed member wrote: "Finding the GriefNet group was the best experience I could have in the midst of the worst time I had ever had in my life. The support and caring that I found from the very beginning was unbelievable. If someone had told me that you could find such compassion from people that you had never met, and develop such close friendships, I wouldn't have thought it was [sic] possible. These bonds of friendship helped me to heal in so many ways."

An adult who lost a parent said, "By reading and writing to each other we learn we are not alone in this world with these overwhelming feelings of grief. That the uncontrollable anger and tears and sometimes fighting in families is something that happens to many. Knowing we can sit down and pour our hearts out in an e-mail form and have it read by someone who understands the place we are in and not get a response like 'get over it' or 'you have to move on' brings comfort."

Although the intimacy that develops is positive for many, the underside of this type of intimacy is that people really do not know each other in many important ways. None of the nonverbal signals people use every day are present. People cannot see another person's reaction when reading their e-mail, or hear tone of voice when someone writes. They do not know how another person looks, their ethnic background, their social class, their education, or their accent. Nothing can be assumed from their clothing, their size, the color of their skin, and in cases where people use only initials, their gender.

Anonymous written communication (as compared with face-to-face communication) provides both freedom and danger. A group member has the freedom to write whatever he or she wishes, but one danger comes from assumptions that one makes about the person to whom one is writing and about their reply to you.

Humans tend to assume that others are like themselves until they find something to the contrary. This assumption can continue much longer in an e-mail group than in person. Members come to consider each other as friends and grow closer so long as the topic remains on grief. When other topics are broached, disagreements can arise. In our first 2 years these problems could be sorted out fairly quickly. There were perhaps two dozen people in each group, and they all operated under the Internet social convention of politeness.

As the Internet grew, that small community feeling was diluted, and some members began being rude online. Our first blowup in a group happened as the 1996 year-end holidays approached. Some of the members of grieving-parents began talking about Christmas, the baby Jesus, their children as angels, and other Christian beliefs. Another member wrote to say she wished they would knock it off, as she was an atheist and did not believe her child continued to exist. Then a third member replied that since she was Jewish, she would appreciate a little less Jesus. One of the Christian members replied with hurt and anger, and soon members jumped into the discussion on many sides. The messages grew angrier and angrier until they were out-and-out flames (personal attacks), and finally, almost the entire group unsubscribed and departed hurt and very angry.

This blowup eradicated the trust that had grown between members. Vulnerable people were attacked in a place they thought to be safe. For many, the hurt was now worse. Elizabeth Edwards was a member of that group, dealing with the death of her son, Wade. Ten years later, as she was writing her book, *Saving Graces* (Edwards, 2006), she phoned me to talk about GriefNet and that blowup. She was still as astounded as we had been at what had happened. She, like we, had lain awake many nights pondering. She was glad to learn that we had found through trial and error ways of keeping such blowups from happening.

When staff discussed how to handle blowups, we disagreed. Some thought we ought to forbid discussions of religion. Others were adamantly against such a rule. We could not reach consensus. Either religion was or was not an OK topic. There was no halfway point. While we were struggling with this, two more blowups happened, both over religion and both similar to the first one. Finally, in 1998, those of us who wanted to stop religious discussions simply took the reins and forbade them. Several of our staff left because of this. Others objected but decided to stay because they thought the survival of GriefNet was paramount.

Many of our members also objected to this rule. Their argument was that the members were all adults who could simply hit the delete key if they objected to what someone said. The fact was, however, that people did not do that. They wrote heated replies; people got stirred up, and nasty e-mails erupted. Some members left, but others asked if we would create a group for people who wanted to discuss religion and who agreed to behave themselves. That seemed workable, so we created grief-religion. A number of people joined it right away, but it soon became clear that they got more help and support from the people in their original group, people who had experienced the same type of loss. It remains, however, as an outlet for some.

We also created "grief-spirits" for people who wanted to discuss spiritual beliefs. This opened another whole can of worms. People began talking about psychics and mediums and soon were recommending that members spend hundreds or even thousands of dollars to consult the psychic du jour, claiming that they had found total peace after they did so. A number of our staff were spiritualists or very close to people of that faith, so this problem was with us for years. Part of the problem was technological; it was not possible to have a group name that used more than a certain number of characters. When we were able to rename it "grief-spirituality," people joined who wished to talk about their own spiritual growth instead of only the spirits of the dearly departed or the possibility of communicating with the dead.

The need for the no-religion rule made clear the mission of GriefNet: to provide safe havens for the bereaved. Staff who remained agreed that safety was paramount and that GriefNet would not be for everyone. We focused on becoming skilled at simply creating and maintaining professional quality safe havens for the bereaved , and that turned out to be a very big job indeed. It was important to learn what the needs of people were who wanted to join, and to decide whether we could fill them. We had to find and train new staff. We had to be able to discuss the deepest issues of grieving with each other if we were going to run groups where members discussed them. We also had to identify the dynamics of e-mail groups and create techniques to handle the dysfunctional ones.

The need for safety brought up the dirty underside of the Internet. Predators found our groups of highly vulnerable people excellent targets. There were opportunists who may legitimately have been bereaved but who sought more than words from other members. They approached members individually seeking money, airline tickets, and other goods.

There were people seeking sex who ranged from lonely widowers to dangerous predators. Many types of assault occurred, from insincere affairs to rape. One widow, having learned trust through our groups, became friends with two other widowed members who lived near her and then joined an online dating site. When she ended the relationship with the man she had met, he murdered her and critically wounded one of the widows. We gave her children free access to GriefNet for as long as they wished.

The scariest predator turned out to be a domestic terrorist. We learned about him when the FBI knocked at the door of one of our widowed staff members at 6:00 a.m. and interrogated her until they could see she had been duped by this man. He was in a relationship with her and engaged to two other members. He escaped from drug rehab in the Federal prison system and phoned me with a long rant. After documenting everything he said, I then contacted the FBI who tracked him down and put him back under lock and key.

Problems evolved that would not normally occur in face-to-face groups but which are endemic to the Internet. We had to create more rules to protect our members and our staff. We also had to find ways to ascertain whether people seeking to join were really who they said they were. We have developed a strategy using online resources that enable us to check the name against the address and phone number given, but of course, we cannot be sure that that is actually the person asking to join. We have no way to know whether potential members actually have suffered a loss or are fabricating one to join. This is where staff training becomes vital.

We learned the hard way that volunteer staff who have not been members of our groups do not really understand our mission, lose interest quickly, and leave us. So staff are drawn only from our members and have the common experience of having found an oasis here in a desert of despair. Current group monitors identify likely members, and I write to ask if they are interested. If they are, I call them. I try to assess their ability to understand and support our mission, whether they use critical thinking, their commitment to our guidelines, their outlook on grief and death, how well they communicate, and whether they will be compatible with our staff group. One essential requirement is a sense of humor and an ability to be silly, which helps one to deal with so many painful e-mails.

Newbies are paired with an experienced monitor (whom we affectionately call a mother hen) who reads the group mail along with the new monitor and suggests, guides, and steps in when needed. It usually takes about a year for a monitor to be able to handle a group alone and 2 to 3 years before they grow into mother hens. I oversee the monitoring of all the adult groups.

No major changes are made at GriefNet until all the staff have had a chance to discuss them and we have reached consensus to proceed. Sometimes, this will take over a year. The two biggest issues we grappled with were our rules and how to raise enough money to keep us going. Although the rules are discussed regularly in our staff group, we have made no changes to them since 2000. The rules, contained in Figure 7.1, are posted on our website and sent to every new member.

We continue to run our groups on e-mail instead of posting comments on a website because we have found that e-mail is a much stronger way to create community. Log-in sites allow users to pick and choose what they will read. With e-mail every member gets a copy of every message which replicates the face-to-face discussions one has at in-person grief groups. Everyone can read what everyone else says and anyone can reply. This facilitates coherent conversational threads, and members quickly feel part of a caring group. Because we run on virtual time, members can read and write when it is convenient for them rather than at a certain time. This also allows the monitors to have better control of the groups. They can stir up conversation when it flags, guide the conversation, set examples of how to communicate, and see when problems arise.

The success of these strategies is reflected within the diversity of our members. We have members from every continent and many walks of life. We have had people from countries where English is not the language, such as the widow of a photo journalist in Ulan Bator, Mongolia. We have many different cultures, ethnic groups, and religions. We have members of every age. As people have come with different losses, we have formed groups for them, now also including loss of siblings, loss of parents, loss of friends, deaths due to substance abuse, war or military service, suicide, violence, and loss of children due to accidents.

Our reputation has grown rapidly and positively. Because we focus closely on safety and quality, we have gained respect and trust. We have been at or near the top of Google searches for 10 years not only because of our web visibility but also because of our quality. Organizations like the American Cancer Society refer people to us. A link to or a description of our site is found on an uncountable number of websites and in numerous books and magazines.

TECHNOLOGY HELPS KIDS GRIEVE

KIDSAID was successful right from the start. Kids took to technology as soon as it was available and quickly found us and liked what we do. The groups evolved into two: k2k for kids younger than 12 years, and k2k-teens for those 12 years and older. Kids are comfortable with e-mail and with conversations which, to an adult, might seem disjointed. They say what is on their minds, which sometimes follows a preceding message and sometimes not. Kids are also straightforward and often blunt when responding to each other. They say things which they would not tolerate from an adult and which adults would not tolerate from each other.

Figure 7.1   Rules for Participation in Adult GriefNet Groups

* **No flaming:** Our primary guideline is that we be polite and respectful in responses to other subscribers. Rudeness or attacks on other people here are not acceptable.
* **Keep this private:** Messages to this group must be kept private and confidential. Do not share messages with someone outside of this list without the author's permission.
* **Stay on topic:** Please restrict topics to those for which the list has been created, which is your grief. Discussions of unrelated issues often confuse new members just joining. Spam, chain letters, forwarded e-mail, and letters requesting replies to off-list addresses are not allowed on any GriefNet lists. They cause our mail system to clog up and do not usually serve the purpose that we are here for: to share our grief and tell our own stories.
* **No religious and spiritual discussions:** Please do not discuss religion or spiritual beliefs. Our membership is composed of people from all over the world who embrace a variety of faiths and religious beliefs. What comforts one person may greatly offend another. We do have two groups for discussion of religious or spiritual beliefs, which you may join by sending a request to Subscribe@griefnet.org.
* **Jokes:** Humor in the form of jokes can be helpful but also possibly destructive, especially when the joke centers on controversial topics, uses overt sexual language, makes fun of someone because of their ethnic background, their sexual orientation, their religious or political affiliation, and probably numerous other antisocial themes. Use extreme discretion and post sparingly, please.
* **Limit contact with other members:** We discourage users from writing to each other privately. If someone has something to say that cannot be shared with the group, then it probably shouldn't be said at all. Never contact another member privately without first asking permission of that person from within the group. Remember that while we do a preliminary screening of our members, we have no way to guarantee that people actually are who they say they are.
* **No identifying information:** Remember also that the Internet is not a totally secure environment. There are many people on the Internet using it for monetary gain or self-glorification and sometimes they will, despite our best efforts, invade our space. We cannot keep all of the offenders out, but we will deal with them appropriately when they are detected. Meanwhile, never give out your personal information to a group. Do not share your phone number, your address, or anything else you would not wish anyone and everyone to know. Never hesitate to contact any of the GriefNet staff if you have concerns about someone in the group.
* **No mentioning products, practitioners, other sites:** Products or services of any sort may not be discussed or recommended, either by supplying web addresses or by describing in detail the commercial venture. This includes recommending individual practitioners or products of any sort, or directing people to other Internet sites.
* **Making sure your mail goes through:** Please do not use multiple addresses when sending messages to the groups, even if you plan to send the same message to other groups of which you are a member. Send each message separately. If you send messages to a number of people or groups at once, they may get stuck in our server or lost. Do not Cc: or Bcc: anyone when writing to the group.
* **No attachments or html:** Attachments are not permitted, as they can easily contain a computer virus, which can totally disable your computer. The same goes for any form of graphics, including messages in html. Use plain text only.

In 2011, our youngest child member is 3 years old, and our oldest 19 years. Kids subscribe from all over the world, mainly the United States, Canada, United Kingdom, and Australia, but we also have members from India, Kazakhstan, Czech Republic, United Arab Emirates, Kenya, New Zealand, Kuwait, Greece, Malaysia, South Africa, Botswana, Costa Rica, Germany, Philippines, Egypt, and Singapore. Most of the children who are active in the groups have experienced the death of a parent; many lost a grandparent or a sibling. However, we also have members who lost a pet, are preparing for the death of a loved one, experienced the death of a friend or relative, or are trying to cope with a divorce or the moving away of a close friend.

When the kids join, we ask for their name, age, city, state, country, and e-mail. We also require a parent's name and e-mail. All this information is given to the KIDSAID administrator, Antje Rath, a child psychologist who joined GriefNet when her newborn son died. She sends the child a welcome letter and sends the parent a letter letting them know who we are, what we do, that their child has joined, and how they can contact us. Often, parents reply saying how grateful they are that their child has the opportunity to reach out to other children because their child does not talk about his or her loss at home or refuses to go to counseling: "Steven has been wanting to find some place he can express his thoughts feelings, etc., on account of his dad's cancer" (mom of a 7-year-old), or "Thanks, this looks like a really helpful place for Madison, and I feel she'll be safe with the monitoring that's in place" (mom of an 8-year-old).

Many parents also ask for advice for their own or their child's grief. "Is it normal that he doesn't talk to me about how he feels? He never cries, either." (father of 15-year-old Dylan). "Is it okay that my 4-year-old wants to go to the funeral? Isn't that too scary?" (Ashley's mom).

When a child writes to a group, the e-mail goes first to Antje. We do not censor the e-mails with regard to spelling, language, or content. We do, however, delete any kind of identifying information, such as e-mail address, surname, address, Facebook or other contact information, location, or the name of their school. This protects the child from being located and contacted by anyone.

The kids usually introduce themselves with their age and a short description of their loss: "Hi my name is Danny. I had a loss in the family when I was three. It was my dad that passed, he died from drugs when he was 24. I'm 8 now." Sandy: "I am 7 daddy died on the 16 before thanksgiving. I am so so sad." "I'm Makayla, my mom died on mother's day of this year, I'm 15 and I was wondering if someone else was going through what I'm going through like blaming God and things like that."

Several kids then respond with expressions of condolence and often candid questions. They ask each other about causes of death, living situations, friendships, support systems, and coping mechanisms. Sixteen-year-old Jason asks, "Why didn't you ever like your dad?" "Can I ask you something bad? Do you ever wanna die to be with your twin again?" are questions that were asked by 10-year-old Sophie. Kia, 15 year old, wants to know: "It is none of my business but why did your grandma commit suicide?" Jake, 9 years old, asks: "Where did your dad shoot himself?"

They are equally candid in their responses. They talk about suicide, over-doses, religious doubts, anger, problems with parents, friends, and school, as well as even more personal issues like nightmares, anxiety, bed wetting, substance use, and the like. One of the concerns the kids have is remembering the person who died. Deb, 15 years old: "I'm sorry if I scare anyone with this, but I'm afraid that we will forget all those memories? Isn't anyone else? I think I am mainly scared of that happening because my grandfather lost his mum when he was 13 and he doesn't remember much about her, and the fact that I might forget just scares me because I always want to remember, you know?" Marie, 14 years old: "Yea I know I'm afraid in a couple years I'll forget about my mom." Jeff, 15 years old: "Me too, I have pictures but I can't remember my brother's voice."

Kids are usually very open about their feelings and are willing to admit a variety of emotions, such as anger, fear, sadness, and sometimes even relief: Terry, 12 years old: "I know it's hard to smile and laugh for me. I feel like there's a big empty spot inside me." Sasha, 16 years old: "I feel nothing BUT empty." Will, 16 years old: "I always seem to bored and tired lately." Samy, 7 years old: "When you lose someone your heart goes with them." Ben, 14 years old: "He was always yelling at me. I mean, I'm not glad he's dead but I'm glad he's not yelling at me anymore."

The kids, no matter what age, often feel guilt around the circumstances of the death or how they behaved toward the person they lost. The older kids often talk about fighting with their parents or even telling them they hate them. If a parent dies shortly after such an argument, the child often feels terrible remorse.

Tara, 14 years old: "When I left for school that morning, she said I should come home right after because I was grounded. I said 'whatever' and just left. She was hit by a car on her way to work an hour later. All I can think of is that the last thing I said to her in this world is 'whatever'."

Ben, 14 years old: "I didn't tell him that I loved him for such a long time. We fought so much. What if he didn't know that I still loved him?"

They discuss all manner of problems: death, their relationship with the one who died, relationships with family and friends, things that hurt them or anger them, bullying, boy- and girlfriends, and how to deal with parents or with teachers. One subject that comes up repeatedly is religion. The group members come from very different backgrounds and are usually not shy talking about it. In adult groups, talking about religion often leads to hurting feelings, preaching, judging, or disengaging from the discussion. The kids are amazingly open and tolerant. They talk about their own religious background and their doubts and hopes; they ask each other questions and state their opinions.

Susan, 17 years old: "Yeah. . . . right after my bro died I pushed God aside. I blamed him for everything I 'till this day do not believe in God . . . Just cause of what happened."

Hannah, 15 years old: "I'm am blaming god and stuff and I know I shouldn't but it's like why did you have to take her now at this moment when my dad has to have surgery and stuff."

Rosa, 13 years old: "Well I think its gods fault because my mom died but I still believe in him."

Kaitlyn, 14 years old: "I blame God, and I go to a catholic school and it really sucks. We were talking about death and stuff the other day in religion, and the teacher asked us for our opinions, so I told her I think God (if there is one) is to blame for taking our loved ones away, and she said he wasn't and then we got into a full-fledged argument about it, and that really brought me down because she made me look like a complete idiot in front of the whole class, most of which are my friends. I was doing ok up until then, but now I feel really bad again."

It is important for many kids to share details about the death, sometimes repeatedly. Their friends want to move on and not talk about the dead person all the time. Their families often become upset and sad and want to protect the child by focusing on the good times. This e-mail group is sometimes the only place where the kids feel comfortable sharing this kind of information. In addition, because of new members joining constantly, they can retell their story again and again. It is fascinating to witness how children grow through their grief and how they start to assist and help other children. For some kids, this process takes only a few months; for some, it takes years.

Although the kids are not shy to give advice or to offer their opinions, there were only two or three instances in the last 5 years in which the kids actually assumed a judgmental stance. Generally, they are amazingly accepting and tolerant, which creates a safe environment and helps everybody to express their opinion and their feelings.

As well as their loss and related topics, the kids talk a lot about aspects of everyday life—school, friends, and family, not always in the context of grief. They seem to have no problems switching topics and talking about a variety of issues. Within the same e-mail, a teenager talks about the suicide of his father and then shares his success at a skating tournament. In the case of 14-year-old Brittany: "Hey, I'm Brittany and I lost my dad to cancer as well. I miss him very much and I'm not the one that breaks down like my mom when we talk about him. I only look at his picture and cry if I wish he were here if my mom is getting on my nerves. I have lots of friends but a certain 2 don't like each other. I like them both and I want to play with them both but they can't stand each other. Do you guys have any advice that I can use to solve this problem?"

The kids often remark that they appreciate not being forced to talk about their grief as in face-to-face grief groups or counseling. They feel comfortable talking to peers with similar experiences instead of adults or even their friends who do not understand what they are going through. Nine-year-old Meghan describes her experience in school: "When we made mother's day gifts my teacher said I didn't have to or I can make it for someone else. I was the only one in my class making it for someone other than their mom! :(." Trenton, 15 years old, states: "I mean, seriously, what do you say when you go back to school in the fall? My summer was great, only my mom died and now I am different from all of you guys? At least here I am not different."

The children vary a lot with regard to how often they e-mail the group. Some of them write more than once daily and respond to every e-mail they receive. Others write less often, sometimes only once a month, if something is bothering them, if an anniversary comes up, or if an e-mail from another kid touched them somehow.

Most of the kids agree on one point: "This group has helped a lot," Noah, 8 years old. "I feel better now, you guys have been so helpful," Amanda, 16 years old. "I like talking here, it makes me feel better, not so alone," Sasha, 13 years old.

TECHNOLOGY HELPS THANATOLOGISTS WITH RESEARCH

Along with phenomenal growth and its concomitant problems, we have acquired tremendous new knowledge about grief. Everyone who found GriefNet helpful has become more educated about grief through sharing the grief of others. The stories and interactions of bereaved people are laid out in endless streams. As a qualitative researcher, I have tried to read, save, and organize the information flowing through GriefNet.

Initially saving it was nearly impossible. During the era of floppy discs, before backup systems came along, memory was very expensive. Home printing was costly, and there was no plausible way to save e-mail to a floppy and let Kinko's print it. Therefore, most of the data of our first few years are available only through human memory. However, the human memory of those early years is remarkably vivid. The way people in groups behaved and the way the groups responded are remembered with great clearness. When Elizabeth Edwards called me in 2006, we talked about what had happened in her grieving parents group and how people had been affected as if it had been just a month previous, not 10 years. Clearly, both having and witnessing grief are deeply imprinted.

Data from 1996 to about 2002 are on all manner of backup hardware: zip discs, data discs, and external hard drives. Recovering it would be a major project, but it is kept safe for the day when that becomes technologically easy. Since 2002, when memory became larger and cheaper, we have been able to save our e-mails in more accessible ways. They live on my computer with a Carbonite backup plus thumb drives. Because I use Outlook, they are difficult to manage, but I expect technology to make that easier as well. When these technological problems are solved, we will have vast amounts of qualitative data and can develop protocols so that members' privacy is not violated.

People have approached GriefNet to do research almost from the start. We protect our members by letting no one approach GriefNet users, found by any means, to solicit any sort of information from or about them. This includes news reporters and magazine writers, as well as social science researchers. We have developed protocols to enable appropriate research. From time to time, I write a letter to each of our members asking whether they would be willing to be contacted by researchers whose project I approve. Those who agree are put onto a list. When a researcher is ready to solicit participants, I send their request letter to everyone on that list. Members can then decide whether they want to participate.

To qualify, researchers must pass our human subjects criteria. We use the same criteria as the Federal government (http://ohsr.od.nih.gov/guidelines/45cfr46.html). Those who meet this guideline are asked to send me an abstract of their proposal or a short description of their article and explain how the human subjects' safeguards will be ensured. I then evaluate the research design and intended use. Usually those seeking a masters or a doctoral degree have well-thought-out research plans. I talk with them on the phone and often I make suggestions of better ways to use our data. I also require a copy of the results.

At the start of 2011, two doctoral researchers were conducting research with GriefNet participants. One was doing a qualitative study on how and when parents deal with the belongings of their deceased child. The other was studying the benefits of online grief support groups. I insisted that she join a group for either her most recent or greatest loss. She had been recently widowed, joined our widowed group, and reported with great excitement that it changed her whole paradigm of how online grief support groups work. Clearly, the availability of a population of bereaved people provides thanatologists with a brand new opportunity to study multiple aspects of grief.

WHITHER WE GOETH?

In December 2011, our web site runs on a Unix-based platform on a 386-based processor at Digital Realm's port in Ann Arbor, Michigan. The software is installed and maintained by Michael Fenimore who is in Dover, Deleware. Our site was designed by Sheri Huffman at Virtual Helping Hand in Texas and is now maintained and updated by Cully Forwend in Australia. Our relational database was designed in Access by David Roach and is stored on his dedicated server in Ann Arbor. Our mail server, Majordomo, runs on our web server. Interfacing between Majordomo and our database is done by humans using Webmin. Our Treasurer keeps our records on his computer using Excel. All staff use their own computers; GriefNet supplies the server computer and its software.

Our Achilles heel is funding. In the beginning, our costs were trivial. In 2011, we have a $30,000 budget, which is insufficient for our needs. We charge members $10 per month per group, although if members claim financial hardship, we allow them to stay without paying. We get small revenue streams from our Bookstore, from Virtual Memorials, and from our gift shop. We pay Michael Fenimore an honorarium but are unable to pay my full salary. We have been reluctant to flood our site with advertising, although we are reconsidering that. We had to cease publication of The *Bereavement Bulletin* in 2008 because of rising costs of printing and postage and are reworking it to be an e-zine. Recently, we have learned that some virtual charities are being funded and have acquired a staff member whose only job is to write grants.

What has held GriefNet together from the start are those incredible people who bring an almost magical quality with them when they join. They grasp the spiritual underpinnings—our essence—and add to them with their presence and their words. They become part of our mission: sharing one's grief and bearing witness to that of others. This ineffable web that holds us is more easily sensed than put into words. However, one of our widowed members captured this shared intangible healing power, and closing with Phil Blown's poignant words seems appropriate:

> My wife died suddenly . . . She passed away in a microsecond. We had been married 53 years. She was barely 18 and I was barely 23 when we married and I had stayed in love for over half a century. I was devastated by the loss. There is a terrible void in losing a loving partner. I knew the meaning of black despair. I descended into the pit of horror. Sometimes I thought I was going insane. Grieving is hard work. You are split in half. To lose a mate is an amputation.
>
> One lonely night I discovered GriefNet and was immediately swept up in e-mail messages, which so often exposed the pain of losing a loving partner. These were people who understood the agony of such a loss. These were people who were suffering. Until it happens to you personally one cannot fully understand and appreciate the depth of despair that such a loss entails. Here was a group who fully understood what I was going through. There were so many of them, all searching for some consolation and understanding. I posted an e-mail message and the replies came flooding back. Many said, "It is too bad that you had to come here but this is a wonderful supporting place."
>
> And it was. And it is. I soon found that many had terrible tales of sickness and lingering death, of angry families, tormenting relatives and of medical errors. I learned that many had had but a very brief time with their partner and that the survivors were frequently young. Many were raising young children who were suffering from the loss of a parent. In spite of the misery there were frequent sparks of humor. But the most compelling spirit, which pervaded the site, was love. I was soon spilling out my innermost feelings and my struggles. Back came advice and counsel based on thoughtful consideration and caring support.
>
> This cyberspace network kept me sane through many difficult months. Well, reasonably sane. We told our stories. We held nothing back. There was such a community of spirit at this website. We all missed the little things of life with a partner: planning each day, shopping together, discussing the news, petting the dogs. We were all different and yet all the same. The Internet can be a grim and ugly place. It can also be a place for caring, loving, and healing. Losing your partner is unlike anything in life. It is a crushing blow and it takes enormous effort to recover. Probably you never do recover. But the outreaching hands on GriefNet helped me bear the pain.

REFERENCES

Edwards, E. (2006). *Saving Graces*. New York: Broadway.

Kehoe, B. (1992, January). *Zen and the art of the Internet: A beginner's guide*. Retrieved from http://www.cs.indiana.edu/docproject/zen/zen-1.0_toc.html

8

Attachment at Distance: Grief Therapy in the Virtual World

Robert A. Neimeyer and Gail Noppe-Brandon

PROLOGUE

This chapter arose from a unique opportunity afforded by the book's editors for two colleagues to reflect on our engagement in grief therapy in a relatively novel context for us both, namely, online videoconferencing and e-mailing as a stand-in for the face-to-face sessions to which we have long been accustomed. Although each of us functioned as "digital immigrants" who came of age in an era that preceded the use of computer technology in clinical practice, we both had naturally accommodated to life in this "brave new world" to a point that constructing web pages, designing online continuing education programs, distributing electronic syllabi, participating in online meetings, and of course, maintaining professional correspondence and connection through e-mail and other social media had become indispensable extensions of our work and personal lives. Nonetheless, the shift to conducting in-depth psychotherapy in the intimate terrain of loss and grief via online sessions—a shift necessitated by the thousand miles that separated us geographically—posed significant challenges to us as therapist and client, just as it afforded equally real advantages. This chapter represents our candid attempt to convey some of the "lessons learned" as a result of our creative use of this "cybertherapy" initiative, with a focus on the unique implications it carries for grief therapy more generally, rather than with a "case study" focus on the details of the therapy itself. Inevitably, however, this experiment bears the imprint of the particular client and therapist who engaged the work, and whose personal and professional predilections shaped our adaptation of technology to our therapeutic ends.

We therefore have chosen to write this chapter as a dialogue in two voices, beginning with an introduction to the players in this particular therapeutic drama to suggest how our unique histories helped configure our response to the virtual therapy that we constructed and reconstructed across our months of contact. In doing so, we make no pretense of addressing all of the complex technical, ethical, or regulative issues regarding online psychotherapy, which are covered more adequately elsewhere in this volume. Instead, we will concentrate on what was most vital and often surprising to us, as the medium in which we worked interacted with the therapy it both supported and constrained. However, first, we begin with some introductions.

AN INTRODUCTION TO THE PLAYERS

Gail: Approximately 2 years ago, my mother was diagnosed with Alzheimer's. As harrowing as this is for any of us to confront, it was uniquely harrowing for me. I had lost my father in a sudden and violent manner (car accident) when I was 4 years old, and having learned thusly that parental mortality was a very real possibility, like many other children of early parental loss, I have always lived in dread fear of losing the remaining one.

This terror was heightened by the fact that the family coping style was one of avoidance. My brother and I were not told the details of how and where our father had met his demise; for a long time we did not even know where or if he had been buried. We were also keenly aware that any discussion of his death, or his life for that matter, induced profound upset in our shocked and overburdened mother. I learned to cover my sorrow, pain, and confusion about this loss at a very young age and did whatever was necessary to ward off the dreaded eventuality of losing my mother, too.

When her mind went last year, I did lose her . . . almost as suddenly as my father had disappeared, and this second trauma invited the reappearance of the first, despite the fact that I thought I had dealt with it adequately during my analysis years earlier. For the first time in over 40 years, I found myself expressing grief, almost uncontrollably. My sister-in-law, a thanatologist, recognized the complicated grief that had so overtaken me and which I have addressed with so many of my own clients and suggested that I consult with her colleague, Dr. Robert Neimeyer. In addition to his expertise with bereavement, she felt that we would find in one another kindred spirits, that my 20-some odd years of work as a narrative coach and later as a therapist, helping people to articulate and revise their life stories (Noppe-Brandon, 2006, 2011), would be *simpatico* with his own therapeutic approach, as would our mutual love of visual art and words. In addition, he, too, had lost a parent as a child.

Although he was located in Memphis, Tennessee, and I in New York City, I sent him an e-mail one night, in which I introduced myself, relayed the story of my grief, and asked for his support. He wrote back a few hours later. With that immediate response began an exploration that changed my life, as well as my style of practice with my own clients. That exploration occurred via telephone calls, e-mails, and eventually Skype. The grief work itself was creative and rich and healing, but it was the mutual challenge of alchemizing this long-distance, virtual relationship into one whose hallmark was intimacy, presence, and even permanence that was, ironically, the most healing aspect of all.

With every session, we dealt with potential loss in a vivid way, as we bumped up against the limits of an imperfect technology that often froze our images in midsentence or abruptly severed the connection entirely. Conversely, we also had a portable laboratory within which to explore the outer limits of attachment anxiety, as we worked together for many months before ever meeting in person. The lessons of this experiment are numerous and complex; that it has also been fruitful speaks to the willingness of two creative clinicians to coconstruct a cyber holding environment and exploit its assets while simultaneously acknowledging that it was a far cry from a human hug.

Bob: At the time Gail contacted me, I had already been practicing therapy for some 35 years in a variety of settings—mental health clinics, psychiatric hospitals, general hospitals, halfway houses, crisis intervention centers, but predominantly in private practice, complementing my ongoing work as an academic psychologist and researcher. Importantly, some of my earliest work with clients was in the context of suicide intervention carried out almost wholly over the telephone, supplemented in the most urgent cases by face-to-face "care team" meetings with the client accompanied by other crisis intervention staff (Neimeyer, 2000). As a consequence, I felt little reluctance to initiate therapy through telephone contacts, a practice I had often enough used over the years with clients who had moved to other cities and who wished to complete our work together or who benefited from the "bridging" of such sessions until they could orient to their new environment and find a new therapist. After several sessions of contact, however, I suggested to Gail that we shift to videoconferencing via Skype, a medium that had served me well in periodic meetings with professional colleagues around the world with whom I was engaged in various projects. In both phases of our work—the purely auditory and the audiovisual—we maximized Gail's penchant for healing through journaling, by using e-mail correspondence to connect, consolidate, and sometimes catalyze our regular Skype sessions. These writing exercises, which we took turns initiating, provided for a narrative strand of the work that made its own distinctive contribution. This said, both e-mail and online sessions also posed their own distinctive limitations, several of which we will consider below.

To understand both the problems and prospects of online grief therapy, however, it could be useful to the reader to know something of my approach to working with loss in the more usual medium of face-to-face contact. As a constructivist psychologist, I find myself drawn to "intervening in meaning," orienting instinctively to the passionate and deeply personal constructs with which we scaffold our experience, building and maintaining a sense of identity in a social world (Neimeyer, 2009). Such work naturally tacks back and forth between the sustaining assumptions, principles, and commitments that structure our lives and the concrete life experiences that validate or invalidate these very premises (Kelly, 1955/1991), shaping and reshaping a self-narrative that is uniquely ours (Neimeyer, 2006a). In the context of bereavement, we commonly find ourselves dislodged from this structure by the loss of a cardinal attachment figure whose life story was woven together tightly with our own, and we struggle to reaffirm or reinvent strands of continuity that preserve or restore our assumptive world and that connect who we were, who we now are, and who we might become in some coherent fashion (Neimeyer, 2006b). Not surprisingly, then, the looming or literal death of a loved one can precipitate a "search for significance" in our loss and in our changed lives, as we struggle to reestablish a sense of secure attachment to relevant projects and people, including the loved one we have lost as a physical presence. A growing empirical literature accords with this "meaning reconstruction" approach to grief (Neimeyer, 2001), documenting the association between an inability to make sense of the loss and profound and protracted mourning (Neimeyer & Sands, 2011), as well as between successful sense making and long-term resilience (Coleman & Neimeyer, 2010). This same perspective fosters a therapeutic emphasis on intensely personal, experientially vivid, improvisational interactions between client and therapist (Neimeyer, Burke, Mackay, & Stringer, 2010), as both seek to symbolize, articulate, and renegotiate the core constructs on which the client has relied but which are in turn challenged by the loss (Neimeyer, 1995). Just how technologically mediated therapy facilitates and impedes such work will find expression in many of the reflections that follow.

EARLY MEMORIES AND EARLY SCENES

Gail: In that first e-mail exchange, in which I had recounted the effects of both my early loss and my current one, I concluded by inquiring as to whether Bob had a referral for me—someone based in New York City who might work in a fashion similar to his own. The reply, which was warm and empathic, stated that *no one* really worked in a similar mode, a mode that I recognized as a unique brew of constructivism, narrative therapy, coherence therapy, and grief work. This was terribly disappointing to me, but he then suggested that we engage in a telephone consultation and take it from there. I had worked over the telephone, as a client and a coach, when in-person meetings were impossible, but I had never imagined this to be a permanent solution. After the first call, however, the limits of my imaginings began to stretch. There is something both intimate and invisible about a voice on a phone; it is both in your ear and beyond your sight, and when the capacity to in-dwell another's circumstance is great, the miles between receivers disappear. In both group and individual work that I have done, my own clients have often remarked that the quality of my vocal presence was a grounding wire. Bob's voice had such an effect upon me. He attended to every utterance with remarkable acuity, and I quickly felt as though he could "see me." In addition, because the particular complications of my complicated grief dictated that others not witness my sorrow, the privacy afforded to my suffering in those early exchanges proved to be a safe space that allowed a greater sharing to build, as I grew more ready to share.

This space encompassed a few weeks of telephone contacts, during which I was free, for the first time ever, to give voice to my newly resurfaced pain without the burden of registering the effect upon my listener. For someone who had grown up covering for the awkwardness that my fatherless status induced in others, this was liberation that cannot be understated. Although I would come to learn that this particular listener shared much of my scar tissue—down to the same paternal death day—and was a deeply emotive human being, I would not yet have been comfortable with the tears that might have welled in his eyes on my behalf; nor would I have been comfortable with his witnessing my own. Despite my comfort in exploring grief with my clients, grieving for *me* was still a solitary activity, and one that was largely *verboten*. That, of course, was precisely the problem, but one that had to be respected as I healed.

After a few weeks of this semianonymous kind of exchange, and as the trust between us grew, the balance began to shift. Suddenly, the embodied absence became more presently felt, and the risk of being seen grieving was not as great as the risk of not fully experiencing he who was helping me to heal. I had never intended my own grief therapy to be conducted within a long-distance relationship, but somehow, poetically, I found myself faced with the challenge of trusting the security of a caretaker that I could not see . . . the very same kind of challenge that I was facing in consolidating an attachment to a father I could not remember but who had nevertheless shaped my core self, and a mother who no longer remembered me but with whom I had shared a lifetime. Learning to trust the solidity of this virtual partner in healing, ironically, proved to be the work of the healing itself.

It was at this time that we switched to Skype-assisted videoconferencing, and the voice grew a face, and that face had reactions. The power of this shift cannot be overstated; suddenly, I had to "face up to" the discomfort of having my feeling state observed and having to observe his in return. This possibility evoked so much anxiety that I did not use my video feature for several sessions. We made the switch because Bob was soon to be traveling to Hong Kong for an extended visit, and the telephone sessions would be too costly to sustain. Conversely, a rupture in the contact at that delicate time in our growing alliance, and the growing crisis, was similarly untenable. I encountered my grief therapist, for the first time, on the other side of the world and at the opposite end of the day. If this highlighted the distance between us even more, it also took that same distance and vanquished it. Our ability to do this said something very visceral about the power of connection, something that could only have been said this literally in this century, and with current technology. In a very plastic way, it taught a lesson about the reach of our presence, the power of our collective imaginations, and the healing value of *intention*: It had been his intention to remain connected, even as he moved further away.

Bob: In a sense, I had met Gail twice before I met her at all—in the medium of our e-mail and in the additional medium of *Listening With Their Eyes*, a documentary about her company, Find Your Voice. Find Your Voice is a unique narrative coaching program that uses playwriting to promote self-discovery across the lifespan.[1] I was fascinated by the work and by Gail, hearing in her compassionate but honest interactions with her clients the same acuity of perception and candor that I had read in her e-mail, where the focus of her reflection was the evolving drama of her own life. Our early weeks of telephone contact added depth and dimension to these preliminary portrayals, as the sometimes astonishing freshness of her imagery, the subtlety of her wordplay, invited novel symbolization of her emotional life: her heart a "monkey" in her rib cage, throwing itself against the bars to find freedom of expression for her grief, her self-censorship a "tiger" that silenced it harshly with a powerful swipe of its paw. As Gail suggested, the telephonic connection (which at least on my end was made with earphones), if anything, *intensified* the sense of presence in her voice, as if it were happening almost inside my head, or as a sustained and surprising conversation I was having with myself. Often, I found myself walking through my home, iPhone clipped to my belt, only vaguely aware of the familiar surroundings as we continued our peripatetic partnership, much as two friends might on a long walk through the park.

One particular sense I recall from these early contacts—refreshed by a more recent experience when Skype failed and we were forced back to the telephone for the first time in many months—was of the sanctity and ambiguity of the silences that would unfold at times, particularly at moments of deep emotion, *both mine and hers*. On the one hand, these seemed to call for simple presence or witnessing, rather than a hurried interpretation, reassurance, or inquiry. On the other hand, as 4 silent seconds turned to 8, I sometimes found myself attempting to discriminate between the possible meanings of muteness, whether Gail was engaged in profound processing of a particular aspect of her grief or whether I had somehow dropped the thread of our developing discourse (Levitt, 2001). In face-to-face therapy I find it easier to remain attuned to the significance of silences, whose function, after all, is usually easily discerned in the quiet tears, furrowed brow, or lost expression of our partner in dialogue. So, as reports of the blind sometimes suggest, being constrained to an auditory contact with another magnified one form of contact, but at a price.

It was in this sense that the shift to Skype felt both liberating and limiting in a different way, which was accentuated for me by the several weeks of sightless interaction. Imagine working for many intensive hours with someone on the deepest questions of their lives—and sometimes yours—blindfolded; and then one day, simultaneously, removing the masks. There, suddenly, was *Gail*, the face in the film, responding to my raised eyebrow, my smile. Even on the flat screens of our respective computers, the other took on *depth*, and—not incidentally— *context*, as we glimpsed a small part of one another's worlds in the form of the walls of our respective studies as a backdrop: her framed print of a Diego Rivera painting hinting at her artistry and her ethic of resistance against oppression, the anthropological *bric-a-brac* on the burgundy walls and walnut shelves of my study suggesting the anachronistic image of a displaced Victorian scholar blinking into

---

1 An excerpt of the film airs on PBS, featuring an ethnically diverse group of inner city teens (*IntheMix@PBS.org*).

the screen of his Macintosh laptop. So began a mutual journey of seeing and being seen, as we each peered into the misty history of sundered attachments that shrouded the landscape of Gail's loss and were oftentimes a mirror of my own.

A CHANGE OF SCENE

Gail: The experience of "meeting" Bob for the first time in Hong Kong, with a world in between us, was one that would be repeated many times in the months to come, as he was on the road a good 20% of the time. As familiar as the burgundy walls of his study were to become, I was to experience the comforting image of his face against the backdrop of countless hotel rooms around the globe, sometimes having to schedule meetings at the crack of dawn or at the close of day to find the 1 hour we might comfortably share in our respective hemispheres. With the security of a more animated respondent, came the constant specter of loss. Would the often-fragile signal sustain, or would we lose it at a delicate moment? If we did—as all too often happened—would we be able to reconnect, and if we could not, how would we seek, find, and signal closure? As I began to accept clients-at-a-distance in to my own practice, I learned well what it was like to be on both sides of that nerve-wracking equation; often resorting to the telephone as a stopgap to back up the Internet, if only long enough to say a proper goodbye.

I think it is fair to say that we spoke to one another in several voices, even that of telegraphic texting on our mobile phones when appointments were delayed by technical problems, and had to learn to "read one another" in a variety of languages (Noppe-Brandon, 2011). Thus, one form of electronic contact began to layer on to the next as we patched in and out across the miles. The early telephone calls were marked by a particular kind of "visual" intensity; the intensity of exploring the terrain of preverbal attachment anxiety and forgotten early childhood traumatic loss. It involved a good deal of imaginal work, with Bob pitching the provocative questions directly in to my ear and the emotional landscape of my brain: *"Where do you notice the pain in your body? If it had a shape, a form, what would it be?" There is a hole in my chest. Sometimes it houses a chimpanzee, jumping wildly to the anxious pounding of my heart. "Look at the monkey. Why is it jumping, what does it need?" It is in a cage . . . my rib cage. It needs to feel calm. "What will calm it?" Soon, a tiger prowling by will swipe it hard with its paw, and knock it to the ground. Then the jumping about will cease.* A painful realization came of the way in which the agony of early parental loss was silenced, without being soothed or healed, a realization followed by the release of quiet tears. Softly, after a pause: *"What is the monkey doing now?"* The concerned voice of a clinician, connected across countless miles only by cyberspace and trust. *The monkey has turned in to a child, is lying down, and is going to sleep.* Another layer of agony is excavated and survived, together.

Moments after the telephone session ends, an e-mail dings to signal its arrival on my laptop. An image flashes on the screen as I open the attachment. It is a photograph of a full-grown chimp, tenderly holding a tiny albino tiger cub.

These are the first characters in what Bob, who is an avid photographer, would dub my "inner jungle book." And here they were, the visible symbols of my inconsolable child-self, grown to a solid and gentle creature, the ferocious parental censor now reduced to a frightened kitten in its arms. *Click*: the representation is enlarged. *Click*: it is minimized. An abstract idea made concrete, at will. It becomes an image I would many times glance at on my tiny Blackberry screen, following the increasingly frequent telephone calls from the nursing facility where my mother now resided. These calls announced in slow motion the event I had dreaded for a lifetime, the loss of my remaining parent: now my mother can't read, now she can't write, now she has stopped walking, now she is on oxygen, now she is angry . . . wants to go home. Home? Another abstraction. A place she is determined to find, with no address and no map. Railing at me for imprisoning her thusly, for mistaking her for someone who is old and demented and dying, is the formerly fierce jungle cat who had promised she would live forever . . . for me. *Click*: there is my representative image, my secular prayer card, called up on my various screens as needed. She is a kitten now; I can hold her lovingly in my arms, and I can grieve. It is safe. It is permissible.

The Skype calls had a different kind of visual intensity entirely. Although equipped with a human presence bearing compassionate eyes, a necessary witness to the incredible pain we were unearthing, there were times when connection was so poor that I would find myself interacting at great length with a still shot of the very person whose lively voice was continuing beyond the moment in the picture. At other times, there were delays in delivery that rendered us perpetually out of synch and forever interrupting one another. Often, I would hear my own thought literally ricochet back to me, leaving Bob's responses somewhere under the waters between our computers. Periodically, I encountered a pixelated version of the face I'd come to know, or the sound would drop out entirely. Though we both favored a constructivist approach to clinical work, these mutations begged the question of how many ways one could rearrange a trusted figure and still recognize in him, or her, the object permanence that was yearned for. Occasionally, the entire system crashed in midsession, leaving me vulnerably regressed and palpably reexperiencing the "sudden disappearance" of an attachment figure and the "no one to process it with" phenomenon that had built the complicated grief the first time around. I would then resort to writing, journaling the sensations and the memories as they wove a braid from past to present, forwarding this to Bob as a kind of therapeutic monologue. And then I would wait for the response to arrive . . . sometimes, when the Internet was particularly uncooperative—as in a German monastery or the Australian outback—for days. Eventually, the journal was received, read, deeply felt, and witnessed. I knew well the healing power of writing and of having that writing shared and responded to (Noppe-Brandon, 2004). I was learning anew a trust that from out of the seeming void of expressed grief a caring response would come; not always immediate, but reliable. A new kind of reliable: caretakers can disappear accidentally, temporarily . . . and then return.

Bob: As Gail implies, the visual aspect of our work in words began before Skype opened the door to literal eye-to-eye contact. Buoyed by a common fascination with metaphor, she and I seemed naturally to steer toward vaguely discerned islands of meaning, ultimately breaking onto some new shore of possibility that offered a sustaining image that we carried forward when we then launched out toward other destinations. One such arose in an early session in which Gail had traced a loss-related feeling of abandonment and panic to a childhood memory: She stood, perhaps all of 4 years old, surrounded by tall, foreboding hedges, lost beyond the backyard of a temporary abode following the death of her father, frozen in terror. Entering the scene in my mind's eye, I encouraged her to turn slowly and to describe the space around her. The shift in perspective proved pivotal; seemingly instantly, the spell of stasis was broken, and she discerned a path around the enclosing walls of vegetation, the path home. Months later, faced with a similar feeling of entrapment and powerlessness in anticipation of a visit to her confused and raging mother, we again found ourselves in session, but this time with Skype contact. Impulsively, I suggested we "go for a walk" and unplugged and picked up my laptop, swiveling first in my desk chair toward the window of my study, her visual field shifting from the familiar dark therapeutic backdrop to the verdant world of a Memphis spring, the great maple on the ivy-covered lawn adorned with fresh growth. Standing, I then took her on a walk through the living room, dining room, study, pausing briefly to peer out each window as we continued our conversation. The effect of this simple intervention was striking, triggering a *pivot into agency* akin to that experienced earlier with the hedges. Suddenly, movement was restored, options opened, childhood trauma was mobilized into adult healing. And just as suddenly, videoconferencing became more than just a convenient stand-in for in-office contact.

As Gail implies, however, not every step on this garden path offered secure footing. Too often, at a crucial juncture, I found myself speaking to an image of her familiar face now rendered by Monet, now by Picasso. One need only conjure a comparably hallucinatory experience in a face-to-face session with a client to imagine the potentially unsettling effect on therapeutic process! But as time went by, partly as a function of our strengthening security with each other and partly through simple habituation, the occasional disruptions became easier to take in stride. The advantages, after all, were palpable: the limitation of geographic proximity as a criterion for matching of client and therapist fell away; some level of consistency in connection was assured across state lines and international frontiers, and with flexibility on the part of both client and therapist, sessions could be arranged before or after office hours, anticipating or responding to sudden upsurges of grief occasioned by decisions about Gail's mother, difficult family discussions, and more. Gradually, the Internet became a safety net, and the high-wire balancing act required to move forward with a long-frozen mourning could be undertaken together with less fear.

REVISING AND REROLEING

Gail: The reappearances after the sudden ruptures, and the unexpected contacts, began to forge a healing strand unique to this kind of virtual alliance. The morning that Bob left for that first departure to Hong Kong, I had e-mailed what I thought would be a final meditation before what was to be our first Skype session, from across the globe, scheduled for some time later. I had composed a monologue that reflected back on our fruitful first weeks of work and the shaky attachment that was beginning to form between myself and the human being behind the voice to whom I was whispering my painful feelings. It was a brave goodbye to a sense of support that had grown floor beneath my feet, as I took my first tentative steps toward obtaining power of attorney for the woman who had been head of house-hold, who served as both my parents, and who could no longer sign her own name. I hit "send" with the forlorn sensation that I would be talking to myself for some time to come. A few hours later, seemingly from midair, Bob's response flashed in; he was in the VIP lounge at an airport, laptop open, availing himself of Wi-Fi before boarding. He encouraged me to respond in-kind, promising to compose further on the plane with the plan of hitting "send" as soon as he landed. Like breadcrumbs on the ocean, we coconstructed a bridge of words on thin air, and each back-and-forth advanced the project. Even our "subject" headings came to be deep-going forms of meaning making, as I signaled feeling states in my communiqués and Bob reframed them in his own, (*hiding/seeking, all ripped up/a stitch in time, wrecking ball/renovation*, etc.). We riffed off of one another's meta-phorical headings like jazz musicians who can tell an entire story in the punctua-tion of a single note . . . and then revise it. Often, the mutual writing and sharing stretched out into such exercises as letters to our respective fathers to mark their shared death day, reciprocal commissions of existential poetry, and the exchange of familial images. Sometimes, the sessions bordered on supervision, as we exam-ined my work with a demented client, and the ways in which the lessons of that work might amplify my attempts at communication with my mother, or the ways in which writing and imaginal exercises with my own grieving clients paralleled my own experience. The therapy played out like a continuous movie across my various screens, punctuated with appearances by the artists behind the scenes, each offering reparation for lost continuity in the past, and the model of a bond that could continue into the future. We used the communication technology like a newfangled classroom "smart board" that provided a ground on which to rerole and revise a lifetime of attachments, bringing the dead to life when needed and traveling back in time when appropriate. Between sessions, we sent letters to one another in the voices of our inner 8-year-olds, our inner summer-campers, our in-ner college students . . . all of whom had a special role to play in the healing.

I have always believed in the efficacy of "the writing cure" (Noppe-Brandon, 2011); in this medium, it became a dialogue. These were not dead pieces of paper brought into a session but a living conversation that was as infinite, and as infi-nitely malleable, as the space left between two people who are separated for life. Clinician and client became cyber pen pals whose letters occasionally morphed into the speaking faces of the writers. Together, we cultivated these possibilities in the soil of fertile imagination, often forgetting that we had never even shaken hands yet, had never even met as physical beings. In some ways, our alliance was as disembodied as the parental figures we had each been severed from early in life; and in my weaker moments, I thought I was leaning on air. In my stronger moments, I sensed that our connection was a richer and more keenly felt presence than ordinarily exists in the confines of a session room, in the limitations of "talk."

So it was a seismic shift, yet again, when a psychotherapy conference in Washington, DC, afforded us the geographic opportunity to finally meet in person. If morphing from voice to face was disorienting after a few weeks, it goes without saying that encountering the whole person, after knowing only a talking head, was completely mind-blowing. When I had this experience with a client of my own recently, meeting in person after months of Skyping across the country, his face seemed oddly shrunken from the 12 × 17 image that I encountered on my desk. I sensed that he, too, was struggling to accommodate the three-dimensional presence that radiated heat and wore cologne, had feet and sported shoes, got up and shook his hand, then held him in a painful goodbye. Separation anxiety is palpably physical and the stuff that grief is made of; it is heightened even further by the flesh and blood connection and disconnection that in-person presence affords. Although we were both eager for this event, it also engendered enormous anxiety. Oddly, it was the reverse of the anxiety I had always lived with—the ghostly presence was about to come to life. And while embracing and walking and eating and sitting with this ghost felt both oddly familiar and not surprisingly strange, it was the departure at the end of the visit that shook the grief work, and the people involved in the work, to their core selves. Suddenly, the real and solid others had to go back into their respective computer boxes, and the actual people were virtual once again.

Bob: Reading Gail's account of our Washington encounter followed by the predictable "dematerializing" as we returned to our usual residence on one another's desktop, I am reminded of countless scenes from the old TV series, *Star Trek*, as Kirk steps onto the transporter and Scotty beams him down to some alien world and the rest of the crew looks on anxiously. With the radiance of a thousand fireflies, the column of light sparkles, and the substantial becomes insubstantial, to reappear magically—if technology does not fail—on another planet. So it was as Gail boarded the train at Union Station, and I turned, already nostalgic, toward the conference and scheduled reconnection in the far thinner atmosphere of cyberspace.

But, like Gail, I sensed that the medium contained a message: that continuing bonds were possible in a nonmaterial form and that these became more elastic even as they stretched across the miles and continents. This conviction, stressed but also strengthened with each coming and going, seemed to have unique relevance in the context of grief therapy, where the need to reorganize an attachment with a physically lost other stands at the core of the work. What our cyberdance demonstrated better than any theory was that a *portable secure base* could be built that could allow both parties to move without threatening a sense of connection. By analogy, at least, this seemed to carry implications for the construction of a durable bond with loved ones that might even survive their ultimate transition— from life to death. The narrative practices that wove naturally through our work, such as writing unsent letters to Gail's parents, corresponding with earlier selves who embodied their own strengths and vulnerabilities, and scripting dramatic dialogues that bravely confronted the specter of (looming) loss, helped (re-) consolidate these relationships, promoting the integration of life experiences in the service of greater wholeness. As the work progressed, I came to recognize that I too had begun to reconstruct some of the meaning of my own childhood loss of my father, as well as the adult loss of my mother, underscoring the reality that full engagement in constructivist therapy offers invitations to growth to the therapist no less than the client (Neimeyer, 2009).

CLOSING ACTS

Gail: I suppose there is a certain sadness in the move toward virtual presence that this very book implies; and it is surely indicative of a broader evolutionary shift. As I traverse the streets of my Greenwich Village neighborhood, I notice that the bookstores are disappearing; you can download and read stories on a device. Gone too are the video stores, for the same reason. The quaint cafes of yesteryear have been replaced by their cyber counterparts, and people seen deep in conversation are often seated alone. At least in New York City, the general food stores, too, are endangered by the growing use of groceries online, and half of my clients met their current or future spouses that way. Perhaps it is the inevitable extension of the airplane and the telephone, both of which connected us to loved ones far away. I know children who have only met certain relatives via Skype, and rare are the families with several generations in the same city. My brother, a tenured professor, now prefers to teach online, and the growing numbers of home-schooled children telegraph the fact that we do not have to sit together to learn together. It is challenging indeed, particularly for someone like myself—who has facilitated the skills of person-to-person engagement for decades and who has battled posttraumatic separation anxiety for a an adult lifetime—to embrace this dematerializing world. In another sense, however, I have always known in my very bone marrow that which the Buddhists teach: that attachment is an illusory thing. That we come in alone and go out alone, and that any positive contact we make with other humans along the journey, in whatever form it comes, is something to be cherished. That even the end of a life does not signal the end of the relationship.

During my work with Bob, my mother deteriorated from being ambulatory in an assisted living unit, to being wheelchair bound and then bedridden in a nursing home; from slowed thinking and poor memory to an almost total lack of recognition and a rejection of all medications. During that same time, I moved from a stance of life review and reminiscence with her, to giving her permission to go when she was ready. And between those hard positions came dozens of imaginary letters written via e-mail and scenes role-played via Skype, preparing me to make this inevitable shift and to face this inevitable loss. This was deep-going and agonizing work, work that allowed the adult that I am, and the traumatized child that I was, to face mortality and loss with meaning, heart and courage . . . and without a loss of self.

When my family headed out for a recent vacation, I got the call that my mother was in congestive heart failure, requiring constant oxygen and declining rapidly. A grueling family decision was made to bring in hospice and to add a do not hospitalize order to the existing do not resuscitate. Although pneumonia was a real and constant threat, that is what she would have wanted, and we all recognized that there was no quality of life ahead. Given that there was no Wi-Fi and little cell service at this most remote end of the Long Island shore, I felt suddenly engulfed in panic. When my children were settled in with my husband to watch a movie, I slipped out of the room for a hastily scheduled cell phone session with Bob, climbing a ladder to the roof of the dining room to establish connection. I stood there, under the evening sky, gazing out at the blackness of the sea and orienting to the existential soundscape of perpetually rising and crashing waves. All I could see was the moon, and a single lonely ship on the horizon. And then, connection . . . here was the voice that had seen me through this turbulent time and would be there—I knew—until the end. We both wept as I relayed the latest news. Following our call I sat on the roof for a long while and stared out at the sea . . . alone, but, finally, not feeling alone.

As I continue the work of healing those confronted with loss (of self or other) in my own practice, I see that work not within the confines of a particular room, on a particular day, but as something that can be shaped and reshaped in infinite ways . . . as infinite as the imaginations of the two human beings who have come together to explore and master the mystery of attachment that is unique to our species.

Bob: Gail's allusion to a Buddhist perspective on loss reminds me of a fundamental truth underlying the welter of constructed meanings: We are wired for attachment in a world of impermanence. Given that fundamental conundrum of human existence, is it any wonder that we as a species keep inventing and reinventing new means of connecting, new ways of bridging our subjective world with that of another, new forms of constructing in discourse a relational reality in which we can find orientation? Viewed in this light, cybertherapy is simply the latest extrapolation of a more basic need to relate, albeit one with its own drawbacks, advantages, and uncertainties. Let me therefore close with some personal reflections on each.

First, I easily resonate to the sadness Gail describes in the shift toward therapy at distance: at least for those of us who are digital immigrants rather than "digital natives," cyberconnection almost inherently seems like a pallid surrogate for "real" contact with another human being who walks into the room with us, perhaps with hesitation, accepts or declines a proffered cup of coffee or tea, sits and arranges his or her body in a chair across from ours or at right angle to ours, leans toward or away from us, fidgets with one foot during a protracted silence, or extends a hand or asks for a hug following a moving session. For those of us marinated in the practice of physical presence, this elaborate language of gesture, of movement, of proxemics, of ritual, and of embodiment speaks volumes, and all of it is lost or greatly compromised when presence is shrunken to what is revealed on even the most generous and high-definition video monitor or efficient exchange of e-mail or "chat." And some form of grief is perhaps appropriate in the face of this loss, and the parallel thinning of community that results when groups of grieving people no longer gather, with or without a therapist, to share a space, a story, and perhaps a snack in the presence of the "grieving bodies" of others.

Beyond this general and perhaps endemic loss entailed by the certain emergence of online therapy, I confess to encountering—partly in the presently available technology and partly in myself—other constraints to the sort of grief therapy I more typically practice. Drawing on my online work with not only Gail but also others—a widow in the northeastern United States, an Argentine family contending with the long-term aftermath of the suicide of a husband/father—I find myself needing to construct creative "work-arounds" when the therapeutic formats or strategies I would prefer seem unworkable for technical reasons. For example, although individual therapy seems feasible to me in an online environment, I balk at the idea of attempting couples or family sessions in this medium, not merely because it would require participants to crowd around a small camera to be within my range of vision, but more significantly because the very substantial reality of the family members' tangible relationships to one another—usually within their own home—easily trumps the level of connection they are likely to feel with me. As a result, I sense that I would have less relational "capital" to guide them into and through difficult but necessary conversations about what are often life-and-death matters. Similarly, some forms of experiential interventions, such as facilitated imaginal conversations with the deceased that I frequently employ in practice (Neimeyer et al., 2010), seem harder to choreograph when I am frozen on the other side of a small virtual window, as I ask the client to shift chairs and voices in a profound and often perturbing encounter with the internalized other. Online grief therapy therefore challenges me to access my own creativity and that of the client to pursue these goals through other means (e.g., "homework" conversations with various family members, "corresponding" with the deceased), though not always with the same effect.

These losses and limitations notwithstanding, the advantages of virtual grief therapy are equally real. As Gail and I have discussed or implied throughout this chapter, the ability to connect with a uniquely relevant therapy irrespective of geographical location is a remarkable benefit, even for someone situated in a city as rich in therapeutic options as New York. For individuals living in rural isolation, access to relevant services at distance is all the more important. Beyond these matters of convenience, the ability to create and sustain connection beyond the usual hour per week of outpatient practice in a fixed location has clear advantages when client needs dictate more frequent or off-hour consultation. Likewise, access to at least head-and-shoulders visual contact with the other adds immeasurably to the capacity of each to orient to the other in an expressive vocabulary that complements and sometimes qualifies the spoken word. Perhaps most fundamentally in the context of grief therapy, virtual partnerships may provide a kind of model of what the bereaved seek: the establishment of a nonmaterial relationship with a significant other through the construction of a continuing bond that is durable and resilient to practical challenges of all kinds. As Gail and I discovered, the achievement of this was no easy feat, but as our cyberattachment consolidated, it became not only the *container* for our work but also a direct *analogue* of desired outcomes as well.

Finally, and perhaps most personally, I have to acknowledge some ambiguity stirred up in me by conducting something as intimate as experientially intense grief therapy in the mediated environment of online practice. For example, I sometimes noticed in my work with Gail my more muted response to her tears or other strong displays of emotion, when in face-to-face sessions with grieving clients tears would almost certainly have been welling in my eyes in response to theirs. At such times, I would find myself wondering whether my greater degree of emotional control represented (a) an appropriate "read" of Gail's need for me to maintain composure to allow her to feel secure in exploring the troubling feelings whose expression had so upset her original caretaker, (b) a simple function of the greater emotional distance introduced by the medium of videoconferencing, which prevented me from even handing her a tissue, or (c) an overextension of my own defensive response of emotional self-control following my own father's early death, triggered in some fashion by Gail's parallel experience. Conversely, at other times I would find myself sharing in our e-mail exchanges more of my own responses to early and recent loss than I typically would with most clients. In such moments I would ask myself whether this reflected (a) a blurring of therapeutic boundaries partly arising from reliance on a communication medium commonly reserved for more ordinary personal and professional relationships; (b) a normative pull to mirror the depth of Gail's disclosures in a written medium that militated against the use of the eye contact, head nods, "umm hmm's," and brief reflections that would be more common in face-to-face conversation; or (c) a natural inclination to "level the playing field" and establish a person-to-person relationship with a liked and admired peer who was quickly becoming a colleague and one with whom mutual disclosure coconstructed a situation that was healing for us both. Such questions have no easy answers under any circumstances, but the additional complexity introduced by the medium of virtual connection called for still further reflection to sort out contributions to a therapeutic process made by the circumstantial and relational factors shaping our interaction.

Perhaps it is appropriate at this early juncture in the exploration of online grief therapy to conclude the report of our experience with open questions rather than definitive answers. As a therapeutic team, Gail and I would agree that the media through which we pursued our work was often challenging, occasionally frustrating, but ultimately indispensable in permitting us to develop a profoundly personal and constructively collaborative partnership in moving through grief to growth. We are hopeful that many other therapists will join us in more fully realizing, researching, and refining the promise of these technologies in the service of companioning others through loss.

POSTSCRIPT

Gail: Since the time of this writing, my mother passed away. In the months immediately preceding and following her slow death, and despite the many extraordinary assets of this creative treatment and clinician, I could not complete my healing through "virtual support" alone. As I have come to understand better in myself, and observed in practice with my own clients, those struggling with complex trauma and complicated grief need a physical presence to help contain and embody responses to the physical loss, as trauma itself is a disconnection to the body (Levine, 1997). Further cultivating the fertile seeds that our work had planted, I gradually segued to a clinician in my own city; one who could also offer a real human hug. Though it can provide essential accompaniment and can model flexibility, virtual treatment alone, for someone who was not "held" in the experience of grief the first time around, can begin to feel insufficient and even re-traumatizing at the time of the next major physical loss. I continue to favor narrative re-construction as a way of making sense of life and loss but, in hindsight, I feel that treatment also must offer, or be augmented by, a literal "holding" environment, especially for those of us who had once been left to grieve alone as children. Bob and I made that adjustment, while also retaining a profound continuing bond as colleagues, friends, and partners in mutual healing.

REFERENCES

Coleman, R. A., & Neimeyer, R. A. (2010). Measuring meaning: Searching for and making sense of spousal loss in later life. *Death Studies, 34,* 804–834.

Kelly, G. A. (1955/1991). *The psychology of personal constructs.* New York, NY: Routledge.

Levine, Peter A. (1997). *Waking the Tiger: Healing Trauma.* Berkeley, CA: North Atlantic Books.

Levitt, H. M. (2001). The sounds of silence in psychotherapy: Clients' experiences of pausing. *Psychotherapy Research, 11,* 295–309.

Neimeyer, R. A. (1995). Constructivist psychotherapies: Features, foundations, and future directions. In R. A. Neimeyer & M. J. Mahoney (Eds.), *Constructivism in psychotherapy* (pp. 11–38). Washington, DC: American Psychological Association.

Neimeyer, R. A. (2000). Research and practice as essential tensions: A constructivist confession. In L. M. Vaillant & S. Soldz (Eds.), *Empirical knowledge and clinical experience* (pp. 123–150). Washington, DC: American Psychological Association.

Neimeyer, R. A. (Ed.). (2001). *Meaning reconstruction and the experience of loss.* Washington, DC: American Psychological Association.

Neimeyer, R. A. (2006a). Re-storying loss: Fostering growth in the posttraumatic narrative. In L. Calhoun & R. Tedeschi (Eds.), *Handbook of posttraumatic growth: Research and practice* (pp.69–80). Mahwah, NJ: Lawrence Erlbaum Associates.

Neimeyer, R. A. (2006b). Widowhood, grief and the quest for meaning: A narrative perspective on resilience. In D. Carr, R. M. Nesse, & C. B. Wortman (Eds.), *Spousal bereavement in late life* (pp. 227–252). New York, NY: Springer Publishing.

Neimeyer, R. A. (2009). *Constructivist psychotherapy.* London & New York: Routledge.

Neimeyer, R. A., Burke, L., Mackay, M., & Stringer, J. (2010). Grief therapy and the reconstruction of meaning: From principles to practice. *Journal of Contemporary Psychotherapy, 40,* 73–83.

Neimeyer, R. A., & Sands, D. C. (2011). Meaning reconstruction in bereavement: From principles to practice. In R. A. Neimeyer, H. Winokuer, D. Harris, & G. Thornton (Eds.), *Grief and bereavement in contemporary society: Bridging research and practice* (pp. 133–186). New York, NY: Routledge.

Noppe-Brandon, G. (2004). *Find your voice.* Portsmouth, NH: Heninemann Press.

Noppe-Brandon, G. (2011). *One vision, many voices.* Bloomington, IN: IUniverse.

9

Bereavement in Online Communities: Sources of and Support for Disenfranchised Grief

Lisa D. Hensley

Imagine for a moment that your homeland, a place both familiar and significant to you where you interacted with loved ones, was about to disappear; you would never be able to return to it. You and the other inhabitants knew what was coming, even the precise time it would occur. You gathered with others in your homeland to say goodbye to it, and to one another, because all of you knew that even if you were able to regroup in another land and recreate vestiges of your home and culture, nothing would be the same after this moment. You are now refugees from a place that no longer exists, and it is clear that people outside this circle will have limited understanding of, and possibly little empathy for, the loss and trauma you have experienced.

Pearce and Artemesia (2009) described such an event concerning the end of *Uru Live*, a multiplayer version of the video game *Uru*. It is a virtual world in which inhabitants explored, solved complicated puzzles, learned the mythological history of their world, and created relationships and communities. As many as 40,000 members participated in the test version (or beta), only to find that *Uru Live* would not be released, and the *Uru* world would be gone within weeks. "Players experienced what they characterized as a 'shock and catharsis' and many described symptoms of posttraumatic stress . . . at this point the players had been made refugees, and the impact of this shared trauma on long-term community building cannot be overstated" (Pearce & Artemesia, 2009, p. 89).

If the reader has limited experience with virtual communities, a number of questions may arise at this point. What was *Uru*? What did people do there? How did they experience a sense of "place" and a sense of themselves in that virtual space? Were they the same people online as they were "in real life?" What kind of relationships did they build with one another? Finally, can people develop attachments to a virtual community and the people within it such that they deeply grieve its loss and the loss of these virtual relationships when they end?

This complex and unusual bereavement situation offers the opportunity to discuss the relationship between virtual communities and the phenomenon of disenfranchised grief, or grief that is not supported or socially sanctioned (Doka, 2002). It is easy to see the potential for disenfranchised grief in the above scenario because those with limited understanding of virtual worlds and online relationships might minimize the loss. At the same time, the opportunity to build those online relationships may offer people an outlet for their grief that they may not have had otherwise, thereby ameliorating disenfranchisement. Doka recognized the possibility of this dual relationship between disenfranchised grief and online communities:

> Nor has the effect of new technology upon the experience of grief been considered. Although thanatologists have explored the role of the Internet in grief education and support (see Martin & Doka, 1999), the effect of this technology upon grief has been largely ignored. Yet many individuals maintain extensive contacts on the Internet, interacting with a range of individuals, developing web-based friendships, and sharing intimacies. In such cases, the only indication of a loss may be unanswered e-mail or a cryptic "host unknown." The Internet is likely to spawn grief as well as inform and support grievers (p. 10).

This chapter will begin with a brief discussion of disenfranchised grief, followed by a description of the general characteristics of online communities. A preliminary survey of individuals who have experienced bereavement in online communities will be described, portions of which were previously presented by Hensley and Arroyo (2010). In discussing the results of this study, characteristics of online communities will be highlighted, particularly those with the potential both for creating disenfranchised grief and for alleviating it. The chapter will conclude with suggestions for assisting bereaved individuals in online communities.

DISENFRANCHISED GRIEF

According to Doka (2002), there are many ways that grief may be disenfranchised. Examples of these include unacknowledged relationships, a significant loss that goes unrecognized, underestimation of an individual's need or ability to grieve, uncomfortable circumstances of a death, or grief expression that is regarded as inappropriate. These sources of disenfranchisement have a common underpinning through the violation of widely held "grief rules." According to Doka (2002), "Each society has grieving rules that define, and in some ways limit, the role of the griever (p. 7)." Experiences that fall outside of these grief rules may lend themselves to disenfranchisement. External agents, such as family, friends, religious groups, or political agents, may disenfranchise grief. However, grief may also be self-disenfranchised if one avoids acknowledging the significance of one's own relationship or loss. Disenfranchisement varies by griever and by circumstances, with the extent of disenfranchisement existing on a continuum and perhaps being an inescapable part of grief. People whose grief is disenfranchised are less likely to receive social support than those with more traditional losses (Corr, 2002), and those with disenfranchised grief often experience an intensification of emotions, such as anger and guilt, which may promote complicated grief and interfere with healing (Doka, 2002).

ONLINE OR VIRTUAL COMMUNITIES: SCOPE AND RELEVANT CHARACTERISTICS

Facebook (2010) reported that it has more than 500 million active users, half of whom log in to their accounts on any given day and spend a total of more than 700 billion minutes per month at the site. According to an August 2010 press release by Blizzard Entertainment, "Since launching in November 2004, *World of Warcraft* has become the world's most popular MMORPG [Massively Multiplayer Online Role-Playing Game], with a current global player base of more than 11.5 million subscribers" (Blizzard Entertainment, 2010, para. 5). Given these statistics, it would be tempting to conclude that virtual communities are so common that most people would be familiar with them and understand their dynamics. According to the Pew Research Center (2010a, 2010b), although 77% of adult respondents were users of the Internet, only 36% of respondents reported having ever played online games. Only 4% of respondents older than 30 years reported visiting a virtual world such as *Second Life* (Lenhart, Purcell, Smith, & Zickuhr, 2010). This means that the person who is heavily involved in online life may be surrounded by those who are not well versed in online communities, which would provide the opportunity for disenfranchisement if a loss occurred in this context. Neimeyer and Jordan (2002) characterized disenfranchised grief as "empathic failure" (p. 95), and there are aspects of online communities that may be ripe for misunderstandings by people outside those communities. Discussions of whether virtual worlds are "communities" in the true sense, stereotypes of those who inhabit virtual communities, and a lack of understanding of the relationships that develop in those environments certainly have the potential to create a sense of disenfranchisement and marginalization.

Pearce and Artemesia (2009) examined the literature related to virtual communities and developed a list of attributes that are characteristic of virtual communities as a whole. First, they can be mapped and explored by inhabitants. Second, virtual worlds are also *persistent*, in that they exist regardless of whether one is logged into them. Virtual worlds are also *inhabitable*, in that it is possible to live inside them, and more than one person can inhabit the world at a time. As such, one's actions inside the virtual world may have consequences for other inhabitants of the world. In addition, inhabitants of virtual worlds have some sort of *player representative* that can persist and evolve over time. If the player representative is graphically based, it is commonly called an *avatar*. Finally, virtual communities have *worldness*, which "is perhaps the most elusive quality of virtual worlds. This term is used to express a sense of coherence, completeness, and consistency within the world's environment, aesthetics, and rules" (Pearce & Artemesia, 2009, p. 20). These characteristics help the inhabitants of virtual worlds to feel immersed in them and thus create a sense of community.

It should be noted that the terms *virtual world*, *virtual community*, and *online community* have been defined in different ways and are often used interchangeably, as they are in this chapter. However, not all online communities include all of the elements of virtual communities as defined by Pearce and Artemesia (2009). Discussion forums, for example, are online communities without elements such as worldness and may or may not have avatars, although text-based communities such as discussion forums usually include a persistent online identity for the individual who frequents them.

The level of immersion that an individual experiences is significantly influenced by the availability of avatars, particularly those that can be customized according to the individual's taste. Originally a Hindu term for a deity's appearance on earth, an avatar is a person's online representation. The avatar allows a person to occupy "space" in the virtual world, interacting with the environment and the people in it in a way that is more analogous to an offline interaction.

Virtual world participants often experience a complex relationship with these online representations. For some, the avatar may bear little resemblance to the person's offline personality, and for others, the avatar is regarded as a faithful representation of the person himself or herself. For most, the relationship between person and avatar is somewhere between those extremes, reflecting a combination of the person's actual characteristics, idealized wishes for himself or herself, traits that are dissimilar to the person, and possibilities for exploration. Pearce and Artemesia (2009) reported, "Research has repeatedly revealed that players often perceive their avatars as a medium through which one's soul, one's deep inner persona, is expressed (p. 22)." For those without online experience, this complex relationship between online and offline identity may be difficult to understand.

Just as it might be difficult to explain one's relationship with one's online self, it may also prove troublesome to explain the nature of many online relationships to those who have never experienced one. Many people have experienced or heard of relationships where people met online, such as through a dating website, but the relationship quickly became offline or "in person." Those sorts of relationships may be inherently more understandable to someone who does not spend much time online. However, what about relationships that rarely, if ever, exist offline? How do these online relationships develop, and are the mechanisms similar to those in "face-to-face" relationships? As with many things, the answer appears to be yes and no. In terms of the level of intimacy and the intensity of feelings, there are important similarities in online and offline relationships, but there are also some noteworthy differences.

According to Baker (2008), traditional models of attraction emphasized physical proximity and physical attractiveness. In online relationships, physical appearance may be less immediately important, whereas common interests and conversational compatibilities tend to be given more weight in the initial stages of an online relationship than they might be in an in-person relationship. Similarly, in an online relationship, physical proximity is likely to be redefined as virtual proximity or being in the same place online at the same time.

Barak and Suler (2008) also found that people in online environments are more likely to self-disclose more personal information more quickly than they are in offline environments because of the *online disinhibition effect*, and the ambiguities in the online environment that make it easier for us to "fill in the blanks" with our own imaginations and mental processes. It is likely that faster and deeper self-disclosures are at least partly responsible for the frequent anecdotal finding that online relationships, whether platonic or romantic, often feel more intimate more quickly than do relationships in the physical world.

Stereotypes of online communities and their participants also persist and are a potential source of disenfranchisement for the bereaved. For example, the common stereotype of the online gamer as a socially maladjusted, immature, late-adolescent or early-adult male is contradicted by studies that indicate that the average gamer is both older and more social than the stereotype indicates (Williams, Yee, & Caplan, 2008). Another commonly held stereotype is that people who frequent chat sites are more likely to have some sort of psychopathology, such as depression or social anxiety, a conclusion which has not been supported by research (Campbell, Cumming, & Hughes, 2006). Finally, motivations for participating in virtual worlds are often stereotyped, as it is often thought that someone who spends a good portion of free time gaming or visiting other virtual worlds is attempting to escape from the "real world." However, the inhabitants themselves report a wide variety of motivations that relate to identity exploration (Matsuba, 2006), as well as achievement, mastery, social relationships, and immersion or escapism (Yee, 2006).

THE BEREAVEMENT IN ONLINE COMMUNITIES PROJECT

With this background information in mind, the Bereavement in Online Communities Project was created to begin the process of understanding the complex dynamics involved in online relationships and the resulting grief and possible disenfranchisement that occur when these relationships end in death. The first phase of this project was a preliminary survey of individuals who have experienced a death in the context of an online community, the results of which will be described in this chapter.

Method

Procedure

Participants were recruited using a page on a social networking site (Facebook) that described the project and contained a link to the anonymous online survey designed to gather information from individuals who had experienced the death of at least one fellow member of an online community. Announcements about the study were also published on the general forums of *World of Warcraft*, *Gaia Online*, *Star Wars Galaxies*, and *Second Life*. Reposting of the announcement was encouraged. Participants indicated consent prior to beginning the survey using PsychData, an online survey program available at http://psychdata.com. Upon completion of the survey, participants were provided with a list of online bereavement and grief resources.

Participants

Fifty-eight individuals responded to the survey, with 41 respondents completing the entire survey. The average age of the participants was 41.2 years. The sample consisted of 49 females (84.5%) and nine males (15.5%). With regard to ethnicity, the sample was 75.9% White, 5.2% African American, 5.2% Hispanic, 1.7% American Indian, and 10.3% multiracial or other ethnicities. With regard to marital status, 22.4% of respondents were single, 36.2% were married, 12.1% reported having a domestic partner, 24.1 were separated or divorced, and 5.2% were widowed.

Respondents came from a variety of online communities. Six came from a social networking site (such as Facebook), 10 came from chat sites (such as Yahoo chat), 10 came from role-playing/gaming sites (such as *World of Warcraft*), 4 came from forums related to specific topics, and 11 came from sites with a mixture of two or more of these elements.

Instrument

Using a combination of Likert-format and free-response items, the Bereavement in Online Communities Survey was developed specifically for this study. The survey included questions about the following issues related to the online relationship and the death:

Frequency of contact. The frequency of different methods of contact was assessed, including in-person, telephone, e-mail, instant messaging, and chat on a 7-point Likert scale, where responses ranged from *never* to *more than once per day*.

Notification of death/access to information. Using free-response items, respondents were asked how they were notified of the person's death, whether they had access to information about the circumstances surrounding the death, and whether they had unresolved questions.

Degree of overlap between online and offline social networks. This was assessed in several ways. Using free-response questions, participants were asked whether people in their offline lives knew about their online relationships and understood the significance of those relationships. Respondents were also asked about the degree to which the bereaved person has been able to share his or her grief and has received support from his or her offline community. Finally, respondents were asked about their participation in any online or offline mourning rituals to honor the deceased.

Grief reactions. Items assessing grief reactions were adapted from a measure developed by Noppe, Linzmeier, Martin, and Wisneski (2008). Respondents were asked about the frequency of reactions such as sadness, fatigue, and yearning for the deceased, both in the first weeks after the death and currently. Answers were recorded on a 5-point Likert scale and ranged from *never* to *all the time*.

Online versus offline bereavement. Using free-response questions, respondents were asked about differences between bereavement experiences regarding the death of someone known only online and other bereavement experiences.

Results

Circumstances of Bereavement

The time since the death ranged from 1 week to more than 10 years, with a wide range of types of death represented, including accidental death, illness, suicide, and homicide. Of the 41 respondents, 12 reported having experienced the deaths of multiple friends and/or romantic partners in their online communities, with some having lost as many as a dozen individuals to death. In answering subsequent questions, respondents who had experienced more than one death were asked to refer to the deceased person to whom they were closest.

Frequency of Contact Prior to Death

Respondents were asked to indicate the frequency of contact with the deceased prior to the death. The most frequent form of communication was online chatting, with 30 of the 41 (73.1%) reporting that they had chatted with the deceased at least once per week and 14 of the 41 (34.1%) reporting multiple chats with the deceased per day. Most reported that they had never talked on the telephone nor met the deceased in person.

Grief Reactions

Respondents were classified as experiencing a grief reaction if they reported that they experienced it either *sometimes, frequently,* or *all the time.* More than half of respondents reported experiencing constant sadness (65.6%), depression (61.8%), yearning for the deceased person (58.8%), and anger (52.9%) in the first weeks after the death. At least one third of the sample reported guilt (44.1%), sleep disturbance (38.2%), emotional outbursts (35.3%), and anxiety (33.3%) in the first weeks after the death.

With regard to current grief reactions, the percentage of respondents who were still experiencing these eight reactions were as follows, in descending order of occurrence: (a) yearning for the deceased (29.3%); (b) depression (23.5%); (c) anger (23.5%); (d) sleep disturbance (20.5%); (e) constant sadness (17.6%); (f) guilt (17.6%); (g) emotional outbursts (11.7%); and (h) anxiety (11.7%). However, it is difficult to generalize about lingering grief reactions from such a small sample because the length of time since the death varied from 1 month for some respondents to more than 10 years for others. Suffice it to say that for some respondents, grief reactions were still very much an issue.

Loss and Disenfranchisement

Participants were asked several free-response questions to assess the degree to which people in their offline communities were aware of the online relationship and of the loss and whether he or she participated in online or offline mourning rituals following the death. Finally, respondents were asked about the most difficult aspect of this person's death.

"How can you form a relationship with someone you've never met in person?" is a common and understandable question. This question may even be asked by the bereaved person himself or herself. One respondent noted, "Part of me felt odd for being so emotional about someone I had never met dying, so I only talked about it in bits and pieces with my husband." In fact, several respondents indicated that they did not feel free to discuss either their online activities or their grief with those in their in-person lives. Others had one or two people in their in-person lives who knew of their online activities and appreciated the significance of them, and a third group was relatively transparent regarding their online activities with individuals known from their in-person lives. Other online friends were the most frequently mentioned resource in coping with online bereavement, mentioned by more than half the sample. Less than one fourth of the sample mentioned significant reliance on family or offline friends in coping with bereavement. One respondent reported, "Mourning my friend was something I did mostly in private, while the mourning of those I lost from 'in person' relationships I could do more publicly. I already knew that many people thought I was 'strange' for having a friendship with someone I had met over the Internet, and so I did not feel I could discuss my feelings with anyone I knew in person."

The stereotype of Internet use as escape from reality has significant potential for disenfranchisement because it calls into question the legitimacy of the entire experience—the community itself, the relationships within it, and the person's online identity. The bereaved person himself or herself may hold this stereotype and may be at a loss to explain the very real grief that is experienced. Several respondents spoke of this perceived lack of legitimacy. One respondent stated, "There is some sort of validity placed on an 'in-person' setting that is not present in the online situation, as if the person means more to you by being an 'in-person' relationship."

The implications of the avatar for bereavement are numerous. One can experience the loss of another person's in-world avatar, the person behind the avatar, or both. When both losses occur, they are often experienced as separate but overlapping losses. One can certainly mourn the loss of one's own avatar, perhaps in a game situation where a character is killed and cannot be resurrected, or when someone has to leave a virtual community because of offline time constraints or loss of Internet access. Finally, deaths and other losses can be felt more acutely in one persona than another. For example, someone who grieves the loss of a person and that person's avatar might feel the loss of the avatar more acutely while "in-game." The difficulty of explaining these concepts to people who have not spent time in virtual settings can contribute to a sense of disenfranchisement.

Because virtual communities are defined by nongeographical space and, in many cases, by anonymity, both geographical distance and lack of access to information are potential sources of distress. More than three fourths of the respondents reported being unable to attend the traditional in-person funeral or memorial service for the person who died either because of distance, because they were not invited to attend, or because they were unable to find out information about the service.

Several respondents were unable even to verify the circumstances of the person's death, and in two cases, they were unable to verify that the death had occurred at all. Internet death hoaxes do occur, of course, because the relative anonymity of the medium makes it possible for someone to fake his or her death. Being unable to verify the death or answer questions about the death for himself or herself makes it more difficult to talk about the death with those in one's in-person life. Other types of deception, such as deception about one's life circumstances, are sometimes discovered after that person's death. This type of deception certainly occurs in offline relationships as well, but it is easier to conceal in online relationships. One respondent reported that he or she had discovered significant deception by a close online friend after her death. The respondent stated, "I was alone in mourning her death twice—the person she was online, and the person I thought she was . . . [I told] no one online. No one would believe me if I told them."

Although it is difficult to quantify closeness or intimacy, one yardstick may be frequency of communication. As previously noted, respondents reported having had frequent communication with the deceased, with more than one third of respondents stating that they had communicated with the deceased via online chat several times per day. Several respondents spontaneously characterized their relationships with the deceased as quite close. One respondent stated, "We always told one another, we were sisters with different mothers." Another reported that she and the deceased had viewed their relationship as one of a godfather to his goddaughter. As with online relationships, there appears to be great diversity in closeness, from merely acquaintances to cherished loved ones. These ties are often not known or acknowledged by people in either the bereaved person's or the deceased's in-person life. One respondent stated, "Although I believe he told others about our relationship, I do not believe they felt it was of any importance."

It is also possible that just as in offline relationships, someone's significance in one's life is not entirely clear until the person is no longer there.

When participants were asked about the most difficult aspect of this person's death, responses often reflected grief at the loss of the opportunity for in-person contact. One respondent said, "I never got to hold her, to hug her, to meet her little dog, and her grandkids." Another reported that the most difficult part was "knowing that we will never get the chance to meet, which was a plan. Knowing that I couldn't go and say goodbye." Another cited "the regret of not making the effort to hang out and actually meet in person." Finally, one respondent reported, "I felt guilt for a period of time because I had turned down an opportunity to meet him in person. I wasn't available that particular day. As it turns out, that was my only opportunity to have met him."

IDENTIFYING AND AMELIORATING DISENFRANCHISED GRIEF IN ONLINE COMMUNITIES

Real losses occur in virtual communities, and lack of familiarity with the significance of online relationships by nonparticipants may contribute to disenfranchisement. However, it is important to note that there are numerous opportunities to ameliorate this disenfranchisement, both through online and in-person means.

At this point, bereavement and grief in virtual communities seem to be handled within the communities themselves. Many people who have experienced losses in online communities find that this community is a potent source of support, especially in situations where those in the bereaved's in-person life are unaware of the loss. Most respondents reported that the support they received from the online community was invaluable.

Several respondents discussed death rituals that took place in the virtual community, including online memorial services, in-game rituals such as an online funeral pyre, or just informal online gatherings for people to share memories of the deceased and express their grief. Online memorial pages have become an important way to express grief, to maintain continuing ties with the deceased, and to create a sense of community (see de Vries & Moldaw in Chapter 10; Roberts, 2004). These may be constructed as independent websites, hosted on general bereavement sites, or housed within the virtual community itself. Hume and Bressers (2009–2010) reported that online memorials are often frequented by friends, whose grief is sometimes disenfranchised when compared with the grief of family members.

YouTube features several in-game funerals and other video or animated tributes to various players of *World of Warcraft*. One example includes an in-game funeral march dedicated to a young man who played a shaman character, Toxiklore (http://www.youtube.com/watch?v=FgDTwg_60g8). The message beneath the video states, "This is a movie dedicated to the shaman Toxiklore, who passed away. Their [sic] was a [sic] hour long funeral march in-game in his honor. He belonged to the guild Ascendency on the Dark Iron server in World of Warcraft . . . " (Toxiklore WoW Funeral March, 2010). According to the information about the video, the actual in-game march featured dozens of characters, took the marchers through the entire graphical space of the *World of Warcraft* game, and lasted more than an hour. The video itself is approximately 4 minutes long and opens with a message from his sister: "Hello, all. This is Toxie's (Chris') sister. He will no longer be online. He passed away yesterday. I'm not sure if he told anyone that he had Muscular Dystrophy. This game was his life, so if everyone could pass the word, that would be great" (Toxiklore WoW Funeral March, 2010). As the music played, the participants' avatars marched slowly in a line across the virtual topography, and the participants typed in comments about the loss, which appeared as text bubbles above the characters and were visible to everyone present. One of the final comments to close the video stated, "You don't have to have that wheelchair anymore, buddy. Rest in peace" (Toxiklore WoW Funeral March, 2010).

These kinds of within-environment rituals are common. According to Taylor (2002):

> Public mourning is not uncommon (generally following the offline death of a user) and avatars will often gather together and set their facial expression to "sad"—which will then typically guide the discussion amongst the group about the departed friend, as well as prompting recent arrivals to inquire as to what has happened. Sometimes they will attach URLs to their avatars which inform the community of the loss and take viewers to memorial web pages. In these instances it is not unusual to find a particular location filled for an entire day with avatars looking sad, holding candles, and creating public memorial space (p. 45).

One respondent stated that the deceased's spouse attended the in-game funeral and was gratified by the expressions of love for the deceased. Another respondent compared online support with in-person support by stating, "Perhaps it is that the written environment allows for a deeper level of expression but people seemed more able to express their emotions in written–spoken language. Of course, the physical hugs and soothing you find at memorial or funeral services [were] not there."

Rituals within the virtual community may be most important if the community itself is what is being lost. Pearce and Artemesia (2009) reported the following ceremony to mark the end of *Uru*:

> The last day of *Uru*, many players assembled in-world, gathering in neighborhoods, or visiting each other's Ages. Owing to varied time zones, not all players were able to be online at the strike of midnight PST, the scheduled shutdown time. A core group of TGU [The Gathering Uru] members gathered in the garden of Lynn's Eder Kemo Age, talked, told each other stories, and played hide-and-seek. As the time approached, they moved into a circular configuration close enough so that their avatars would appear to be holding hands. Several players recall the clocks in their "rl" (real-life) homes striking midnight, the screen

freezing, and a system alert message appearing on the screen: "There is something wrong with your Internet connection," followed by a dialogue box saying "OK." As one player recalled: "I couldn't bring myself to press that OK button because for me it was NOT OK (pp. 88–89)."

Although it is reassuring that virtual communities provide opportunities for sharing and expression of grief, these are necessary but not sufficient. Both online and in-person resources outside those virtual communities are needed as well. Online bereavement education sites are plentiful, but they typically do not include information about losses in virtual communities. In addition, although websites for online bereavement support groups have become numerous (e.g., Feigelman, Gorman, Beal, & Jordan, 2008), at this point there are no groups specifically designed for losses experienced in virtual communities. Studies of online support groups underline the role they can play in ameliorating disenfranchisement; for example, Hollander (2001) stated, "Just the amount and intensity of the exchanges made the importance of the dialogue obvious. The 'talk' was going on in a kind of cyberrefuge from the larger social order where grieving was perceived as unwelcome (p. 140)."

However, it is unclear what kind of reception a person who is mourning a death from an online community might receive in a general support group. Although it is certainly possible that a support group would welcome such a member, it is also possible that the loss of a virtual community member might not be perceived as a "real loss," and the bereaved person would experience disenfranchisement there as well. Relying on the community itself to handle these bereavement issues, without proper support from those with knowledge and experience in death education and counseling, is akin to leaving family and friends to handle their own grief in an in-person bereavement situation, no matter how complex the relationships are or how complicated the grief is.

There are several ways that death educators and grief counselors can provide education and/or intervention for this population. These efforts should take the following factors into account: (a) the dispersion of online communities throughout cyberspace and the potentially insular nature of these groups; (b) the need for education targeted to multiple audiences, including online community members, organizations that develop and administer those communities, and those who work in the area of bereavement; and (c) the need for multiple levels of intervention that may include general educational information about bereavement and disenfranchised grief, the availability of online support groups both within and outside those virtual communities, or referral to resources for professional intervention, if needed, by grief counselors who are well versed in the dynamics of online communities.

The need for general educational information should be addressed through multiple avenues. There is a need for a centralized website that could be publicized through social networking sites, other online communities, and professional organizations that deal with bereavement. The Bereavement in Online Communities Project is in its infancy, but with sufficient interest and support, it could grow to serve that function. General information about bereavement, the dynamics of online communities, and disenfranchised grief should be included on this website. This information should be adapted to multiple audiences, namely, bereaved individuals, administrators of online communities, and thanatology professionals. Opportunities for interaction and self-expression among the participants, such as discussion forums or monitored blogs, would be especially useful features of this website. An online support group could be hosted either on this site or on sites that already host bereavement support groups. Such a support group would particularly serve the needs of individuals who, for whatever reason, do not feel comfortable dealing with their grief within their "home" communities.

Although a centralized website would be extremely helpful, it is also important to disseminate this information to online communities themselves because much of the mourning takes place inside those communities or even in subgroups within those communities. Although it would be challenging to reach them all directly, forming partnerships with those who create and administer some of the major online communities would be a good step toward that end. Partnerships such as these would allow for educational information to be hosted on the community's own servers and publicized through the administrators' normal communication channels within that community.

Perhaps most importantly, death educators and counselors who work with people with active online lives should educate themselves about the types of online environments frequented by their clients and the relationships that exist within them. A list of death educators and counselors with expertise in virtual environments should be made available and publicized, and more structured referral relationships could be sought with some of the major online communities. However, it is likely that only a small number of professionals would consider themselves "experts" in this area. Grief counselors who encounter a client who has experienced a death in an online community can use the following questions to assess the significance of this death:

- How frequently were you in contact with the person who died? (Include both online and offline modes of communication.)
- How would you characterize your relationship with the deceased person? (e.g., friends, romantic partners, chosen family, other?)
- Did you find yourself sharing things with this person that you might feel uncomfortable sharing in your offline life? (This relates to the level of intimacy and self-disclosure in the relationship.)
- How much do people in your offline life know about this online relationship? Do they understand the significance of this relationship to you? Who in your offline environment might be considered a source of support for you as you grieve this loss?
- Are there people in the deceased person's offline life who know about his or her relationship with you and understand the significance of it? (This also goes to an understanding of how much information and support may be available to the client.)

- If the person was ill, how much communication, if any, was possible before the person's death? To what extent were you able to gain information about the person's condition? Were you able to say your goodbyes?
- How did you find out about the person's death? Did you have access to information about the circumstances of the person's death? The person's "real-life" name? An obituary and/or funeral notice? If so, were you able to attend an in-person funeral or memorial service?
- Did you make any significant discoveries about the person after his or her death? On a related note, are there lingering unanswered questions about the person's life or death that trouble you?
- Was there some sort of memorial or tribute to the deceased person within your online community? Are there people in the online community who are or could be a source of support for you?

Identifying potential strategies to assist grievers in these situations is important. Recognizing that those in virtual communities may sustain real losses and feel real grief is a crucial first step in this process. Understanding some of the facets of virtual communities that may result in disenfranchisement of that grief is also valuable. The individuals may also self-disenfranchise their grief. They may not even recognize that they are grieving or may feel as though they should not be grieving an online relationship. For example, a counselor who understands that bereavement may occur because of the loss of an avatar, the loss of the person behind the avatar, or both would be better prepared to explore the dimensions of these separate but overlapping losses.

Identification of secondary losses would also be useful, particularly if one of those secondary losses is the loss of the community itself or the loss of the positive feelings that membership in the community once engendered. Evaluation of a client's participation in online communities without resorting to stereotypes of those communities or the individuals and relationships within them is also essential. A counselor should assist the client in exploring online and offline possibilities for healing.

Experts predict that the divisions between physical and virtual reality will be further erased in the future for everyone who is connected to a virtual community (Anderson & Raine, 2008). Although virtual communities have existed in cyberspace for years, research exploring the loss of online relationships is in its infancy and merits further attention by thanatologists. Participants in this survey who experienced the loss of an online relationship reported that being able to talk to at least one offline person about their grief was beneficial. A grief counselor may very well be that person.

Author's note: Individuals who are interested in learning more are encouraged to contact the author at lhensley@txwes.edu or at the Bereavement in Online Communities Project at http://www.facebook.com/profile.php?id=1068147223#!/pages/Bereavement-in-Online-Communities-Project/309500351772.

REFERENCES

Anderson, J. Q., & Rainie, L. (2008, December 14). *The future of the Internet III.* Retrieved July 25, 2011, from http://www.pewinternet.org/~/media//Files/Reports/2008/PIP_ FutureInternet3.pdf.pdf

Baker, A. J. (2008). Down in the rabbit hole: The role of place in the initiation and development of online relationships. In A. Barak (Ed.), *Psychological aspects of cyberspace: Theory, research, and applications* (pp. 163–182). Cambridge, England: Cambridge University Press.

Barak, A., & Suler, J. (2008). Reflections on the psychology and social science of cyberspace. In A. Barak (Ed.), *Psychological aspects of cyberspace: Theory, research, and applications* (pp. 1–12). Cambridge, England: Cambridge University Press.

Blizzard Entertainment. (2010). *World of Warcraft: Wrath of the Lich King* to launch in mainland China on August 31, 2010. Retrieved from http://us.blizzard.com/en-us/company/ press/pressreleases.html?100823

Campbell, A. J., Cumming, S. R., & Hughes, I. (2006). Internet use by the socially fearful: Addiction or therapy? *CyberPsychology & Behavior, 9*(1), 69–81.

Corr, C. A. (2002). Revisiting the concept of disenfranchised grief. In K. Doka (Ed.), *Disenfranchised grief: New directions, challenges, and strategies for practice* (pp. 39–60). Champaign, IL: Research Press.

Doka, K. (2002). Introduction. In K. Doka (Ed.), *Disenfranchised grief: New directions, challenges, and strategies for practice* (pp. 5–22). Champaign, IL: Research Press.

Facebook (2010). *Statistics.* Retrieved September 6, 2010, from http://www.facebook.com/ press/info.php?statistics

Feigelman, W., Gorman, B. S., Beal, K. C., & Jordan, J. R. (2008). Internet support groups for suicide survivors: A new mode for gaining bereavement assistance. *Omega, 57*(3), 217–243.

Hensley, L. D., & Arroyo, X. (2010, April). *Narrative analysis of bereavement in virtual communities.* Poster presentation at the annual meeting of the Association for Death Education and Counseling, Kansas City, MO.

Hollander, E. M. (2001). Cyber community in the valley of the shadow of death. *Journal of Loss and Trauma, 6,* 135–146.

Hume, J., & Bressers, B. (2010). Obituaries online: New connections with the living—And the dead. *Omega, 60*(3), 255–271.

Lenhart, A., Purcell, K., Smith, A., & Zickuhr, A. (2010, February 3). Social media & mobile Internet use among teens and young adults. Retrieved July 25, 2011, from http://pewinter net.org/Reports/2010/Social-Media-and-Young-Adults.aspx

Martin, T. L., & Doka, K. J. (1999). *Men don't cry: Transcending gender stereotypes of grief.* Philadelphia, PA: Brunnel/Mazel.

Matsuba, M. K. (2006). Searching for self and relationships online. *CyberPsychology & Behavior, 9*(3), 275–284.

Neimeyer, R. A., & Jordan, J. R. (2002). Disenfranchisement as empathic failure: Grief therapy and the co-construction of meaning. In K. Doka (Ed.), *Disenfranchised grief: New directions, challenges, and strategies for practice* (pp. 95–117). Champaign, IL: Research Press.

Noppe, I. C., Linzmeier, E., Martin, R., & Wisneski, M. (2008, May). *Forging a pathway through college during bereavement and grief: Preliminary findings of the National College Student Grief Study.* Paper presented at the annual conference of the Association for Death Education and Counseling, Montreal, Quebec.

Pearce, C., & Artemesia. (2009). *Communities of play: Emergent cultures in multiplayer games and virtual worlds.* Cambridge, MA: MIT Press.

Pew Research Center. (2010a, December). Trend data. Retrieved from http://pewinternet.org/Home/Static%20Pages/Trend%20Data.aspx

Pew Research Center. (2010b, December). What Internet users do online. Retrieved from http://pewinternet.org/Trend-Data/Online-Activites-Total.aspx

Roberts, P. (2004). Here today and cyberspace tomorrow: Memorials and bereavement support on the Web. *Generations, 28*, 41–46.

Taylor, T. L. (2002). Living digitally: Embodiment in virtual worlds. In R. Schroeder (Ed.), *The social life of avatars: Presence and interaction in shared virtual environments* (pp. 40–62). London, UK: Springer-Verlag.

Toxiklore WoW Funeral March. (2010). Retrieved from http://www.youtube.com/watch?v=FgDTwg_60g8

Williams, D., Yee, N., & Caplan, S. (2008). Who plays, how much, and why? A behavioral player census of virtual world. *Journal of Computer Mediated Communication, 13*, 993–1018. doi:10.1111/j.1083-6101.2008.00428.x

Yee, N. (2006). Motivations for play in online games. *CyberPsychology & Behavior, 9*(6), 772–775.

10

Virtual Memorials and Cyber Funerals: Contemporary Expressions of Ageless Experiences

Brian de Vries and Susan Moldaw

Our ways of living and dying have encountered significant changes over the past century (e.g., Charmaz, 1980; Walter, 1996). These changes include dramatic medical advances and concomitant increases in life expectancies or, as framed in another way, the fulfillment of life span potentials. The corollary of these successes includes what Bouvard (1988) has referred to as the medicalization of life's end through the objectification of illness and the perspective on death as failure. de Vries and Rutherford (2004) proffer that such changes naturally extend into the ways in which individuals mourn and grieve, the latter of which is increasingly seen as a "medical condition," replacing previous community norms (Parkes, 1972) and evidenced in the recent debate of the inclusion of grief in the *Diagnostic and Statistical Manual of Mental Disorders, Fifth Edition*.

Death largely has been left to take place behind institutional walls; according to recent National Death Statistics, more than two thirds of all deaths in the United States now take place in hospital or long-term care settings. Mourning has become "morbid" (de Vries & Rutherford, 2004); memorialization has not been actively encouraged (Bouvard, 1988; Cable, 1998); and grief is a "problem" of the individual, not the community (Charmaz, 1980). In short, death has become deritualized (Kamerman, 1988), and our responses to death have lost some of their structure.

Unchanged is the fact that the death of a loved one continues to have a profound effect on the psychological and physical health of those who survive (Stroebe, Stroebe, & Hansson, 1993), and who seek a venue for the expression of their response to loss, even as such responses are "treated," questioned, or ignored. In this clouded context, survivors are "more likely to alter and customize standard ritual practices to inject personal meaning . . . death may take on a collage of meaning and opportunities, which could result in new social patterns" (Haney et al., 1997, p. 168).

Such "new social patterns" may be evident in the NAMES Project AIDS Memorial Quilt, for example, or in the spontaneous memorialization of groups of persons to unanticipated and/or violent deaths (the deaths of Princess Diana; John F. Kennedy, Jr.; or those following the terrorists' attacks on the World Trade Center and the Pentagon). In such efforts, individuals create a role for themselves as mourners and extend the boundaries of who is allowed or expected to participate in the mourning process (de Vries & Rutherford, 2004) and alter the face and shape that mourning assumes.

In this same context, many individuals have turned to cyberspace to seek new opportunities to express their grief, commemorate the deceased, and create and find community—an appropriately odd pairing of the amorphous "out there" with the "great unknown" (de Vries & Roberts, 2004). This is the area of exploration of this chapter. We first review the emerging literature on memorialization on the World Wide Web (hereafter referred to as "web")—a body of research that describes who submits memorials and their content, with a more recent turn to an accounting of the communities that are established around these memorials. The extent to which more traditional media have captured this trend is discussed in segue into a discussion of the extent to which the funeral industry has adopted this nontraditional memorialization movement. We draw attention to the potential benefits and drawbacks of these virtual manifestations of real-world loss.

MEMORIALS AND CEMETERIES IN CYBERSPACE

Who Writes Memorials and What is Written

Sofka (1997) and Roberts (1999) may be credited with introducing to the academic community the presence of web cemeteries, charting their beginnings in about 1995. They clearly have an appeal to those grieving the death of a loved one; dozens of cemeteries now exist with thousands of memorials in each. Web cemeteries provide a place to honor and remember the deceased with few restrictions: on length or format, unlike obituaries; on time and place, unlike land cemeteries. Web memorials are primarily text based, although some cemeteries allow for pictures and sounds as well. In most cases, posting a memorial is a simple procedure, accomplished by sending text and demographic information through e-mail. As such, web memorials are a low-cost and easy access opportunity to commemorate the deceased—from anyone, at almost anywhere, at almost any time. They serve as a force of democracy in the world of grief, a point to which we return. It should be noted that these memorials found in web cemeteries are in addition to the thousands of memorial sites that have been created by the bereft for either a particular individual or group of individuals; these memorials have not been studied as systematically and are only modestly considered herein.

The memorials found in these web cemeteries also hold some allure to researchers, for many of the same reasons listed above: they provide an environment inclusive of those who are often neglected or uninvited in the more traditional grief settings; they offer up for examination a wide array of issues often unavailable to researchers (Strobe et al., 2008). Web memorials are accessible and unobtrusive data (Roberts, 1999), with "responses" unchanged by the research enterprise of which they have become a part. Web memorials reveal much about their authors, the grieving process and the relationships that existed (and continue) between the deceased and the bereft. The review of research in the area of web memorials is made necessarily brief by its recent history and modest empirical base, although researchers have noted that bereavement Internet-based methods are a suitable and valid alternative to traditional paper-and-pencil methods of research (Tolstikova & Chartier, 2010). The description that follows draws largely upon the studies of Roberts and Vidal (2000), de Vries and Rutherford (2004), and Blando, Graves-Ferrick, and Goecke (2004). In general, women are the primary authors of web memorials, although a sizable number of memorials are also written by groups of individuals and by authors whose gender could not be determined. The research of Blando et al. (2004) represents an exception to this pattern, wherein it was found that men were the largest group of authors in their study. It is perhaps both noteworthy and explanatory that their study focused on AIDS-related memorials found on an AIDS information website; partners and friends of those memorialized authored the greatest proportion (almost half) of the memorials.

Not surprisingly, men are the primary subjects of the memorials across the studies, replicating the gendered patterns of memorializing reported by Kastenbaum et al. (1977) years ago. Relationally, children of the deceased are the majority authors in the studies (almost 70% in one study, although only about 5% in the Blando et al. study). Evocatively, friends are noted as authors in significant proportions across all studies, perhaps turning to this untraditional venue to express their grief in an environment within which they have been disenfranchised (Doka, 1989). That is, the bereaved peers tend to be ignored; an experience regularly reproduced by family, doctors, and the legal system (Deck & Folta, 1989). Close friends are not conventionally recognized as grievers, not identified by norms, expectations, or rights (or even the terms *friend-grievers* [i.e., Deck & Folta, 1989] or *survivor friends* [e.g., Sklar, 1992; Sklar & Hartley, 1990]). In web memorials and in cyberspace, they have a presence.

Roberts, Williamson, and Clemens (1998) examined another disenfranchised group in their exploration of memorials created by individuals for deceased companion animals, found in significant proportion in several web cemeteries. Interestingly, approximately one half of these memorials had some direct message to the deceased (rendering the memorials more similar to personal letters than obituaries). In fact, few of the memorials had qualities of standard obituaries, favoring instead narratives about the deceased. Poignantly, many of the companion animal memorials listed the death of previous animals and the presence of current animals along with statements that the deceased pets could either be with animals that had gone before or watch over those currently living.

Memorials in the form of letters were not unique to companion animal tributes; between one quarter and one half of the memorials in the other studies assumed similar forms. This pattern has been interpreted as suggestive of the continuing bonds of the living with the deceased (Silverman & Klass, 1996), an aspect of grief response not freely endorsed in other settings. Authors write on salient anniversaries, update the deceased on the activities of the bereft, offer eulogies and stories, and provide examples that illustrate the character of the deceased as if to reinforce that people know the deceased was a person of value, meaning, and substance. Just as 21st century grievers are searching for novel and meaningful venues to express themselves, so too are they challenging accepted models of grief that dictate who is entitled to grieve and how one should grieve—models which suggest that the ties between the living and the dead are severed with the death and which encourage individuals to "recover" from their loss and "get over it." Web memorials highlight that grief is not restricted to socially sanctioned or legally defined relationships, nor is it restricted to particular forms of expression and standard timelines.

As intimated in the above comments about the letters to the deceased, these memorials are more than factual presentations of the group memberships held over the course of a life and/or a listing of those left to grieve common to the more traditional death notices and even obituaries (although this content is often included); these memorials contain often very personal information presented in often deep emotional tones. This was the more particular focus of Blando et al.'s (2004) article, finding that almost all memorials contained positive affective content (more than 98%), with more than half coded as evidence of high emotional intensity (and just over 20% coded as low emotional intensity). The emotion expressed, similar to the other studies referenced above, included longing, love, grief/sadness, gratitude, guilt, and emotional pain. Web memorials are deeply personal and moving tributes to the deceased and reveal much about those grieving in the process. Nager and de Vries (2004) studied bereaved daughters who had created online memorials for their deceased mothers; these daughters were contacted and asked to complete online surveys about their reasons for creating the memorials, personal and relational characteristics, and their experiences of grief. Nager and de Vries found a lower frequency of secure attachment styles and a somewhat higher level of grief than would be expected among the bereaved daughters; they suggested that the nature of the ties that exist between daughters and their mothers, perhaps in life and death, may be associated with the extraordinary efforts to memorialize in this format and may represent their unexpectedly intense grief.

Roberts, Bruce, Izarraraz, and Soni (2000) were interested in how often authors of memorials visit the sites and their experiences in doing so. They invited individuals who had created a memorial web page connected to the Empty Arms webring (linked web pages dedicated to deceased children) to complete an online survey about their experiences creating, visiting, and sharing their memorial web page. The survey respondents indicated that they frequently visited the web memorial; almost three quarters visited at least daily in the first month after creating the memorial, with 83% visiting at least weekly in the first 6 months and 68% visiting at least weekly in the first year (Roberts, 2004). It is worth noting that more than three quarters of the respondents had a physical memorial to visit, but web memorials, which can be visited quickly, at any time and from any location, were visited much more frequently (Roberts, 2004). Poignantly, more than 90% of the authors updated the memorials as they visited them—perhaps the verbal equivalent of speaking to urns and grave markers and/or leaving objects at burial sites.

Roberts (1999) noted that creating and visiting web memorials adhere to Kollar's (1989) four steps of effective postdeath rituals: entering into a special time or place, engaging in a symbolic core act, allowing time to absorb what has occurred and is occurring, and taking leave. Web memorials also enable the positive postdeath ritual of writing; Lattanzi and Hale (1985) found that writing to or about the deceased assisted in the expression of emotion and sharing of perspective.

Web Memorials and Virtual Community

Web memorials—text-based homages to and remembrances of the deceased—are deeply personal tributes to lost lives and changed relationships; so too have they become a venue for the creation of community around a loss and/or the experience of loss. Most sites offer "buttons," the clicking of which allows visitors to leave messages about the memorial, sometimes to the author and sometimes just to the site in general. Some sites allow visitors to leave "virtual flowers" or "stones" at the memorials they have visited. Guest books are features in some of the Web cemeteries, allowing visitors to offer comments and/or condolences. Hollander (2001) believes that the Internet connects grieving people who otherwise would likely not have met.

Roberts, Neal, and Shamitz (1999) studied the guest books linked to each web memorial in the World Wide Cemetery; they examined each guest book for number of entries and number of repeat visits per guest, as well as the content expressed. Interestingly, and related to the nature of the memorial itself as described above, most (more than 80%) of the guest book entries from those who knew the dead were written *to* the deceased rather than the memorial author or a general audience (replicating the pattern noted above wherein memorial authors communicate to the deceased in their tributes). Some of the repeat notes provide updates on relationships with the living and the dead, also consistent with the above. Just under one third of the entries in guest books were written by the memorial author returning to visit after posting their memorial, whereas another quarter identified themselves as either family or friends. Many of these visitors signed the guest book more than once, offering an ongoing virtual sign of support.

Returning to the Empty Arms survey research of Roberts et al. (2000), it was revealed that almost 20% of the memorials had been developed with spouses, and another 10% had involved other family members and friends. Authorship of web memorials also often included groups of individuals. This collaborative effort is comparable to work on the AIDS quilt, which authors have proposed both strengthens bonds and creates community while facilitating a construction of a shared reminiscence of the deceased (Ruskin, 1988).

In the Roberts et al. (1999) survey, respondents were asked why they had created the memorials; more than half of those surveyed identified that "giving others a place to visit" was an important reason. Respondents to the survey also noted that the online memorial offered opportunities for communication not available in everyday contact. Respondents indicated that reviewing guest book entries provided support for the bereaved and a sense of connection with others. Similarly, Roberts et al. (2000) report that 84% of their respondents indicated that they had visited the memorial they had created with at least one other person, most of whom were friends. The extent of sharing Web memorials with others runs counter to the isolating stereotype; "it suggests the computer being used as a tool for interacting with others about a very difficult subject" (Roberts, 2004, p. 66).

Evocatively, the communities around virtual memorials are not restricted to those previously known to each other. Almost half of the guest book entries in the Roberts et al. (1999) study either commented that they did not know the deceased or the bereft or gave no indication of such familiarity. They often spoke of how moved they were by the memorial; many were bereaved themselves and had come to visit a memorial and remained at the site noting the memorial which they then felt compelled to acknowledge. Authors of memorials also noted that their memorial creation was in part based on a search for community, either sharing experiences or offering insights.

Web Memorials and Traditional Media

The accounts and experiences of web memorialization may not be dissimilar to those associated with more traditional print media. That is, memorials are created to honor the deceased, to share information, and to engage community; obituaries and death notices in more traditional media are submitted for many of the same reasons. Notwithstanding these similar bases, however, there are dramatic contrasts between what have been presented in these online tributes and those in more traditional media (e.g., messages to the deceased, personal stories and references, memorials to companion animals and humans alike), as has already been suggested and referencing older research on death notices and obituaries. That is, obituaries chronicling the life of the deceased tend to be restricted for those who have been deemed, by the newspaper, as newsworthy in some way. "Ordinary" persons who have died are identified by time-sensitive death notices that typically consist of little more than a list of survivors, funeral or memorial service time and place, and information about contributions, although the more recent *In Memoriam* sections of newspapers offer an exception to this (de Vries & Rutherford, 2004). The more egalitarian and democratic web memorials offer fewer such restrictions and constraints in terms of who writes and what is written, and the popularity of these web cemeteries and alternative forms of memorializing has caught the attention of traditional print media—finally (Hume & Bresser, 2009).

Hume (2000) has written about the consistent framing of obituaries over many years, surprisingly resistant to change, with an exclusive and homogenous focus. That is, "newspapers appeared not to notice the deaths of the vast majority of African Americans. Children, the poor, socially outcast, or disabled Americans also failed to fit a social ideal that would allow them to be part of public memory" (Hume, 2000, p. 161). This resistance to change not only reflects on this media but also on the collective portrait of community identity and values that are presented therein (Hume & Bresser, 2009). There is evidence of recent change, however.

Hume and Bressers (2009) examined online obituary pages at the top circulating daily U.S. newspapers in each of the nine geographic areas defined by the U.S. Census. They found that these paid obituaries were generally scripted and formulaic, much like their more traditional print form. Unlike these more traditional forms, however, these newspaper sites included guest books, linked to the paid obituaries, which included messages from a wide range of visitors, both known and unknown to the bereft sponsors of the obituaries, once again implicitly creating community—ephemeral, elusive, or tangible—along the lines studied by Roberts et al. (1999, 2000), for example. Similarly, unlike more traditional obituaries, Hume and Bressers (2009) noted that visitors and others were participating in the same kinds of bereavement activities that scholars have attributed to private web memorials—sending messages to the dead, expressing emotion, and telling stories. The obituary page also facilitates fascinating connections among readers, shedding light on the complex nature of community. Largely distinct from the mostly nonprofit web cemeteries, all of the websites studied by Hume and Bressers offered additional features included in their fees, such as searchable archives of the obituaries and the opportunity to add photographs, music, and even voice messages. The extent to which this paid and more traditional media will fully embrace this technological wave of memorializing remains to be seen, but initial steps have been taken. The same might be said of the funeral industry, which is the focus of the following sections of this chapter.

The Funeral Industry

Most of the literature on postdeath experiences and rituals focus on funerals (e.g., Weeks, 1996), with some recognition that funerals do not always serve to comfort the bereaved (Wolfelt, 1992) and that further rituals have value (e.g., Worden, 1991). Several authors have commented, often with some amazement or amusement, on virtual funerals as a potential next step in this unfolding technological influence into life's endings. Research has not yet responded to this observation, although the funeral industry has given it some (preliminary) thought.

Funeral homes and crematories in the United States generated 11.95 billion dollars in revenue in 2007, according to Jessica Koth, Public Relations Manager of the National Funeral Directors Association. There were 19,902 funeral homes in 2010; in 2008, there were 25,680 funeral directors employed; and in 2007, 102,877 workers were employed (J. Koth, personal communication, June 22, 2010).

A survey of funerals directors in 2009 in several eastern states noted that the funeral industry is one of changing customs, declining death rates and falling profit margins. Although the industry "reacts slowly and cautiously to change," this same survey shows that funeral directors are increasingly embracing technology; a growing minority are interested in offering their customers more options, and a small, but increasing number, value greater flexibility and are adapting to change (2009 Funeral Directors Survey, Connecticut, New Jersey, New York, & Pennsylvania, with additional data from elsewhere in the United States, Strategic Report, September 2009).

Koth has noted that the National Funeral Directors Association does not yet have any data on the number of funeral homes offering virtual memorials and/or virtual cemeteries, given their relative newness. Services appear to vary widely among funeral homes—they might offer simple online guest books to more elaborate online video tributes and photos. What is offered depends on the funeral home, the size of the community they serve, and the needs of the community.

Funeral homes offer a variety of online services to the bereaved. One website lists services such as tribute videos, personalized printing, memorial websites, and live funeral webcasting. A short video explaining the services begins: "Every life has a story; we let you tell it; as a life tributes provider; celebrate your loved ones lives in the most meaningful ways." A tribute wall on the site is interactive and participatory. A funeral home director states that their website is about a year old, and although the funeral home's customers like what's offered, not many use the services, currently provided at no cost. The director estimates that about 10% of the customers use webcasting of funerals (M. Schoedinger, personal communication, August 5, 2010).

Funeral Webcasting

Within this large, conservative industry challenged by the economy and changing funeral practices, a new service has emerged during the past decade: webcasting funerals. No national data exist, although anecdotally, the growth in this feature can be seen in the increased attendance of webcasting vendors at the annual convention, according to Koth, who estimates that in 2009, eight or nine vendors attended, whereas when webcasting began, there were far fewer (J. Koth, personal communication, June 11, 2010).

Webcast funerals are funerals that are shown over the Internet. They are also known as funeralcasting, memorial webcasting, or cyberfunerals. The funeral can be shown live or archived for showing at a later date. Funeral homes may supply a password to family and friends. Some funerals are available online to anyone. Families or funeral homes contract with a webcasting service, or the funeral home can handle the technology independently.

The 10-year-old service has become increasingly user-friendly and is being aggressively marketed to funeral directors as a "turnkey" offering to funeral homes, dramatically increasing their attractiveness, according to an owner of a funeral home. In *Spectrum Magazine*, Karlin (2009) writes that the service is benefitting from cheaper broadband and the increasing costs of travel. Koth comments there is now a fairly general consensus among funeral directors that webcasting is a great service to offer families.

As families and social networks become more geographically dispersed and find it harder to travel to the location of a funeral, webcasting allows everyone to participate in the funeral, giving all participants a chance to participate. Along such lines, Sofka is quoted in *The Family Plot Blog* as follows: "With a significant number of funerals, at least one person would like to be there but can't, whether from work or family obligations, geographic distance, travel costs, physical or health-related challenges, military deployment overseas, or complicated or disenfranchised relationships." (http://thefamilyplot.wordpress.com/category/trends-in-death-care). These observations are echoed by a number of funeral directors describing the service and webcasting companies that sell the service to funeral homes.

Roman Dabrowski of Virtual Memorial Services, a Canadian webcasting company, states that many Canadians live all over the world, and live webcasting allows family members to participate in the funeral in real time, so that they are " . . . given a way to be part of the healing process associated with the death of a loved one." He further comments that a live webcast rather than a prerecorded one may provide a "sense of closure." In agreement with the above, Vandermeersch (2010) notes that webcasting " . . . truly uses the power of the Internet to help families everywhere with the healing process."

The June 2010 issue of *International Cemetery, Cremation and Funeral Association* recently gave a KIP (Keeping It Personal) honorable mention award for the Most Personalized Service or Memorial to a funeral home offering webcasting services that the judges asserted should be a " . . . best practice" and that the video availability was a "highlight of the service . . . for those who could not attend." The article goes on to note that there were 100 or more viewings of the webcast, including two overseas. Images shown included the graveside service, the casket carried to the grave, the attendees at the cemetery, and the musicians at the service.

Other organizations and publications echo their support and endorsement for this best practice. Funeral One, a company that markets webcasting to funeral homes, for example, states that "family and friends . . . are able to take part in the private viewing of memorials at anytime, anywhere—around the country or around the world—over the Internet, in a safe, secure location, in the privacy of their own home" (www.funeralone.com).

The Perfect Memorials Funeral and Cremation Blog notes that "by allowing mourners who would otherwise be unable to attend a funeral to share the experience with loved ones, webcasting allows survivors to participate in an important part of the grieving process." (http://www.perfectmemorials.com/blog/funeral-webcast-popularity-rising-rapidly/).

A funeral director recounted these two stories supporting this observation (B. Hanner, personal communication, June 10, 2010). The first was about the death of a 17-year-old girl, the daughter of a minister, who died after several months in the hospital. Because her brother was stationed in Iraq, the sister's funeral was webcast and password protected. Her friends requested that they be able to post a link to Facebook and to her memorial Facebook page, and within an hour, the local network called to say there had been an upsurge in traffic. In that hour, 147 had watched her service, and after a few days, 300 people, presumably unrelated to her, had viewed her service.

In another case, there was a missionary from Puerto Rico who died in an Ohio nursing home and still had family in Puerto Rico. The funeral home worked with the Puerto Rican family to record eulogies and then posted them to YouTube. The eulogies were played at the funeral in Ohio and were part of the funeral webcast that was watched in Puerto Rico.

Funeral directors have reported that the main reason webcasting is requested is so that those overseas can participate, and so far, no family has asked for a passcode. The families want the funeral on the web for everyone to see (F. Fergerson, personal communication, June 11, 2010).

Issues and Concerns

The "problem" of grief in North American culture, including our awkwardness around such emotions and clumsiness around interactions with those grieving (Cable, 1998; de Vries & Rutherford, 2004), has led to the bereft seeking venues and opportunities to express their reactions to loss; one such venue is cyberspace. Notwithstanding, an emerging literature exploring this opportunity and this experience, Moss (2004, p. 79) has noted that we do not know the conditions that lead a person to create or return to Web memorials: "Is it at a regular time? Is it in response to a disturbing memory or heightened feeling of intense loss? Do professionals who counsel the bereaved find that their clients go to ("visit") these Web memorials?"

Even as authors (e.g., Roberts, 2004) suggest that web memorials and the surrounding activities satisfy the core principles of postdeath rituals (e.g., Kollar, 1989), there remain unanswered experiential questions and questions about the support anticipated, offered, and received. Niemeyer (as quoted in Hart, 2007) asks: "Are mediated relationships satisfying surrogates for face-to-face relationships, in which you literally can be held in someone's arms?" (p. 89). The question he poses could be asked about viewing a webcast funeral rather than attending the funeral in person.

In an article in *American Funeral Director*, it is noted that although on-line memorials and electronically sharing condolences may aid in the process of mourning, they could also be methods of grief avoidance. Does a funeral webcast hurt or help the bereaved? (Kenvich, 2009).

Funeral directors and others in the industry make the same point. In an article in the *New York Times*, Rabbi Jeffrey A. Astrachan saw webcasting as a valuable service, but cautioned that it should not "replace coming to a funeral." In the same article, Kevin Gray, owner of a funeral home on Long Island, says, "You can't hug someone over the Web" (2006, p. 6). Jessica Koth believes there is a value in being present, in that it is a source of mutual support; nothing replaces actually being there (personal communication, June 11, 2010). Nevin Mann, a consultant to the funeral industry, found that when he ran a large cemetery outside of Philadelphia, there was very little interest in webcasting funerals. There, the attitude was that if someone really wanted to get home they would (personal communication, June 11, 2010). Protecting the privacy of the deceased is a related, important issue. In webcast funerals, cameras focus on family, on eulogies, the minister, the procession, and the gravesite; others focus only on public images (B. Hanner, personal communication, June 10, 2010).

Webcast funerals are not a substitute for attendance. One funeral director has yet to find that people who can attend do not (F. Fergerson, personal communication, June 11, 2010).

Looking Forward

David Kessler, Tribute.com's grief expert, is quoted in *American Funeral Director* about the future of memorial technology. He states: "There are endless possibilities to be expanded still." John Heald, vice president of sales and business development for Tributes.com, adds: "It's going to happen . . . It's not if, it's when" (March, 2009). In fact, some of the "endless possibilities" are already beginning to take shape. In an Internet posting from the Episcopal Café (http://www.episcopalcafe.com/lead/liturgy/a_cyber_funeral.html#more), the funeral of Lee Davenport is described. On April 3, 2009, an online service was orchestrated by Deacon Larry Shell and attended online, in individual homes, by friends who could not be at Davenport's Virginia service and only knew Davenport from blogs, Facebook, and other Internet sites. The service was followed on Shell's blog and Facebook page and included the Book of Common Prayer and music. One of the comments on the blog was: ". . . It was as 'live' a service as it gets." Deacon Shell said: "the reaction was awesome." He noted virtual attendees were from all over the world. Another blogger wrote: "this evening, several of us attended his (Lee's) cyber-funeral on Facebook . . . Lee's home church priest . . . was going to consecrate all our elements via the Internet." He attended from "his sacred spot in the yard." This blogger typed in responses in the comments section of Shell's report and noted the "'Amens' and 'Thanks be to Gods'" that were coming in from all over the country" and that he listened to prerecorded music according to instructions. He writes: "I was NOT alone in the dark. I was standing . . . with . . . other people slung all over the country, at that moment who were all in their 'sacred spaces for the evening,' reciting the Creed . . . Facebook friends were all exchanging the peace, LIVE, with me, just as if we were right there in church together!" And further: "It was one of the most real Sacraments I have ever felt." (http://kirkepiscatoid.blogspot.com/2009_04_01_archive.html).

Facebook friends memorializing a friend they knew only from the Internet–experiencing a live service via the Internet—all part of the 21st century funeral and emerging postdeath rituals. It brings to mind Woody Allen's well known comment: "90% of life is just showing up." The new question is: how do we show up?

REFERENCES

Blando, J. A., Graves-Ferrick, J., & Goecke, J. (2004). Relationship differences in AIDS memorials. *Omega, 49*(1), 27–42.

Bouvard, M. (1988). *The path through grief.* Amherst, NY: Prometheus Books.

Cable, D. G. (1998). Grief in the American culture. In K. J. Doka & J. D. Davidson (Eds.), *Living with grief: Who we are, how we grieve* (pp. 61–70). Bristol, PA: Taylor & Francis.

Charmaz, K. (1980). *The social reality of death: Death in contemporary America.* Reading, MA: Addison-Wesley.

Deck, E. S., & Folta, J. R. (1989). The friend-griever. In J. K. Dota (Ed.), *Disenfranchised grief: Recognizing hidden sorrow* (pp. 77–89). Lexington, MA: Lexington Books.

de Vries, B., & Roberts, P. (2004). Introduction. *Omega, 49*(1), 1–3.

de Vries, B., & Rutherford, J. (2004). Memorializing loved ones on the World Wide Web. *Omega, 49*(1), 5–26.

Doka, K. J. (1989). Disenfranchised grief. In K. J. Doka (Ed), *Disenfranchised grief: Recognizing hidden sorrow* (pp. 3–11). Lexington, MA: Lexington Books.

Fischler, M. (2006, October 8). Technology: Funeral home Webcast allows out-of-town mourners to pay respects. *The New York Times*, p. CT-6.

Haney, C. A., Leimer, M. A., & Lowery, J. (1997). Spontaneous memorialization: Violent death and emerging mourning ritual. *Omega: Journal of Death and Dying, 35*, 159–171.

Hart, J. (2007, March/April). Grief goes online. *Utne. Topeka, 140*, 88–89.

Hollander, E. M. (2001). Cyber community in the valley of the shadow of death. *Journal of Loss and Trauma, 6*, 135–146.

Hume, J. (2000). *Obituaries in American culture.* Jackson, MI: University Press of Mississippi.

Hume, J., & Bressers, B. (2009–2010). Obituaries online: New connections with the living—and the dead. *Omega, 60*(3), 255–271.

International Cemetery, Cremation and Funeral Association. (2010, June). KIP awards: Most personalized service or memorial. *ICCFA Magazine*, pp. 16–20.

Kamerman, J. B. (1988). *Death in the midst of life: Social and cultural influence on death, grief and mourning.* Englewood Cliffs, NJ: Prentice Hall.

Karlin, S. (2009, October). Funeral Webcasting is Alive and Well. *IEEE Spectrum Magazine.* Retrieved from http://spectrum.ieee.org/at-work/innovation/funeral-webcasting-is-alive-and-well

Kastenbaum, R., Peyton, S., & Kastenbaum, B. (1977). Sex discrimination after death. *Omega: Journal of Death and Dying, 7,* 351–359.

Kenevich, T. (2009, March). Next generation of grief. *American Funeral Director.* Retrieved from http://www.nxtbook.com/nxtbooks/katesboylston/nxtd/index.php?startid=18

Kollar, N. R. (1989). Rituals and the disenfranchised griever. In K. J. Doka (Ed.), *Disenfranchised grief: Recognizing hidden sorrow* (pp. 271–286). Lexington, MA: Lexington Books.

Lattanzi, M., & Hale, M. E. (1985). Giving grief words: Writing during bereavement. *Omega: Journal of Death and Dying, 15,* 45–52.

Maybury, K. K. (1996). Invisible lives: Women, men and obituaries. *Omega: Journal of Death and Dying, 32,* 27–37.

Moss, M. (2004). Grief on the Web. *Omega: Journal of Death and Dying, 49,* 77–81.

Nager, L., & de Vries, B. (2004). Memorialization on the World Wide Web: Patterns of grief and attachment in adult daughters of deceased mothers. *Omega, 49,* 43–56.

Parkes, C. M. (1972). *Bereavement: Studies of grief in adult life.* London, England: Tavistock.

Roberts, P. (1999). Tangible sorrow, virtual tributes: Cemeteries in cyberspace. In B. de Vries (Ed.), *End of life issues: Interdisciplinary and multidimensional perspectives* (pp. 337–358). New York, NY: Springer.

Roberts, P. (2004). The living and the dead: Community in the virtual cemetery. *Omega, 49*(1), 57–76.

Roberts, P., Bruce, J., Izarraraz, L., & Soni, R. (2000, November). *"A little sad, a lot stronger": The impact of Web memorialization on bereaved parents and others.* Poster presented at the Gerontological Society of America meetings, Washington, DC.

Roberts, P., Neal, N., & Shamitz, S. (1999, November). *Who left the flowers? Visiting in virtual cemeteries.* Poster presented at the annual meetings of the Gerontological Society of America, San Francisco, CA.

Roberts, P., & Vidal, L. A. (2000). Perpetual care in cyberspace: A portrait of memorials on the Web. *Omega: Journal of Death and Dying, 40,* 159–171.

Roberts, P., Williamson, B., & Clemens, S. (1998, November). *"Who will I toss a snowball to now?" Grief at the death of companion animals.* Paper presented at the annual meeting of the Gerontological Society of America, Philadelphia, PA.

Ruskin, C. (1988). *The quilt: Stories from the NAMES project.* New York, NY: Pocket Books.

Silverman, P. R., & Klass, D. (1996). Introduction: What's the problem? In D. Klass, P. R. Silverman, & S. L. Nickman (Eds.), *Continuing bonds: New understanding of grief* (pp. 3–27). Bristol, PA: Taylor & Francis.

Sklar, F. (1992). Grief as a family affair: Property rights, grief rights, and the exclusion of close friends as survivors. *Omega: Journal of Death and Dying, 24,* 109–121.

Sklar, F., & Hartley, S. F. (1990). Close friends as survivors: Bereavement patterns in a "hidden" population. *Omega: Journal of Death and Dying, 21,* 103–112.

Sofka, C. (1997). Social support "internetworks," caskets for sale, and more: Thanatology and the information superhighway. *Death Studies, 21*(6), 553–574.

Stroebe, M., Stroebe, W., & Hansson, R. (1993). Bereavement research and theory: An introduction to the handbook. In M. Stroebe, W. Stroebe, & R. Hansson (Eds.), *Handbook of bereavement: Theory, research, and intervention* (pp. 3–19). New York, NY: Cambridge University Press.

Stroebe, M., van der Houwen, K., & Schut, H. (2008). Bereavement support, intervention, and research on the Internet: A critical review. In M. Stroebe, R. Hansson, H. Schut, & W. Stroebe (Eds.), *Handbook of bereavement research and practice: Advances in theory and intervention* (pp. 551–574). Washington, DC: American Psychological Association.

Tolstikova, K., & Chartier, B. (2009–2010). Internet method in bereavement research: Comparison of online and offline surveys. *Omega: Journal of Death and Dying, 60*(4), 327–349.

Vandermeersch, A. (2010). VirtualMemorialServices.com performs Ontario's first live funeral Webcast. Retrieved from http://www.marketwire.com/press-release/VirtualMemorialServices com-Performs-Ontarios-First-Live-Funeral-Webcast-1267968.htm

Virtual Memorial Garden (VMG) Information [online]. (1999). Retrieved from http://catless. ncl.ac.uk/Obituary/aboutvmg.html

Walter, T. (1996). Facing death without tradition. In G. Howarth & P. C. Jupp (Eds.), *Contemporary issues in the sociology of death, dying and disposal* (pp. 193–204). Basingstoke, UK: McMillan.

Weeks, O. D. (1996). Using funeral rituals to help survivors. In K. J. Doka (Ed.), *Living with grief after sudden loss* (pp. 127–138). Bristol, PA: Taylor & Francis.

Worden, W. (1991). *Grief counseling and grief therapy.* New York, NY: Springer Publishing.

Wortman, C. B., & Silver, R. C. (1987). Coping with irrevocable loss. In G. R. VandenBos & B. K. Bryant (Eds.), *Cataclysms, crises and catastrophes: Psychology in action* (pp. 189–235). Washington, DC: American Psychological Association.

Part III

Sharing and Gathering Knowledge in Cyberspace

11

Open to Hope: An Online Thanatology Resource Center

Gloria Horsley and Heidi Horsley

THE ORIGIN, GOALS, AND BENEFITS OF THE OPEN TO HOPE FOUNDATION

When Dr. Gloria Horsley's son Scott was killed in an automobile accident in 1983, there were few resources available for individuals and families in grief. Although Elisabeth Kübler-Ross's seminal book *On Death and Dying* (1969) had been published two decades earlier and had given some voice to those dealing with dying, death, and grief, nevertheless, the overwhelming expectation at the time of Scott's death was that grievers should "just get over it and move on." After a few weeks, mourners were forgotten by the world, leaving them feeling abandoned and disenfranchised in their seemingly endless struggle to absorb the loss.

Although Gloria's work as a clinical nurse specialist on the faculty of the University of Rochester School of Nursing and her role as liaison to the medical center at the time of Scott's death exposed her to issues related to loss every day, she was totally unprepared for the suffering that she, her husband Phil, and their surviving children, Heidi, Rebecca, and Heather, would experience. Over the following 18 years, as she worked as a licensed marriage and family therapist and published texts, books, and articles on individual, family, and in-law therapy, Gloria used her clinical knowledge to support the family in their grief as best she could. However, the traumatic loss of their beloved son and brother ultimately influenced the career direction of both Gloria and Heidi.

Heidi earned her undergraduate, master's, and ultimately, her doctoral degree in psychology. In addition to her thriving practice as a clinical psychologist in New York City, she serves as a researcher on Columbia University's study of the families of firefighters killed on September 11 and as an adjunct faculty member at the Columbia University School of Social Work. In 2003, Gloria retired from private practice and decided to devote her professional expertise to helping families and individuals who had experienced profound losses. She volunteered with The Compassionate Friends, a nonprofit organization supporting bereaved parents, siblings, and grandparents. She became a member of the National Board of The Compassionate Friends (TCF) in 2005 and, with husband Phil, established a chapter in Burlingame, CA. She and Heidi became frequent presenters at TCF conferences.

In 2005, at the request of TCF, Gloria began writing, producing, and hosting *Healing the Grieving Heart*, a weekly Internet-based radio show on the web's largest radio broadcasting network, VoiceAmerica. The plan was for the show to run for 13 weeks. After 10 weeks, Gloria received the following e-mail: "Dr. Gloria: I have noticed that you have only two more shows listed on TCF website. I hope you are not going to quit. You are my life-line."[1] This message moved Gloria to make the decision to produce the show indefinitely.

In 2006, Heidi joined the show as a cohost to provide a sibling loss point of view. In 2007, they were again moved by a specific e-mail: "Dear Dr. Gloria and Dr. Heidi: I just wanted you to know how much I have learned and been supported by your radio show. Although I have not lost a child, I find that many of the things you and your guests are saying help me to deal with the death of my husband." This and similar comments inspired Heidi and Gloria to launch *The Grief Blog* at www.thegriefblog.com, an interactive website for all bereaved people. Much of their inspiration and motivation continued to come from website visitor comments, such as Myra's: "There have been many nights like this night when I honestly feel that I will cry until I die. That is why I love this blog. There are real people here who know what pain and loss means and who don't mind sharing in hopes of helping someone else. Thank you for being here. Thank you for caring."

By 2008, the Horsleys and their volunteers were sponsoring over 10 grief and loss blogs, as well as continuing the weekly radio show. In response to the over 1 million visitors to the sites, they decided to consolidate all of the separate websites, loss-specific blogsites, and ventures into a centralized source under one umbrella, www.opentohope.com, and create a 501(c)(3) nonprofit family foundation, The Open to Hope Foundation. Their desire was to provide an "open platform" for grief experts and organizations to reach out and serve the grieving public with a combination of expert articles, news, research, radio, and video. The Foundation's mission is simple: To help all people find hope after loss.

The Open to Hope foundation uses a disciplined approach to fulfilling its mission and provides the following primary benefits to website visitors and www.opentohope.com participants: empowering the bereaved and validating their experiences with "heart-based" resources, filling the information gap, and fitting the time frame of actual grieving. These benefits will now be described.

---

1 All names, identities, and comments cited are those provided by actual users of the Open to Hope website.

EMPOWERING THE BEREAVED AND VALIDATING
THEIR EXPERIENCES WITH HEART-BASED RESOURCES

The Open to Hope Foundation mission is based on the belief that despair and suffering, although painful, are all part of a normal process of grief and adaptation to loss. The website has been designed to empower the griever and help each person feel that his or her own unique needs are not only heard but also understood. For many in active grief, the site might be their first opportunity to reach out and obtain practical advice and simple support, and to be reassured that their experience is within the realm of normal. The griever can be angry, critical, and depressed, and Open to Hope and its contributors are there to support them on their journey. Opentohope.com is a heart-based website, and each user experience enables the griever to know there are actual people behind the machine. There is a human touch as expressed through the site's invitation to "write your story" and space for comments after articles, videos, and radio shows. The site—and all its writers and contributors—is there for those in grief, their families, and their friends, not only during the immediate aftermath of death and most acute period of grief but also to support them through future losses. Metaphorically, the opentohope.com site assures grieving visitors that "we will hold your hand and hear your story, you are not alone."

The Open to Hope site offers users the opportunity to explore and understand their own experiences with loss in a safe, caring online community. With the help of the Internet and an open forum, there is no need to be limited to the familiar grief paradigms for categorizing grief. Every user has his or her own voice and knows that he or she is not alone. Although a number of Open to Hope writers are professional therapists or health care givers, the site also includes opportunities for grievers themselves to share their own stories and experiences with others. No one has the last word or is looked to as the expert on the user's experience.

FILLING THE INFORMATION GAP

Although copious research on grief and loss has been published professionally in books and journals, the information that has been generated seldom reaches those who have lost loved ones. This disconnect, combined with the Internet's ability to easily capture and disseminate information, was recognized as a vacuum that could be uniquely filled by the Open to Hope online community.

Steele, Mummery, and Dwyer (2007) noted that innovative information technology applications such as the Internet have the potential to offer support to large numbers of people worldwide, as compared with face-to-face interventions. According to the latest mortality statistics (Centers for Disease Control and Prevention, 2010), around 2.5 million people die in the United States yearly. Considering relatives and close friends of those who are grieving, a multiple of that number would more accurately reflect the total number of people who are actively experiencing grief.

The Open to Hope Foundation site has become the most widely visited site for grief support on the net. In January 2010, the Open to Hope network served over 1 million website visitors, plus an additional half million radio listeners. According to Internet World Statistics (2009), almost three quarters of the population in the United States are currently using the Internet, offering the potential for millions of bereaved people to find community, support, and information in their journey of loss, hope, and healing. In 2009, by far the most common language of the Internet was English. However, the Open to Hope Internet family is international, with commentators and participants from around the world, including the UK, Australia, United Arab Emirates, Puerto Rico, Germany, South Africa, Singapore, and beyond.

Content on the site is provided by grief professionals and survivors of loss, with 300 contributing authors and a library of nearly 3,000 original articles, 500 original radio shows, and 75 original videos. The bereaved are able to find articles, archived radio shows, and video resources that resonate, finding their own unique and special issues discussed. Those who desire more interaction and higher levels of connection can write their own stories, and others can respond. There is also the opportunity to connect off the site because those who leave comments and stories have an option to provide their own e-mail addresses.

FITTING THE TIME FRAME OF ACTUAL GRIEVING

The Internet site is available 24/7—whenever there is a need, people can connect. The Internet offers not only intimacy but also the safety of distance, as the computer that allows for the connection can be turned on and off at will. The Open to Hope site gives individuals the opportunity to compartmentalize their grief as the Internet can be accessed at will before and after work or on those long endless nights when grievers often explore the magnitude of their loss. One can be in individual or group counseling or therapy and can still access Open to Hope as an online support or supplement. Unlike time-limited (or brief) therapy sessions, online communities are available 24/7. The users may select an article, listen to a 30-minute radio show, or watch a 2-minute video clip.

Coming to terms with the loss of a loved one can be a long-term process, especially if there are mitigating factors that delay or complicate the grieving process, such as suicide, litigation, or homicide (Lobb, Kristjanson, Aoun, & Monterosso, 2010; DeSpelder & Strickland, 2008). To get professional help for what is seen as "normal grief," grief must be pathologized. There are universal aspects and responses to grief, which were first identified by Lindemann (1944). Today, it is recognized that one's personal grief is like a fingerprint, unique and special. Although humans can sympathize with others' losses, only through personal experience can one fully embrace the physical and emotional response to a major loss.

When it comes to integrating a major loss, research and observations from practitioners (practice wisdom) provide support for the conclusion that adaptation, healing, and the integration of loss into one's life occurs in *years*, not weeks or months (e.g., Heinz, 1999; McBride & Simms, 2001; Murphy, Johnson, Wu, Juan Fan, & Lohan, 2003; Feigelman, Jordan, & Gorman, 2008–2009). Because loss is unpredictable and can present a multitude of challenges and issues, a great advantage of the Internet is that it can be dipped in and out of as needed. It may be years before an anniversary reaction such as a graduation, marriage, or birth will influence someone's decision to seek support, reassurance, or validation of his or her grief. Anniversary reactions are notorious for being triggered unexpectedly by events like a change in a season, holiday, or the death of another family member or associate (Vanderwerker & Prigerson, 2004).

With the exception of hospice bereavement support programs funded by Medicaid and Medicare, it is a rare program that supports bereaved families beyond a 6-week window after the loved one's death. Although studies have shown that the recovery process from a sudden, unanticipated death is longer than that from a loss that was anticipated (Patricelli, 2007), the typical 6- to 12-session allotment of therapy sessions covered by most insurance providers and employee assistance plans is brutally inadequate. For those who need long-term support, few have the financial resources to afford it. Insurance generally covers only a few sessions, and funded grief programs often terminate after a few months. Support from Open to Hope has no time limits.

The Open to Hope Website

In February 2010 alone, 2.1 million people searched the Internet for "grief," and 16.6 million people searched for "hope." The Internet provides the information grievers seek, and Open to Hope puts it at their fingertips. The website visitors are men and women experiencing grief, each at his or her own stage in the grief healing process.

When visitors come to www.opentohope.com, the information is organized by categories of information on the navigation bar: family loss, other losses, grief and healing, and special topics.

Family loss categories include the death of a child, pregnancy loss, the death of a sibling, death of a spouse, death of a parent, and death of other family. Nonfamily losses are validated in a category that includes the death of a coworker, friend, or pet.

The Open to Hope website provides support for unique populations and also acknowledges the power of creativity as a resource for coping with loss. Visitors will find information about "Grief and Healing" that relates to "Children and Grief," "Art, Hope, and Healing," and "Poems and Reviews." The "Special Topics" section includes information "For Men Only," with information about male styles of grieving. The "Spirituality" section offers insight into how grievers experience challenges with faith, dreams, and signs and offers support for those in the pastoral community. The section on "Traumatic Deaths" provides information about homicide, suicide, and death by overdose. In addition to a section about "Hospice," an "Other" section includes material about recent events and other unique topics. A search engine is available to help users find information specific to one's current needs.

A Multitude of Internet Modalities to Engage Users

The Open to Hope site engages users across a multitude of Internet modalities. As well as providing easy access to information about grief in a centralized source, the Open to Hope site also offers numerous possibilities to engage users—whether visitors are those in grief or professionals who are seeking information. These include (a) becoming an author of articles of the site (this category of user is typically drawn from the professional community, or those who have written books relating to loss, hope, and recovery); (b) listening to archived streaming audio radio shows or participating on the radio show as a guest; (c) viewing video clips created for Open to Hope Television (as well as being available on YouTube); (d) blogging on the site to tell a personal story or to comment on other content; and (e) being involved with social media including Facebook and Twitter. Each of these modalities is discussed below.

INVITING AUTHORS TO WRITE ARTICLES FOR THE WEBSITE

The Open to Hope site currently has more than 3,000 articles, with more published each week. To facilitate connecting the public with the academic community, the site gives voice to both professionals and those who experience loss. Research from universities and professionals often does not reach the general public. Unless it involves a high-profile person's death, the traditional publishing world and the media do not view grief and loss as a "top-selling category." It is very difficult for even well-known grief experts to find an audience, let alone those who have gained comfort from writing about their experiences and perhaps published their own books in memory of their loved ones.

On the other hand, the Internet provides an opportunity for authors, both professional and amateur, to pen articles that will have a strong chance of getting published. Particularly in the case of the Open to Hope site, writers have expressed their pleasure in the opportunity to publish their ideas and experiences pertaining to grief, loss, hope, and recovery in a well-organized, heavily trafficked forum. The site also enables authors to link to vendors such as Amazon.com to encourage the Open to Hope visitors to read even more. Authors also benefit from the Open to Hope site's "Author Profile Pages," which provide a web presence to professionals, along with a place for valuable links to increase the author's position and exposure on Google and other search engines.

OPEN TO HOPE RADIO

The Healing the Grieving Heart radio program, currently called *Open to Hope*, was launched by Dr. Gloria Horsley in July 2004. A year later, her daughter and fellow therapist Dr. Heidi Horsley joined as cohost, providing Internet radio access around the globe, with Gloria broadcasting from San Francisco and Heidi from New York City.

Until April 2010, their syndicated talk radio show was heard live weekly and was one of the top-ranking shows on Voice America, World Talk Radio, and CBS Internet. At this time, the decision was made to shift from live Internet broadcasting to podcasting. Producing commercial-free shows and having control of the listener/visitor traffic data has enabled Open to Hope to better serve their listeners. These *Open to Hope* shows focus on weekly topics featuring various guest speakers, with the common thread being that each guest has survived a major loss or are experts on a topic related to grief, loss, hope, and healing. New shows are posted weekly, and all current and past shows are available on the Open to Hope site.

Interviews on the *Open to Hope* show include grievers and professionals who work in the area of grief and loss. Open to Hope makes it a request of those who write for the site, are guests on the radio show, or make a video to discuss their personal experience with loss. The idea is that others have been there and survived and thus so can the radio show's listeners and website visitors. This goes against the traditional psychoanalytic model, in that Open to Hope believes that giving people the opportunity to provide service and using one's personal experience are extremely healing. The message is "If you have lost hope, lean on ours until you find your own."

According to data reported in the 2008 Arbitron/Edison Media Research Internet and Multimedia study, one in seven 25- to 54-year-olds is listening to online radio on a weekly basis. The study notes that the audience for both audio and video broadcasts has grown tremendously since 2007. This underscores that there is tremendous opportunity for topics that may not have enough mass appeal to be sustainable at the local level by a broadcast radio station but could generate very sizable audiences nationally or globally.

Challenges of Podcasting

Recording and broadcasting a weekly radio show is not without its challenges. The expense of doing Internet radio is considerable, with each show averaging $300 in recording costs. High-grade audio, skilled technicians, and sound engineers using advanced equipment are necessary to ensure a consistently high-quality listener experience. One of the advantages of moving to independently produced podcasting is the control it affords over the unique URLs for each show. In the past, the URLs were frequently changed by the broadcasters, necessitating immense staff time to fix the broken links. The URLs are now stable.

Open to Hope Television

The Open to Hope video segments provide an ideal medium to enable users to connect. Kinship and bonds can be formed between people around the world who find themselves in similar circumstances. The site currently broadcasts 75 videos on topics that range from "Reinvesting In Living After Loss of a Loved One" to "African American Funeral Rites" to "Men and Depression" to "Normalizing Grief." Many of the videos were filmed at the 2009 Association for Death Education and Counseling Conference. In addition to broadcasting on the site, the Open to Hope videos are featured on YouTube. Those who were interviewed in the video segments have created numerous links between their videos and other sites, which significantly impacts the number of visitors the Open to Hope site has received.

Grievers in the depths of loss have posted messages on the site indicating that video is often the most accessible way to enter the site and get a quick hit of information. Because of the filming costs and time involved in editing the segments, the video clips are one of the most expensive aspects of the Open to Hope site. However, positive user feedback indicates the added value is well worth the expense, and Open to Hope plans to continue producing quality video for the site.

INVITATION TO VISITORS TO TELL THEIR OWN STORIES

Throughout the Open to Hope site, users are encouraged to chime in and respond to the articles, stories of others, radio shows, or videos. Users are also encouraged to tell their own stories, and these sometimes take on a life of their own. These stories are very personal and range from very literary to very stream of consciousness. The only requirement is that they reflect the user's personal experiences. Grieving visitors also use their postings as an outlet to announce deaths and funeral arrangements and to keep talking about how much they miss the people who have passed away. In the past, those in grief were counseled to gain closure and to move on. However, as Open to Hope Foundation board member Dr. Robert A. Niemeyer stresses, "Closure is for bank accounts, not for love accounts."

The Open to Hope community of website visitors very generously share their experiences, good and bad. They also, very caringly, offer advice and comments to other users. Such was the case with Phil, who wrote on the Open to Hope site, "I felt depressed at work today and I left early, when I got home I typed the following into my computer's Google search, 'My son died and I need help.' The Open to Hope site came up and I knew that I was not alone." Phil has been a contributor ever since. He often expresses his own grief experiences and connects with others, thus letting them also know that they are not alone. The following exchange took place later on the site, when "Big B" posted: "My son died recently of cancer; I am in a living hell." In response, Phil wrote: "Dear Big B: I don't know you but my son died of cancer also. I know your pain. Phil."

Although one might expect some misuse of a site such as Open to Hope, it is surprisingly free from typical website "blazing" or harsh treatment of other users, which is rife on many other sites. The Foundation believes this is attributable to not only the content but also to the fact that the website users actually feel part of a larger community of caring and shared pain. Because those who visit have "been there" and have a real "passion point," they seem to be extremely reluctant to step on the toes of others who are in grief. Because the site is staffed with "real people" and all new content is monitored, if any abusive content is posted, the inappropriate material can be immediately removed.

The website does include a legal disclaimer, which is frequently reviewed (see http://www.opentohope.com/terms-conditions/). All website staff members and volunteers are encouraged to keep the Open to Hope mission statement in mind when considering whether to pull comments that may be questionable by holding them up to the challenge: "Is this comment related to *helping people find hope after loss*?" If not, the comment can be deleted without qualms. Open to Hope offers a unique forum for real people dealing with real feelings in real time, with comments appearing immediately on the site. Because the site has experienced so few problems with inappropriate material being posted, visitors' comments and stories go directly onto the site and are reviewed daily by staff, thus enabling visitors to feel validated as their words are posted immediately and without delay.

SOCIAL NETWORKS

The Open to Hope Foundation online social media channels include Facebook, Twitter, and YouTube. Visitors initially come to our sites as strangers but quickly get to know one another, often forming friendships based on their grief experiences and becoming part of a virtual Internet community. Website visitor comments indicate that those in grief are not only looking to find some hope and to make meaning out of their own experience, but also there is a desire to reach out and touch others.

Facebook is a place where current events, guests on our radio shows, upcoming articles, and current news and events related to our authors and other grief-related organizations are posted and shared. Twitter is used when a show is being broadcast, and participants are "tweeted" with the call-in number or URL to make it easy to connect. The social networking sites also include photo albums showcasing attendance at conferences such as TCF or the Association for Death Education and Counseling.

Experts say that as people share more of their lives online, grief moves with them. In addition, the nature of sites such as Facebook, Twitter, and even online guest books allows people suffering from tragedies to find others just like them, without anyone censoring their emotions.

BEHIND OPEN TO HOPE:
EXECUTIVE SUPPORT, BOARD OF DIRECTORS, AND FUNDING

Employees of the Open to Hope Foundation include Heidi Horsley, Executive Director; Heather Johnson, Video and Newsletter Editor; and Neil Chethik, Executive Editor. Gloria Horsley and her husband Phil Horsley volunteer their time. With his background in venture finance, Phil serves as the Foundation's chief financial officer.

The Open to Hope Foundation board of directors is made up of highly regarded professionals who offer depth and breadth of experience from a variety of backgrounds, including an attorney with a major international law firm who serves as the Foundation's General Counsel; one of the world's leading grief therapists and educators; the head of a major broadcast network; a marketing expert; and published writers who focus on grief and loss.

Open to Hope is a family foundation and is currently funded by the Horsley family. Authors are unpaid for their efforts but receive Author Profiles, as mentioned earlier. As the visitor numbers increase and the Open to Hope site continues to become recognized as a major source of grief support on the web, the Board plans to broaden the support base to ensure the future success of the Foundation. Open to Hope plans to continue to focus on its primary mission and believes that in doing so, it will attract the visitors who truly will benefit from the information and community it offers, who are given the opportunity to make online contributions, thus providing financial support beyond that of the founders.

Open to Hope was awarded a Google Grant in 2009. The Google Grants program empowers 501(c)(3) organizations to achieve their goals by helping them promote their websites via advertising on Google. Google ads appear when users search on Google. Organizations that receive a Google Grant are awarded an in-kind online advertising account that can be used in a variety of ways, including general outreach, fundraising activities, and recruitment of volunteers.

THE IMPACT, IMPLICATIONS, AND RESEARCH OPPORTUNITIES

Open to Hope radio, video, and articles posted on the site provide a unique archive for medical students, nursing student, social work, and thanatology students, among others, to read first-hand accounts of the problems facing those who have suffered loss. Hearing and reading of the resilience and courage of those who have moved on to support and help others can inspire visitors to also have hope and let their voices be heard. Teachers can give students the opportunity to access material from the site and to write response papers.

One college professor from Canada requires her students to watch the Open to Hope YouTube video segments because watching the leaders in the field of grief and loss gives them a more personal experience when they read the author's material in their textbooks. Students are often reluctant to conduct research studies on grief and loss, as it is difficult to identify an appropriate sample. The Open to Hope community provides a unique resource for students who will be working with bereaved clients.

Open to Hope is committed to supporting studies on the impact of normal grief and techniques or ideas that might ease the suffering of the bereaved, and it allows researchers to post requests for research participants. Open to Hope supports bereavement research projects that have gone through the appropriate institutional review board process. The website also includes a link to a list of professionals who provide a range of services related to thanatology.

Other allied areas of use for the Open to Hope content are in the education of the general public through the performing arts. The Foundation received an e-mail from Brian Kavanaugh Jones, husband of Shana Feste, who wrote and directed the movie *The Greatest*, starring Pierce Brosnan, Susan Sarandon, and Carey Mulligan. The story focuses on a family who loses their son in a car accident, their grieving process, and their redemption through refinding each other. The story and movie were heavily influenced by Open to Hope, and according to Kavanaugh Jones, "Shana listened to Healing the Grieving Heart many, many times while she wrote the script—and was so deeply moved by many of the stories on your show."

Open to Hope has created a path of progressively increasing reach. On a segment of the *Open to Hope* radio show, distinguished author and Stanford University professor emeritus Dr. Irvin Yalom discussed his book *Staring at the Sun* (Yalom, 2009). He described the rippling effect that people produce through their good works. Open to Hope has created a strong ripple effect not only by helping the grieving find hope but also by informing the general public about the challenges faced by those who suffer loss. It is the Foundation's sincere hope that this ripple effect will continue to expand, so that all who have lost loved ones and have broken hearts can find hope again.

REFERENCES

Arbitron/Edison Media Research. (2008). The Arbitron/Edison Media Research Internet Media Study. Retrieved from http://www.edisonresearch.com/internet_studies.php

Centers for Disease Control and Prevention. (2010, May 20). *National Vital Statistics Reports*. Retrieved from http://www.cdc.gov/nchs/data/nvsr/nvsr58/nvsr58_19.pdf

DeSpelder, L. A., & Strickland, A. L. (2008). *The Last Dance—Encountering Death and Dying* (8th ed.). Boston, MA: McGraw Hill.

Feigelman, W., Jordan, J. R., & Gorman, B. S. (2008–2009). How they died, time since loss, and bereavement outcomes. *Omega—Journal of Death and Dying, 58*(4), 251–273.

Heinz, D. (1999). *The last passage—Recovering a death of our own*. New York, NY: Oxford University Press.

Internet World Statistics. (2009). Retrieved from http://www.internetworldstats.com/

Kübler-Ross, E. (1969). *On death and dying.* New York, NY: Macmillan.

Lindemann, E. (1944). *Symptomatology and management of acute grief. American Journal of Psychiatry, 101,* 141–148.

Lobb, E., Kristjanson, L., Aoun, S., Monterosso, L., Halkett, G., & Davies, A. (2010). Predictors of complicated grief: A systematic review of empirical studies. *Death Studies, 34*(8), 673. Retrieved August 5, 2011, from Research Library. Document ID: 2128557821.

McBride, J., & Simms, S. (2001). Death in the family: Adapting a family systems framework to the grief process. *American Journal of Family Therapy, 29*(1), 59–73.

Murphy, S. A., Johnson, L. C., Wu, L., Fan, J., & Lohan, J. (2003). Bereaved parents' outcomes 4 to 60 months after their children's deaths by accident, suicide, or homicide: A comparative study demonstrating differences. *Death Studies, 27*(1), 39–61. Retrieved August 5, 2011, from Research Library. Document ID: 272441321.

National Vital Statistics Reports. (2009). Retrieved from http://www.cdc.gov/nchs/data/nvsr/nvsr58/nvsr58_19.pdf

Patricelli, K. (2007, March 7). *Factors influencing the grief/bereavement process—unexpected death vs. expected death.* Retrieved August 1, 2011, from http://www.mentalhelp.net/poc/view_doc.php?type=doc&id=12002&cn=174

Steele, R. M., Mummery, W. K., & Dwyer, T. (2007). A comparison of face-to-face or internet-delivered physical activity intervention on targeted determinants. *Health, Education & Behavior, 4*(3), 245–260.

Vanderwerker, L. C., & Prigerson, H. G. (2004). Social support and technological connectedness as protective factors in bereavement. *Journal of Loss and Trauma, 9*(1), 45–57.

Yalom, I. G. (2009). *Staring at the sun—Overcoming the terror of death.* San Francisco, CA: Jossey-Bass.

12

DEATH EDUCATION

*Illene Noppe Cupit, Carla J. Sofka, and
Kathleen R. Gilbert*

In many respects, death education is at the heart of thanatechnology. Despite all of the graphic multimedia representations of death that have increased in number and intensity, many thanatologists, particularly those in the western-northern hemisphere, decry that we still are in an era of "death denied" (Aries, 1981). We all experience death and loss, but few of us truly know how to negotiate this thanatological territory. Death education, in its both experiential and didactic forms, is essential for the training of practitioners, for the advancement of knowledge about dying, death, and loss through the work of scholars and researchers; and for the consumers of death-related information. It is the responsibility of death educators, taking an interdisciplinary approach (Noppe, 2010), to emphasize the importance of learning about theories of grief, the significance of evidence-based practices in grief therapy, how to interpret the literature, and the psychosocial and physiological consequences of dying in the 21st century.

Although death education courses have proliferated on college campuses during the past two decades, there remains a great need at all levels of the life span to educate and guide the critical problem solving that is necessary to make intelligent and informed death-related decisions (Noppe, 2007b). Perhaps an effective way in which to meet the needs for death education is through technologically based formats. In this chapter, we begin by exploring what is meant by death education. This is followed by a discussion of the current state of the art of online education in general and how the lessons learned can be applied to online death education. We then offer several examples of what seem to be effective practices developed by those educators who have spent many a night in their pajamas designing Internet-based educational experiences in thanatology.

WHAT IS DEATH EDUCATION?

According to Kalish (1989), death education refers to planned educational experiences that pertain to issues involving understanding the meaning of death, dying, and factors involved in grief and bereavement. Some of the goals of death education are to promote discourse about death; integrate the dying with the living; explain the developmental processes of death understanding and grief; heighten sensitivity about cultural variations in dying, death, and grief; and appreciate the universal and individual course of the grief experience (Corr, Nabe, & Corr, 2009; Feifel, 1959; Kalish, 1989).

Over the past decade, death, dying, and grief have increasingly become legitimate topics of study. In part, this is because of the Internet and other forms of computer-mediated communication that have made the transmission of thanatological information, whether accurate or not, immediately accessible on a global scale. A quick "Google Scholar" search with the keywords *death, dying*, and *grief* yielded 124,000 links in a matter of seconds. In addition, as Sofka (2007b) aptly notes, the Internet has opened up the door to ever-increasing exposure to death and dying, especially in terms of violence. This fact of life has led to a greater need for rational and realistic information about dying, death, and loss, delivered in ways that appeal to cohorts raised on seeking information via the Internet.

Death education occurs in a variety of formats (Corr, Nabe, & Corr, 2009). Of course, there are boundless opportunities for informal instances of death education in the form of "teachable moments." Death education modules may appear in limited numbers in high school curricula or even in lower grades, although not without controversy (Dean, 1995). Informal death education occurs through the print media (including children's books) and popular press, television shows, late night discussions among friends, and popular movies (Durkin, 2003). Just as their grandparents may have learned about death by watching the events surrounding the assassination of John F. Kennedy in 1963, many of today's college students learned about terrorism and death by repeated televised viewings of the horrific events of September 11, 2001.

Immersion in popular culture provides young adults with numerous opportunities for exposure to thanatology-related topics through music on their iPods, music videos online via YouTube or Vevo, television programs, and movies. Even a trip to the public library can provide opportunities for death education because of the proliferation of young adult literature that prominently features topics of dying, death, and grief (Sofka, 2011).

As noted by Simpson (2011), students who participate in online gaming or play video games that involve killing or war, when provided with opportunities to read memoirs of soldiers and participate in discussions about the actual consequences of these "simulated" behaviors, demonstrate increased empathy toward the soldiers they are playing. As fatalities from war continue to rise and the incidence of mental health-related challenges for veterans increases, further sensitivity to those impacted by war and terrorism would be a beneficial outcome.

Formal versions of death education occur in college and university courses, workshops, and in-service training sessions. In nursing and medical programs, material on death and dying typically is integrated within the curriculum (Downe-Wamboldt & Tamilyn, 1997). The number of such classes has mushroomed from a few renegade courses in the 1970s to the present where courses exist on most campuses. Formal courses in death education tend to lean toward being primarily didactic, emphasizing knowledge and information, and/or experiential, where learners are encouraged to relate their own personal experiences and feelings about death to the material (Durlak, 1994). Most of these courses are housed in psychology, sociology, health sciences, religious studies, and human services or social work departments. The most common topics (in order) are medical ethics, funerals, process of dying, cross-cultural views, public tragedy and death, hospice, spiritual issues, bereavement and grief, and death and children (Noppe, 2007b). Most courses cover cognitive content and assess student knowledge gains via examinations and research papers, but they also include journals of personal experiences and applied experiences, such as visits to funeral homes, cemeteries, hospice patients, and hospitals. Hannelore Wass (1995) claims that effective death education is composed of knowing the research, understanding its usefulness, and translating it into "educational action." In accordance with Wass (1995), what has been unique about the field of thanatology is that it has always deliberately included death education as a significant component of its scholarship.

During the past decade, death education has evolved so as to reach out to new "consumers" and to incorporate newer teaching formats. Community death education programs are becoming more common through local health care organizations (particularly hospice programs), senior centers, and adult education programs (Sofka, 2007a). Use of the Internet has expanded both formal (e.g., online credit-bearing and noncredit courses and webinars) and informal death education experiences. In terms of the informal version of online death education, anyone who has access to a computer can bring to his or her screen what seems like an infinite number of death-related Web sites. Creative partnerships have been formed to provide death education materials online to families and children (e.g., Sesame Street, 2010). Courses now are offered online, potentially reaching a much wider, more diverse audience (Gilbert, 1997).

World events (such as the bombing and attack on the children's camp in Norway; September 11, 2001 terrorist attacks; natural disasters; or the wars in Iraq, Afghanistan, and Sudan) have also moved death to the forefront of our nation's consciousness. Death educators have played a pivotal role in studying and disseminating information about responses to public tragedy (Sofka, 2009). The shared public trauma over large-scale tragedies, the wide reach of the media to produce secondary exposure, and the long-term consequences of these experiences have led to an increased demand for resource materials that educate mental health professionals, parents, and teachers about how to talk about death. Such materials have also provided information on the identification of individuals who may need extra help and the types of intervention efforts that may be most effective for traumatized individuals (Lattanzi-Licht & Doka, 2003). For example, in the wake of the events of September 11, 2001, many organizations, such as the National Association of School Psychologists, the National Educational Association, and the National Association for the Education of Young Children, were called upon to post advice on their websites on how to talk to children about death, terrorism, and violence (Noppe, 2004).

THE NEW WORLD OF ONLINE EDUCATION

Mehrotra and McGahey (2012) have written an excellent overview of online teaching in which they define online education as:

> . . . the form of distance education delivered across the Internet, as contrasted with remote instruction provided by means of video or audio tapes, CD or DVD discs used on a single computer, or even paper-and-pen correspondence courses. (n.p.)

Online education may be totally web based with no face-to-face interaction, or it may appear as a *hybrid* of online class sessions and in-class meetings, referred to as "web enhanced" by Palloff and Pratt (2001). In addition, online education may appear in synchronous (material is presented in "real time" such as with webcasting or chat rooms) or in asynchronous (teacher and students do not have to interact at the same time such as with e-mail or a discussion forum) delivery formats. The Sloan Commission estimated that as of 2007, over 3.9 million U.S. students were enrolled in at least one online course—20% of students in U.S. higher education (Allen & Seman, 2008). More impressive was their claim that the growth rate of online student enrollments was much higher than the general growth of the number of students in higher education.

Because of the logarithmic increase in the number of online offerings, the U.S. Department of Education (2009) commissioned a meta-analytic study of research from 1996 through 2008 that compared the learning outcomes of students who took courses that were totally online or hybrid with similar courses that were completely face to face. Most of the studies included in the meta-analysis were based on higher education courses spanning a variety of undergraduate and graduate fields. Also included were investigations based on courses in medicine and the health sciences and a few studies involving K-12 learners. The most important findings were that students who took online courses, particularly those that are hybrid, outperformed those in traditional classroom settings. Drilling down further into the analysis, the study concluded that when students receive a greater variety of "instructional elements," such as links to videos, podcasts, articles, and when they are given more time to learn the material, these superior outcomes were seen. The authors of this important study indicated that these two factors may not be inherent to online learning per se, but it is easier to include such course features in web-based courses. These findings provide a convincing case for the further development and promotion of online death education.

DEATH EDUCATION ONLINE: THE ADVANTAGES AND DISADVANTAGES

The use of the computer for online education has opened up many new opportunities for learning about dying, death, and grief. On an informal level, information about virtually any aspect of thanatology can be accessed via online resources or computer-mediated communication. Perhaps the largest informal death educator is Facebook, wherein many lessons about dying, death, and grief occur. In addition, websites devoted to sharing information and promoting discussion among the dying, their loved ones, and grieving survivors (e.g., the CaringBridge and Griefnet.org—see Chapters 3, 4, 5, and 6) also offer many informal lessons about dying and death. Consumers of such social networking sites share information and links to other sites and provide social support to the bereaved. They may also learn about the grief experience through postings by those whose sorrow and condolences almost instantaneously appear on the homepage of a friend, family member, or loved one who has just died. In the process, they may gain multiple perspectives on meaning making and death. The challenge for the consumer of such education is to know where to find reputable resources. Information about death and dying may be more prone to misinformation and misinterpretation than many other areas, and this may truly be a case of "buyer beware" (see Appendix A in the back of this book for resources to assist with the evaluation of websites).

On a formal level, many universities now offer their courses online, and advocates of such courses refer to the inherent advantage when geographic or schedule limitations to accessing information about death and dying are removed. These courses also can incorporate both the didactic and experiential elements by having content accompanied by students participating in online discussions. These discussions may include the sharing of opinions, beliefs, and personal encounters with death in addition to discussions of course content. Interestingly, the resources that serve as informal opportunities for death education provide a wealth of material for case studies in formal death education courses. The exchange of information via computers has also contributed to a blurring of distinctions between the students and the scholars, thus leading to a more open dialogue and mutual exchange of interesting and scholarly ideas (Noppe, 2007b).

The Internet has also helped to promote global education about dying, death, and grief, and this too has greatly influenced the perspectives that death educators take as they respond to an increasingly diverse student body. Web-based learning management systems (LMS) such as Vista, Blackboard, and D2L are popular among death educators. In terms of course design, using the Internet has opened up many possibilities for using original source materials. As long as copyright laws are respected, instructors now have many cost-effective options for creating readers and anthologies of original writings, journal articles, and chapters from several textbooks. Students can now get their textbooks online, perhaps downloading theses, E-chapters, and PDFs of journal articles to their electronic readers, or they may opt to read these materials online via links on the course site. Some universities are now moving to e-reserve systems, in which course readings are available to enrolled class members on secured servers.

In addition to opening access across the globe, the online death educator can teach in the comfort of his or her own home; recruiting high-quality off-site instructors is easier, and for both student and teacher alike, the class schedule is more flexible (Harris, 2007). In a world where time has become the scarcest commodity of all, such flexibility (perhaps at the cost of sleep) is quite appealing, especially when child care costs and job conflicts are minimized. Although student diversity can be a welcome addition, diversity and the wide range of time zones within which people reside can create challenges when determining the best times to hold "virtual office hours" or interpreting deadlines. If the class is asynchronous, the instructor may choose to use an alternative to office hours, particularly if students live in time zones that are widely distributed or significantly different from that of the instructor. (It is helpful to include a website such as http://www.timezoneguide.com/ to assist students in translating between their own time zone and that of the instructor.) However, the instructor might end up offering office hours at all times of the day, as discovered by one of the authors (Gilbert), who taught one class where students were from the disparate time zones in Israel and Hawaii!

One student population that has truly taken advantage of the online educational opportunity involves members of the U.S. military (Allen & Seaman, 2008). Thanatological insights can be shared by those in the midst of overseas military action or by the many returning veterans who frequently report feeling isolated from their college peers. However, as Harris (2007) astutely notes, teaching easily can become a 24/7 activity if the instructor is not careful (particularly with the proliferation of smart phones); class sizes need to be limited, ideally, not to exceed 25; as such courses are intense, the integration of learning with discussion can be challenging; and the logistics of assessment (e.g., paperless marking, returning papers, storing assignments) must be carefully considered.

Regarding the student perspective, Harris (2007) raises the caveats of an increased sense of impersonality and isolation from the lack of face-to-face interaction, access to technological support, and understanding of course expectations. Unless there is a discussion time wherein all students synchronously participate with the instructor, there may be no opportunity to take questions about assignments with all students present. Yet, it may be difficult, if not impossible, for classes that draw from around the world to have simultaneous engagement of all students (Gilbert, 2004). For the instructor, it may be a challenge evaluating potential negative reactions to the material because there is little opportunity for nonverbal cues. For potentially at-risk populations of students (e.g., military personnel, those who experience a loss while enrolled in the class), providing information about how to access mental health professionals is a necessity.

Students may be surprised to find that online death education courses are demanding, with extensive reading, course projects, and online discussion groups an integral part of the educational experience. Students need to know that personal reflections and thoughts, so important to a death education course, should be shared within the constraints of an intellectual, academic setting with confidentiality honored by all (Harris, 2007). Suggestions to educate students about the appropriate use of self-disclosure are discussed in more detail by Gorman in Chapter 13. Another advantage of thanatology courses that use online materials is that they offer the potential for greater student engagement in active learning (Mehrotra & McGahey, 2012). Although this finding is for online courses in general, this outcome may be particularly relevant for students who might be reticent to actively grapple with the emotionally laden material about death and dying while their classmates are watching. Young adults (particularly men) may be more comfortable doing so in the quiet solitude of the wee hours of the night in front of the glowing monitor, as was the case for one of Gilbert's students, a young man whose grandfather became ill and entered hospice care while the student was enrolled in a class on grief. This young man only worked on the class between 1:00 and 4:00 a.m. while his roommates were asleep to avoid their seeing any tears triggered by readings or fellow students' postings. Furthermore, Boettcher and Conrad (2010) and Harris (2007) encourage the creation of online learning communities, which can be particularly helpful for those students who tend to hang back in class participation. In courses on death, dying, and grief, feeling safe to comment is essential for course and student success (see Gorman in Chapter 13). This safety must extend to the student–teacher interaction, as computer-mediated communications may decrease the power differential between such online dyads. Mehrotra and McGahey (2012) also note that online students, in comparison with their classmates on campus, tend to be older students who are further along in their college careers. As encounters with death increase with age, it is plausible that more of these students would have experiences and insights about death to share in the online classroom community.

Since the days of B.F. Skinner's (1965) "teaching machines," educators have recognized the efficacy of feedback tailored to the individual learner afforded by "the new instructional technology." This finding certainly has not changed with the newness of online education. Thus, online education seems to be particularly effective when explanatory feedback is individualized for each learner (Mehrotra & McGahey, 2012). Given the diversity of experiential and cognitive learning that accompanies the thanatological student who comes to the real or virtual classroom with a multiplicity of learning situations (including cultural), feedback customized for their learning may be an especially noteworthy dimension of online death education. Not only may feedback be personalized, but instructional techniques can also be modified for the individual needs of the student in dying, death, and grief courses (known as *adaptive education*). More work for the instructor, of course, but perhaps the positive results for the committed educator provide the incentive to continue the practice.

Perhaps, the most difficult issues that can arise involve "missing" or delayed postings or problems with e-mail and assignment submission because of "technical glitches." Instructors should carefully consider using the online tools available within their LMS to assist with monitoring deadlines for assignment submission (e.g., Turnitin, Digital Dropbox). If possible, they should discuss a backup plan with students in the event of problems with the LMS around the time of a deadline (e.g., assuming the student has e-mail capacity, an e-mail submission to the instructor with a "cc" to the student and saving a copy of the "sent" e-mail with the file attached).

EVALUATING "GOODNESS OF FIT" FOR TEACHING AND LEARNING ONLINE

Although online death education opportunities have many advantages for students and educators alike, it may not always be wise for a particular student or faculty member to choose to learn and/or teach in this manner. The goodness of fit between a student's learning style, an educator's strengths and preferred style of teaching, and the information that has been gathered about online education merits consideration (Vai & Sosulski, 2011; Wolfe, 2001). The developmental level of the online learner must also be carefully considered. Most of the research literature is based upon higher education, but it is possible that death education may expand into lower grades because of the technology.

Death educators have a responsibility to be mindful of and to gain information about potential "mismatches" (e.g., visual vs. verbal learners; interpersonal vs. intrapersonal learners) that can place different demands on the student as a reader and processor of information. These mismatches can create dilemmas not only for students but for the instructor (Wolfe, 2001). Personality factors (e.g., tolerance for ambiguity), cognitive factors (e.g., cognitive flexibility), and social factors (e.g., the online coursework can have an impact on social interaction) can also play a role in the student experience (Wolfe, 2001).

With respect to online death education, instructors also need to be aware that emotional issues may hamper learning and interactive experiences. Keeping in mind the necessity of student confidentiality, it may be helpful to ask students at the onset of the course if there is anything they wish to disclose about themselves that potentially could affect their performance. This is particularly significant in a death education course because of the possibility that a student's loss history may impact his or her reaction to course material and his or her willingness to participate in class discussions.

When considering whether to teach a course online, death educators must also reflect upon their own traits and characteristics in relation to what is known about those faculty who may be well suited to teach online. The following have been identified by Palloff and Pratt (2001) as important to consider: (a) the impact of extroversion versus introversion on establishing an online presence;

(b) relationships between the factors of time (asynchronous vs. "real" time), one's processing style (reflective vs. reactive), and the perceived need for immediacy of response; (c) willingness to give up "control" in the teaching and learning process to empower the learners and build a learning community; and (d) comfort with the use of collaborative learning techniques and personal interaction. Contemplation about one's ability to be a "Guide on the Side" as opposed to the "Sage on the Stage" is particularly important because the former style is much more effective in an online teaching environment (Collison, et al, 2000). In addition to this self-evaluation of "faculty readiness," these authors note that "institutional readiness" (e.g., institutional support for distance education as evidenced by appropriate compensation for faculty time, support for training, technology access) is also crucial to successful online educational offerings (Palloff & Pratt, 2001).

Overlaying the need to know about best practices in online education is the specific demands that a death educator must meet. Durlak (1994) notes that effective death educators must be comfortable with thanatological material. This requires that the death educator is well versed in the literature on dying, death, and grief and is apprised of current theories and research findings. In the process of his or her own death education, instructors need to carefully examine and acknowledge their own attitudes, values, and beliefs about thanatological issues. Modeling such self-reflection will encourage students to do the same (see Collison et al. 2000 for guidance). In addition, the thanatechnological instructor should be willing to invite collaborative learning. Although collaborative learning is important in face-to-face death education courses, such learning is especially important in the online classroom environment. (For guidance in creating supportive and accepting classroom climates, see Collison, et al., 2000; Palloff & Pratt, 2001; Vai & Sosulski, 2011). According to Durlak (1994), the effective death educator needs to be skilled in conducting group discussion, be able to deal with conflicting opinions (frequently strong ones!) among the students, and be an attentive and good listener who is responsive to the diverse needs and backgrounds of students. Mastering these qualifications in addition to the technology is a tall order!

TEACHING TIPS FOR ONLINE DEATH EDUCATORS

A range of resources are available to assist death educators in efforts to create and implement effective online courses. Table 12.1 presents a compilation of information based heavily on Mehrotra and McGahey's (2012) teaching tips for online courses combined with information and strategies for success from the following additional sources: Vai and Sosulski (2011); Harris (2007); Sofka (2007a and 2007b); Palloff and Pratt (2001); Wolfe (2001); and Collison, Elbaum, Haavind, and Tinker (2000). The corresponding right-hand column provides additional implications and examples for the online death educator.

Table 12.1   Teaching Tips for the Online Death Educator and Moderator*

Teaching Tips for All Online Instructors	Implications and Examples for Online Death Educators
Tip 1 Consider "Who are your learners?"** • Level of experience and comfort with technology (see Chapter 2) • Demographic traits • Learning styles • Levels of experience with written communication (younger learners vs. nontraditional students) • Language barriers (international learners) ** See Chapter 13 for additional information	Life experiences and loss histories may vary tremendously across students. "Family rules" or cultural norms about disclosure of personal information may vary and influence participation levels, particularly during student introductions. These variations among students may also influence comfort with and response to self-disclosure. In classes with students who have significant professional experience in the field of thanatology, carefully consider wise use of their experience (serving as a "guest lecturer"). Technical support is a crucial factor for those who are "new" to online learning.
Tip 2 Students need to be encouraged to monitor their own course progress.	Students can be required to maintain a reflective journal integrating the content on dying, death, and grief with their own personal encounters and evolving understandings. If a student experiences a loss while enrolled, special accommodation may need to be made.
Tip 3 The syllabus should have a detailed section on course expectations, expectations for assignments, their due dates and times (clarifying the appropriate time zone), and where they should be posted. Clear guidance should be provided regarding grading criteria, including definitions of and expectations for participation (including rules for self disclosure), particularly for postings.	Provide detailed rubrics and encourage students to self-monitor and self-evaluate levels of participation. Students take courses in dying and death for personal as well as academic needs. There is a challenge with the sharing of very personal experiences—"therapy" as a need versus academic goals. The syllabus must carefully address the appropriateness of self-disclosure to create a learning community that is sensitive to the reality of loss among students but specifies the expectations as to whether (or to what degree) such personal revelations are appropriate.

(continued)

Table 12.1   (*continued*)

	Special consideration must be given regarding the role of self-disclosure in relation to requirements for participation (e.g., the absence of self-disclosure regarding one's loss history should not result in a penalty to the student's grade).
	In addition, resources for students who may need to seek professional mental health assistance should be listed.
Tip 4 The syllabus, the substantive content of which should not be modified once the course commences, should have embedded materials (e.g., assignments, policies, learning resources). Timeframes/due dates may need to be shifted if technical challenges or other circumstances merit a change.	The "virtual poster session" on death and dying assignment (see Exhibit 12.1), links to web-based readings, and other web-based requirements for the course learning should appear as links in the syllabus. The tone of the syllabus needs to be carefully constructed to account for student sensitivities to thanatological materials.
Tip 5 Instructors need to make sure that they build in enough time to interact with students in a respectful manner. Instructors have a responsibility to plan sufficient time to moderate online discussions in a timely manner and gain the knowledge and skills to do this effectively. Effective moderation takes place in a professional and social context. Balance is the key to creating an effective learning community.	Effective student-instructor interactions are crucial in a course about dying, death and loss. Instructors need to keep in mind how much students read (what may be unintentionally) "between the lines." Instructors who have an unusually high dropout rate may want to review the ways in which they respond to students as well has how their responses serve as a model to other students in the class.
Tip 6 The structure of simulations and games (e.g., rules, activities) should be in accord with course outcomes.	Online death educators have a variety of death-related simulations The "Death Clock," (e.g., "Second Life" the "Death Clock") and games (e.g., "Heavy Rain") that can be used in a thanatechnological course. It is important, particularly if violence is involved, to be sure that students are given advance preparation and are told the expected educational outcomes of these exercises.

(*continued*)

Table 12.1 (*continued*)

Tip 7 Use the technology! Relevant visual material needs to be presented with audio and written commentary. The one caveat is that, if visually impaired students are in the class, an audio or textual substitute must be made available.	Cognitive dissonance and high emotionality may be an unintended consequence of learning death-related material. For example, a video of a funeral may be disturbing to a student who has just suffered the loss of a close friend. Instructors may want to make it easier for students to assimilate such material by including commentary in a variety of modalities that can address student needs.
Tip 8 The most effective online courses promote active learning with the teacher being an active participant in the learning process. Be a "Guide on the Side" as opposed to a "Sage on the Stage."	Thoughtful questions for online discussion promote critical thinking. Students should be given appropriate reading materials on contemporary issues (e.g., assisted suicide, green funerals, the use of social media to communicate about death and dying) and be asked to comment on carefully constructed questions. Students can also be asked to identify relevant online materials ("death website of the week" – Harris, 2007, participatory sites such as virtual cemeteries, or pop culture links) and construct appropriate discussion questions to facilitate active student engagement and deeper processing.
Tip 9 Online courses need to be designed to promote student-content, student-instructor, and student-student interactions.	Following from Tip 8, online discussions, learning communities, group projects, and reflective journaling (shared or private) use the power of the Internet to help students learn what is reliable material about death and dying and to share knowledge and opinions about death and dying. Wikis (web pages that can be edited by several individuals or groups) can be used to create a repository for such information. Students should be given a grading rubric in order to understand what is considered appropriate to write as well as how frequently postings are expected (for online discussions). Death educators need to gain assessment skills to evaluate the impact and effectiveness of the material presented in online death education courses. (See Vai & Sosulski, 2011, for guidance.)

(*continued*)

Table 12.1   (continued)

Tip 10

Online educators, their students, and host institutions must learn about additional ethical/legal issues specific to the virtual educational format.	Students in online thanatology courses need to be apprised of the appropriate times to disclose information about themselves or others. Information about forwarding e-mails, and using copyrighted materials about death and dying should be available. Honor codes should be used on all assignments and examinations.
Student-related issues need to be explicitly addressed in syllabi and built into course assignments. Faculty-related issues must be addressed with the appropriate administrators and committees in relation to intellectual property rights and promotion/tenure criteria.	

* Note: Resources to assist with the development of effective online facilitation skills are available: Collison, et al, 2000; Palloff & Pratt, 2001; Vai & Sosulski, 2011.

HOW DO WE "DO" DEATH EDUCATION ONLINE: LET ME COUNT THE WAYS

Despite the newness of online death education, a number of death educators have taken on the challenge of using technology to optimize the learning experience and to engage their students with the course material. For many of those in the Internet-trenches of online instruction, thanatechnology affords the possibility for developing new and creative teaching ideas. Most of these original teaching practices have not been formally assessed for their pedagogical efficacy, but positive student feedback and informal evaluation indicate that there are many original ways to "do" thanatechnological education. The following list includes strategies that have been successfully used by online death educators:

- Sofka has her students posting links to news stories as events occur during the semester in threaded discussions or in a "wiki."
- Discussion boards, discussion threads, online discussion groups (Harris, 2007; Sofka, 2007b; for guidance in constructing questions and facilitating effective discussions, see Vai & Sosulski, 2011, and Collison et al., 2000).
- Creative uses of thanatology-related online resources (news archives, blogs, podcasts, and virtual cemeteries/memorials).
- Pairing of students to discuss books, TV programs, and movies (Harris, 2007).
- Virtual field trips through the use of websites (World Trade Center Exhibit and Oklahoma City National Museum and Memorial virtual tours; thanatourism websites; cemetery websites; Sofka, 2007b). See Culture, Grief in a Family Context, http://www.indiana.edu/~famlygrf/units/culture.html, for an example of the use of cultural sites to trigger class discussion.

- Students post the "website of the week"—something related to thanatology that may be of interest to the rest of the class (e.g., music videos, information on green burials, creative grief therapies) and can be discussed by the rest of the class (Harris, 2007).
- For Sofka's "death in pop culture" web-based course, students located online examples of thanatology-related music, TV episodes, books/book reviews, and posted links for the class (in threaded discussions, or you can compile a "wiki" of these resources). Links to current news stories are posted as they occur.
- Require each student to create a discussion question for one unit of the course that is counted toward participation (student selects the unit and receives instructor feedback about the question prior to posting). Students frequently draw and discuss conclusions from readings and group discussion during each unit.
- Virtual guest lecturers can contribute to discussion threads to provide contact with professionals in the community or academic colleagues of the instructor to discuss their writing or research (can also create podcasts or webcasts). Because the Internet does not restrict participation to a limited geographic area, Gilbert has invited guests to the class from around the world because the delivery method in Grief in a Family Context is asynchronous.
- Incorporate links to thanatology-related cartoons (e.g., http://www.gocomics. com/ for popular strips; http://www.caglecartoons.com/ for editorial cartoons) to balance humor with serious subjects, to illustrate thanatology-related subjects on the editorial pages, and to educate students about gallows humor/dark humor.
- Cupit has created a folder on her LMS entitled "Death in the News" where online newspaper articles on a current issue of thanatology (e.g., assisted suicide, the Haitian earthquake, recent criticisms of grief therapy, home funerals) are posted. Students must select two of the articles on two separate entries, discuss how the material affected them personally, and integrate the article with course readings.
- In addition to specific questions on the topic of the week, students in Gilbert's class are provided with open discussion forums centered on the topics of the week, as well as a general "café" that is available throughout the semester for students to discuss any aspect of loss and grief that is of interest, often triggered by current events in the news.
- The Virtual Poster Session: Cupit's hybrid course on Dying, Death, and Loss combines face-to-face learning with a web-based program (D2L or "Desire to Learn"). Rather than using trifold presentation boards, students upload their projects into a discussion folder. For extra participation points, class members are invited to provide substantive feedback to at least six posters. See Exhibit 12.1 for a copy of the assignment.
- The cultural interview: Gilbert's fully online course includes an assignment in which students interview someone who is culturally different from him or her, regarding various aspects of grief and mourning. This assignment is posted to the class conferencing site for discussion among class members. The instructions for this assignment can be accessed from the course website at http://www.indiana.edu/~famlygrf/sitemap.html.

Thanatechnology for Use in Web-Enhanced Classes:

- Simulations by Lambrecht—Death: A Personal Encounter (1989) and Bereavement Counseling (1993).
- "Clickers"/polling devices used in hybrid classes. These audience response tools provide opportunities for testing mastery of content and anonymous sharing of opinions regarding topics that can be value-laden or polarized (Sofka, 2007b).

ASSESSMENT FOR ONLINE DEATH EDUCATION COURSES

Most formal educational endeavors have assessment as an integral part of the learning and evaluation experience. Many forms of assessment, such as examinations, papers, projects, and class participation appear in traditional face-to-face, hybrid, and completely web-based courses. However, the ways in which these assignments are implemented and evaluated need to be tailored to the course format. Teaching thanatology online may offer opportunities for more creative forms of assessment, such as E-portfolios, group contributions on shared websites such as wikis, and original multimedia productions including YouTube videos, student-designed video games, and simulations about dying, death, and grief. If class postings/discussions are central elements of assessment, students will benefit from regular feedback on the quality of their work and ways of improving their performance. Successful online learning is dependent upon continuous opportunities for assessment and evaluative feedback (Mehtrotra & McGahey, 2012; Vai & Sosulski, 2011), and students appear to react favorably to multiple opportunities for evaluation.

In a comprehensive study of student preferences of the various components of online strategies, Buzzetto-More (2008) found that over the course of several semesters, college students appreciated the opportunity to submit their assignments online. They also were particularly positive about receiving immediate feedback and having the ability to check their grades throughout the semester. Although death educators may be reticent to administer examinations online, Filz, Gurung, and Wilhelm (2011) found that online multiple-choice testing and similar in-class examinations yielded comparable results. The researchers also found that online examinations were less stressful for students, but a number of students also reported that they had gotten help taking the examinations. One way to attenuate the "cheating" factor is to administer open-book online essay questions that assess critical thinking and transfer of learning. One of this chapter's authors has done this successfully for several years in her Dying, Death, and Loss courses. A major requirement of the examination is that the students reference their points from course readings and discussions. Students find these timed essay examinations challenging but more rewarding than in-class essays, and the superior quality of the writing and reflection of controversial issues (e.g., assisted suicide, efficacy of grief therapy) has made for a much happier instructor!

Vai and Sosulski (2011) offer detailed guidance regarding strategies for the evaluation of online learning. First and foremost, as would be the case for a traditional face-to-face course and an online course, assessment must be directly tied to the learning objectives for the course, with learner expectations and requirements articulated clearly from the start. Grading criteria must be evident, teacher feedback must be timely, and forms of assessment should be varied and ongoing. In addition to self-assessment and instructor feedback, peer-to-peer feedback is also encouraged.

Determining what constitutes "attendance" and/or participation and how to attach a grade or score to these components of an online class are important but can be challenging tasks. Palloff and Pratt (2001) note that an instructor must clearly define participation requirements in terms of not only "frequency" but also "substance." For example, a student may believe he or she can meet the minimum number of weekly posts easily by simply acknowledging another student's post without adding any original commentary that includes evidence of critical thinking—what Gilbert has informed her students are "you go, girl/boy" postings. Reactions to others' comments can also vary in the "additive" or "substantive value" to the course dialogue. Sample rubrics for evaluating postings that include criteria such as "quality," "accuracy," and "timeliness" of the postings can be found in Vai and Sosulski's (2011) helpful guidebook as well as on the companion website for the book (see http://www.marjorievai.com/Marjorie_Vai/B-Chapter_8.html). Instructors must also learn to carefully balance one's own level of participation between too much (which can impede student comfort with posting) and too little (which can result in being perceived as "uninvolved and uncaring"). Stepping in and setting limits if the quantity and types of postings are headed in the wrong direction is crucial, as is sending private invitations to participate to individuals who are not involved.

CONCLUSIONS

Death educators hope to provide an environment wherein open discourse on a generally taboo topic can be promoted not only for personal enrichment but also for the betterment of social policy and political decision making. Many death educators believe that understanding thanatology could ultimately lead to increased efforts to prevent war, nuclear proliferation, and global warming (Noppe, 2009).

Thanatechnology provides endless possibilities for creative ways to provide death education, both informally and formally. How wonderful would it be for a thanatologist to modify a program developed by Sato, Asakura, and Tsubakimoto (2011) for use with grieving families to help families create a narrative memorializing a deceased loved one, facilitating open communication about grief in the process. Online resources continue to facilitate community death education efforts, and the potential to expand the level of outreach is tremendous.

In one of the earliest articles published on the subject of death education, Leviton (1977) insisted that the learning outcomes of such courses be measurable and testable. Both process measures (i.e., the structure of death education courses) and outcome measures (i.e., examinations, attitude measures) must be subjected to empirical study—what is currently known as the Scholarship of Teaching and Learning or SoTL research. To implement evidence-based classroom practices, Noppe (2007a) argued that SoTL is particularly important for death education courses. We now argue that SoTL research needs to be an inherent component of online death education courses.

The impact of web-based instruction on content knowledge, values, and emotions pertaining to the multidisciplinary field of dying, death, and grief begs for assessment so that best practices can be used in the online classroom. Research comparing online death education courses with online courses in other fields can help to identify course elements, issues, strengths, and weaknesses that are unique to teaching and learning about thanatology. Death education has a tradition of using evidence-based practice since the first courses appeared on college campuses, and the thanatechnological researcher (see Chapter 14) in collaboration with course instructors (i.e., practitioners) can continue this tradition in cyberspace.

Death educators are becoming increasingly skilled and experienced with providing formal opportunities for learning online. The challenge now becomes how to form creative partnerships between practitioners, death educators, researchers, and tech-savvy individuals to study and document the impact of these death education opportunities and share the wisdom being gained. We look forward to being part of this exciting dialogue.

EXHIBIT 12.1

INSTRUCTIONS ON THE VIRTUAL POSTER SESSION FROM I. CUPIT'S DYING, DEATH, AND LOSS CLASS AT THE UNIVERSITY OF WISCONSIN-GREEN BAY

Preparing Your Poster Presentation

A well-constructed poster is self-explanatory and addresses the questions a reader is likely to have about your project. Successful posters achieve both coverage of the topic and clarity of presentation. In order to effectively communicate the nature of your work, your poster should be succinct, clearly presented, well written, and checked for spelling and grammatical errors.

Coverage and Clarity

Posters must be easy to read. In preparing text for your poster, aim for clarity of communication. Your goal is to educate your readers about what you have

(continued)

EXHIBIT 12.1 (*continued*)
learned through studying an interesting topic. The APA guidelines for posters include the following points about coverage and clarity:

> Have you provided all the obvious information? Will a casual observer walk away understanding your major findings after a quick perusal of your material? Will a more careful reader learn enough to ask informed questions? Ask yourself, "What would I need to know if I were viewing this material for the first time?" Then state the information clearly. If you have additional information that you wish to share, you can put it in the "Notes" section of the PowerPoint slides.

Preparing Graphics

You can use graphs, illustrations, photographs, videos, recordings, and other supplementary materials to enhance your work and make it clearer to your readers. This is one of the advantages of posting these online. A professional poster presentation is not decorated just to make it "pretty." Each visual element relates to the study. You can include links to sites to illustrate your points. The computer program PowerPoint may give you ideas for planning and preparing your graphics.

THE VIRTUAL POSTER SESSION:

IN ORDER FOR THIS TO WORK AS A POSTER SESSION, EVERYONE IN THE CLASS NEEDS TO "VISIT" POSTERS AND "TALK" TO THE AUTHORS. FOR PARTICIPATION POINTS, STUDENTS ARE INVITED TO VISIT UP TO SIX POSTERS AND POST A COMMENT OR A QUESTION (MORE SUBSTANTIVE THAN "GOOD JOB") TO THE AUTHOR. EACH COMMENT WILL EARN 2 CLASS PARTICIPATION POINTS.

REFERENCES

Allen, I. E., & Seaman, J. (2008). *Staying the course. Online education in the United States, 2008*. Needham, MA: Sloan Consortium.

Aries, P. (1981). *The hour of our death*. New York, NY: Alfred A. Knopf.

Boettcher, J. B., & Conrad, R. M. (2010). *The online teaching survival guide: Simple and practical pedagogical tips*. San Francisco, CA: Jossey-Bass.

Buzzetto-More, N. A. (2008). Student perceptions of various E-learning components. *Interdisciplinary Journal of E-Learning and Learning Objects, 4*, 113–135.

Collison, G., Elbaum, B., Haavind, S., & Tinker, R. (2000). *Facilitating online learning: Effective strategies for moderators*. Madison, WI: Atwood Publishing.

Corr, C. A., Nabe, C. M., & Corr, D. M. (2009). *Death and dying: Life and living* (6th ed.). Belmont, CA: Wadsworth/Thomson Learning.

Dean, P. V. (1995). Is death education a "nasty little secret"? A call to break the alleged silence. In L. A. DeSpelder & A. L. Stricklund (Eds.), *The path ahead. Readings in death and dying* (pp. 323–326). Mountain View, CA: Mayfield Publishing.

Downe-Wamboldt, B., & Tamlyn, D. (1997). An international survey of death education trends in faculties of nursing and medicine. *Death Studies, 21,* 177–188.

Durkin, K. F. (2003). Death, dying, and the dead in popular culture. In C. D. Bryant (Ed.), *Handbook of death and dying* (Vol.1; pp. 43–49). Thousand Oaks, CA: Sage.

Durlak, J. A. (1994). Changing death attitudes through death education. In R. A. Neimeyer (Ed.), *Death anxiety handbook. Research, instrumentation, and application* (pp. 243–260). Washington, DC: Taylor & Francis.

Feifel, H. (1959). *The meaning of death.* New York, NY: McGraw-Hill.

Filz, T., Wilhelm, T. M., & Gurung, R. A. R. (2011, August 4–7). *The utility of online examinations in face-to-face classes: Empirical evidence.* Poster presented at the annual meeting of the American Psychological Association, Washington, DC.

Gilbert, K. R. (1997, June). *Death education on the World Wide Web: The course development process.* Paper presented at the 19th Annual Meeting of Association for Death Education and Counseling, Washington, DC.

Gilbert, K. R. (2004). Death education on the "Net": Development and delivery of "grief in a family context." In G. Cox & R. Bendikson (Eds.), *Teaching the Sociology of dying and death* (pp. 83–91), Washington, DC: American Sociological Association.

Harris, D. N. (2007, April 12–15). *Online death education: Strategies for learning.* Presented at the 29th Annual Conference of the Association for Death Education and Counseling, Indianapolis, IN.

Kalish, R. A. (1989). Death education. In R. Kastenbaum & B. Kastenbaum (Eds.), *Encyclopedia of death* (pp. 75–79). Phoenix, AZ: Oryx Press.

Lambrecht, M. E. (1989). Death: A personal encounter [computer program, instructor manual]. New York, NY: American Journal of Nursing Company.

Lambrecht, M. E. (1993). Bereavement counseling: Bereavement issues [videodisc program, instructor manual]. New York, NY: American Journal of Nursing.

Lattanzi-Licht, M., & Doka, K. J. (Eds.). (2003). *Living with grief. Coping with public tragedy.* New York, NY: Brunner Routledge.

Leviton, D. (1977). The scope of death education. *Death Education, 1,* 41–56.

Mehrotra, C. M., & McGahey, L. (2012). Online teaching. In Schwartz, E., & Gurung, R. A. R. (2012). *Teaching using evidence instead of intuition.* Washington, DC: American Psychological Association.

Noppe, I. C. (2004). Death education and the scholarship of teaching: A meta-educational experience. *The Forum, 30,* 1, 3–4.

Noppe, I. C. (2007a). Life span issues and death education. In F. Balk (Ed.), *Handbook of thanatology* (pp. 337–344). Northbrook, IL: Association for Death Education and Counseling.

Noppe, I. C. (2007b, April 12–15). *Bridging research and teaching: The marriage of SoTL and death education.* Presented at the 29th Annual Conference of the Association for Death Education and Counseling, Indianapolis, IN.

Noppe, I. C. (2009). Death education. In C. D. Bryant & D. L. Peck (Eds.). *Encyclopedia of death and the human experience.* Thousand Oaks, CA: Sage.

Noppe, I. C. (2010, April). *Teaching that matters: Interdisciplinarity and death education.* Presented at the 32nd Annual Conference of the Association for Death Education and Counseling, Kansas City, Missouri.

Palloff, R. M., & Pratt, K. (2001). *Lessons from the cyberspace classroom: The realities of online teaching.* San Francisco, CA: Jossey-Bass.

Sato, T., Asakura, T., & Tsubakimoto, M. (2011). "PeKay's Little Author": Developing a storybook creation software for family narratives. In T. Bastiaens & M. Ebner (Eds.), *Proceedings of the world conference and educational multimedia hypermedia and telecommunications 2011* (pp. 1203–1208). Chesapeake, VA: AACE.

Sesame Street. (2010). When families grieve. Available at http://www.sesamestreet.org/parents/topicsandactivities/topics/grief

Simpson, E. (2011). Teaching empathy: Teacher mediation of a violent video game. In M. Koehler & P. Mishra (Eds.), *Proceedings of Society for Information Technology & Teacher Education International Conference 2011* (pp. 1208–1210). Chesapeake, VA: AACE.

Skinner, B. F. (1965). Review lecture: The technology of teaching. *Proceedings of the Royal Society of London. Series B, Biological Sciences, 162*(989), 427–443. Retrieved from http://www.jstor.org/stable/75554

Sofka, C. J. (2007a). Death education: Ethical and legal issues. In D. Balk (Ed.), *Handbook of thanatology* (pp. 355–367). Northbrook, IL: Association for Death Education and Counseling.

Sofka, C. J. (2007b, April 12–15). *Death education: Changing places, new pedagogical resources, and changing faces.* Presented at the 29th Annual Conference of the Association for Death Education and Counseling, Indianapolis, Indiana.

Sofka, C. J. (2009). History and healing: Museums as healing spaces. *International Journal of the Inclusive Museum, 2*(4), 79–90.

Sofka, C. J. (2011, June 22–25). *Vamps, suicide and grief, oh my! Death Ed in the library.* Paper presented at the 33rd Annual Conference of the Association for Death Education and Counseling, Miami, Florida.

U.S. Department of Education, Office of Planning, Evaluation, and Policy Development. (2009). *Evaluation of evidence-based practices in online learning: A meta-analysis and review of online learning studies.* Washington, DC: Centre for Learning Technology.

Vai, M., & Sosulski, K. (2011). *Essentials of online course design: A standards-based guide.* New York, NY: Routledge.

Wass, H. (1995). Visions in death education. In L. A. DeSpelder & A. L. Stricklund (Eds.), *The path ahead. Readings in death and dying* (pp. 327–334). Mountain View, CA: Mayfield Publishing.

Wolfe, C. R. (2001). Learning and teaching on the World Wide Web. In C. R. Wolfe (Ed.), *Learning and teaching on the World Wide Web* (pp. 1–22). San Diego, CA: Academic Press.

13

Death Education in the Cyberclassroom: Creating a Safe Space for Student Learning

Eunice Gorman

The Web 2.0 revolution coupled with the astounding growth of learning management systems such as Moodle, Blackboard/Web CT, and countless others has proven a boon to death education. Expert information on dying, death, and bereavement is now accessible to anyone with a computer and Internet access, thanks to social networking and media. The scope and relative ease of online participation has allowed widespread access to specialized training in many thanatology topics, including bereavement, grief, trauma, palliative care, suicide, and associated subjects. However, high-quality content requires one to attend to risks and benefits associated with distance education.

THE ONLINE CLASSROOM

Much has been written about creating meaningful online learning opportunities through the use of evolving technologies (Amhag & Jakobsson, 2009; Ashburn & Floden, 2006; Hannon & Bretag, 2010; Inoue, 2007; Moore, 2007). These new technologies allow users contacts, relationships, interactions, sharing of cultural experiences and learning in ways that traditional classroom environments cannot.

Flexibility and convenience make online education an increasingly attractive alternative to in-class learning. Coconstruction of knowledge and negotiation of meaning online in synchronous (real time) and asynchronous (off time) learning communities also motivate students to opt for online courses (Hull & Saxon, 2009). Distance education permits them to collaborate using cost-effective technology and interactive modules while at the same time allowing instantaneous feedback and opportunities to reflect (Lynch, 2004). Success in online venues requires self-motivation and time management skills, as well as the capacity to learn with limited support and to build relationships with online facilitators and fellow students (Beaudoin, Kurtz & Eden, 2009). Achievement requires the ability to express one's ideas well, to cope with nonstructured settings, and to be comfortable with technology (Palmer & Holt, 2009).

Guidelines supporting online learning have lagged behind interest. Students or instructors who do not fully understanding how online classes operate are often disappointed, frustrated, and dissatisfied. Dropout rates for online courses are as high as 30% to 50% (Stanford-Bowers, 2008). Many students drop out because of concerns about teachers; lack of interaction, support, or time; and workload management problems. Surprisingly, online death education often has higher retention rates because of factors such as prescreening, ongoing support, one-to-one contact for struggling students, small supportive classes, mini work groups, detailed information packages, and similar features. The course content is relevant and readily applicable to students' daily lives. In some cases, regular postings to the class and the instructor allow students to notice and respond to deviations of peers from normal class engagement.

Posted and enforced rules for appropriate behavior are critical for effective online courses (Cimino, 2009; Palloff & Pratt, 2007). Rules create a safe environment for open discourse. Examples of such rules would include standard expectations (students will not plagiarize, will maintain confidentiality, and will post to the class on time) and rules more specific to the class. Topics in death education classes may trigger strong emotion. Students should be reminded that the class is educational, not therapeutic. Online students may feel they must reveal extremely personal information, which they would normally not reveal in the presence of others. Students should be discouraged from seeing the class as their "interactive diary." Students should also be reminded to stop and think before posting something that might offend their peers.

BUILDING COMMUNITY ONLINE: LEARNING COMMUNITIES

Communities provide individuals with a sense of belonging, emotional connection, shared purpose, and cosmological/ideological perspectives (Habermas, 1971). Ideally, they also allow for accessibility and diversity, a sense of membership, the fulfillment of needs, and the development of trust and influence. They also provide gathering places (Harris-John, 2006; Rovai, 2001).

To build this sense of community, students must engage in class discussion. Students may engage in many on-campus classes without speaking. Such lack of engagement is penalized in interactive online courses, where weekly posts may be worth 10% to 40% of the student's final grade (Gulati, 2008).

Strategies for creating effective online collaboration include transparent expectations, clear instructions, appropriate work tasks, relevance, embedded motivation for participation, learner readiness, timing of group formation, respect for learner autonomy, and ongoing monitoring and feedback (Brindley, Walti, & Blaschke, 2009). Audiovisual tools; personal e-mails; discussion forums; live, real-time chat; and chat rooms facilitate collaborative online learning.

THE INSTRUCTOR: SAFETY PATROL

Bradley (2010) maintains that the instructor's facilitation skills are integral to successful online courses. Instructors serve as role models and coaches. They promote success while delineating course expectations. They set the tone of the course by providing a respectful, open learning space.

Brookfield (1995) writes about the importance of viewing teaching and learning through a critically reflective lens. Our ability to integrate our own and our colleagues' experiences with the scholarly literature and student needs and expectations is essential for success. We instructors must not only master the subject and stay current within our area of expertise, but we must also convey the spirit and love of learning to others. We must examine our own personal responses to dying, death, grief, and loss if we are asking students to undertake such emotionally challenging work.

Banner and Cannon (1997) encourage instructors to be open to the knowledge of others by integrating independent thought and imagination with patience, character, compassion, and ethical comportment. It is important for instructors, as well as students, to feel safe in the online classroom. Rules and guidelines are as important for instructors as they are for students.

Students can usually intuit their instructor's beliefs, thoughts, theoretical biases, and viewpoints. Instructors, on the other hand, do not know as much about their students, especially in a large university. In the online classroom, instructors can learn more about their students than is possible in a lecture hall. This more intimate knowledge of how individuals are responding to course content raises questions about our responsibility to intervene, redirect, and actively support students: yet another compelling reason to pay close attention to the comfort and safety of online students.

CREATING SAFE SPACES

To teach is to create a space, not necessarily fill the space (O'Reilly, 1998). To that end, online instructors set the stage for learning but give up the role of expert. They maintain order and authority so as to encourage shared student influence (Banner & Cannon, 1997). Ultimately, teaching goes beyond technique. It includes heart, integrity, identity, connectedness, and creation of space (Palmer, 1993). Commitment to learning, devotion, expertise, openness to change, willingness to learn, and caring for the students are critical attributes of an instructor.

Palmer recommends inviting and honoring the voice of the individual, the voice of the group, the little stories of the individual, and the big stories of the tradition and discipline.

Livesay and Palmer (1999) describe "space" as including physical, emotional, and intellectual dimensions: we do our own reflection, look inward, engage with course material, and step back from it. In essence, the instructor in the electronic environment provides a holding environment, a safe space, or containment in a reliable, consistent, and cooperative fashion.

Palloff and Pratt (2005) recommend posting a welcome note for students with information about the instructor, course expectations, and instructions for navigating the site and interacting with other students. The students are invited to post similar information, and photographs, if they wish, introducing themselves to the instructor and to their peers. Students thus engage with each other and coalesce into a community. The welcome page for the course may include any elements the instructor deems important. Welcome pages often include an array of folders containing such diverse content as catalogues of web pages, teaching philosophy statements, academic writing guidelines, downloadable video clips, blogspots, wikis to support group work, bibliographies with linked in articles, and similar interactive modalities to reinforce engagement and learning.

Emotional safety in the cyberclassroom requires that "netiquette" rules be made clear from the beginning. In addition, the processes followed by the class should ensure that students feel safe when fully engaged. A statement addressing power differentials among students that might influence participation is helpful, including explicit warnings about expressing strongly held and potentially unusual beliefs or the use of offensive language. Class structures should allow students to express their viewpoints, knowing that their input will be valued and that discussion will be respectful.

Mechanisms for balancing levels of student engagement should also be in place. Students should not lurk (i.e., remain silent observers) nor monopolize discussion; rather, they should seek a balance when trying to understand the course material and each other.

CULTURE, DIVERSITY, AND INCLUSIVITY ONLINE

Hunt (2001) maintains that culture is a dynamic and complex sharing of responses, beliefs, values, relationships, and behaviors. Issues of culture and inclusivity concern all instructors and not just those teaching international students. Important cultural dimensions they must consider include power and authority language, family roles, sex roles and differences, sexual orientation, independence, spirituality, success, conflict history, socioeconomics, acculturation and internalized culture, and worldviews (Hofestede, 2005; Lynch, 2004).

Hunt (2001) calls for cultural humility: the ability to look at our own worldview with reflection, self-awareness, and respectful attitudes toward other points of view. Humility requires openness, flexibility, and ability to compromise in the face of conflict. Any effort to address dying, death, and bereavement will encounter occasional, and often significant, cultural variations among our students. An important role of the instructor is to model humility in the treatment of these cultural differences.

Cultural safety requires that students and instructors respect the nationality, culture, age, gender, political, and religious beliefs of all. It requires commitment to social justice and understanding of racialization, power imbalances, institutional discrimination, the lasting impact of colonization, and the centrality of trust and politicized knowledge (Browne, Varcoe, Smye, Reimer-Kirkham, Lynam, & Wong, 2009). Ensuring cultural safety requires a commitment to avoid that which would intentionally diminish the cultural identity or well-being of any student in the class.

Palloff and Pratt (2007) warn that subtle (or overt) oppression can pressure those in the online classroom to agree unwillingly with others. A student who does not feel part of the dominant culture may feel ill at ease, unsafe, or silenced: an outsider fearing ostracism. Unaddressed differences may lead to self-doubt and a sense of separateness from others. Alternately, cultural sensitivity can lead students to silence themselves out of fear, which runs counter to the goal of respectful discourse. A balance must be struck to allow for full expression of ideas, opinions, and responses in the online classroom.

In a review of 27 studies that looked at questions of culture and distance learning, Uzuner (2009) identified a number of inclusivity challenges. Cultural hegemony is most common, where the customs of the dominant culture come to be viewed as the best, most commonsense way to think or behave. Ignorance of cultural references can also be a challenge, as well as the management of students who are excessively critical or opinionated or who balk at unfamiliar cultural practices. Unclear course designs threatened people from cultures that strongly value certainty. In addition, the power and authority of the instructor are highly important in some cultures, so that the instructor's feedback may be sought out and valued more often than peer feedback.

The students in the online classroom may evolve a distinct culture over time, combining elements of the culture of each student and the instructor and the developing norms of the group. As many online instructors will affirm, no two online groups are alike; they are all unique, organic, and dynamic entities.

Students in an online death education course can be provided with the opportunity to create a chat room or café or suggest a special topic for discussion, allowing them to correct misunderstandings and common misconceptions. For instance, after 9/11, a young Muslim student educated her fellow class participants about Islam and the Koran to clarify and correct erroneous cultural and religious beliefs held by other students in the class. Her response to angry stereotyping by some of her fellow students resulted in a respectful exchange of information about her faith among most students. Where a student was unable to get past his anger, the instructor stepped in to exchange personal e-mails and to remind the student of appropriate classroom behavior and the need for respectful discourse (Gilbert, personal communication, August 5, 2011).

For the most part, students are highly supportive of peers from other cultures. The excitement and curiosity about how things are done in other cultures can be palpable. Students are often anxious to ask questions, get clarification, and share their own responses to culturally different life experiences, norms, values, and rituals. This opportunity to look beyond stereotypes and to discuss the meaning making, rituals, and practices of other groups is often the richest result of the depth and detail of experience attained from online posts, group work, and discussion threads.

TRANSFORMATIVE LEARNING AND CULTURE ONLINE

Much of learning is emergent. Perspective transformation, meaning making, conscientization, and acceptance of alternative paradigms can occur through sudden insight or, more slowly, through a number of incremental transitions (Habermas, 1971). Transformative learning (Mezirow, 2003), requiring reflection on ideas and assumptions, experiences gained through prior learning, the questioning of personal assumptions, and the process of meaning-making, is something for which skilled instructors strive. It challenges the learner to let go of limiting perspectives, paradigms, and stereotypes—of that which they take for granted—and to examine his or her psychological assumptions. The goal of transformative learning is to create more open, critically reflective, discriminating observers; in this case, students.

The exposure of students to the critical reflections of their peers (as well as their instructor) produces a richness of meaning usually absent in the on-site classroom. Transformative learning requires that students feel safe and included in the group. If the case studies, video clips, web pages, and notes address only the point of view of the dominant culture, any deviation from this point of view exposes the student, making him or her feel vulnerable.

One of the most rewarding moments comes when students share flashes of insight online. In one case, a nursing student enrolled in a bereavement theory and interventions course revealed how her engagement with the course content brought her to understand, and subsequently forgive, her mother for the distance in their relationship that followed the death of her twin sister many years before. The young woman went on to describe how her new learning, self-awareness, and appreciation for the impact of death and grief on the individual and the family would likely change how she would interact with patients in her future professional practice.

LANGUAGE

Many of us who teach online thanatology courses find increasing numbers of students whose first language is not English. These students often struggle with language, as well as cultural differences, making the learning experience that much more challenging. Those contemplating online thanatology programs are not limited by their lack of ease or facility with the English language, however. Some students successfully use translation packages to assist them with longer posts or with online readings.

That said, students must be made to feel welcome. Gentle teasing or constant correction of their posts and discussions, even when well intentioned, may be annoying and disconcerting for participants. Absence of the nonlinguistic cues and clues common in face-to-face interactions may leave those in the online classroom at a loss, especially in matters of culture, diversity, and inclusivity. This is where compassion and patience must ensure that students are not judged or humiliated. Those students from outside of the dominant paradigm often add immeasurably to the learning experience of all students and instructors.

THE CONCEPT OF TIME ONLINE

Many new instructors of online courses are shocked to find out how much time is needed to set the stage; deliver course content; facilitate, mentor, and support the students; monitor discussions; and maintain safety. For instance, an off-handed comment by a student racing to post something by the weekly deadline can mean hours of damage control addressing hurt feelings or other reactions to the post, which, while perhaps not well thought out, was not meant to upset anyone.

Morse (2003) reminds us that the online environment is perceived as more informal than the traditional classroom. The online classroom allows for access 24/7. Some students expect the instructor to be perpetually online. Instructors need to set clear limits and model appropriate engagement so that students feel safe enough to create their own parameters for time spent online. Furthermore, given the nature of the course content, careful monitoring is required to guide discussions back from the brink of chat, gossip, titillation, therapy, or battles for position. Chatter, while potentially interesting, is not the goal of learning communities.

CYBERSELF: "I'M SO MUCH COOLER ONLINE" BRAD PAISLEY

In the online classroom, it is crucial to create safe places where all feel able to enter discussion (Atkinson & De Palma, 2008). They need to be assured of confidentiality; they must know that their posts will not be forwarded without their permission. Moreover, all students must understand that their posts can become a permanent record on someone else's computer. Members of the class may not all embrace limits or understand the need for them; therefore, it can be a challenge to set boundaries and enforce confidentiality. Students must receive periodic reminders about privacy, copyright, plagiarizing, and respectful communication

(Orvis & Lassiter, 2008). The needs of the group must be balanced with the needs of the individual at all times.

Continuous support is necessary for those asking questions and challenging existing assumptions in an online environment (Dzakiria, 2008; Magnan, 2008). Attempts at online humor often fall flat, or they are misconstrued as angry, antagonistic, or critical statements. The relative anonymity of the online classroom may result in an online social presence that does not conform to the boundaries of the day-to-day world. It can also create a sense of isolation.

Students who are active users of social networking on the Internet may find ongoing, and sometimes intense, online social interaction appealing. Asynchronous discussion boards, e-mail announcements, and streaming videos seed their sense of community and allow for a social presence (Drouin, 2008). Students accustomed to measuring themselves against their contemporaries may find their anxiety heightened as they learn more about their online colleagues than they would about their fellow classmates in the lecture hall. They may judge themselves to be lacking in depth of understanding or in their ability to make connections that other students seem to make readily. Students less comfortable with the online environment, or those who are in the beginning stages of their university educations or careers, may move into the shadows unless they are urged to remain engaged as fully valued participants.

How students experience themselves and others online is important (Aboujaoude, 2011). Sharing private experiences in public spaces may prove challenging to students who are internally negotiating lines between their personal and professional lives. Early and deep self-disclosure may be promoted in online death education, but it also raises concerns about privacy and personal safety, and, in rare cases, cyberbullying or cyberstalking.

BOUNDARIES AND BUNNY SLIPPERS

The online classroom lacks the formality associated with the university lecture hall, laboratory, or seminar room. Students often work on their online classes late at night in their pajamas and bunny slippers (or the equivalent) in the privacy of their own homes. For this reason, the guidelines for interacting with each other, with the material, and with the instructor, need to be transparent.

The traditional orientation in the first class session does not translate easily to materials online. Welcome posts, introductions, and "how to's" must be spelled out at the beginning and reinforced throughout the duration of the course (see Figure 13.1 for an example of how to do this).

Interactive communication, in contrast with the occasional question or comment in an onsite class, is a constant and integral part of distance learning. Discussion posts provide opportunities for higher level thinking: for the evaluation of alternative points of view that, when managed well, lead to extremely positive experiences for students and instructors alike. Although learning communities

Figure 13.1   Suggestion for syllabus statement regarding safety and conduct expectations

---

_____ is an academic university level course. While the course may contribute to the student's personal growth and development, grades will be assigned on the basis of academic achievement and mastery over the material covered. All participants are required to complete the course requirements to a high standard in order to receive credit. One's strong feelings or experiences will not substitute for effort and academic achievement. It is recommended that a student who is recently bereaved consider delaying taking _____. Please see the instructor privately if you have any questions or concerns at the outset.

There will be opportunities to present personal experiences and case examples to the class. We must respect each person's contribution of what may often be painful memories and the strong feelings they evoke (at the same time appropriate limits to self disclosure or to the time allotted to individuals will be upheld when personal narratives are shared) and agree to hold each other's contributions *strictly confidential*. For further clarification about online participation and posting guidelines please refer to the "Netiquette" notes on the front page of the course. The purpose of participation in university courses related to dying, death, grief and loss is to build a learning community and not to function as an online support group, or therapeutic community despite the fact that some students may wish to share personal loss experiences in their postings.

It should be acknowledged by all who join the class that the content may be difficult to discuss and challenging to examine. For some of the participants' painful memories, fears or concerns may be brought to the surface. In order to ensure that all students feel that their needs are being met there will be other supports put in place including a separate chat room, personal contact exchange opportunities, lists of supportive services at university/college, local, regional, national, and international levels, optional assignments and private correspondence and/or telephone contact with the instructor.

---

are not therapeutic communities, they can prove therapeutic through exposure to new information, group work, fresh realizations, shared experiences, and supportive dialogue.

CHARGED CONTENT

Images of death are commonplace in television and films, where they are viewed from a relatively comfortable psychic distance. This is not the case in the online classroom. Here, the shared narratives are real and potentially disturbing in ways that may surprise the students. Proximity to real pain and suffering in posts or work groups means that the instructor must be aware of the potential that students will need support. Learners enter the course with their personal history of loss, and their reactions to the course text, readings, and discussions may be dramatic.

Emotional reactions to past losses may bubble to the surface. Disclosure by others of their losses and tragedies overwhelm some students and make them feel unsafe. For some students, this may be more than they bargained for.

This is especially true for students who have suffered a recent death in their family and are very raw emotionally. They may encounter initial "silence" on the computer screen when they post about their intense feelings. They may also receive well-meaning condolences offered by students who are struggling with what to say, who then quickly move to another topic. Either way, the student who has disclosed a difficult or tragic experience and deeply felt emotion may feel abandoned.

Balk (2001) estimates that as many as one quarter to half of college-aged students have suffered a loss within the last 2 years. Instructors need to be exquisitely aware of the risks of engaging young vulnerable people in a course focused on loss while they are grieving, especially as they are in the presence of watchful peers. Prescreening students for losses within the previous year might reduce (or at least anticipate) difficult situations. However, many students (even with prescreening) will forge on ahead, believing that their recent losses are irrelevant to a university theory course.

Recently bereaved students may struggle with their own psychological and personal responses to the learning materials. In a recent course, one student could not move beyond several recent tragic losses. The student did not respond to questions from the weekly postings and was unable to engage with others in the class. Other students became uncomfortable and felt overly responsible for providing comfort and support to the student in question.

In subsequent weeks, two actions were taken to remedy this situation. First, the student was encouraged to use the course chat room for more in-depth and personal conversations. This way, students who felt overwhelmed by their colleague's intense pain were able to opt out of the discussions. Secondly, and simultaneously, the instructor maintained ongoing one-to-one contact and provided the student with resources in the local community in an attempt to provide gentle redirection and much needed support and guidance. This level of one-to-one involvement may well be relatively rare but shows how the safety of the student and the group may be thrust to the forefront of course management and maintenance.

WHEN LIFE/DEATH INTERVENES

For some students, death intrudes in their lives while they are enrolled in a death education course online. They may have enrolled in the course for personal growth or job requirements or as an elective or required course. Each of these motivations comes with differing sets of expectations and commitment levels. Regardless of the reason, students who experience a death during the course period may struggle with material that, up to that point, had not been emotionally charged.

No preventative measures will allow for unforeseen tragic losses in a student's life, no matter what the age of the student. Students who are faced with a death in their family or circle of friends must decide whether to continue the course. Many will need one-to-one support from the instructor and group contact from their online peers. Those in a thanatology-related course of study may remain in the class but opt out of the next class in the rotation of death education courses.

AGE

Older students who are not comfortable with technology may struggle with the requirements of an online course. Adult learners, especially those who have been out of school for a while, may experience feelings of uncertainty about interacting with others in cyberspace (Chatterjee & Moore, 2009). They may begin to feel incompetent despite having experiences to offer.

Keeping such students engaged and committed may require the patience and the support of the instructor, instructional technology services, and fellow students. In some cases, mature students with advanced work or life experience become very popular with other students as they share their personal narratives. An older student willing to share a wealth of experiences in ways that support learning can be a wonderful addition to the course.

GENDER

Thanatology courses appeal to students in social work, nursing, education, and the social sciences. As a result, many courses find themselves filled with female students. This may create discomfort for some male students, who are often reticent about discussing their feelings and experiences in depth with others. Male students may struggle with gender roles in their culture and with how these roles play out in the online classroom ethos. Being outnumbered by female students can benefit some males by allowing them to delve more deeply into the personal meanings of the readings and discussion posts than might be allowable with more male peers. The gender mix also allows female students the opportunity to engage with male colleagues in the relative confines and safety of the discussion threads, potentially deepening understanding across genders.

Women may feel more comfortable in dealing with the strong feelings that may surface in reaction to the readings, downloads, and other course materials. In some cultures, women are permitted to express their emotions more freely than men are. In one case, a male student taking a death education course when both his grandfather and an old high school acquaintance died reported having to find ways to shield himself from his roommates to complete the readings and posts because he would often become tearful and overwhelmed with sadness. Logging on to the site in the wee hours of the morning allowed him privacy.

HOW DISTANT IS TOO DISTANT IN DISTANCE EDUCATION?

Powering up your computer from the comfort of your office on campus makes it easy to forget that not all students will have similar access or technical support. Many students from rural or remote areas do not have high-speed access and so are unable to participate as fully as those who can download the full spectrum of course materials. Even being an hour outside of a metropolitan center can mean that students are contending with dial-up connections and high cost, or with timed access to high-speed internet service. Some students may have older computers with limited abilities to perform all the necessary tasks online. Although the linked-in articles may be available to these students, video clips, podcasts, or other more advanced social media and web 2.0 applications will not be. Some students may be able to access the course only through the terminals at their local library. They will be severely limited in their ability to participate in the course. Even in relatively wealthy nations, advanced computer and Internet capability are not available to everyone.

DIFFERING ABILITIES

Online courses may appeal to students with serious mobility handicaps, sight restrictions, learning disabilities, and health issues because they offer access to students who cannot readily attend classes on a campus. The online environment is thus enriched tremendously by these students who can share their unique stories and insights with others. Students with learning challenges may feel safer in the online classroom, where they can set their own pace and ask for help from the instructor anonymously (without raising their hands) and without disclosing their special needs to relative strangers.

Students with special needs should be encouraged to contact their instructors early if they wish to be accommodated in some reasonable way or if they require special assistance or have concerns about their ability to engage fully in the class.

The Americans with Disabilities Act, the Accessibility for Ontarians with Disabilities Act, and other state and national policies may provide important and useful guidelines for supporting students with special needs. They include concrete suggestions with regard to web page design, ways to facilitate braille and audio readers, use of varied ways to provide content, tips for arranging technical and online assistance, and other invaluable resources.

CONCLUSIONS

Success in the virtual classroom requires simultaneously delineating spheres of responsibility and acknowledging a certain degree of lack of control (O'Reilly,

1998). The best courses offer presence, trust, hospitality, listening, attention, nurturing, stories, and compassion, facilitated by good pedagogy, instructor empathy, authenticity, and humor.

Safety strategies, codes of conduct, mutual respect guidelines, active participation principles, and explicit responsibilities, all anchored to the course's front page, are essential for building spaces where students can actively construct new knowledge. Through careful attention to design, instructors can support students in safely bringing their current and past experiences to bear on the theory and content of the coursework, thus enhancing the experience for all those who seek transformative learning in the online environment.

REFERENCES

Aboujaoude, E. (2011). *Virtually you: The dangerous power of the E-personality.* New York, NY: W. W. Norton & Company.

Amhag, L., & Jakobsson, A. (2009). Collaborative learning as a collective competence when students use the potential of meaning in asynchronous dialogues. *Computers and Education,* 52(3), 656–667.

Ashburn, E., & Floden, R. (2006). *Meaningful learning using technology: What educators need to know and do?* New York, NY: Teachers College Press.

Atkinson, E., & DePalma, R. (2008). Dangerous spaces: Constructing and contesting sexual identities in an online discussion forum. *Gender and Education, 20*(2), 183–194.

Balk, D. E. (2001). College students, bereavement, scholarship, and the university: A call for university engagement. *Death Studies, 25,* 67–84.

Banner, J. M., & Cannon, H. C. (1997). *The elements of teaching.* New Haven, CT: Yale University Press.

Beaudoin, M. F., Kurtz, G., & Eden, S. (2009). Experiences and opinions of e-learners: What works, what are the challenges and what competencies ensure successful online learning. *Interdisciplinary Journal of E-Learning and Learning Objects, 5,* 275–289.

Bradley, J. (2010). Promoting and supporting authentic online conversations: Which comes first—The tools or the instructional design? *Online Pedagogy in Practice, 5*(3), 20–31.

Brindley, J. E., Walti, C., & Blaschke, L. M. (2009). Creating effective collaborative learning groups in an online environment. *International Review of Research in Open and Distance Learning, 10*(3), 1–18.

Brookfield, S. D. (1995). *Becoming a critically reflective teacher.* San Francisco, CA: Jossey-Bass.

Browne, A. J., Varcoe, C., Smye, V., Reimer-Kirkham, S., Lynam, J., & Wong, S. (2009). Cultural safety and the challenges of translating critically oriented knowledge in practice. *Nursing Philosophy, 10*(3), 169–179.

Chapman, C., Ramondt, L., & Smiley, G. (2005). Strong community, deep learning: Exploring the link. *Innovations in Education and Technology International, 47*(3), 217–230.

Chatterjee, M., & Moore, P. (2009, September 28–30). Issues of inclusivity for online distance learners: An academic learning support perspective. Educational integrity: Creating an inclusive approach. Presented 4th Asia Pacific Conference (4APCEI), University of Wollongong, NSW, Australia. Refereed paper 1–14.

Cimino, M. (2009). *Netiquette (online etiquette): Tips for adults and teens: Facebook, MySpace, Twitter! Terminology and more.* Baltimore, MD: Publish America.

Drouin, M. A. (2008). The relationship between students perceived sense of community and satisfaction, achievement and retention in an online course. *Quarterly Review of Distance Education, 9*(3), 267–276.

Dzakiria, H. (2008). Students' accounts of the need for continuous support in a distance learning programme. *Open Learning, 23*(2), 103–111.

Gulati, S. (2008). Compulsory participation in online discussion: Is this constructionist or normalization of learning? *Innovations in Education and Teaching International, 45*(2), 183–192.

Habermas, J. (1971). *Knowledge and human interests.* Boston, MA: Beacon Press.

Hannon, J., & Bretag, T. (2010). Negotiating contested discourses in learning technologies in higher education. *Educational Technology and Society, 13*(1), 106–120.

Harris-John, M. (2006, December 6). Creating meaningful online discussions. National Council of the Professors of Educational Administration (NCPEA). *Connexions.* Retrieved from the Connexions Web site at http://cnx.org/content/m14135/1.1/

Hofstede, G. (2005). *Cultures and organizations: Software of the mind.* New York, NY: McGraw-Hill.

Hull, D. M., & Saxon, T. F. (2009). Negotiations of meaning and co-construction of knowledge: An experimental analysis of asynchronous instruction. *Computers and Education, 52*(3), 624–639.

Hunt, L. M. (2001). Beyond Cultural competence: Applying humility to clinical settings. *The Park Ridge Center for Health, Faith and Ethics Bulletin, 24*(Dec), 1–20.

Inoue, Y. (2007). *Technology and diversity in higher education.* Hershey, PA: Information Science Publishing.

Livesay, R. C., & Palmer, P. J. (1999). *The courage to teach: A guide for reflection and renewal.* San Francisco, CA: Jossey-Bass.

Lynch, M. M. (2004). *Learning online: A guide to success in the virtual classroom.* New York, NY: Routledge Falmer.

Magnan, S. S. (Ed.). (2008). *Mediating discourses online.* Amsterdam, the Netherlands: John Benjamins Publishing.

Mezirow, J. (2003). *Learning as transformation: Critical perspectives on a theory in progress.* San Francisco, CA: Jossey-Bass.

Moore, M. (Ed.). (2007). *Handbook of distance education* (2nd ed.). Mahwah, NJ: Lawrence Erlbaum Associates.

Morse, K. (2003). Does one size fit all? Exploring asynchronous learning in a multicultural environment. *Journal of Asynchronous Learning Networks, 7*(1), 37–55.

Nagel, G. (1998). *The Tao of teaching: The ageless wisdom of Taoism and the art of teaching.* New York, NY: Plume/Penguin.

O'Reilly, M. R. (1998). *Radical presence: Teaching as contemplative practice.* Portsmouth, NH: Boynton/Cook Heinemann.

Orvis, K. L., & Lassiter, A. L. R. (Eds.). (2008). *Computer-supported collaborative learning: Best practices and principles for instructors.* London, England: Information Science Publishing.

Palloff, R. M., & Pratt, K. (2005). *Collaborating online: Learning together in a community.* San Francisco, CA: Jossey-Bass.

Palloff, R. M., & Pratt, K. (2007). *Building online learning communities: Effective strategies for the virtual classroom* (2nd ed.). San Francisco, CA: Jossey-Bass.

Palmer, P. J. (1993). *To know as we are known: Education as a spiritual journey.* San Francisco, CA: Jossey-Bass.

Palmer, S., & Holt, D. (2009, March 5). Students' perceptions of the value of the elements of an online learning environment: Looking back and moving forward. *Interactive Learning Environments, 18*, 135–151.

Rovai, A. P. (2001). Building classroom community at a distance: A case study. *Educational Technology Research and Development, 49*(4), 33–48.

Stanford-Bowers, D. E. (2008). Persistence in online classes: A study of perceptions among community college stakeholders. *Merlot Journal of Online Learning and Teaching, 4*(1), 1–10.

Stepich, D. A., & Ertmer, P. A. (2003). Building community as a critical element of online course design. *Educational Technology, 43*(5), 33–45.

Uzuner, S. (2009). Questions of culture in distance learning: A research review *International Review of Research in Open and Distance Learning, 10*(3), 1–19.

14

Research in Thanatechnology

Illene Noppe Cupit

INTRODUCTION

It is impossible to deny the profound impact that communication technology has had on all dimensions of human endeavor. It is difficult to even consider a world in which e-mail, the Internet, and social networking sites did not exist. What has made such change even more significant is the universal applications of such technologies that have linked people across the globe, as well as the incredibly rapid changes in which technological advances have taken place.

Research has also been profoundly affected by the "revolution" in communication technology. From their desktop or telephones, social science researchers now share data files with colleagues in institutions thousands of miles away and jointly write in the same document either synchronously or asynchronously. Perhaps most importantly, researchers now can be in contact with large numbers of individuals who may or may not be invited to participate in an empirical investigation.

Researchers in thanatology have become increasingly enamored with information technology. Not only has use of communication technology served as a useful tool for conducting research, but it has also been necessary for thanatological researchers who are interested in tracking current movements in the field to be apprised of how technology has influenced coping, thinking, and relating to issues of death and dying.

Thanatological research has characteristics in common with most social science research that is based on communication technology. For example, issues of sampling, methodology, data analysis, survey design, and research ethics are some of the areas of the new "Internet Social Science Research" that must be addressed by all relevant disciplines. However, there are also methodological concerns specific to thanatology. Beginning with what we currently and broadly know about doing Internet-based social science research and narrowing it down to the specific issues of research in thanatology will be the major focus of this chapter. Because thanatological research is anchored in the methodologies and principles of social science research, what has been learned in general about studying *computer-mediated communication* (CMC), as it is called by Joinson and Paine (2007), is instructive to researchers studying death and dying. The issues faced by thanatologists, however, including the recruitment and representativeness of dying or grieving participants, ethical concerns specific to working with potentially at risk participants, research design appropriate to the field of death and dying, and self-disclosure regarding sensitive topics have their unique stamp when dealing with thanatological content. The intent of this chapter, then, is to explore the terrain and provide a roadmap to this exciting way of studying dying, death, and bereavement.

INTERNET SOCIAL SCIENCE RESEARCH

A number of publications have attempted to transpose social science methodology into a computer-driven virtual environment. Much of this work concerns the Internet, although technology using handheld data collection devices (such as computers to record observational data and surveys loaded onto smart phones) may become increasingly popular ways of conducting such research. Computer-mediated communication can be used for laboratory-type psychology experiments, collecting survey data, or qualitative research. For example, Birnbaum (2004) and Reips (2007) address how psychological experiments may be conducted on the World Wide Web. The differences and similarities between the experimental method via the Internet and real time-real laboratory work are detailed. Many social scientists are keen on using the Internet for empirical psychological studies because recruiting large diverse samples, standardizing procedures, and collecting data are easy to do with the potential for rapid turnaround times (Birnbaum, 2004). Access to groups of people other than the ubiquitous college sophomore in an Introduction to Psychology class enables greater generalizability of research findings. The cost of research may also be greatly reduced because sophisticated and expensive equipment, travel expenses, and employee time can be eliminated. Reips (2007) also notes that such Internet-based methods may make it easier for individuals to participate in the study; because the study is brought directly to them, their participation truly may be voluntary (unless, of course, they are that ubiquitous college sophomore), and there are fewer time constraints. In addition, the minimal presence of the examiner reduces their potential influence on the participants (experimenter effects), and the entire research process is more transparent. This in particular may enhance the ethical nature of such research. Birnbaum (2004) suggests that comparisons between Internet findings and laboratory findings indicate similar conclusions, although there may be differences because of the distinctions between Internet-based and non-Internet-based participants. It is no wonder that many social scientists (including thanatologists) applaud such research.

However, there certainly are concerns that must be addressed. From the standpoint of the researcher, it is imperative that adequate training be obtained in technological research methods (Reips, 2007). The training should address, for example, how to communicate with participants, especially when the only contact is digitized (Reips, 2007). The rapid transformation and updating of software and hardware for data collection and analysis can create havoc in a researcher's life and should be considered in the planning stages of the project. Longitudinal research in particular may suffer from technology, as it often appears to be out-moded the moment it becomes available for use. From the standpoint of the par-ticipants, there also are a number of concerns: The requirement that participants have the requisite programs, computers, and computer savvy, and the assurance of confidentiality and security of the data, are of utmost importance. Using e-mail, for example, as a method of collecting survey information, would make it easy to track down the respondent. In addition, the participants at the monitor typically are better educated, older, more likely to follow directions, and more highly motivated to participate in the study than those recruited for a labora-tory experiment (Birnbaum, 2004). And what about participant behavior? Does it change, for example, because of the technology (Reips, 2007)? Only studies that can compare online participation to more traditional methods can answer this question. Even if there is evidence, the researcher must proceed with cau-tion if the phenomena he or she wishes to study has not been supported by such comparative research.

Despite the potential for greater interest in participation, Internet-based so-cial scientists also must be vigilant about multiple submissions and selective drop-out (Reips, 2007). Another great concern involves the issue of self-disclosure. Making the self known to other people is a perennial problem in social science research, but research specific to this topic suggests that individuals are very will-ing to honestly present themselves on the Internet (Joinson & Paine, 2007). This may be particularly the case in studies using surveys, as responses to very per-sonal and sensitive information may be more truthful when they are delivered to a respondent's monitor and not through face-to-face contact with an interviewer (Joinson & Paine, 2007). However, some forms of inquiry, such as using e-mail for surveys, do not assure participants of their anonymity. Even when anonymity is assured, media reports of hacking into e-mail and supposedly secure databases have made many users of technology nervous about protecting their identities. Such fears, as well as fear for one's safety and the safety of loved ones, promote outright deception when demographic information is sought (Green, 2007). The lack of face-to-face contact between the researcher and respondent renders such deception very difficult to detect. Finally, the migration of CMC from comput-ers to mobile phones has led to severely truncated messages, which may limit the amount of information available to the researcher. Despite such concerns, psychology research that compared online with paper-and-pencil methods has found the differences between the two approaches to be negligible—a finding corroborated by Tolstikova and Chartier (2009/2010), who compared the results of responses to an online version of the Core Bereavement Inventory with those of the paper-and-pencil survey.

CONDUCTING THANATECHNOLOGICAL RESEARCH

Thanatology research over the past 50 years has amassed an impressive array of findings that have led to an interdisciplinary knowledge base that is important, interesting, and necessary (see Balk, 2007). On a pragmatic level, this research in thanatology has led to the understanding that bridging research and clinical practice is necessary for the effective treatment and assessment of those suffering from dying, death, and bereavement.

Most of the empirical work in thanatology rests within the traditions of social science research methodology. Out of this backdrop comes the expediency and excitement generated by the potentials of the Internet for conducting research to learn about death and dying. What methodological concerns specific to thanatology need to be considered in examining dying, death, and bereavement in this way? The following section will address these issues and then provide several examples of CMC thanatological research that illustrate the specific ways in which technology can be used to further understand dying, death, and loss.

METHODOLOGICAL CONCERNS FOR THANATECHNOLOGICAL RESEARCH

Research in thanatechnology can use several different methodological strategies. The first involves the actual use of technology to facilitate the research process. Collecting information via online surveys may be an example of this methodology. Another direction may involve examining how those facing life-threatening situations (caregivers and/or patients) or those who are bereft use technology to cope. Analyzing social networks and blogs exemplifies this approach. How this is done, given the sensitive issues raised above in conducting thanatological research, typically involves much creativity on the researcher's part. Throughout the process of studying death and dying using CMCs, the researcher faces a number of decision points that will affect the way in which the research is conducted. Keeping in mind that some research principles that have been the mainstay of more "traditional" research also apply to thanatological research, these decision points, as illustrated in Figure 14.1 (concerning research questions and types of analysis) and Figure 14.2 (examples of types of thanatechnological research and research ethics), will help to conceptualize and illustrate the issues that are specific to thanatechnological research. It also is important to note that this decision process is of value not only to researchers but also to consumers of research, such as practicing clinicians and educators, who will need to use research findings if they wish to follow an evidence-based practice model. Knowing if the research

Figure 14.1   Thanatechnological research: Methodological decision points

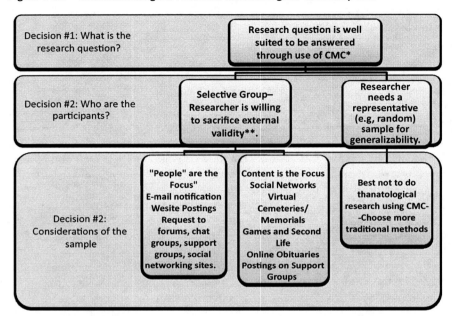

*CMC= Computer Mediated Communication.
**External validity= Leads to the ability to generalize to a broader group of people.

is appropriately designed and interpreted is becoming increasingly more important in many fields, from medicine to psychotherapy. It may be especially vital to thanatology, a field often viewed as being out of the mainstream of more traditional fields of study.

Decision Point 1: What is the Research Question?

As noted in Figure 14.1, what the thanatologist wishes to study should direct the methodology of the study. Some research (e.g., the content of Facebook tributes to deceased friends) can only be studied via the Internet. Some questions may be easier to answer in more traditional formats as seen in a recent study looked at the narrative themes expressed during meetings of a support group for bereaved parents (Umphrey & Cacciatore, 2011). However, many thanatology-oriented research questions (e.g., attitudes toward therapeutic intervention for the bereaved) may lend themselves to either traditional or online approaches. When the research question can be studied using either approach, it may be helpful to move to Decision 2 (Figure 14.1) in planning the research to determine whether to use a computer-mediated option or a traditional format.

Figure 14.2   Thanatechnological research: Decision points for quantitative and qualitative analyses

What Types of Analyses Best Answers the Research Question?		
Quantitative Analysis ⬇	Qualitative Analysis ⬇	Mixed Models/Mixed Methods ⬇
Examples:	Examples:	Examples:

• Questionnaires
• Rating Scales
• Demographic
  Surveys
• Word Counts
  Number of Postings
• Numbers in
  Categories ⬇
	• Content Analysis
	• Ethnography
	• Grounded Theory
	• Narrative Analysis
	• Discourse (spoken
	  language) Analysis
	• Life Story Research
	• Focus Groups ⬇
		• Includes both quantitative
		  and qualitative methods
		• Rating scales plus open-
		  ended questions
		• E-mail linked surveys with
		  interactive forums. ⬇

Ethical Concerns:

• Anonymity and Identification of Respondents

• Deception

• Informed Consent

• Permission to contact members of Social Networking Groups

• Test Security/Security of Data Sets

• Debriefing

• Maintaining trust and confidentiality, especially if researcher is participant in group

Decision Point 2: Who are the Participants and What are the Sample Considerations?

If the potential study is dependent upon the involvement of human participants, their characteristics need to be considered before determining if the study lends itself to a technological format. Using online surveys, questionnaires, and interviews for understanding death and dying is an expedient way to obtain large numbers of cases from a potentially global participant pool. Multiple submissions may be curtailed by how these assessment tools are set up. However, the sample may be limited by who is using the Internet. Sending an e-mail to college students or university personnel is relatively easier than accessing a large number of elderly persons. Thus, studying widowhood or the experience of facing the end of life with a chronic degenerative disease with our current cohorts will yield information from a small group of younger participants and a highly selective group of older individuals. Research conducted in the future may not have to deal with our contemporary generational digital divide. For now, these participants most likely will be non-Hispanic Whites with relatively high incomes (see the Pew Research Center's reports on the Internet and American life Project, 2010). Where the survey is posted or to whom an e-mail request is sent also affects the outcome of the study. Birnbaum (2004) reminds us that requesting participation in a study via e-mail may be treated as "spam." Worse yet is the possibility that caregivers who see the request would consider such a survey in poor taste or damaging to the morale of the participant. Grieving survivors who have access to e-mail accounts of their deceased loved ones might become distraught if they find requests for participation in research about the end of life sent to the person who has died. Of course, gaffes such as these can occur in nontechnological research as well, but the anonymity of cyberspace makes it difficult to assess the psychological impact of these potentially harmful communications. Social networking sites serves as a potentially rich source for research participants and data. Members of these sites not only use them to report on the quality of their daily latte, but they also have turned to their networks, in the face of death, to inform others, for online communal support, and to contribute to online memorials. Chapters 3, 5, 6, 9, and discuss such uses and their implications in greater detail. The research opportunities linked with these social networking sites are potentially immense, as they can be used to recruit participants and to query the bereaved or dying as to how they use social networking as a source of social support and information or a place for memorialization. The postings themselves often become the actual data.

Linking a survey or questionnaire to such social networking sites or websites might be one way to expand the demography of the participant pool, but the researcher must always keep in mind that this may be an at-risk population. Therefore, the researcher must be wary about how his or her intent and words regarding death, dying, and bereavement will be interpreted by individuals with diverse and different cultural worldviews, who might take offense, not understand, or respond in a manner that may be misinterpreted by the researcher as well.

Having access to a large pool of respondents who may be accessed anytime and anywhere is a seductive lure for any researcher, but perhaps even more so for the thanatological investigator who frequently has a limited group with whom to work. Given the current "digital divide," there may be a willingness to sacrifice the ability to generalize to a broader population, as generalizability is best served by an experimental approach wherein people are randomly assigned to experimental or control groups or randomly selected from a larger group.

For the present, therefore, thanatological online surveys will predominantly be geared to adolescents (parental permission required), college students, and younger adults.

Gaining permission to link a survey or questionnaire to a particular social networking group or website may also be a delicate matter, particularly for those that are designed for the grieving. Thanatologists are keenly aware that they must present a highly professional stance (Wogrin, 2007), and they may be wary to link surveys to their websites. Finally, there may be an inherent bias in terms of the characteristics of those who are drawn to particular websites associated with dying, death, and grief. As for many studies reliant upon an Internet-based population, it is hard to differentiate between the information gatherers, the support seekers, and those with "morbid" curiosity. In addition, ethical decision making is paramount for working with potentially at-risk populations (see Figure 14.2). The ethics of such research are uncharted as well. For example, does the researcher have an ethical obligation to follow up (if this is possible) on a respondent whose answers suggest suicidal intent?

Decision Point 3: What Types of Analyses Best Answer the Research Question?

Quantitative methodology and analysis: Many areas of research in thanatology lend themselves to quantitative analyses often using descriptive and inferential statistics to analyze the data. Examination of aspects of dying, death, and bereavement that can be accessed via Internet surveys, attitude scales, word counts, and hits on Internet sites would lend themselves to quantitative approaches. The thanatechnological researcher needs to pay special attention to specific problems that may arise from using the CMC format considering the "touchy" nature of the topic being studied. Clarity of instructions and ease of use for a computer can make all the difference in participant cooperation and enhance the reliability and validity of the responses. Unlike surveys and scales that are administered over the telephone or face to face, there is little opportunity to check to see if the respondent understands how to answer using radio buttons, text only boxes, and submission bars. In addition, how questions and choices are worded can make it difficult to avoid socially desirable responses. This may be particularly true for affect-laden words—*dying, death, cancer, suicide,* and/or *funeral*. Although the faceless examiner may be a blessing for soliciting honest responses about such content, their sincerity and genuine interest in the participant might not be seen in an online survey. Depending upon the characteristics of the sample, there may be an even greater paranoia to give the socially "correct" response as opposed to a true and honest opinion. Other risks might include a failure to respond, typos or unintelligible responses, angry responses, fabricated answers, and/or incomplete surveys. Internet surveys and questionnaires on death and dying might be particularly prone to missing data, and there is only so much interpolation that can be handled by inferential statistics. As more and more people become comfortable filling out online surveys and as the technology gets increasingly user-friendly, such problems may diminish, and the added benefits of accessing a wider pool of participants may outweigh the disadvantages.

Examples of Thanatechnological Research Using Quantitative Analyses

A study by Stroebe, Stroebe, Schut, Stroebe, and van den Bout (2009) that examined the outcomes of online mutual support for grief exemplifies the value of a quantitative approach. In this investigation, three measurement points were taken for participants in an intervention for bereavement that involved e-mail-based writing. Recruitment of the participants occurred through websites, forums, and e-mail groups focused on bereavement with the restrictions that they were older than 18 years of age, spoke English, had experienced the loss of a significant other, and were notably upset about the death (Stroebe et al., 2009). Participants were then randomly assigned to treatment and controlled conditions and received questionnaires at three points during a 6-month period. The questionnaires queried about demographics and about the death, measured grief reactions, depression, positive and negative mood, physical health, coping behaviors, social support, engagement in online mutual support groups, and involvement in religious communities. A number of valuable findings emerged from this research. In particular, Stroebe et al. (2009) found that those who completed all the surveys were older and more educated than the 13% (a reasonable selective dropout rate) who did not complete all measures, were younger than those who did not use online support groups, were more likely to have lost a child, and less likely to be involved with a religious community. They seemed to spend a good deal of time on the Internet. In addition, one of the main findings of this study was that using the online mutual support group was not predictive of mental health changes over the duration of the study, and a number of reasons for this finding are insightfully offered by the authors. Of particular relevance to the issue of Decision 2 ("Who are the participants?"; see Figure 14.1), the authors indicated that their participants were very savvy about their use of the Internet and thus were a selective, nonrepresentative group (see Figure 14.1), something that the authors acknowledge is typical of bereavement research. An additional challenge involved standardizing demographic information across different countries (e.g., there was no way to categorize place of residence for participants of different nationalities). However, this research is significant for its rigorous quantitative analyses, the care and ethics involved in participant recruitment, the longitudinal design, and the desire to subject the results of online mutual support groups to a rigorous empirical test.

Another important illustration of such research comes from a study by Dominick et al. (2009), which was an evaluation of an Internet self-help tool (*Making Sense of Grief*) to educate and support bereaved individuals who have suffered a loss in the prior 6 months. Although there was a qualitative component, this study primarily was a quantitative experimental study. In comparison to the control group, the researchers found that as a result of the intervention, there was a significant change toward more positive attitudes and knowledge gained about grief, an increase in feelings of self-efficacy, and modifications in anxiety.

Qualitative Methodologies and Analysis

The use of qualitative methods to learn about social and psychological phenomena has gained increasing acceptance over the past two decades. This is particularly the case in thanatology, where using a phenomenological lens to uncover the underpinnings of experience associated with dying, death, and bereavement has occupied an important position in the literature (Carverhill, 2007). Central to these approaches is the search for how individuals construct meaning in the face of death (Neimeyer, 2001). It is not surprising, therefore, that thanatological CMCs would have a natural affinity for such analyses, given the verbal, interactive, and content-rich pool of data.

There actually are a number of methodologies associated with qualitative research that stem from several disciplines, including psychology, human development, nursing, communication processes, anthropology, history, and sociology. The thanatological researcher who is interested in the experiences of death and loss from a descriptive, participant observer perspective and who is willing to bend on the rigors of psychometric measurement, external validity, and inferential statistics would find such qualitative methods appealing. Qualitative researchers argue in favor of multiple-constructed realities as opposed to logical positivism and profess that "data" should be viewed within the context from which it emerges (Johnson & Onwuegbuzie, 2004). Qualitative research does not necessarily imply that numbers are eliminated. For example, researchers may extract themes from verbal content and look at their frequencies within certain demographic features. Most likely, the statistics that are used in such cases would be more descriptive in nature. These methods use the analysis of verbal content as in narrative analysis, storytelling, content analysis, and themes emerging from ethnography and discourse (see Figure 14.2). By not imposing theoretical constructs and specific research hypotheses beforehand, researchers who use qualitative methods ideally are allowing the data of the participants to "speak for themselves."

There is a blossoming array of literature that has benefitted from qualitative analysis and the interdisciplinary focus that it has afforded, and the many forms of technological content that lend themselves to qualitative analysis have been richly heuristic. Because qualitative analysis centers on subjective content, some empirical researchers believe that this approach may be lax in methodological rigor. Thus, having multiple eyes and perspectives, cross-validating the researchers' interpretation of the content, and replicating findings in additional studies—perhaps using different methodological approaches—are imperative to knowledge accumulation in thanatology.

Examples of Thanatechnological Research Using Qualitative Analysis

Because there so many different forms of qualitative methodologies that lend themselves to thanatechonological research, two examples are provided to clarify the decision to use qualitative methods and to illustrate how this is done. One such example uses social networking sites, recognized as providing rich data sources for qualitative analyses of the grief experience as it is expressed in digitized format. Sanderson and Cheong (2010) investigated how postings on Facebook and TMZ.com, and tweets on Twitter were used to communicate and receive social support when pop singer Michael Jackson died in 2009. The authors mention that it was challenging to decide which of the large number of websites, blogs, and social networking sites to use for their study. This was compounded by the dizzying number of postings and comments that they could analyze. Although such verbiage is considered to be part of the public domain, Sanderson and Cheong (2010) were careful not to use information that could help to identify its author. Classification of the postings and tweets, each treated as a unit of analysis, was done on a weekly basis. Using the constant comparative methodology of Glaser and Strauss (1967), thematic categories were derived from line-by-line analyses, and then relationships among these categories were established. By looking at the content of over 1,000 messages, Sanderson and Cheong learned that these sites provided a place for fans to express their grief. The authors' thematic analysis suggested that these communications also helped the grieving fans of Michael Jackson by allowing them to share their feelings within a sympathetic digital community.

Hollander (2001) was a participant observer of e-mail based support groups composed of survivors of suicide. Inviting some of the support group survivors to submit their stories via e-mails and cybermessage boards, Hollander immersed herself in the verbal content by using a textual analysis. Some of her many observations were that the messages indicated a social reconstruction of the self as the survivor of the suicide moved through the grief experience, a sense of social isolation, and recognition of the importance of the connection to others in the community of the bereaved.

The Mixed Methods Approach And Analyses

According to Johnson and Onwuegbuzie (2004), mixed methods research is the ". . . class of research where the researcher mixes or combines quantitative and qualitative research techniques, methods, approaches, concepts or language into a single study" (p. 17).

Johnson and Onwuegbuzie (2004) argue that the multiple approaches inherent to mixed methods research lead to a more creative and expansive way of examining social science phenomena and often better suit the overriding research question (see Figure 14.1). Combining the quantitative and qualitative strategies in research on thanatechnology permits both inductive and deductive analyses ranging from an emphasis on one paradigm over the other to a fully mixed study, and from using both approaches throughout the stages of the research process (mixed-models) to including sequential quantitative and qualitative phases (mixed methods). The advantages of using the mixed models or mixed-methods approaches is that they reap the benefits of both qualitative and quantitative methods because the researcher can select the methods that best suit the research questions rather than be constrained by the methodological rules of a singular paradigm (Johnson & Onwuegbuzie, 2004). As such, mixed models and methods designs require that quantitative and qualitative methodologies are considered from the initial planning stages to the writing up of the results and not as "add ons" to be used in post hoc analyses (Carverhill, 2002). As exemplified below, this pragmatic approach may be particularly useful in the newly emerging research questions affiliated with thanatechnology.

Examples of Thanatechnological Research Using Mixed Method Analyses

Swartwood, Veach, Kuhne, Lee, and Ji (2011) analyzed the written messages posted on three unrelated grief forum websites. These criteria that were used in the selection of the websites were as follows: (a) they were public places where discussions about grief-related issues could appear in weblogs; (b) the websites had at least four "types of deaths" (i.e., loss of a spouse/partner, loss of a sibling, loss of a parent, and loss of a child) under discussion; and (c) grief therapists were not involved in the management of the content. First responses to an original message were analyzed in terms of the length of each message, readability of message content, types of messages (e.g., self-disclosure, influence, self-involving, and advice), and the emergent themes that were determined upon analysis of the content of the messages . Thus, both the structural characteristics of the posts (the *quantitative* aspect) and the emerging themes (the *qualitative* aspect) were examined. Some of the findings from the Swartwood et al. (2011) research were that self-disclosure (i.e., responders telling the original messenger about themselves) were most prevalent, with the central themes of exchanging hope and validating the grief experience seen in the content of the posts.

A second example is seen in a study by Odom et al. (2010). Using survey and interview techniques, these researchers interviewed 11 bereaved individuals to learn, in part, how they used digital means to maintain social interactions with their deceased loved one. The researchers, who recruited their participants in part, through advertisements in online grief forums and bereavement e-mail lists, found that in addition to the bereaved inheriting "tools of rememberance" in the form of physical objects such as diaries and artwork, there also were digital inheritances, such as photos, blogs, or personal narratives. Other interesting findings were in regard to interviewees' opinions about online funerals and the tensions of digitized inheritances. Similarly, Massimi and Baecker (2010), using a web-based survey and semistructured interview, learned that bereaved individuals shared photos on social networking sites, eulogized the deceased on memorial websites, and engaged in reminiscence with relatives via e-mails. For Massimi and Baeker's (2010) research, social networking sites such as Craigslist was one of the ways in which potential participants were found.

Finally, Cupit, Servaty-Seib, Parikh, Walker, and Martin (under review), using a mixed-methods research, studied the incidence of college student bereavement over a 24-month period and the ways in which such students negotiate the demands, expectations, and social interactions on a campus as they proceed with their grief. Complete data were collected from 837 students at two universities, a "regional comprehensive" university and a Research 1 institution using an on-line survey (SurveyMonkey) that was linked to an e-mail sent to the students. This mixed-method study, using both survey data and thematic analyses of open-ended questions, revealed that a sizable number of college students (almost 48%) experienced a significant loss within a 24-month period and that their college experience was affected in terms of their academic motivation and priorities, school-based social experiences, and interactions with professors.

ETHICAL CONCERNS IN THANATECHNOLOGICAL RESEARCH

Conducting social science research is inherently challenging, but investigating phenomena about dying, death, and bereavement in death-phobic and hetero-geneous populations, such as those found in the United States, has its unique pitfalls and concerns. Because of the sensitive nature of the content, institutional review boards examine proposals with the fear that the research will cause un-due psychological or emotional harm. Getting informed consent, particularly if the research involves minors, can be difficult. Wording surveys, questionnaires, and interviews so as to not be offensive is a concern, as is leading participants into socially desirable responses. Cautious about being perceived as "ambulance chasers," thanatological researchers also must determine the appropriate timing for approaching potential participants. Deciding whether some research ques-tions are beyond the pale, such as when studying survivors of traumatic events (suicide, homicide, disasters of all types), also befalls the thanatologist.

Concerns specific to the use of e-mail need to be heeded, especially when the content of these e-mails involves matters of death. Frankel and Siang (1999) underscore the vulnerability of e-mail messages to be routed to the wrong ad-dress, sent to computers that are not secure, opened by an unintended audi-ence because of the "reply to all" function, or being mistakenly sent to an entire listserve. It is incumbent upon the researcher to make the research participants aware of these risks—harmonious family relationships might be at stake!

Knobel (2003) notes that the distinction between public and private space is significant to thanatology research conducted online. He notes that a researcher should carefully consider participating in the online community prior to the start of research about that community because it is the responsibility of the re-searcher to determine the public versus private nature of the space. Spaces that are password protected should be viewed as private, and archivable discussions are generally presumed to be public spaces. Thus, the greater the acknowledged public nature of the venue, the less obligation there may be to protect the privacy, confidentiality, and right to informed consent of the individual (Ess et al., 2002).

Tolstikova and Chartier (2009–2010) point out that it may be easier to main-tain the privacy of Internet respondents because of the lack of physical contact. Although web-based communications that are publicly open are considered to be a part of the public domain, it might also be considered a breach of confidential-ity to use such data without contacting the participants (Tolstikova & Chartier).

In addition, given how easy it is to falsify personal information, researchers may be surveying minors without knowing their true age or receiving parental consent. Research ethics dictates that vulnerable populations should have access to follow-up treatment. Although such information may be provided, the ability for a researcher to truly know the psychological or social impact of the research may be compromised by the lack of actual interaction.

Some of the methods used in thanatechnological research require that researchers take extra steps to protect the anonymity of their participants. This is especially true when e-mails are used, when there is an incentive (e.g., money or a prize) to participate that requires recording personal information, when pictures or videos posted on sites such as YouTube are a part of the study, and when tests or data obtained from online surveys, telephone applications, or text messages must be securely stored. Simply hitting delete buttons does not necessarily wipe out data, and researchers need to use password-protected storage devices. Collaborative research, in which data are shared among multiple researchers who span the globe, entails taking extra precautions. Although the Internet certainly has facilitated international collaboration, researchers may find that they have to consider the institutional review board or ethical requirements of a foreign university, language and translation issues, differences in customs in the use of CMCs, and further selection biases inherent in the digital divide in countries outside of the Northwestern hemisphere. Finally, participants in online public spaces may not be aware that their postings can be the subject matter of researchers, and resulting publications may perpetuate breaches in confidentiality. There also may not be an easy way to debrief participants in a virtual community, a practice that most likely is of utmost importance in thanatological research (Frankel & Siang, 1999). Certainly, participants usually are not aware that researchers may be part of the audience (Moreno et al, 2008). Guidance is available regarding research ethics that involve issues of perceived "intrusion," "lurking," and disclosure of one's presence as an observer (Knobel, 2003; Leandor & McKim, 2003; Moreno et al., 2008). Perhaps the best advice comes from Knobel's three maxims: (a) be informed, (b) be honest and open, and (c) be prepared to invest in online communities. Failure to honor these maxims can result in "smash and grab" research that has the potential to alienate participants and make them wary of involvement in future studies (Knobel, 2003).

CONCLUSIONS

Revisiting Figures 14.1 and 14.2 makes it apparent that there are many decisions that must be made in the planning of thanatechnological research. In particular, it is imperative that the thanatological research question determines whether the study should involve CMCs, that the researcher consider the costs/benefits of working with online samples, and that the researcher determine a priori the best type of analyses to adequately answer the research question(s). In addition, thanatological researchers need to be aware of the expense of such research, the difficulties involved in securing funding for such "out of the mainstream" types of investigations, and whether such research would be appealing for publication by journal editors.

Because this is such a new way of investigating issues related to dying, death, and bereavement and especially because of the rapid growth and transformation of the technology, such decisions must be adaptive and flexible. For example, several years ago, Noppe, Noppe, and Servaty-Seib (2008) attempted to assess continuing bonds and adolescent bereavement using the digital device of Palm Pilots. In 2011, this outmoded technology would not be as appealing to adolescents as using text messages and smart phone applications. It is difficult to do replication studies when technology from 3 years ago is viewed as antiquated.

Despite the speed with which technology evolves and the ethical concerns associated with thanatechnological research, researchers have much to gain. Examining death and dying through the lens of technology is rich and creative. The possibilities range from participant recruitment, to the content of social networking sites, to the evaluation of online support groups, to the death-related content of gaming, to blogs and virtual cemeteries. Thanatologists would be remiss to ignore the ways in which people, throughout the world, are using technology to negotiate dying, death, and bereavement.

Similarly, practitioners need to avail themselves of these research findings to make informed decisions about best-practice methods. Evaluation of online therapeutic interventions (see Chapter 8) is paramount, as these forms of support and care are becoming increasingly prevalent. Documenting what aspects of intervention are appropriate and perhaps even better in a computer-mediated environment, and for whom this would be true is essential because the value of grief therapy has recently been criticized (Balk, 2011). Mental health practitioners frequently are overwhelmed by the demands of their practice to make a regular habit of reading journal articles, so it would be important that the latest research findings of relevant thanatechnology research (including their unique methodological considerations) be available through webinars, workshops, and conferences that offer continuing education credit. Included in these continuing educational experiences should be a thorough discussion of the nature of research in thanatechnology and some of the significant decisions researchers need to make for their investigations and their associated ethical concerns.

In the end, it is the user of technology who is the central figure moving through the multiple terrains of online issues related to dying, death, and bereavement. It is a new world "out there," but the questions about death, the contextually defined meanings connecting the living, the dying, and the dead, are rooted in our past and are a bridge to our future, leading to an exciting arena of possibilities for research.

REFERENCES

Balk, D. (Ed.). (2007). *Handbook of thanatology. The essential body of knowledge for the study of death, dying, and bereavement.* New York, NY: Routledge.

Balk, D. (2011). Ruth Konigsberg's demythologizing project. A review of "The Truth About Grief: The Myth of Its Five Stages and the new Science of Loss." *Death Studies 35*, 673–678.

Birnbaum, M. H. (2004). Human research and data collection via the Internet. *Annual Review of Psychology, 55*, 803–832.

Carverhill, P. A. (2002). Qualitative research in thanatology. *Death Studies, 26*, 195–207.

Cupit, I. N., Servaty-Seib, H. L., Parikh, S. T., Walker, A., & Martin, R. (under review). Forging a pathway through college during bereavement and grief: Findings of the National College Student Grief Study.

Dominick, S. A., Irvine, A. B., Beauchamp, N., Seeley, J. R., Nolen-Hoeksema, S., Doka, K. J., & Bonanno, G. A. (2009). An Internet tool to normalize grief. *Omega, 60*, 71–87.

Ess, C., & the AoIR ethics Working Committee. (2002). *Ethical decision-making and Internet research: Recommendations from the AoIR Ethics Working Committee.* Retrieved June 10, 2008, from www.aoir.org/reports/ethics.pdf

Frankel, M. S., & Siang, S. (1999, November). *Ethical and legal aspects of human subjects research on the Internet. Report from a workshop convened by the AAAS Program on Scientific Freedom, Responsibility and Law, Washington, DC.* Retrieved July 3, 2010, from http://www.aaas.org/spp/sfri/projects/intres/eport.pdf

Glaser, B., & Strauss, A. (1967). *The discovery of grounded theory.* Hawthorne, NY: Aldine.

Green, M. C. (2007). Trust and social interaction on the Internet. In A. N. Joinson, K. Y. A. McKenna, T. Postmes, & U. Reips (Eds.), *The Oxford handbook of Internet psychology* (pp. 43–52). New York, NY: Oxford University Press.

Hollander, E. M. (2001). Cyber community in the valley of the shadow of death. *Journal of Loss and Trauma, 6*, 136–146.

Johnson, R. B., & Onwuegbuzie, A. J. (2004). Mixed methods research: A research paradigm whose time has come. *Educational Researcher, 33*, 14–26.

Joinson, A. N., & Paine, C. B. (2007). Self-disclosure, privacy and the Internet. In A. N. Joinson, K. Y. A. McKenna, T. Postmes, & U. Reips (Eds.), *The Oxford handbook of Internet psychology* (pp. 237–251). New York, NY: Oxford University Press.

Knobel, M. (2003). Rants, ratings, and representations: Issues of validity, reliability and ethics in researching online social practices. *Education, Communication and Information, 3*(2), 187–210.

Leander, K. M., & McKim, K. K. (2003). Tracing the everyday "sitings" of adolescents on the Internet: A strategic adaptation of ethnography across online and offline spaces. *Education, Communication, & Information, 3*(2), 211–240.

Massimi, M., & Baecker, R. M. (2010). A death in the family: Opportunities for designing technologies for the bereaved. In *CHI 2010: Proceedings of the 28th International Conference on Human Factors in Computing Systems* (pp. 1821–1830). New York, NY: ACM.

Moreno, M. A., Fost, N. C., & Christakis, D. A. (2008). Research ethics in the MySpace era. *Pediatrics, 121*(1), 157–161.

Neimeyer, R. A. (Ed.). (2001). *Meaning reconstruction and the experience of loss.* Washington, DC: American Psychological Association.

Neimeyer, R. A. (Ed.). (2004). *Death anxiety handbook: Research, instrumentation, application.* Washington, DC: Taylor & Francis.

Odom, W., Harper, R., Sellen, A., Kirk, D., & Banks, R. (2010). Passing on & putting to rest: Understanding bereavement in the context of interactive technologies. In *CHI 2010: Proceedings of the 28th International Conference on Human Factors in Computing Systems* (pp. 1831–1840). New York, NY: ACM.

Pew Research Center. (2010). Internet and American Life Project. Retrieved from http://www.pewinternet.org/Static-Pages/Trend-Data/Whoe-Online.aspx

Reips, U. -D. (2007). The methodology of Internet based experiments. In A. N. Joinson, K. Y. A. McKenna, T. Postmes, & U. Reips (Eds.), *The Oxford handbook of Internet psychology* (pp. 373–390). New York, NY: Oxford University Press.

Sanderson, J., & Cheong, P. H. (2010). Tweeting prayers and communicating grief over Michael Jackson online. *Bulletin, of Science, Technology & Society, 30*, 328–340.

Stroebe, H. K., Stroebe, M., Schut, H., Stroebe, W., & van den Bout, J. (2009). Online mutual support in bereavement: An empirical examination. In H. K. van der Houwen (Ed.), *The psychological aftermath of bereavement: Risk factors, mediating processes, and intervention* (pp. 44–62). Utrecht, the Netherlands: Royal Netherlands Academy of Arts and Sciences.

Swartwood, R. M., Veach, P. M., Kuhne, J., Lee, H. K., & Ji, K. (2011). Surviving grief: An analysis of the exchange of hope in online and grief communities. *Omega, 63*, 161–181.

Tolstikova, K., & Chartier, B. (2009–2010). Internet method in bereavement research: Comparison of online and off line surveys. *Omega, 60*, 327–349.

Umphrey, L. R., & Cacciatore, J. (2011). Coping with the ultimate deprivation: Narrative themes in a parental bereavement support group. *Omega, 63*, 141–160.

Wogrin, C. (2007). Professional issues and thanatology. In D. Balk (Ed.), *Handbook of thanatology. The essential body of knowledge for the study of death, dying, and bereavement* (pp. 371–386). New York, NY: Routledge.

Part IV

Thanatechnology: Responsibly Looking Forward

15

Ethical Considerations When Conducting Grief Counseling Online

Louis A. Gamino

Picture the following scene: A client enters a coffee shop on the entry level of a large office building in a major U.S. city on the Eastern seaboard and selects a comfortable, overstuffed chair in a secluded corner. With the technological assistance of a very smart phone and local wireless access to the Internet, the client participates in a real-time counseling session via videoconferencing with an expert provider located on the West Coast, who was recommended as the best counselor available for the client's particular loss. The client wears a wireless headset to hear the counselor's comments and responds into a sensitive microphone that transmits clearly what the client says when speaking no louder than a "library voice." On the telephone screen, the client can see the grief counselor, who is seated at a desktop computer with a Webcam in an office at the counselor's home 3,000 miles away. When the client's cup of coffee is finished and the 50-minute therapy "hour" is over, both parties sign off, and the bill is paid over the Internet by credit card.

In a brave new world of grief counseling on the Internet, and with the help of increasingly sophisticated video phone technology, this scene could certainly become more common. In some parts of the United States and around the world, it already is a regular occurrence. In a recent survey of mental health providers, Centore and Milacci (2008) reported the prevalence of several types of Internet counseling: e-mail counseling (28%), online text chat counseling (6%), and videoconference counseling (1%). Given that online mental health service delivery is underway and likely to expand in the future (Rochlen, Zack, & Speyer, 2004),

---

Major sections of this chapter appeared in a work previously published by L. A. Gamino and R. Hal. Ritter, Jr. (2009). *Ethical practice in grief counseling*. New York NY: Springer Publishing Company, 2009. Used with permission.

contemporary grief counselors need to be apprised of the ethical challenges associated with providing professional services via the Internet. For example, one must consider how practicing grief counseling on the Internet as a "place" (e.g., in "cyberspace" or "in the cloud") creates unique demands and challenges. Other ethical issues to consider include the various forms of online counseling, the advantages and disadvantages of Internet counseling, and potential ethical problems linked to Internet modalities.

UNIQUE CHALLENGES OF INTERNET COUNSELING

Internet counseling is an emerging field of practice. Therefore, grief counselors should exercise appropriate caution and seek special training and preparation before attempting to include Internet counseling in their repertoire of professional services. Professionals who want to offer Internet counseling need to consolidate the foundational ethical steps of establishing competence, obtaining informed consent, and maintaining confidentiality. As Maheu (2001) warns, "it is imprudent to use e-mail and chat rooms to establish or maintain psychotherapeutic relationships with unscreened, undiagnosed, unseen, unheard, and unknown consumers through the Internet" (p. 7). Instead, grief counselors interested in Internet modalities will have to modify their administrative procedures and adjust their practice styles to meet the specific demands of the Internet as a medium. How does one authenticate the identity of prospective clients and conduct the process of informed consent both before grief counseling begins and during sessions?

In their seminal text on ethical practice in grief counseling, Gamino and Ritter (2009) introduced the Five P Model for ethical decision making that takes into account variables of person, problem, place, principles, and process when trying to resolve an ethical dilemma. The hypothetical case of grief counseling via transcontinental videoconferencing described at the beginning of this chapter illustrates how the element of *place* is particularly important to consider in addressing the specific ethical challenges presented by Internet counseling. Internet counseling happens over an electronic network instead of in a geographic location. So how does one ensure confidentiality and keep others from "eavesdropping" on the teleconference? Furthermore, cyberspace is a virtual place not governed by licensing boards and jurisdictional statutes, even though electronic transmissions of protected health information is regulated by federal statute under the Health Insurance Portability and Accountability Act (1996). One metaphor in the field likens online counseling to practicing "with one foot in the jurisdiction where the counselor works and one foot in the jurisdiction where the client resides." The Internet as the place of service delivery requires grief counselors to make special arrangements for intervening in the event of a crisis and to take special precautions for meeting state or jurisdictional rules to conduct themselves in an ethically sound manner.

However, the same basic ethical principles (cf. Beauchamp & Childress, 2008) that govern grief counseling in traditional practice settings apply also to Internet counseling: respecting a client's *autonomy* to choose counseling and negotiate the terms of a working agreement for online services; making the client's welfare a priority and striving to obtain a good outcome for the client—*beneficence*; avoiding any harm to the client through misuse or mishandling of the Internet as a medium—*non-maleficence*; treating the client fairly within the parameters of available resources, especially using online sources of mental health information—*justice*; and keeping trust and good faith by honoring the professional integrity of the counselor–client relationship—*fidelity*.

TYPES OF INTERNET COUNSELING

Teletherapy, e-therapy, online counseling, Internet-mediated psychological services, telehealth, web counseling, cybertherapy, e-mail counseling, Internet therapy, web-based counseling, and *distance counseling*—a variety of names are found in the scholarly literature to describe mental health services delivered on the Internet (Heinlen, Welfel, Richmond, & Rak, 2003). For purposes of this chapter, the term *Internet counseling* is used as a convenient description. Borrowing from Rochlen et al. (2004), Internet counseling is defined broadly as any professional interaction that makes use of the Internet to connect qualified mental health providers and their clients. Potentially, Internet counseling is available to any client with Internet access via computer or telephone that can connect with a grief counselor. Related options would be cell phone "texting" or "tweeting," as well as "telemedicine," delivered through closed-circuit television or satellite. However, the content of this chapter does not include consideration of computer-administered mental health treatments where the computer effectively replaces the human therapist (Cavanagh & Shapiro, 2004; Cavanaugh, Zack, Shapiro, & Wright, 2003; Dominick et al. 2009-2010).

Some have argued that Internet communication, or e-therapy, between a provider and a client is not really counseling or psychotherapy because it does not consist of diagnosing and treating mental disorders (Grohol, 1999; Manhal-Baugus, 2001). In the view of this author, making a distinction between e-therapy and formal grief counseling or psychotherapy is superfluous hairsplitting. Barnett and Scheetz (2003) cite how courts tend to see the existence of a professional relationship when an individual pays a fee to a professional for advice given, especially when multiple communications occur. Thus, grief counselors are encouraged to acknowledge that offering help and advice online to clients for a professional fee constitutes grief counseling and requires them to adhere to all applicable rules of professional conduct and ethics in providing such service.

Internet counseling can be either *asynchronous* or *synchronous*. Asynchronous means the parties respond to one another on a time-delayed basis, such as exchanging e-mail or posting entries to a web-based message board.

Synchronous means the interchange occurs in real time with both parties online simultaneously, such as "chat" modes like instant messaging, live voice streaming, or videoconferencing (such as with Skype) as in the hypothetical scenario portrayed at the beginning of this chapter (Recupero & Rainey, 2005; Rochlen et al., 2004; Stofle, 2002). Communication through texting represents a hybrid function—both parties can be operating online simultaneously but time delays can make the medium "feel" more asynchronous. As a function of technology, Internet counseling began mainly through asynchronous e-mail (Heinlen et al., 2003; Rochlen et al., 2004). As technology advances, live videoconferencing is likely to be the preferred modality.

Providing some form of Internet counseling can be an adjunct to traditional, face-to-face sessions. For example, some counselors give out their e-mail address for brief communication between sessions. As with telephone calls, the counselor then must set clear boundaries about what kind of information will be acknowledged between sessions and what will be carried over to the next session. Should a client whom the counselor knows well move to another locale, they may agree to continue via Internet counseling with e-mail or videoconference, or some grief counselors may encourage clients, especially adolescents, to "stay connected" electronically through e-mail, weblogs known as "blogs," or designated chat rooms to build rapport and give clients the opportunity to communicate on their terms.

Some practitioners may offer Internet counseling as an independent, stand-alone service without ever having any in-person contact with the client. Interestingly, survey data show that Internet counseling for grief and bereavement is much less common than online treatment for depression, anxiety, family problems, and relationship difficulties (Cook & Doyle, 2002; Maheu & Gordon, 2000). On the other hand, Vanderwerker and Prigerson (2004) studied a community-based sample of bereaved persons and found that 59% reported using the Internet and 50% used e-mail, although their data did not indicate whether this usage included health information seeking or Internet counseling. Perhaps, because of the intensely personal nature of grief counseling, an Internet modality may be less preferred than traditional face-to-face sessions (J. Bissler, personal communication, September 29, 2008).

IS INTERNET COUNSELING ADVISABLE?

Like it or not, Internet counseling appears to be here to stay and will likely only increase in the future (Maheu, 2001; Nickelson, 1998; Rochlen et al., 2004; Skinner & Latchford, 2010). Skinner and Zack (2004) trace the history of "indirect" treatment back to Freud's practice of providing psychoanalysis by letter when necessary because of geographic distance. In other words, communication with clients through writing is not really a new idea. Still, many scholars continue to debate the potential advantages and disadvantages of Internet counseling (Centore &

Milacci, 2008; Fenichel et al., 2002; International Society for Mental Health Online, 2000; Leibert, Archer, Munson, & York, 2006; Maheu, 2001; Manhal-Baugus, 2001; Ragusea & VandeCreek, 2003; Robson & Robson, 2000; Rochlen et al., 2004; Shaw & Shaw, 2006). For discussion purposes, we summarize in the following sections with the principal issues involved in the debate over the advisability of Internet counseling.

Advantages of Internet Counseling

Convenience and ease of use are often mentioned as prime advantages to Internet counseling. In short, clients can "reach out" to their counselors when the moment of need occurs, regardless of whether it is the middle of the night or they are traveling away from home (cf., Ainsworth, 2002). There is no telephone tag, there are no obstacles to getting an appointment, and conceivably, the client can choose from a more extensive panel of providers. In addition, Internet counseling increases access to mental health treatment by dissolving geographic boundaries and empowering clients in remote locations with few providers or in areas where there is a language barrier. Internet counseling may provide an avenue for mental health treatment for the homebound, those disabled with mobility problems, the deaf, and those reluctant to seek treatment face-to-face because of shame, embarrassment, or perceived social stigma (Centore & Milacci, 2008).

Suler (2004; 2010) is credited with describing the "online disinhibition effect" as one of the potential advantages of Internet counseling. Without the perceived necessity of negotiating social personas and expectations, clients may feel less restrained and engage more quickly in a high degree of intimate self-disclosure. Clients may reveal personal material to an online counselor that they would never admit in person. Suler believes that the anonymity of Internet counseling and the fact that clients are "invisible" physically to their counselor give them the courage to speak out more, an assertion supported by early empirical data (Cook & Doyle, 2002). However, Suler also describes how the disinhibition effect can enable acting-out behavior, making it a disadvantage at times.

Another advantage to Internet counseling is that both the client and the counselor have the capability of downloading the conversation and printing out a transcript of the counseling session(s). Clients can reread and ponder the words of the counselor any time after their exchange. Rereading can help promote a reflective stance, extend the therapeutic value of the counselor's input, and enhance the client's internalized sense of the counselor's ongoing presence (Fenichel et al., 2002). The time delay involved in asynchronous forms of Internet counseling affords freedom from having to respond immediately to the other party, thus allowing both counselors and clients an opportunity to contemplate the therapy dialogue and formulate their thoughts by writing.

Related to this, the fact that clients must write out their responses in e-mail or message board-style could make Internet counseling a salutary process in and of itself (cf., Pennebaker, 1997; Smyth & Pennebaker, 2008; White & Epston, 1990), especially for bereaved clients (Neimeyer, van Dyke, & Pennebaker, 2008).

For clients who enjoy writing, e-mail exchanges with an Internet counselor may be a natural way to think through various concerns, identify potential strategies for coping, and find connections or patterns in their responses and relationships. Because journaling and letter-writing are therapy techniques frequently employed with bereaved clients (cf., Gamino & Ritter, 2009), a text-based Internet modality may be a natural extension of traditional counseling practice.

Two other advantages to Internet counseling concern finances and educational resources. As a general rule, professional fees for Internet counseling, particularly text-based options like e-mail and message-posting, may be less than fees customarily charged for face-to-face counseling (Heinlen et al., 2003; Manhal-Baugus, 2001), although some have challenged this assertion (Centore & Milacci, 2008). Presumably, this is because overhead costs such as office space, staff salaries, supplies, and so forth are significantly less, particularly for those practitioners who offer Internet counseling as a stand-alone service or who work from home. Finally, because clients often ask for educational materials pertaining to their specific problems, such as books or websites, Internet counseling has the advantage of enabling the counselor to create hyperlinks easily when typing a response to direct clients to web locations with helpful information or resources.

Disadvantages of Internet Counseling

The most frequently mentioned disadvantage to Internet counseling with text-based modalities is the absence of nonverbal cues. Most therapists trained in traditional, face-to-face counseling pay close attention to numerous nonverbal signals, including facial expression, "body language," and voice stylistics, in making an assessment of a client and conducting therapeutic interventions. The totality of data accrued from visual, aural, olfactory, tactile, and intuitive channels contribute to an accurate anamnesis of the client. Ekman and Friesen (2003), citing decades of research, assert that facial signals are the primary system for expression of emotion. Mehrabian (2007) hypothesizes that, in any conversation, 93% of the meaning is communicated through nonverbal cues such as facial expression, behavior, and voice quality, with only 7% of the actual message communicated by the words themselves.

Consider the following examples. An acutely grieving client who states, "I'm doing pretty well with the loss," while leaking tears throughout the session presents an incongruity that a counselor will explore. A client with terminal lung disease who smells of tobacco and has a pack of cigarettes in a shirt pocket will have a difficult time convincing the counselor that very little smoking is occurring. A bereaved parent whose voice conveys angry overtones while describing "forgiveness" for the driver at fault for the fatal car crash that killed the child may be in a state of denial that needs to be addressed. The client who responds with a fearful "deer in the headlights" expression when asked why the opportunity was not taken to say goodbye to the loved one dying in the hospital is telling the counselor something that would never be conveyed through asynchronous e-mail. Many practitioners admit readily that they would not be comfortable forgoing these important nonverbal aspects of grief counseling and consider such information vital to a complete understanding of the client.

Proponents of Internet counseling counter by arguing that novelists and poets throughout human history have succeeded in capturing the richness of the human experience in the written word alone (Fenichel et al., 2002). Supporters of Internet counseling believe that enterprising clients can use a variety of compensatory techniques to enliven and imbue their writing with an emotive, conversational quality. Examples include use of "emoticons" (either symbols formed from aggregated keystrokes, such as "frowny faces," or cartoon-like icons representing a wide array of moods and affects); parenthetical expressions that convey subvocal nuance, such as (sigh); CAPS for emphasis; bracketed labels of [emotion]; use of similes and metaphors; and trailers (. . .) for transitions, to name a few (Fenichel et al., 2002; Manhal-Baugus, 2001). Proponents like Fenichel (2010) believe such adaptations can successfully ". . . ensure accurate communication and allow for expression of feeling and mood to be accurately and mutually understood; in short to promote *online empathy.*" (p. 5).

These arguments on the adequacy of the written word to convey truth about the human heart and spirit have not persuaded everyone. Shaw and Shaw (2006) worry that developing adequate rapport can be a problem with a client never seen face-to-face; a worry founded on data indicating that as much as one fourth of the therapeutic effect of counseling is based on establishing a working alliance (Hubble, Duncan, & Miller, 1999). Barnett and Scheetz (2003) warn that cultural differences may be even more difficult to detect and account for in a text-only interchange. Others have charged that relying on text-only communication modes in Internet counseling results in a subtle form of socio-intellectual "elitism" by selecting only those clients most adept at a written medium, thus neutralizing arguments of increased access and availability (Manhal-Baugus, 2001; Ragusea & VandeCreek, 2003).

There are other potential disadvantages such as the time delays that occur with asynchronous Internet counseling. The immediacy of the client's ability to "talk to" the counselor any time of the day or night can create an unrealistic wish or expectation for an expedited response. Clearly, e-mail or message-posting modalities require some mutual understanding between clients and counselors about the time frame in which the client can reasonably expect a response, typically within 24–72 hours (Manhal-Baugus, 2001). Just as traditional therapists have "office hours" during which appointments are taken, Internet counselors are not online all the time, and clients need to be prepared for inevitable time delays.

Internet counseling depends on technology in a manner that face-to-face counseling does not. Anyone with a computer is aware of the many exasperating ways that technology can break down as a result of hardware failure, software malfunction, transmission problems with one's Internet provider, power outages, "bugs" and "viruses," and many other potential problems. Obviously, when technical problems occur, interruptions in the anticipated schedule of Internet counseling will follow, and this is a major disadvantage. Counselors who plan to offer services over the Internet need to become skilled at troubleshooting and solving technical problems that interrupt service provision, both as a business practice and as a model for clients who rely increasingly on the Internet for vital life activities, including their counseling (Ragusea & VandeCreek, 2003; Skinner & Zack, 2004).

Many scholars suggest that certain types of emotional disorders are not amenable to Internet counseling. Usually, this list includes unstable bipolar disorder, borderline and other personality disorders, eating disorders, substance misuse, dissociative disorders, psychotic disorders with a perceptual distortion of reality, sexual abuse, and violent relationships. A client in an abusive or violent relationship who accesses Internet counseling from home may risk the perpetrator finding out that family "secrets" are being revealed and incur additional risk as a result (Robson & Robson, 2000). Although everyone may not agree on what kind of problems should be excluded from consideration, there appears to be broad consensus that depression, anxiety, and relationship or interpersonal problems lend themselves most readily to Internet counseling. To the extent that there are limits to which problems can be addressed suitably through Internet modalities, this can be considered a disadvantage.

Finally, Centore and Milacci (2008) found that mental health counselors engaged in providing Internet-based counseling services perceived a diminution of their ability to fulfill their ethical duties as therapists when working online. Although it was unclear whether this finding represented an actual disadvantage to providing Internet counseling or a lack of confidence in doing so, grief counselors engaged in the practice of Internet counseling need to address the ethical challenges involved (cf., Kraus, 2010).

RESEARCH DATA ON INTERNET COUNSELING

As an emerging treatment modality, Internet counseling does not yet have a substantial body of research validating its efficacy. Yet, early tests of its effectiveness compared with face-to-face counseling or wait-list controls are promising (Rochlen et al., 2004). One early test of the therapeutic effectiveness of Internet counseling came from Cook and Doyle (2002), who compared the relative strength of the perceived therapeutic alliance by clients in both Internet and face-to-face counseling. In their small, mostly White female sample of volunteers, empirical ratings of the counselor–client working alliance were higher in the group of online clients than in the norm group of clients in face-to-face counseling on whom the empirical scale was validated.

In a similar study, Leibert et al. (2006) investigated client perceptions of Internet counseling and the therapeutic alliance. They noted that previous research showed that individuals who were lonely, socially anxious, and struggling with forming relationships in person were more likely to develop relationships online. Online clients in their study were predominantly female, White, unmarried, young adults (average age was 29 years) who had some college, were already regular Internet users, and enjoyed the convenience and anonymity of the service. Almost one third of the sample mentioned cost considerations as a factor. Regarding modality of Internet counseling, 59% reported e-mail contact, and 33% had used instant messaging. Only 2% used videoconferencing. Interestingly, nearly 80% of the sample had *previously* attended face-to-face counseling. In their study, online counseling clients were generally satisfied with their counseling, but their satisfaction ratings were not as high as a comparative group of clients who received only face-to-face counseling. Clients who received face-to-face counseling reported a stronger therapeutic alliance with the counselor than those clients who received counseling online. The researchers concluded that some people are clearly at ease with Internet counseling. Their sample of young adult women may represent a generation that has grown up using the Internet on a daily basis, so they embrace the anonymity and convenience of Internet counseling and generally feel safe online.

A randomized controlled trial of Internet counseling for complicated grief was reported by Wagner, Knaevelsrud, and Maercker (2006). German-speaking clients in Europe and elsewhere who responded to Internet notices of the study were carefully screened online and eliminated from consideration if they met any of the following exclusion criteria: younger than 18 years, receiving mental health treatment elsewhere, time since death less than 14 months, abusing substances, reporting severe depression or suicidal intentions, and indicating dissociative or psychotic tendencies. It is noteworthy that this screening process began with 213 requests for the questionnaires, of which 143 were returned. After screening, only 55 persons entered the random treatment allocation. The authors' efforts to ensure an appropriate sample for their study illustrate how important it is to screen Internet applicants for research or counseling.

Wagner et al.'s (2006) study sample was predominantly younger females (average age was 37 years), of whom 61% were bereaved parents. This suggests they closely resemble the population of troubled grievers who seek mental health treatment because of problems coping (cf., Gamino & Ritter, 2009). Clients were randomly assigned either to 5 weeks of cognitive–behavioral treatment delivered entirely through e-mail communication or to a 5-week waiting-list control group (who then received the treatment sequence). Based on Stroebe and Schut's (1999; 2010) dual-process model of grief, the treatment focused on deliberate exposure to bereavement cues such as thinking about the most distressing aspect of their loss, cognitive restructuring to begin thinking of the deceased in a more comforting way that incorporated new perspectives, integrating the death by reflecting on how the loss had changed them, and envisioning the future. Clients receiving the cognitive–behavioral treatment showed significant symptom reduction after 5 weeks compared with the waiting list group. They maintained those gains at follow-up 3 months later. Most clients felt that the contact between the therapist and them was "personal" and expressed satisfaction with the Internet counseling. Only 20% of the clients reported missing face-to-face contact with the therapist. Wagner et al. concluded that Internet counseling for complicated grief can be as effective as, if not more effective than, traditional therapy.

ETHICAL CHALLENGES WITH INTERNET COUNSELING

Five major areas of ethical challenges emerge from the scholarly literature available on Internet counseling. These include authenticating identity, obtaining informed consent, securing confidentiality, intervening in a crisis, and establishing jurisdictional and administrative governance.

Authenticating Identity

Most readers of this text will probably have heard at least one news story, personal account, or client disclosure of an individual impersonating someone else on the Internet for purposes of voyeurism, exploitation, criminal activity, or other mischief. An example was the case of Missouri teenager Megan Meier (Scott & Huffstutter, 2008). The mother of one of Megan's neighborhood girlfriends enlisted the help of some other teenage girls to fabricate an identity as a male admirer and begin chatting with Megan on her MySpace page. The hoax was intended as an effort to learn what Megan was saying about the neighbor's daughter. Later, the fictitious "boy" broke off contact with Megan in messages that turned vindictive and mean, "The world would be a better place without you." Megan subsequently hanged herself. The ringleader mother was indicted by the state of California for violating the rules of MySpace, creating a false identity, and using it to solicit personal information from a minor. In a controversial verdict based on a federal statue designed to combat computer crimes, the mother was convicted of misdemeanor charges of computer fraud in creating the phony account (Steinhauer, 2008). The point of this vignette is that anyone can impersonate someone else on the Internet, and this can happen in the course of Internet counseling as well.

Authentication of identity is critical, and the process starts with the counselor. Counselors who plan to practice Internet counseling should be willing to provide their real name and their educational credentials, training experiences, state license, and pertinent certifications. A web page listing this information should include hyperlinks to licensing boards or professional associations enabling potential clients to verify independently a counselor's identity and licensure status. Legitimate counselors with appropriate training and credentials should have no hesitation providing this basic information.

An example of how large, online clinics handle authentication is http://www.letstalkcounseling.com. The site lists numerous counselors from various locations around the United States and Canada. There is also a thorough list of topics addressed, including "grief and loss." Each counselor for the site has a page that includes a picture, an address, and the counselor's training, license and certification, and fees for service. Fees vary for e-mail, telephone counseling, chatting online, videoconferencing, and face-to-face counseling in the office. The website lists the professional organizations that certify the various counselors. Potential clients can select a topic, such as grief counseling, and enter their state of residence, and the site will list counselors who are geographically close.

Authenticating the identity of potential clients is trickier. Specifically, an individual must be at least 18 years old to give consent for counseling. Because Internet counseling is paid for by credit card, one cross-check is to match the client's reported demographic information with credit card information. It is always possible for minors to masquerade as their parents for purposes of engaging a counselor online and to use the parents' credit card to pay for it. That is why it is sometimes helpful to ask for a second form of identification, such as a photocopy of a driver's license, to verify identity. Of course, in order for clients to feel safe providing this kind of personal information about themselves, they must first be convinced of the counselor's authenticity.

Obtaining Informed Consent

Moving from traditional office practice to Internet counseling is not a reason to abandon a dynamic model of informed consent as a continuous consensual process (Gamino & Ritter, 2009). The same information that would be contained in a client information brochure used in a traditional office practice needs to be conveyed to potential online clients, together with modifications appropriate to Internet modalities, such as the time window in which a response can be expected, the nature of emergency backup, confidentiality safeguards (and the client's responsibilities in that regard), fee schedules for different types of service, and so forth. The challenge is ensuring that the client not only understands the parameters of grief counseling but also freely agrees to the proposed course of action.

In lieu of face-to-face discussion between counselor and client about informed consent, some interchange verifying the client's understanding and noncoerced agreement is necessary. When initial consultations are conducted in person, by telephone, or through videoconference, this interchange resembles customary discussions of informed consent prior to the initiation of counseling. When e-mail is the intended format, some exchange between prospective client and counselor is necessary to confirm consent. Providers are well advised to consider such e-mail communications concerning consent to be part of the counseling record and part of one's professional actions (Bradley, Hendricks, Lock, Whiting, & Parr, 2011). What is *not sufficient* is using "click-wrap agreements," in which the client reads a consent form or information page and indicates consent for counseling simply by clicking on a button saying, "I accept" or "I agree." Such shortcuts do not constitute discussion "informing" consent for grief counseling (Recupero & Rainey, 2005).

Securing Confidentiality

Conducting Internet counseling through e-mail or real-time chat via "open air" transmission with a commercial Internet service provider is open to eavesdropping and does not at all secure confidentiality. The only way to have the kind of privacy that clients enjoy in traditional face-to-face counseling behind a closed office door is to use encryption technology to protect the communications over the Internet. No system is completely foolproof, but there are some alternatives available that meet the Health Insurance Portability and Accountability Act (1996) standards for securing protected health information "in transit."

Most readers will have at least some familiarity with encryption technology from making purchases over the Internet or banking from home. Financial transactions over the Internet commonly employ an encryption process called *Secure Sockets Layer* (www.verisign.com). Applied to the situation of Internet counseling, Secure Sockets Layer would originate with the counselor's website. Conceptually, it creates an encrypted "tunnel" between the client's computer and the counselor's website destination that protects the information as it travels online. The primary advantage of Secure Sockets Layer is that it can be activated by most common Internet browsers such as Internet Explorer, AOL, and Netscape Navigator and usually does not require the client to add or install hardware.

Another alternative is to use an encryption program such as Pretty Good Privacy (www.pgp.com), which encrypts files prior to sending them over the Internet. It requires the recipient to enter a password to "decrypt" the file and thereby access it. Thus, the password or "key" must be shared between the sender and the recipient. In addition, the software program has to be installed on both computers in order for encryption and decryption to take place. For Internet counseling, the client would have to have the same encryption program as the counselor in order for a system such as Pretty Good Privacy to operate. Without encryption technology, it is possible for clients to install a Trojan horse program on the practitioner's computer and download all the contents of the practitioner's computer onto a remote computer (Maheu, 2001).

It is important to acknowledge to clients that e-mail and text-based messages are stored on local servers and that agency or institutional supervisors and information technology personnel have the right to read e-mail records of counselor-employees (Manhal-Baugus, 2001). Another security consideration with Internet counseling is the fact that texts that are deleted do not really disappear. Whatever has been typed into the system is discoverable by legal process. All the documents that have been a part of the counseling can be ordered legally from the online service provider. Under subpoena, these documents are discoverable for use in a court of law. Further, some countries outside of the United States regularly intercept e-mails and messages. Any international Internet counseling may be subject to these intercepts.

Ensuring client confidentiality demands that electronic data downloaded to discs or remote storage devices, or printed on paper, require the same secure storage as conventional counseling records. Lax procedures by practitioners who work from home computers that are either shared by family members or located in common living areas of the house can breach confidentiality, even if elegant encryption programs are in place. With wireless Internet access becoming more commonplace, Internet counseling could be conducted from almost anywhere via laptop computers, which are particularly vulnerable to security breaches resulting from human error or theft (Zur & Barnett, 2008). Practitioners' intent on providing Internet counseling can refer to Fisher and Fried (2003) for an excellent summary of how to protect confidential counseling information online.

Intervening in a Crisis

A grief counselor's responsibilities in instances when clients pose danger to themselves or others certainly apply to Internet counseling (Kraus, 2010). However, the geographic distance that may be insignificant for an Internet connection between a counselor in one locale and a client in another can become, in turn, a formidable barrier to intervening effectively in a crisis if advance arrangements have not been made. This is another reason, in addition to authenticating a client's identity, for knowing where clients live.

Even if potential clients do not see the reason or need, certain basic information about the client's locale is needed to activate a crisis intervention plan in the heat of the moment. At a *minimum,* this includes telephone numbers for the local police department and a local hospital emergency department. Also helpful are telephone numbers for community crisis lines or hotlines where distraught individuals can call at any hour of the day or night, as well as telephone numbers for local support groups. Ideally, a practitioner providing Internet counseling to a client in a remote location would also have the name and telephone number of a nearby mental health or medical provider to link the client to a local resource should a crisis develop. Of course, lack of qualified local providers may be the very reason that the client is seeking Internet counseling in the first place, so this recommendation may be difficult to carry out in some instances.

Establishing Jurisdictional and Administrative Governance

Cyberspace is not a specific geographic location, so it is not immediately clear what entity has jurisdictional governance of Internet counseling activity. Does it take place in the state or jurisdiction where the counselor works and holds a license? Do the laws of the client's home state or jurisdiction apply? Is it a case of interstate or international commerce where federal regulations prevail? Given these unanswered questions, to whom can one complain if the counseling process goes awry or if clients believe they have been harmed or mistreated? Koocher and Keith-Spiegel (2008) offer a humble, straightforward admission regarding these vexing questions about Internet counseling: "We simply do not know the answers at this time" (p. 144). However, knowledgeable consultants (Barnett, 2005; Barnett & Scheetz, 2003; Kraus, 2010; Mallen, Vogel, & Rochlen, 2005) strongly endorse the position that a professional license is needed in the jurisdiction where the client resides.

Grief counselors legitimately interested in offering Internet counseling as part of their service line must address this jurisdictional dilemma. The most conservative approach would be restricting one's online practice only to clients who reside in the state(s) where the counselor is licensed. A cavalier approach would be interpreting the lack of regulatory guidelines as a carte blanche to offer Internet counseling to any willing, paying client from anywhere. A study by Finn and Barak (2010) showed that such disregard for jurisdictional authority may be the norm as most of the counselors working online whom they surveyed had not even considered such questions and, instead, assumed they could treat anyone through the Internet from their "virtual office" as if operating in their own state. In addition, unlicensed individuals may exploit lack of regulations to pass themselves off as "counselors" to unsuspecting or naive clients, as evidenced by survey studies of websites that advertise Internet counseling (cf., Heinlen et al., 2003; Shaw & Shaw, 2006).

Koocher and Morray (2000) polled U.S. state attorneys general about regulations governing the practice of Internet counseling. At that time, only 3 of 42 responding jurisdictions had statutes in place that specifically addressed provision of psychotherapy by telephone, Internet, or other electronic means. However, almost half of the responding attorneys general claimed regulatory authority over mental health practitioners residing outside the state who offer Internet therapy to residents of that state. Thus, these states consider Internet counseling to be an instance of "crossing state lines." Koocher and Morray urge practitioners who provide Internet counseling to consult in advance with their professional liability carrier to make sure that coverage is in force (cf., Bradley et al. 2011; Heinlen et al., 2003).

In a recent chapter on legal issues for online counselors, Zack (2010) explained how both the client's state and the therapist's state have an interest in controlling what happens in an online counseling interaction, such as ensuring that practitioners are qualified and protecting (resident) clients. Zack suggested that providers contact licensing boards in jurisdictions where clients reside to determine the status of the counselor's ability to offer Internet counseling as well as the office of the state's attorney general to determine whether any special statutory or credentialing obligations exist. Sometimes, states make provision, with limits, for professionals to practice temporarily in their jurisdiction without a license. At the same time, states may differ in statutory regulations governing duty of care, and prudent practice requires knowing such state-specific requirements.

A related administrative issue concerns charging third-party payers for Internet counseling. Conscientious grief counselors must make it clear to third-party payers if they are providing services via the Internet, rather than face-to-face, to avoid any fraudulent representation in charges. Medicare authorizes reimbursement for some "telehealth" services, including psychotherapy, rendered to individuals residing in geographic areas with provider shortages, but such coverage is by no means automatic or universal (Nickelson, 1998). There is now a billing code, 98969, for online patient management services by a qualified nonphysician health care professional to an established patient using the Internet or similar electronic communications network (Ingenix, 2010). In all cases, the best policy is to clarify in advance the client's eligibility for insurance coverage of Internet counseling.

Haberstroh, Parr, Bradley, Morgan-Fleming, and Gee (2008) raised another question about billing when online counselors using text-based media work with more than one individual during a given therapeutic hour, because of the relatively slower pace of online sessions. Although providers in older age cohorts may find such a prospect mind-boggling, more youthful providers who have grown up with the Internet and mobile communication devices may find it a natural extension of established communication patterns. In effect, Meshriy (2009) argued against such multitasking by claiming that online counseling in text formats *magnifies* the amount of attention that must be paid to the client because the absence of visual cues requires application of intense listening skills. As a matter of practice, conducting multiple online counseling sessions simultaneously appears inadvisable, and billing multiple persons for the same therapeutic hour presents ethical challenges in avoiding fraud and misrepresentation.

CONCLUSIONS

Because Internet counseling is a new and emerging practice option for grief counseling, providers bear an additional burden of mastering the techniques of online communication needed for Internet counseling—demonstrating competence, authenticating the identity of the parties involved, ensuring the integrity of the informed consent process, securing confidentiality, intervening in a crisis, and establishing jurisdictional and administrative governance. Many of these challenges are a function of the Internet as a unique *place* of service delivery as outlined in Gamino and Ritter's (2009) Five P Model.

Fortunately, detailed guidelines from several professional associations and societies are available to provide recommendations for the ethical practice of Internet counseling (see Appendix B of this book). By acquiring the specific knowledge needed and adequately addressing the ethical issues raised, grief counselors can offer Internet counseling as an option to clients who have a legitimate reason for choosing this treatment modality.

REFERENCES

Ainsworth, M. (2002). My life as an e-patient. In R. C. Hsiung (Ed.), *e-Therapy: Case studies, guiding principles, and the clinical potential of the Internet* (pp. 194–215). New York, NY: W. W. Norton.

Barnett, J. E. (2005). Online counseling: New entity, new challenges. *The Counseling Psychologist, 33,* 872–880.

Barnett, J. E., & Scheetz, K. (2003). Technological advances and telehealth: Ethics, law, and the practice of psychotherapy. *Psychotherapy: Theory, Research, Practice, Training, 40,* 86–93.

Beauchamp, T. L., & Childress, J. F. (2008). *Principles of biomedical ethics* (6th ed.). New York, NY: Oxford University Press.

Bradley, L. J., Hendricks, B., Lock, R., Whiting, P. P., & Parr, G. (2011). E-mail communication: Issues for mental health counselors. *Journal of Mental Health Counseling, 33*, 67–79.

Cavanagh, K., & Shapiro, D. A. (2004). Computer treatment for common mental health problems. *Journal of Clinical Psychology, 60*, 239–251.

Cavanagh, K., Zack, J. S., Shapiro, D. A., & Wright, J. H. (2003). Computer programs for psychotherapy. In S. Goss & K. Anthony (Eds.), *Technology in counseling and psychotherapy: A practitioner's guide* (pp. 143–164). Hampshire, England: Palgrave Macmillan.

Centore, A. J., & Milacci, F. (2008). A study of mental health counselors' use of and perspectives on distance counseling. *Journal of Mental Health Counseling, 30*, 267–282.

Cook, J. E., & Doyle, C. (2002). Working alliance in online therapy as compared to face-to-face therapy: Preliminary results. *CyberPsychology & Behavior, 5*, 95–105.

Dominick, S. A., Irvine, A. B., Beauchamp, N., Seeley. J. R., Nolen-Hoeksema, S., Doka, K. J., & Bonanno, G. A. (2009–2010). An Internet tool to normalize grief. *Omega, 60*, 71–87.

Ekman, P., & Friesen, W. V. (2003). *Unmasking the face: A guide to recognizing emotions from facial clues.* Cambridge, MA: Malor.

Fenichel, M., Suler, J. Barak, A., Zelvin, E., Jones, G., Munro, K., . . . , Walker-Schmucker, W. (2002). Myths and realities of online clinical work. *CyberPsychology & Behavior, 5*, 481–497.

Finn, J., & Barak, A. (2010). A descriptive study of e-counselor attitudes, ethics, and practice. *Counselling and Psychotherapy Research, 10*, 268–277.

Fisher, C. B., & Fried, A. L. (2003). Internet-mediated psychological services and the American Psychological Association Ethics Code. *Psychotherapy: Theory, Research, Practice, Training, 40*, 103–111.

Gamino, L. A., & Ritter, R. H., Jr. (2009). *Ethical practice in grief counseling.* New York, NY: Springer Publishing.

Grohol, J. M. (1999). Best practices in e-therapy: Definition & scope of e-therapy. In *Online Mental Health Issues: Current Research and Publications.* Retrieved September 24, 2008, from http://www.ismho.org/builder//?p=page&id=216

Haberstroh, S., Parr, G., Bradley, L., Morgan-Fleming, B., & Gee, R. (2008). Facilitating online counseling: Perspectives from counselors in training. *Journal of Counseling & Development, 86*, 460–470.

Health Insurance Portability and Accountability Act of 1996. (1996). 45 C.F.R. Parts 164.508–512. Retrieved April 13, 2006, from www.cms.hhs.gov/HIPAAGenInfo/

Heinlen, K. T., Welfel, E. R., Richmond, E. N., & Rak, C. F. (2003). The scope of Web counseling: A survey of services and compliance with NBCC standards for the ethical practice of Web counseling. *Journal of Counseling & Development, 81*, 61–69.

Hubble, M. A., Duncan, B. L., & Miller, S. D. (Eds.). (1999). *The heart and soul of change: What works in therapy.* Washington, DC: American Psychological Association.

Ingenix. (2010). *The 2011 current procedural coding expert.* Rocky Hill, CT: Author.

International Society for Mental Health Online. (2000). *Suggested principles for the online provision of mental health services.* Retrieved September 23, 2008, from http://www.ismho.org/builder/?p=page&id=214

Koocher, G. P., & Keith-Spiegel, P. (2008). *Ethics in psychology and the mental health professions: Standards and cases* (3rd ed.). New York NY: Oxford University Press.

Koocher, G. P., & Morray, E. (2000). Regulation of telepsychology: A survey of state Attorneys General. *Professional Psychology: Research and Practice, 31*, 503–508.

Kraus, R. (2010). Ethical issues in online counseling. In R. Kraus, G. Stricker, & C. Speyer (Eds.), *Online counseling: A handbook for mental health professionals* (2nd ed.; pp. 85–106). New York, NY: Elsevier.

Leibert, T., Archer, J., Jr., Muson, J., & York, G. (2006). An exploratory study of client perceptions of Internet counseling and the therapeutic alliance. *Journal of Mental Health Counseling, 28*, 69–83.

Maheu, M. M. (2001). Telehealth: Practicing psychotherapy on the Internet: Risk management and great opportunity. *TelehealthNet*. Retrieved September 23, 2008, from http://telehealth.net/articles/njpa.html

Maheu, M. M., & Gordon, B. L. (2000). Counseling and therapy on the Internet. *Professional Psychology: Research and Practice, 31,* 484–489.

Mallen, M. J., Vogel, D. L., & Rochlen, A. B. (2005). The practical aspects of online counseling: Ethics, training, technology, and competency. *The Counseling Psychologist, 33,* 776–818.

Manhal-Baugus, M. (2001). E-therapy: Practical, ethical, and legal issues. *CyberPsychology & Behavior, 4,* 551–563.

Mehrabian, A. (2007). *Non verbal communication.* New Brunswick, NJ: Transaction.

Meshriy, N. (2009). Technology in counseling. *Career Planning and Adult Development Journal, 25,* 82–88.

Neimeyer, R. A., van Dyke, J. G., & Pennebaker, J. W. (2008). Narrative medicine: Writing through bereavement. In H. Chochinov & W. Breitbart (Eds.), *Handbook of psychiatry in palliative medicine* (pp. 454–469). New York, NY: Oxford University Press.

Nickelson, D. W. (1998). Telehealth and the evolving health care system: Strategic opportunities for professional psychology. *Professional Psychology: Research and Practice, 29,* 527–535.

Pennebaker, J. W. (1997). Writing about emotional experiences as a therapeutic process. *Psychological Science, 8,* 162–166.

Ragusea, A. S., & VandeCreek, L. (2003). Suggestions for the ethical practice of online psychotherapy. *Psychotherapy: Theory, Research, Practice, Training, 40,* 94–102.

Recupero, P. R., & Rainey, S. E. (2005). Informed consent to e-therapy. *American Journal of Psychotherapy, 59,* 319–331.

Robson, D., & Robson, M. (2000). Ethical issues in Internet counseling. *Counseling Psychology Quarterly, 13,* 249–257.

Rochlen, A. B., Zack, J. S., & Speyer, C. (2004). Online therapy: Review of relevant definitions, debates, and current empirical support. *Journal of Clinical Psychology, 60,* 269–283.

Scott, G., & Huffstutter, P. J. (2008, May 16). L.A. files 'cyber bully' charges against Missouri mother in connection with girl's suicide. *Los Angeles Times.* Retrieved July 3, 2008, from www.latimes.com/news/local/la-me-myspace16-2008may16,0,3642392.story

Shaw, H. E., & Shaw, S. F. (2006). Critical ethical issues in online counseling: Assessing current practices with an ethical intent checklist. *Journal of Counseling & Development, 84,* 41–53.

Skinner, A., & Zack, J. S. (2004). Counseling and the Internet. *American Behavioral Scientist, 48,* 434–446.

Skinner, A. E. G., & Latchford, G. (2010). International and multicultural issues. In R. Kraus, G. Stricker, & C. Speyer (Eds.), *Online counseling: A handbook for mental health professionals* (2nd ed.; pp. 257–269). New York, NY: Elsevier.

Smyth, J. M., & Pennebaker, J. W. (2008). Exploring the boundary conditions of expressive writing: In search of the right recipe. *British Journal of Health Psychology, 13,* 1–7.

Steinhauer, J. (2008, November 27). Verdict in MySpace Suicide Case. *The New York Times,* p. A25.

Stofle, G. S. (2002). Chat room therapy. In R. C. Hsiung (Ed.), *e-Therapy: Case studies, guiding principles, and the clinical potential of the Internet* (pp. 92–135). New York: W.W. Norton.

Stroebe, M., & Schut, H. (1999). The dual process model of coping with bereavement: Rational and description. *Death Studies, 23,* 197–224.

Stroebe, M., & Schut, H. (2010). The dual process model of coping with bereavement: A decade on. *Omega, 61,* 273–289.

Suler, J. (2004). The online disinhibition effect. *CyberPsychology & Behavior, 7,* 321–326.

Suler, J. (2010). The psychology of text relationships. In R. Kraus, G. Stricker, & C. Speyer (Eds.), *Online counseling: A handbook for mental health professionals* (2nd ed.; pp. 21–53). New York, NY: Elsevier.

Vanderwerker, L. C., & Prigerson, H. G. (2004). Social support and technological connected-ness as protective factors in bereavement. *Journal of Loss and Trauma, 9,* 45–57.

Wagner, B., Knaevelsrud, C., & Maercker, A. (2006). Internet-based cognitive–behavioral ther-apy for complicated grief: A randomized controlled trial. *Death Studies, 30,* 429–454.

White, M., & Epston, D. (1990). *Narrative means to therapeutic ends.* New York, NY: W.W. Norton.

Zack, J. S. (2010). Legal issues for online counselors. In R. Kraus, G. Stricker, & C. Speyer (Eds.), *Online counseling: A handbook for mental health professionals* (2nd ed.; pp. 107–127). New York, NY: Elsevier.

Zur, O., & Barnett, J. (2008, September/October). Laptops threaten confidentiality. *The National Psychologist, 17,* 22.

16

Dying, Death, and Grief in a Technological World: Implications for Now and Speculations About the Future

Illene Noppe Cupit, Carla J. Sofka, and Kathleen R. Gilbert

In the field of medical ethics, it frequently has been said that we are in an age where the rapidity of technological evolution has far outpaced our capacity to comprehend and anticipate its consequences. The same can be said for the multidisciplinary field of thanatology, where the issues of dying, death, and grief have increasingly become digitized, virtual, and shared around the globe. *Dying, Death, and Grief in an Online Universe* is an attempt to distill and synthesize a range of important thanatechnological issues, research findings, narratives, and theory pertaining to this critical juxtaposition of the new digital age with timeless traditions and time-honored beliefs surrounding dying, death, and grief. As more and more people gain command and rely upon their digital devices, how they die and how their survivors grieve will increasingly be affected by the informational resources, products, online support, and social networking/commemorative opportunities that are available on a global scale.

Reviewing the contents of this book, we are struck by the myriad of ways in which this new digital age affects and is affected by our mortal concerns. For example, computer-mediated communications have become a new strategy for coping with loss, from social networking sites, to narrative writing that appears in blogs, to virtual grief therapy and finally, to virtual commemoration. Online communities have appeared as websites of support and as places where those who are disenfranchised in the "real world" can "get together." Information abounds through online resource centers, via Internet courses and webinars, e-mails and text messages, and the sharing of information by those who forward their favorite online finds to their distribution lists of friends, family, and colleagues.

Thanatological researchers have found such phenomena rich fodder for empirical investigation and have developed ways in which to gather data online and form online research collaborations on topics ranging from the types of content found in online obituaries to the efficacy of online grief support groups. Overlaying such thanatechnological events is the amazing rapidity of transmission of information across oceans, mountaintops, and once-impassible political boundaries. In the "Wild West" of the information age, ethical concerns and netiquette specific to the use of thanatechnology need to be considered by thanatological practitioners, researchers, and educators.

THANATECHNOLOGY: COMMON THEMES

Although each chapter offers a unique aspect and perspective on thanatology issues in an online universe, there are a number of common themes that help to create a "book-wide-web":

Theme 1: Thanatechnology and Social Support

Many of the chapters in this book refer to the facilitation of social connection and attachment resulting from online discourse on dying, death, and grief. Time and distance are irrelevant to mourners, educators, and researchers. Social support is achieved through social networking sites (Chapter 3), within the blogosphere and other internet communities of support (Chapters 5, 6, 7, 9, and 10), virtual therapy sessions (Chapter 8), and online thanatology resource centers that combine multiple elements, including Internet radio (Chapter 11). Those who have experienced social isolation in the past can now reach out to others in similar circumstances, thus removing barriers to grieving and reducing disenfranchisement over the loss of a pet, an ex-spouse, or an online relationship (Chapter 9). The bereaved can participate in a funeral even though they are at a military encampment or have a mobility impairment that prevents them from leaving a nursing home (Chapter 10). Technology can also facilitate one's ability to visit a terminally ill family member even though distance requires the visit to be "virtual" rather than in person (Chapter 6).

During the stages of finishing this book, two of the coeditors had personal experiences with the use of thanatechnology to cope with loss. The son of one of the coeditors was able to participate in his grandmother's memorial service despite not being able to book a flight out of Louisiana in time to attend the actual event. Instead, this musician composed a piece in honor of his grandmother, digitally recorded it, and attached it to an e-mail sent to his aunt in New York, who burned it onto a CD and played it less than 12 hours later at the memorial service. Because of technology, this grandson was able to share in the commemoration of his beloved grandmother with his family.

Following the sudden death of another coeditor's aunt, cousins in the states of Washington, California, New York, and Florida fondly remembered their aunt via posts on Facebook because of their inability to book flights within 24 hours of the funeral in St. Louis. This coeditor's daughter was vacationing with a family friend in Florida. Discussion and debate occurred regarding whether the news should be delivered by telephone or in person, and it was decided that she should be allowed to enjoy her vacation without the distraction of this news (and without expecting her friend or her friend's mother to be responsible for handling her reaction). At this point, the embarrassed coeditor suspects that you have guessed what happened. Yes, it was unwise to assume that said daughter had no access to the Internet while vacationing at a resort in Daytona Beach! Of course, she saw the memorial postings on Facebook and told her friend and her friend's mother, but failed to tell her own mother until 4 days later when she was being informed in person of the news she already knew. (Note: The coeditor's family has teased her unmercifully, saying "Gee, if only someone would write a book about how to handle these things!") Live and learn.

In addition to the use of thanatechnology by practitioners and laypeople in everyday life, researchers now can connect and collaborate with like-minded scholars in other countries (Chapter 14). Educators can teach students from anywhere in the world within a virtual classroom. The caveats abound—we are not alone out in cyberspace, and yet we also are disembodied and virtual. Because strangers can participate in the most private segments of our online emotional lives, we are intimately involved with people whom we have never met. As noted by Nardi, Schiano, and Gumbrecht (2004), whether bloggers realize it or not, 900 million people may be reading any post that is made on a public blog.

Although more and more research is being published about the impact of participation in online activities to cope with illness, dying, death, and grief, it is crucial to generate empirical data that build on the premise that "technological connectedness" is a protective factor in bereavement (Vanderwerker & Prigerson, 2004). However, as Neimeyer and Noppe-Brandon point out (Chapter 8), perhaps a virtual "hug" or a two-dimensional visual of the other cannot replace real flesh and blood.

Although the benefits of thanatechnology are numerous, the potential risks that one can encounter in cyberspace must be acknowledged. Examples of cyberbullying, insensitivity of others in online communities, and predatory behavior have been provided in Chapters 4, 5, 7, and 9 of this book. Practitioners, educators, and researchers have an ethical obligation to our clients, our students, and those who participate in online research to do what is in our power to ensure their safety.

Theme 2: The Blurring of Realities—Real Versus Virtual

The experience of dying, death, and grief is frequently accompanied by ambiguity and confusion. Many societies have elaborate, evolved patterns of behavior that create order and a sense of security out of the chaos. As noted throughout the book, thanatechnology is evolving within contemporary societies around the globe; ancient rules and traditional rituals to cope with illness, death, and grief are being supplemented with, or potentially replaced by, virtual ones. As noted by Hensley (Chapter 9), individuals can digitally create a funeral whose participants involve the created avatars of online gamers from around the world. Although the emotions may be heartfelt, how does the lack of a tangible experience affect the grief process? How does the lack of actual student–teacher and student–student contact affect the learning process (Chapters 12 & 13)? How does the absence of visual/nonverbal cues between a practitioner and a client (or between two friends) impact the process of providing support, whether that support is "professional" or "social"? As pointed out by Hieftje (Chapter 3) and de Vries and Moldaw (Chapter 10), how does ongoing communication with the deceased via messages on Facebook or MySpace, achieved in the absence of a physical presence, impact the development of a new representation of the deceased? Such blurrings between the virtual and the actual may be particularly difficult in times of sudden, unanticipated death, tragic deaths from suicide or homicide, or the numerous deaths from natural and human-made disasters.

It seems prudent to recognize that certain situations may benefit from the differences that exist between real and virtual. For instance, consider the person who desperately wants to support a family member, friend, or colleague during a time of crisis or loss but is incredibly challenged to find the "right thing to say" when face-to-face with a distressed or grieving individual. Perhaps, the absence of "virtual time pressure" makes it possible for this same person to craft an incredibly sensitive, compassionate response (with the help of an online resource at his or her fingertips) and increase the sense of technological connectedness experienced by the person in need of support.

Theme 3: Thanatechnology Opens Up Options

The online universe is one of invention. Encountering dying, death, and loss in an online universe may be a significantly more democratic experience than what happens in reality. Such experiences typically are not scripted or formulaic, and who gets to participate and what he or she can do online frequently is not restricted. With every upgrade, new device, and previously unimaginable type of technology, one has the option of reexamining the rules, the rituals, and the expectations. If one really is not comfortable with things the way that they are, one can even make them up anew.

For those who have had extensive experience with computer-mediated communications, adaptation and use of the online options may come more easily than to those who are limited by lack of accessibility and familiarity (Chapter 2). Many of the computer-mediated communications in thanatology offer a mind-boggling array of options, from digitized photos, videos, voice messages, written content on websites, animated creations, and three-dimensional opportunities seen through specially created head gear and computerized programs. This necessitates continual invention on the part of the survivors of the deceased, the funeral director, the practitioner, the developer of webinars on death and dying, the death educator, and the researcher who wishes to study all of the above. For some dealing with such highly emotional content, or for those to whom the technology is unfamiliar, the array of options may be unsettling. As discussed in Theme 2, the rituals of the past are giving way to an amorphous amalgam of expectations, communications, and online "behaviors"—hardly what many need when a death occurs or when grief is challenging to manage.

For others, thanatechnology is commonplace and inherently appealing. Adolescents and emerging adults have venues for discussion about thanatology-related issues and opportunities for creative expression of their thoughts and reactions that did not previously exist (Chapters 3, 4, and 7). The task of preserving one's digital legacy over a lifetime takes on a different meaning for someone who is 10 years of age as opposed to someone who only started to use technology 10 years prior to his or her death. The new generation of thanatologists who are currently being trained have a different thanatechnological skill set—a higher level of comfort and familiarity with technology in general, extensive experience with social media, and potentially more openness to doing things differently, particularly if they have limited life experience that was influenced by traditional ways of dealing with dying, death, and grief. Mentoring relationships between the thanatology "digital immigrants" and the thanatology "net generation" has the potential to be incredibly interesting and perhaps much less one sided than they have been in the past. Such new options mean that we will certainly be living and dying in interesting and novel ways!

Theme 4: Ethical Issues Permeate All Aspects of Thanatechnology

Creating new rules (Theme 3) requires that we contemplate and anticipate their consequences, giving deep consideration to the issues of protection, safety, and preservation of social justice. Unfortunately, the potential for sensitive information to be mishandled, inadvertently forwarded to unintended recipients, or accidently posted on the World Wide Web is high. The learning curve for death educators who begin teaching students online is steep. Therefore, protecting the privacy and identities of consumers receiving online services or those of participants in online research merits special consideration. Responsibly managing a virtual classroom is an important obligation. Thus, every aspect of thanatechnology must be examined for ethical considerations and concerns, maintaining safety for all who interact with thanatologists online and ensuring that members of highly vulnerable populations are not placed at greater risk for increased distress. Thanatologists must also be wary of distress that can result from the disturbing online behavior (intended or not) of those over whom we have no control or our own actions that inadvertently have an unintended consequence.

Professional organizations and associations are beginning to recognize the need for ethical codes that reflect the unique nature of online service provision (see Appendix B). Sadly, it is not uncommon for practitioners to state that they have limited or no specialized training to prepare them to provide services to consumers online and to report limited familiarity with or awareness of ethical issues that would be relevant while providing services in this manner (Chapter 15; Appendix B). It is our hope that this book will be a useful resource in the quest to enhance the knowledge base and skill set of any death professional who provides services online.

Themes and the Thanatechnological Death System

Revisiting the Thanatechnological Death System (see Figure 1.2, Chapter 1), it is apparent that the previously discussed themes (social support, the blurring reality between real and virtual, opening up options, and ethical issues) tap into all of the Thanatechnological Death System's elements and functions. For example, the themes common to all chapters concern the people (e.g., social support, the blurring of reality between real and virtual, ethical issues); objects, symbols, places, and times (e.g., the options, the blurring of reality); social consolidation (e.g., social support, options); care of the dying (e.g., social support, ethical issues); disposal of the dead (e.g., the blurring of reality, ethical issues); and perhaps most importantly, making sense of death (seen in all four common themes: social support, blurring of reality, options afforded by computer-mediated communications, and ethical and nonethical behaviors).

IMPLICATIONS OF THANATECHNOLOGY FOR NOW AND SPECULATIONS FOR THE FUTURE

Implications for Practitioners

Neimeyer and Noppe-Brandon (Chapter 8) and Gamino (Chapter 15) all characterize online therapy as part of a "brave new world." As in many other aspects of confronting dying, death, and grief via the Internet, approaches to grief counseling may have to be modified or created anew. Few graduate programs in the helping professions address dying, death, and loss, and there may be even fewer that would consider how this is done online (see Chapter 12). Evaluating the availability of training to provide online services is difficult because a Google search to identify such programs largely results in educational institutions that provide online courses for counseling rather than training in how to deliver online counseling.

This lack of training compounded by the absence of published materials that evaluate the effectiveness of online counseling makes it challenging to state whether the provision of online grief counseling can be considered a legitimate evidence-based practice. Evaluation research is needed before we can determine what forms of treatment are best provided in an online environment and for whom such treatments are effective. Even in the absence of empirical support for online counseling and online support groups, these thanatechnological interventions are occurring with increasing frequency. Such opportunities hold great promise for bereaved individuals who are not geographically close to a grief counselor.

However, the clinician should be wary about only screening potential clients online. Jordan and Neimeyer (2007) suggest that the clinician first assess the mourner's narrative of the death. Ordinarily, this would be a verbal response (and can happen that way via videoconferencing). However, dependence on the written word may hamper understanding a client whose written skills are not well developed. In addition, Jordan and Neimeyer recommend that the clinician assess the coping skills of the mourner. Both of these tasks would be more effective through face-to-face contact in an office to allow for use of nonverbal information and observation skills that contribute tremendously to an accurate assessment. Determining the appropriate time frame for termination of the helping relationship presents another concern. Frequently not an easy process in the "real" world, it may be necessary to create a new set of criteria and modify the process of termination for virtual grief counseling.

Technological problems have the potential to present additional complications. It is not hard to imagine that technological difficulties can exacerbate the agitation of a client in the throes of acute grief. The Internet can make grief counseling available to individuals who ordinarily would not have such services available, but the accessibility, of course, is limited to those who are computer savvy and have the hardware, software, and reliable Internet access. Grief counseling, at present, therefore may be a service for a younger, educated, and wealthy group—a "psychotherapeutic divide." An online grief therapist may have the opportunity to work with people from diverse cultural, religious, and national backgrounds. If this is the case, it is important that the therapist have a high degree of cultural competence regarding death-related beliefs and practices (Shapiro, 2007). It is equally important that potential consumers of online counseling services, whether individual or group, verify the credentials of the online clinician. For example, http://checkatherapist.com/ is an online resource provided as a public service by the Family and Marriage Counseling Directory that allows consumers to check whether a potential counselor or therapist is licensed to practice in his or her state. It is important to remind consumers that this type of check does not verify experience or skill with the provision of online counseling. Those who specifically are seeking an online therapist for grief counseling need to query about the therapist's level of training in thanatology. The home page of the website of the Association for Death Education and Counseling (www.adec. org) has a link entitled "Find a specialist." In this case, the thanatological training is not being questioned but rather the ability of the therapist to provide services online.

As discussed in Chapter 15 and Appendix B, there are crucial elements that define ethical practices when providing online services. An important aspect of the therapeutic relationship involves the definition and maintenance of appropriate boundaries. Computer-mediated communication carries with it the potential expectation of almost instantaneous, 24/7 access. If this is truly an expectation of a client, he or she may feel distressed or abandoned if immediate responses are not forthcoming. Respecting confidentiality is inherent to competent clinical practice, but clients may not recognize the importance of maintaining the confidentiality of group members or the potential consequences of disclosing comments made by their counselor or therapist. Practitioners must be vigilant about establishing appropriate guidelines for participants in online groups and educating clients about the implications of confidentiality when receiving individual online services.

As noted earlier in this chapter, some professional organizations and associations are developing ethical codes for the provision of online services and are encouraging increased technical competence However, practitioners may not be aware that this guidance is available and would be well advised to gain familiarity with these resources (see Appendix B).

Although a great deal of attention is focused on the provision of counseling or therapeutic services, death professionals should remain mindful that informational support can be equally important in the process of assisting individuals who are dealing with illness, dying, death, and grief (see Chapters 4, 5, and 11 and Appendix A). Thanatologists may want to consider how they routinely use an intervention strategy called *information therapy*, defined by Kemper and Mettler (2002) as "prescribing the right information to the right person at the right time" (p. 43). Although this intervention is used largely in health-oriented contexts, death education can be an important component of the grief counseling/grief therapy process (Vespia, 2004). In an online universe, such thanatechnological resources lead to a number of thought-provoking questions: What is the impact of providing accurate, targeted information to an individual dealing with an illness, impending death, or grief? Does the guidance or reassurance provided by this informational support facilitate resilience? Might it possibly prevent complications in one's ability to adapt to the challenges inherent in dealing with change? It is exciting to consider the new interventions that will evolve as a result of technology-tolerant and technology-savvy death professionals working side by side with clients who are receptive to or have already discovered thanatechnology resources. Mesch and Talmud (2010) note that the use of information and communication technologies can result in societal coviewing—sharing the experience of viewing information with one or more other individuals. How often do parents and children or adolescents share the experience of going online to deal with illness or loss? Might it be useful to prescribe an intervention like this to deal with challenges or conflicts within a family that arise from different grieving styles or by differing views about how an illness should be treated ? The online universe is rife with such opportunities provided that individuals use appropriate levels of caution, foresight, and critical thinking.

Implications for Researchers

It is an exciting time for creative questions and new methodological approaches that can shed light on topics that once were difficult to assess. Cupit (Chapter 14) outlines a research process that can guide thanatechnological research, and the Internet offers a plethora of research possibilities, from attitude surveys to examination of content such as those found on online obituaries, memorials, and blogs. The chapters in this book are rich with a wide range of potential topics for study by thanatologists.

Because of the large number of individuals who are dealing with dying, death, and grief in online communities, there is a larger pool of participants available. However, as noted by Lynn and Rath (Chapter 7), Horsley and Horsley (Chapter 11), and Cupit (Chapter 14), the rights of online participants must be protected, and new challenges created by online recruitment and data collection must be evaluated with care.

The power of technology also creates opportunities to collaborate with researchers around the globe that were previously challenging to develop. The new era of thanatechnology needs its researchers for they may be at the forefront of helping us to discern the efficacy of therapeutic intervention, the impact of online memorials, and meaning making that is associated with blogs and computerized diaries. The dissemination of research results may also be facilitated by the Internet via websites, e-newsletters, e-books, and journals. It is imperative that researchers learn best methodological practices that make online research reliable and valid, while maintaining research ethics.

Several major foundations (the Pew Foundation and the Kaiser Family Foundation) have invested tremendous resources (financial and human capital) to study and document society's ever-increasing use of and dependence upon technology. Perhaps, thanatologists can find a way to engage these groups to help us document the manner in which thanatechnology is impacting the death system.

Because researchers in the field of human–computer interactions are doing creative methodological and theoretical work on thanatechnology, it is also crucial for thanatologists to gain familiarity with their work and consider reaching out to form partnerships with researchers in this discipline (such as the partnership that generated Chapter 2 of this book). Perhaps, it will become commonplace to see thanatologists presenting at the annual meeting of the Association of Computing Machinery conferences on human factors in computing systems, computers and society (which addresses the ethical and societal impact of computers), health infomatics, or other special interest groups that may be relevant to thanatechnology. Publications by thanatologists may find a home in journals such as *Internet Research, Cyberpsychology, Behavior, and Social Networking,* or *Cyberpsychology: The Journal of Psychosocial Research on Cyberspace.* Or perhaps, someday—there will be a *Journal of Thanatechnology?*

Implications for Educators

The Association for Death Education and Counseling (www.adec.org) defines death education as "formal and informal methods for acquiring and disseminating knowledge about dying, death, and bereavement" (Balk, 2007, p.301). As noted in Chapter 12, the online universe has increased the availability of both informal and formal death educational experiences (see Appendix A for a typology of sites). On the informal side, there are numerous sites offering information from casket building to cryonics—literally hundreds of websites loaded with valuable information can be accessed via an Internet search. However, one's understanding of dying, death, and grief may also take on unrealistic proportions, particularly for youth whose "informal" death education may stem from the murder and mayhem portrayed on the Internet games found at on-the-fringe websites.

On the formal side, death educators have created online courses, workshops, webinars, majors, and certificates that cover topics ranging from introductory surveys of dying, death, and loss to death in pop culture to webinars on translating theory into practice. A number of death educators have worked hard to translate the real classroom experience to the virtual classroom (Chapters 12 and 13; Harris, 2007) so that students can "walk" through a virtual cemetery instead of experiencing one during a class field trip. Death education online can truly occur in a global classroom, giving students from around the world an opportunity to directly learn from each other about differing paradigms and cultural experiences regarding dying, death, and loss. While online death education may be more appealing to children and adolescents who have no formal education about thanatology, Facebook should not be the only venue for learning about these topics. The literature comparing the outcomes of online classes to in-classes of similar content has yielded a mixed grab bag of results (e.g., Summers, Waigandt, & Whittaker, 2005). As in clinical practice, evidence-based research findings on best practices for death education will help to advance the field and open increased opportunities for the training of thanatological practitioners and researchers.

Perhaps, death educators should consider using some of the technology that is available to create a niche community in the blogosphere designed to share stories from the trenches, curriculum materials (syllabi, assignments, activities, and exercises), and links to online resources that are used in death education efforts (see Chapter 12). Social networking sites and other thanatechnology resources could be used to facilitate partnerships between seasoned death educators and current students. The students can help their professors to successfully navigate the technology, allowing the professors to concentrate on mentoring at a pedagogical level. Social networking sites could provide venues for problem solving and discussion regarding research questions, methodological challenges and measurement strategies, recruitment of participants, and resolution of any ethical dilemmas that may arise in the process. Online support groups could potentially be formed—one for students to provide assistance in coping with the pressures of student life, and one for academics to provide assistance in coping with pressures of the tenure and promotion process. Online writing groups could benefit both the students and the academics who are interested in publishing.

CONCLUSION

On May 20, 2010, the first "Digital Death Day" conference was held in London, bringing together the businesses of social networking, data management, and death care. The 2nd conference, held in the San Francisco Bay area in May of 2011, was described as follows: "This un-conference will be primarily concerned with provoking discourse around the social, cultural, and practical implications of Death in the Digital World. Thus stimulating a reconsideration of how death, mourning, memories and history are currently being augmented in our technologically mediated society." (www.digitaldeathday.com). How exciting that thanatechnology seems to have a following and its own conference!

Each day that we use computer-mediated communication technology in our work and our personal lives, our digital legacy grows. In recognition of the significance of electronic communication in modern life, the British Library in London now has "digital curators"—staff who curate the e-manuscripts and digital legacies owned by the library (Paul-Choudhury, 2011). Walker (2011) describes sifting through the "digital litter" of one's life to determine which of the information (much of which was meant to be private) should be preserved in a potentially public manner. It seems that the task involves sifting through "digital trash" to find "digital treasure." Rita King, an online identity expert, encourages caution "about the mindless expression of everything, the default veneration of 'sharing' over 'curating.' If people thought about dying more often, they'd think about living differently" (as quoted in Walker, 2011, n.p.).

Theoretically, each of us can become a digital curator to preserve information about and examples of the ways that thanatechnology is being used in our work as death educators, grief counselors, and thanatology researchers as well as how thanatechnology is being used within society both on a personal level and on a global scale. However, it seems important to do the sifting wisely and purposefully.

Although "thanatechnology" is not a familiar concept even among thanatologists, it is our hope that this book will begin to change the degree to which death professionals consider the role that technology can play in helping society to deal with issues related to dying, death, grief, and loss. In fact, thanatologists are an important component of our "Thanatechnological Death System," and as these thanatologists explore and study new and evolving concepts such as "digital immortality," "cybersoul," "technological connectedness," "mourning netiquette," and other components of the rapidly growing thanatechnological death system, we look forward to the fascinating conversations (possibly using information and communication technology or computer-mediated communications to host them) that lie ahead. See you on Digital Death Day!

REFERENCES

Balk, D. (Ed.). (2007). *Handbook of thanatology. The essential body of knowledge for the study of death, dying, and bereavement.* New York, NY: Routledge.

Harris, D. (2007, April 13). *Online death education: Strategies for learning.* Symposium presentation to 29th Annual Conference of the Association for Death Education and Counseling, Indianapolis, IN.

Jordan, J. R., & Neimeyer, R. A. (2007). Historical and contemporary perspectives on assessment and intervention. In D. Balk (Ed.), *Handbook of thanatology. The essential body of knowledge for the study of death, dying, and bereavement* (pp. 213–226). New York, NY: Routledge.

Kemper, D. W., & Mettler, M. (2002). Information therapy: Prescribing the right information to the right person at the right time. *Managed Care Quarterly, 10*(4), 43–59.

Nardi, B. A., Schiano, D. J., & Gumbrecht, M. (2004). Blogging as a social activity, or would you let 900 million people read your diary? *Proceedings of the 2004 ACM conference on Computer Supported Cooperative Work, 6*(3), 222–231. Retrieved July 31, 2011, from http://citeseerx.ist.psu.edu/viewdoc/download?doi=10.1.1.102.3591&rep=rep1&type=pdf

Paul-Choudhury, S. (2011, May 6). Digital legacy: Respecting the digital dead. *New Scientist*. Retrieved August 1, 2011, from http://www.newscientist.com/article/dn20445-digital-legacy-respecting-the-digital-dead.html

Shapiro, E. R. (2007). Culture and socialization in assessment and intervention. In D. Balk (Ed.), *Handbook of thanatology. The essential body of knowledge for the study of death, dying, and bereavement* (pp. 189–202.). New York, NY: Routledge.

Summers, J. J., Waigandt, A., & Whittaker, T. A. (2005). A comparison of student achievement and satisfaction in an online versus a traditional face-to-face statistics class. *Innovative Higher Education, 29*, 233–249.

Vanderwerker, L. C., & Prigerson, H. G. (2004). Social support and technological connectedness as protective factors in bereavement. *Journal of Loss and Trauma, 9*(1), 45–57.

Vespia, K. M. (2004). The clinician as a death educator. *The Forum, 30*, 5.

Walker, R. (2011, January 5). Cyberspace when you're dead. *The New York Times*. Retrieved August 7, 2011, from http://www.nytimes.com/2011/01/09/magazine/09Immortality-t.html

Appendix A

Informational Support Online: Evaluating Resources

Carla J. Sofka

In 1997, this author used the conceptual framework of mediated interpersonal communication to describe the types of websites that were available as resources for social support when dealing with dying, death, and grief (Sofka, 1997). Definitions from classic social support literature and the previously developed framework are included in this appendix to briefly summarize the types of websites available to individuals seeking information about thanatology-related topics. Resources available to facilitate information literacy and the evaluation of websites, particularly those with health-related information, are also included.

RESOURCES FOR SOCIAL SUPPORT

Opportunities to gain social support on the Internet and the web are numerous and diverse, creating the potential for dynamic "social support Internetworks" among individuals who use these resources. Three types of social support are available: informational or guidance support, emotional or affective support, and instrumental or material support.

Informational support (Schaefer, Coyne, & Lazarus, 1981), or guidance support (Barrera & Ainlay, 1983), involves sharing advice, suggestions, directives, or factual information that a person can use in coping with personal and environmental problems. Emotional or affective support consists of behaviors or acts that involve the provision of caring, love, empathy, and trust (Cobb, 1976; Pattison, 1977). Instrumental or material aid involves the provision of tangible resources such as financial assistance or physical objects for use in care or the provision of services (Gottlieb, 1978; House, 1981; Pattison, 1977).

Resources for Informational and Emotional Support

Sponsored by service providers and organizations or created by individuals, numerous sites for informational support are available. When working with individuals coping with the diagnosis of a life-threatening or terminal illness, it is not uncommon to hear concerns about the limited time available for direct communication with doctors or the difficulties in finding current information about the illness and treatment options. Websites containing frequently asked questions and medical information can serve as an adjunct resource to be used in conjunction with the advice and guidance of a physician. For example, clients coping with cancer can benefit from accessing the website of the National Cancer Institute (http://www.cancer.gov/), Cancer.net, sponsored by the American Society of Clinical Oncology, or OncoLink (www.oncolink.org), developed by the Abramson Cancer Center at the University of Pennsylvania. These sites offer information to patients with cancer and their caregivers about cancer diagnoses, potential treatment options, psychosocial aspects of the cancer experience, and resources for coping and support. As with any health-related information that is available online, it is crucial to evaluate the quality of the information, and a resource to assist with this task developed by research fellow Sue Childs is included (see Figure A1).

Online information about grief and coping with loss is plentiful and is written from factual and experiential perspectives. Factual information should be carefully scrutinized using established criteria for website evaluation. A tool created by Kapoun (1998) is included (see Figure A2). If more in-depth rating of website criteria is desired, consider use of the checklist developed by Anderson, Allee, Grove, and Hill (1999). Types of websites written from experiential perspectives will be described momentarily.

Opportunities are also available for computer-mediated discussion with professionals or members of the bereaved community. At one such site, individuals can participate in a live interactive chat to discuss mental health issues with Dr. John Grohol at specified times (http://psychcentral.com/chats-grohol.htm). Clinicians and clients can access websites that provide descriptions of available services and resources. In addition to information about formal services such as medical treatment or hospice, these online directories may describe opportunities for informal emotional support through self-help or support groups. The types and specificity of information vary significantly, influenced by the goal and purpose of the Web site as well as sponsorship of that particular site (e.g., a national organization, local agency, nonprofit group, or individual). Sites may also include automatic connections to other relevant sites ("hotlinks") that can be accessed via the click of a mouse. GriefNet and Open to Hope (see Chapters 7 and 11 of this book) are excellent places to learn about communities of informational and emotional support that are available online.

Figure A1

Consumer Guidelines:
Evaluating Websites for Health Content

Sue Childs, Research Fellow
School of Computing, Engineering and Information Sciences,
Northumbria University, UK

These guidelines aim to help health consumers make informed decisions about websites and summarize the things to look for that will help you judge if a website is of good quality.

- **Trust and reputation**

Look for sites of trustworthy organizations with a good reputation, e.g. well-known, reputable organizations; organizations you already know and trust; sites recommended by a health professional or a support group.

- **Who produced the site**

Find out which organization or individual has produced the site, e.g. professional organizations, support groups, government departments, commercial organizations, individuals.

- **Purpose of the site**

Find out the purpose of the site, e.g. its aims or mission, its audience, how the site was developed and if health consumers were involved.

- **Funding sources**

Find out where the site gets its funding from, e.g. financial accounts, names of sponsors, the types of advertisements on the site.

- **Date**

Look for the date when the site was last updated or reviewed. Information on the site should also be dated, with an update / review date given.

- **How the information is written**

Look at how the information is written, e.g. discussing different sides of an issue; not sensational or extreme; with correct grammar and spelling; simply written and easy to understand if aimed at health consumers; in other languages if aimed at non-English speakers.

(continued)

Figure A1 (*continued*)

- **Descriptions of conditions and treatments**

Look for the following details that indicate that the information is likely to be reliable, e.g. the name of the author, their job title, place of work, qualifications, potential conflicts of interest; the date the information was written, with an update or review date; the sources of information the author used; the author's contact details; links to related resources; descriptions of quality checks or editorial processes.

Detailed assessment of the correctness of medical information requires help from a health professional or a lay-expert. A lay-expert is a member of the public who has spent a lot of time reading and learning about a specific medical condition.

- **Medical research**

Medical research literature is very complex and needs specialized knowledge to understand it fully. Support groups often explain about research on their websites or in their newsletters.

- **Personal experiences**

Personal experiences of patients and their caregivers are important sources of information. Check that they are clearly marked as personal experiences. Be cautious about individual patient or carer sites. Check the medical information they give carefully.

- **Foreign sites**

Find out the country of origin of the site. Health information on non-UK sites can be different to that provided on UK sites, e.g. different health systems and cultural practices, use of different terminology, recommending different treatments, different availability of treatments and drugs.

- **Communication**

Look for ways you can contact the organization to discuss issues, ask for advice or comment on the site, e.g. an e-mail address, a postal address, a phone number, electronic forms.

- **Links**

Assess links to other websites too. The site should explain why and how they have chosen these links. It should be made clear that you are linking to another site.

- **Disclaimers**

Look at the site's terms and conditions and disclaimers. These should cover issues such as, medical information, privacy, copyright, responsibilities for accuracy of information and for any harm caused by using the site.

(*continued*)

Figure A1 (*continued*)

- **Kitemarks**

Kitemarks are signs or logos indicating that the site has been 'endorsed' in some way by another organization. They do not necessarily mean that the health information is correct. The absence of a kitemark is not a sign of poor quality. Only a minority of sites apply for them.

- **Design**

Look at how well the site is designed, e.g. personal information should be kept private and secure; the site should be easy to use; the site should be easy to access; advertising should be clearly marked as such, and discrete; the site should have an attractive appearance, without the need to use extra software.

- **Interactive facilities, e.g. e-mail lists, bulletin boards, chat rooms**

Assess the quality of interactive facilities too. Look for the presence of experienced members; requirement for rules of polite, supportive behavior; presence of people ensuring the rules are followed; requirement to register to use the facility.

These guidelines were produced by Contact a Family, Northumbria University, and the Centre for Health Information Quality, through a project supported by the Health Foundation in the UK. Author: Sue Childs, Research Fellow, School of Computing, Engineering and Information Sciences, Northumbria University. Published February 2003. Last updated December 2009. Review date December 2010.

Resources for Instrumental Support

Although it has been traditional to speak directly with funeral directors or memorial societies for preneed planning or at-need assistance following the death of a loved one, online resources to assist consumers with a variety of decisions related to the funeralization and memorialization process have proliferated. In addition to education about the process of planning a funeral and the ability to purchase caskets, sites offer information about cremation (the Internet Cremation Society at www.cremation.org), green burial options (http://www.greenburialcouncil.org/), and products to assist with memorialization (e.g., cremation jewelry, memorial books, and various other products).

Sites such as these may assist in decreasing the sense of mystery and taboo that have surrounded the funeral industry. Individuals who need such services or those who are simply curious may visit these funeral homes in cyberspace at their convenience.

Figure A2

Five criteria for evaluating Web pages
Jim Kapoun (1998)
Reproduced with permission of the author

Evaluation of Web documents	How to interpret the basics

1. Accuracy of Web Documents
 	
   • Who wrote the page and can you contact him or her?
   • What is the purpose of the document and why was it produced?
   • Is this person qualified to write this document?
	Accuracy
	
	   • Make sure author provides e-mail or a contact address/phone number.
	   • Know the distinction between author and Webmaster.

2. Authority of Web Documents
 	
   • Who published the document and is it separate from the "webmaster?"
   • Check the domain of the document, what institution publishes this document?
   • Does the publisher list his or her qualifications?
	Authority
	
	   • What credentials are listed for the authors?
	   • Where is the document published? Check URL domain.

3. Objectivity of Web Documents
 	
   • What goals/objectives does this page meet?
   • How detailed is the information?
   • What opinions (if any) are expressed by the author?
	Objectivity
	
	   • Determine if page is a mask for advertising; if so information might be biased.
	   • View any web page as you would an infommercial on television. Ask yourself: why was this written and for whom?

4. Currency of Web Documents
 	
   • When was it produced?
   • When was it updated?
   • How up-to-date are the links (if any)?
	Currency
	
	   • How many dead links are on the page?
	   • Are the links current or updated regularly?
	   • Is the information on the page outdated?

(*continued*)

Figure A2 (*continued*)

5. Coverage of the Web Documents	Coverage
• Are the links (if any) evaluated and do they complement the documents' themes? • Is it all images or a balance of text and images? • Is the information presented cited correctly?	• If page requires special software to view the information, how much are you missing if you don't have the software? • Is it free or is there a fee to obtain the information? • Is there an option for text only, or frames, or a suggested browser for better viewing?

Putting it all together

- **Accuracy.** If your page lists the author and institution that published the page and provides a way of contacting him/her and . . .
- **Authority.** If your page lists the author credentials and its domain is preferred (.edu, .gov, .org, or .net), and, . .
- **Objectivity.** If your page provides accurate information with limited advertising and it is objective in presenting the information, and . . .
- **Currency.** If your page is current and updated regularly (as stated on the page) and the links (if any) are also up-to-date, and . . .
- **Coverage.** If you can view the information properly—not limited to fees, browser technology, or software requirement, then . . .

You may have a Web page that could be of value to your research!

Narrative, Commemorative, Expressive, and Experiential Sites

Although the following types of sites do not appear to be captured within the framework of mediated interpersonal communication, they do make important contributions to the value of the Internet and the web as a resource for death professionals in their work with clients, other professionals, and students. These sites include narrative sites, commemorative sites, expressive sites, and experiential sites, many of which span more than one category of website.

Narrative sites are defined as those that include the telling of a story or descriptions of a personal experience with illness or loss. Prior to his death on May 31, 1996, Timothy Leary's home page provided the most highly publicized example of a narrative site. In addition to mental and physical status reports, Leary described his activities to achieve "hi-tech designer dying" and his efforts at pain control, which included a menu of his average daily intake of neuroactive drugs. A similar site documented the struggle of Austin Bastable, a Canadian who fought to legalize physician-assisted suicide until his death by assisted suicide on May 6, 1996. Because this site is sponsored by the Right to Die Society of Canada, there is an advocacy component, sensitizing readers to the legal and policy-oriented issues involved in the individual's experience.

Other sites include narratives about grief and loss situations that are more commonplace, such as "A Place to Honor Grief." At this site, sponsored by social worker Tom Golden, bereaved individuals can read about others who have experienced similar losses. The site could also be described as a "commemorative site," one that not only includes personal stories but also incorporates aspects of memorialization and ritual. In addition to opportunities to describe the life and death of a significant other (human or pet) through the creation of a memorial, these sites allow an individual to participate in a variety of meaningful activities and rituals. Detailed information about these types of sites, including virtual cemeteries, is included in Chapter 10 of this book.

Expressive sites are forums for the expression of thoughts, emotions, and experiences through the use of writing, poetry, artwork, and, potentially, music or sound. Individual home pages may also incorporate photographs as a means of capturing moments in time or ideas. For example, the use of creative artwork by children as a means of coping with illness or grief is captured by the gallery of pediatric oncology patients' artwork within the OncoLink site. This unique gallery provides an outlet for the children as well as a place for reflection by others. As noted in Chapter 4, technology provides numerous opportunities for creative expression by adolescents (and perhaps some adults).

Humor has been defined as the mental faculty of discovering, expressing, or appreciating the ludicrous or absurdly incongruous or as an instance of being comical or amusing. Although most would not define impending death, events involving loss, or the experience of grief as amusing or comical, the existence of "gallows humor" certainly indicates the need for comic relief from the anxiety generated by these serious subjects. Brain (1979) supports this notion with the statement that "evidently we laugh at what we find most threatening" (p. 22). Canonical joke lists often include jokes about death professionals, particularly doctors, nurses, morticians, and coroners. Humor archives frequently contain "sick joke cycles" precipitated by highly publicized tragic events. Individuals searching for thanatology information on the Internet and the web are likely to encounter sites that include examples of dark humor, some of which may be offensive to those not seeking it out. A relatively innocuous site called "The Graveyard" contains humorous epitaphs (and crickets) and may come in handy at Halloween (http://www.kraftmstr.com/graveyard/). However, some sites containing gallows humor can also be gruesome. Although some of these sites include user-friendly notices of potentially objectionable content, one may stumble upon offensive material without warning.

Experiential sites provide an opportunity to explore one's own reactions to or attitudes about a thanatological issue or topic. Individuals can confront their own mortality through The Death Clock. This site uses figures on the average life span of a human to estimate how many seconds a visitor has left to live, forcing the person to consider the implications of limited time in this life. The site notes that the death clock is "the Internet's friendly reminder that life is slipping away . . . second by second. Like the hourglass of the Net, the Death Clock will remind you just how short life is." Although these sites are still relatively rare, experiential sites will most likely become more common and more sophisticated as the programming skills required to create these sites are gained at younger ages (e.g., programming with "Alice").

Although possessing the skills required for locating information online is practically universal, it cannot hurt to share the links for several tried and true sources of thanatology-related information and other tools to explore these topics.

▪ Explore approximately 900 topics (Note: Although death and grief are not included in the topic list, there will be multiple "hits" when these terms are used)

Yahoo "Society and Culture" Directory, Death and Dying subdirectory: http://dir.yahoo.com/Society_and_Culture/Death_and_Dying/
About.com: http://www.about.com/

▪ To identify patterns or trends in the volume of "hits" on a topic

Google Trends: http://www.google.com/trends

▪ "Classic" Thanatology-related Sites with Multiple Hotlinks

http://www.trinity.edu/MKEARL/death.html
http://www.deathreference.com/

REFERENCES

Anderson, P. F., Allee, N., Grove, S., & Hill, S. (1999). *Web site evaluation checklist*. Retrieved July 25, 2011, from http://www-personal.umich.edu/~pfa/pro/courses/ WebEvalNew.pdf

Barrera, M., Jr., & Ainlay, S. L. (1983). The structure of social support: A conceptual and empirical analysis. *Journal of Community Psychology, 11*, 133–143.

Brain, J. L. (1979). *The last taboo: Sex and the fear of death*. Garden City, NY: Anchor Press/ Doubleday.

Cobb, S. (1976). Social support and health through the life course. In M. W. Riley (Ed.), *Aging from birth to death: Interdisciplinary perspectives* (pp. 93–106). Washington, DC: American Association for the Advancement of Science.

Gottlieb, B. H. (1978). The development and application of a classification scheme of informal helping behaviors. *Canadian Journal of Behavioral Science, 10*, 105–115.

House, J. S. (1981). *Work stress and social support*. Reading, MA: Addison-Wesley.

Jerome, R., Duignan-Cabrera, A., Arias, R., & Longley, A. (1996, August 5). Beyond sorrow. *People*, 36–41.

Kapoun, J. (1998, July/August). Teaching undergrads WEB evaluation: A guide for library instruction. *C&RL News*, 522–523.

Pattison, E. M. (1977). A theoretical–empirical base for social system therapy. In E. F. Foulks, R. M. Wintrob, J. Westermeyer, & A. R. Favazza (Eds.), *Current perspectives in cultural psychiatry* (pp. 217–253). New York, NY: Spectrum.

Schaefer, C., Coyne, J. C., & Lazarus, R. S. (1981). The health-related functions of social support. *Journal of Behavioral Medicine, 4*, 381–406.

Sofka, C. J. (1997). Social support "internetworks", caskets for sale, and more: Thanatology and the information superhighway. *Death Studies, 21*(6), 553–574.

Appendix B

Resources to Assist With Ethical Issues in Online Service Provision

Carla J. Sofka, Joyce Rasdall Dennison, and Louis A. Gamino

As noted in Chapter 14 by Gamino, the provision of grief counseling services via online technology raises a host of challenges and ethical issues that must be carefully considered and addressed. In 2003, Ragusea and VandeCreek noted considerable controversy regarding whether online therapy was ethical. In 2008, Centore and Milacci reported that individuals providing distance counseling through a variety of modalities perceived their "ability to fulfill ethical duties" to be decreased (p. 277). In 2010, Finn and Barak noted the continued lack of consensus about ethical obligations among individuals providing e-counseling. To provide guidance, several professions and organizations have created ethical standards designed to create an implied social contract with the public to "balance professional privilege with responsibility and a commitment to consumer welfare" (Koocher & Keith-Spiegel, p. 27). As noted by Shaw and Shaw (2006), "each time a new field in counseling is created, this delicate balance is challenged" (p. 41). Service providers must become familiar with the resources that have been developed to assist with these professional challenges and obligations. This appendix is designed to supplement Gamino's discussion with the following resources: (a) a brief summary of the technology-affiliated topics typically addressed within ethical codes designed for helping professionals (this includes a chart identifying sections of professional and organizational ethical guidelines that were specifically written for use while providing technology-assisted services; URLs for the complete guidelines are included) and (b) checklists to assist in the review of website and practitioner compliance with recommended ethical standards.

TECHNOLOGY-AFFILIATED TOPICS WITHIN ETHICAL CODES/PROFESSIONAL AND ORGANIZATIONAL ETHICAL GUIDELINES FOR TECHNOLOGY-ASSISTED SERVICE PROVISION

Providing services online requires a practitioner to carefully consider the ways in which the use of technology potentially alters one's ability to deliver services in a responsible and ethical manner. Documents from six professional organizations or associations that guide the provision of online services were identified during research for this appendix. Rather than include these documents in their entirety, a chart (see Figure 1) has been constructed that guides a reader to specific content within the organizations'/associations' documents that are readily available online at the URLs listed below the chart. The following organizations/associations are represented: the American Counseling Association, the American Mental Health Counseling Association, the Commission on Rehabilitation Counselor Certification, the International Society for Mental Health Counseling Association, the National Board for Certified Counselors, and the National Association of Social Workers/Association of Social Work Boards. The information in the chart is organized according to these categories: (a) the impact of technology on access to services; (b) potential risks and benefits (the appropriateness) of online services; (c) aspects of service provision that are unique when services are provided online; (d) issues related to the identity of the consumer or provider of services; (e) legal requirements to practice/issues related to jurisdiction; (f) components of technical competence; (g) privacy and confidentiality issues created by the use of technology; and (h) safety and emergency-related situations related to online practice.

In addition to remaining sensitive to the potentially prohibitive cost of computer equipment and access to online resources for some consumers (and advocating for assistance with access for those who may have no other alternative to receive services), practitioners must acknowledge that language and physical disability may also prevent access to online services for some individuals. Competence regarding cultural issues that may also influence access is crucial. All consumers of services should be informed of the potential risks and benefits of online services, and it goes without saying that professionals should receive specialized training in the provision of these services before advertising services that are provided in this manner. Practitioners should also anticipate and educate consumers about potential challenges that may arise when communication occurs without the benefit of nonverbal cues or in light of the possibility of a power outage that could prevent communication from occurring for an unknown period. Additional suggestions to manage the "anomalies" of online service provision are included in the checklist at the end of this appendix.

Consumers have the right to verify the identity of their service provider, and practitioners must make provisions to verify the identity of the consumer of services, including special permissions in the case of a minor. As noted previously

Figure B.1

Ethical Practice Online: Guidance from Professional Organizations and Associations

Organization or Professional Group	Ethical, Legal, or Skill-based Aspect of Online Practice							
	Factors Impacting Access to Services	Risks and Benefits (appropriateness) of Online Services	Unique Aspects of Online Process	Issues Related to Identity	Requirements to Practice / Jurisdiction	Technical Competence	Technology-related Privacy and Confidentiality Issues	Safety / Emergency Situations / Local Backup
ACA	A.12.d A.12.h6-7.	A.12.a-c.	A.12.g.10-11.	A.12.h3-5.	A.12.e. – f. A.12.g3.	A.12.f.	A.12.g.	A.12.g.1-3. A.12g.5-9. A.12.h.2
AMHCA	-	6c.	-	6a.	6d. – 6e.	-	6b.	6a.
CRCC	J.2	J.1, J.12	J.1	J.3.	J.7	J.1, J.4	J.3	J.10
ISMHO	-	1c. – 1d.	1a., 1e., 2c.	1b. & 1g.	2a. - 2g.	2a.	2f.	3a. - 3b.
NASW/ ASWB	2.	9.	9.	6.	1. & 5.	4.	7. - 8.	1.
NBCC	7. – 8.	-	3., 5., 9.	1.-2.	13.-14.	-	10. - 12.	6.

Each cell on this chart identifies the relevant section within each organization's ethics code addressing the specified topic. URLs for each organization are as follows:

American Counseling Association (ACA): http://www.counseling.org/Resources/CodeOfEthics/TP/Home/CT2.aspx

American Mental Health Counseling Association (AMHCA):

  https://www.amhca.org/assets/news/AMHCA_Code_of_Ethics_2010_w_pagination_cxd_51110.pdf

Commission on Rehabilitation Counselor Certification: https://www.crccertification.com/filebin/pdf/CRCC_COE_1-1-10_Rev12-09.pdf

International Society for Mental Health Online (ISMHO): https://www.ismho.org/suggestions.asp

National Association of Social Workers / Association of SW Boards (NASW/ASWB):

  http://www.socialworkers.org/practice/standards/NASWTechnologyStandards.pdf

National Board for Certified Counselors (NBCC): http://nbcc.org/Assets/Ethics/internetCounseling.pdf

by Gamino, "cyberspace is not a specific geographic location" (Chapter 14), and practitioners have a responsibility to fully investigate and communicate legal and jurisdictional aspects of the helping relationship that are impacted by this reality to the consumers they serve. On a disconcerting note, research indicates that there is no consensus, even considerable misunderstanding, regarding the role of jurisdiction in e-counselling, with 61% of the respondents in one study agreeing with the statement "People come to my virtual office so I am working in my own state" (Finn & Barak, 2010, p. 272).

Technical competence is a complex skill set, and practitioners have a responsibility to be personally well-versed with hardware and software-related issues or have a knowledgeable consultant readily available. Practitioners must also be able to vouch for the security of all aspects of the system that is used, protecting the privacy and confidentiality of all communications. Last, but certainly not least, the list of topics included in this chart involves issues of safety and having clearly defined strategies for managing emergency situations with local backup to assist in the event of a crisis.

With the proliferation of involvement on social networking sites by consumers and professionals alike, the issue of "dual relationships" should be briefly addressed. Practitioners have an ethical obligation to avoid involvement in relationships with consumers that "blur" professional boundaries.

Although not detailed in nature, three additional professional organizations have noted the importance of honoring standard ethical guidelines when delivering services using technology. The Association for Death Education and Counseling has a detailed code of ethics for work with thanatology-related issues that "applies across a variety of contexts, whether in person or by postal service, telephone, internet, and/or other electronic transmissions" (http://www.adec.org/Code_of_Ethics/1725.htm). Section IIIE of the Association for Death Education and Counseling Ethics Code also notes that "Members who offer services, products or information via electronic transmission inform their clients and students of the risks to privacy and the limits of confidentiality." Section B17 of the Canadian Counselling and Psychotherapy Association Code of Ethics states: "Counsellors follow all additional ethical guidelines for services delivered by telephone, teleconferencing and the Internet, including appropriate precautions regarding confidentiality, security, informed consent, records and counseling plans, as well as determining the right to provide such services in regulatory jurisdictions" (http://www.ccacc.ca/en/resources/codeofethics/). The American Psychological Association published a statement in 1997 (http://www.apa.org/ethics/education/telephone-statement.aspx) noting that their "Ethics Code is not specific with regard to telephone therapy or teleconferencing or any electronically provided services as such and has no rules prohibiting such services" and that "delivery of services by such media as telephone, teleconferencing and internet is a rapidly evolving area." The Ethics Committee recommends that psychologists follow Standard 1.04c, Boundaries of Competence, which indicates that "In those emerging areas in which generally recognized standards for preparatory training do not yet exist, psychologists nevertheless take reasonable steps to ensure the competence of their work and to protect patients, clients, students, research participants, and others from harm." The statement notes additional standards considered to be particularly relevant to this modality of service provision: 1.03, Professional and Scientific Relationship – 1.03, the Basis for Scientific and Professional Judgments 1.06, Describing the Nature and Results of Psychological Services – 1.07a, Avoiding Harm – 1.14, Fees and Financial Arrangements – 1.25, Assessment 2.01–2.10, Therapy 4.01–4.09, especially 4.01 Structuring the Relationship and 4.02 Informed Consent to Therapy, and Confidentiality 5.01–5.11. It is also noted that standards under Advertising, particularly 3.01– 3.03, merit special consideration. Psychologists are encouraged to review the characteristics of the services, the service delivery method, and the provisions for confidentiality, as well as licensure board rules governing this type of practice.

With the advent of "e-health" initiatives that blend the provision of informational support (see Appendix A) and the use of communication technologies in support of health and health-related fields, it is important to note the availability of three resources to assist with the ethical provision of e-health services. The first was written by the Internet Health Coalition, an international, nonpartisan, nonprofit organization dedicated to promoting quality health care resources on the Internet. The goal of the eHealth Code of Ethics is to "ensure that people worldwide can confidently and with full understanding of known risks realise the potential of the Internet in managing their own health and the health of those in their care" (http://www.ihealthcoalition.org/ ehealth-code/). This code highlights the following ethical principles: candor, honesty, quality of information and services, the right to informed consent, privacy, professionalism in the provision of online health care, responsible partnering, and accountability. The second—the HONcode—was written by the Health on the Net Foundation as a response to the lack of a guarantee for the quality of information found online and is based on eight essential ethical, quality and accessibility principles (http://www.hon.ch/Global/ copyright.html). A third example from the Health Internet Coalition (Hi-Ethics—http://www.wellspan.org/body.cfm?id=348) outlines 14 ethical principles to guide the provision of internet health services to consumers. Readers are encouraged to review these codes to assist with the evaluation of ethical issues regarding informational support online for health-related websites.

CHECKLISTS FOR WEBSITE AND PRACTITIONER COMPLIANCE WITH ETHICAL GUIDELINES

This appendix has summarized a wide range of factors that influence a practitioner's ability to deliver online services in an ethically responsible manner. To assist readers in honoring these ethical guidelines, two additional resources will be provided: (a) the Ethical Intent Checklist (Shaw and Shaw, 2006) and (b) an additional checklist compiled by Sofka for this appendix to assist with the provision of ethically responsible online services.

Concerned with the degree to which online service providers were complying with the ethical standards developed by the American Counseling Association for online counseling, Shaw and Shaw (2006) created a checklist that could be used to evaluate levels of compliance based on information that can be gathered from a practitioner's website (see Figure B.2). Based on information that has been gathered through a literature search for this appendix (e.g., Barnett & Scheetz, 2003; Fisher & Fried, 2003; Heinlen, Welfel, Richmond, & O'Donnell, 2003; Mallen, Vogel, & Rochlen, 2005; Haberstroh, Parr, Bradley, Morgan-Fleming, & Gee, 2008; Meshriy, 2009; Lehavot, Barnett, & Powers, 2010; Rummell & Joyce, 2010; Taylor, McMinn, Bufford, & Chang, 2010; Bradley, Hendricks, Lock, Whiting, & Parr, 2011; Ross, 2011) and professional experience, a practitioner checklist has been compiled by Sofka (See Figure B.3). To encourage ethical practices and the continued evaluation of compliance, both checklists are included.

Figure B.2   The Ethical Intent Checklist (Website Compliance) by Shaw and Shaw (2006)

Following are the 16 items that make up the Ethical Intent Checklist. In parenthesis after each item is the reference to the ACA (1999) standard or standards from which the item was derived.

1. Is the full name of counselor given? (Confidentiality: b.2., Professional Counselor Identification)

2. Does the site clearly identify the state from which they are operating? (Establishing the Online Counseling Relationship: d., Boundaries of Competence)

3. Are degrees listed? (Confidentiality: b.2., Professional Counselor Identification)

4. Are areas of study and university given for degrees? (Confidentiality: b.2., Professional Counselor Identification)

5. Is the address or the phone number of the counselor given for backup purposes? (Establishing the Online Counseling Relationship: c., Continuing Coverage)

6. When requesting client information, does the site require client's full name and address? (Must be a required field for client to fill in.; Confidentiality: b.3., Client Identification)

7. Does the site clearly state that clients must be 18 years or older or have consent of a legal guardian? (Establishing the Online Counseling Relationship: e., Minor or Incompetent Clients)

8. When requesting client information, does the site require client's age or birth date? (Must be a required field for client to fill in; Establishing the Online Counseling Relationship: e., Minor or Incompetent Clients)

9. Does the site have an intake that clients must fill out before counseling can begin? (Must be a required field for client to fill in; Establishing the Online Counseling Relationship: a., The Appropriateness of Online Counseling)

10. Does the site have a statement stating that online counseling is not the same as face-to-face counseling? (Establishing the Online Counseling Relationship: a., The Appropriateness of Online Counseling)

11. Does the site have a statement stating that not all problems are appropriate for online counseling? (Establishing the Online Counseling Relationship: a., The Appropriateness of Online Counseling)

12. Does the site refer clients to traditional forms of counseling, or provide other suggestions (crisis lines, etc.) for clients who are not deemed appropriate for online counseling? (Establishing the Online Counseling Relationship: b., Counseling Plans)

13. Does the site have a statement indicating that ensuring complete confidentiality over the Internet is not possible? (Confidentiality: a., Privacy Information)

14. Is e-mail secure via a Secure Sockets Layer (SSL) or via encryption software? (Confidentiality: a.1., Privacy Information, Secured Sites)

15. Does the site have a statement about conditions under which confidentiality must be breached for legal reasons? (Confidentiality: a.4, Privacy Information, Limits of Confidentiality)

16. Does the site have a waiver that clients must electronically sign or mail in before beginning counseling that specifically states the limits of ensuring confidentiality over the Internet? (Confidentiality: a.4., Limits of Confidentiality; Confidentiality: c., Client Waiver)

Figure B.3   Checklist for Ethical Practice Online

Competence (Professional, Technical, and Cultural)

Practitioner has:

□ current professional training/access to continuing education regarding online service provision
　　and computer-mediated communication
□ access to counsel to interpret relevant legal and jurisdictional statutes
□ up-to-date knowledge regarding technology issues relevant to the provision of online services
　　and/or access to an information technology professional
□ the knowledge and skills necessary to provide culturally-competent services

---

Consumer Access to Services

Practitioner has assessed for and worked to eliminate barriers to service:

□ financial	□ language-related / literacy-based
□ technical	□ cultural/ethnic
□ physical / ability-oriented	□ other

Consideration of the Unique Aspects of the Process of Online Service Provision

Consumer has been informed and educated about:

　　□ potential benefits and risks of receiving services online
　　　　□ appropriateness of service provision based on consumer needs has been determined
　　□ "netiquette" / strategies to facilitate effective online communication
　　□ the potential for challenges and misunderstandings in the absence of visual / non-
　　　　verbal cues; practitioner has invited consumer to directly address any concerns
　　□ the anticipated range of time within which a response from the practitioner will be sent

□ Messages to and from a consumer are sent with a "return receipt" requested to document
　　receipt of a communication

Safety / Emergency Situations / Local Backup

□ Emergency contact information has been provided to each consumer to facilitate receipt of
　　face-to-face services during a crisis
□ Local back-up service provider has been identified and approved by each consumer should the
　　practitioner decide that professional intervention is necessary;　policy regarding duty to
　　warn and duty to protect has been discussed

Emotional Safety in Online Services, Websites or in Chat Rooms / Community Discussion Forums

□ Webcams will only be used with prior consent of both consumer and professional;　decisions about
　　the presence or absence of video streaming should be made prior to the beginning of each contact

---

(continued)

Figure B.3 (*continued*)

Emotional Safety in Online Services, Websites or in Chat Rooms / Community Discussion Forums

☐ Professional or volunteer monitors have an obligation to screen postings or comments for appropriateness and to remove any postings that could be considered offensive or discriminatory

☐ Guidelines for chat rooms, bulletin boards, or community discussion forums should contain clear instructions that facilitate the following:
  ☐ non-judgmental communication
  ☐ creation of an environment of tolerance and acceptance of divergent points of view
  ☐ dialogue that is not value-laden or discriminatory in nature

☐ Proselytizing or harassment will not be tolerated and offensive comments will be removed / offending participants will be banned

---

Assessment of Non-Professional Online "Presence" and Practices

☐ Practitioner is mindful of the potential for "deprofessionalization" of communication and boundaries during e-mail exchanges and maintains professional style and boundaries

☐ Policy about "friending" consumers is communicated clearly; appropriate professional boundaries are maintained (also assess the appropriateness of contact with family, friends, or close acquaintances of consumers)

☐ Ethical principles of privacy and honesty should be carefully considered before seeking out information about consumers on social networking sites or other public websites

☐ Practitioner's profile settings and content posted on professional and non-professional social networking sites are "professionally" appropriate

☐ Practitioner will not participate in "sharking" or monitoring chat rooms and bulletin board services for the purpose of offering online services when no request has been made. This includes sending out mass unsolicited e-mails. Advertisement of services should only be done observing proper "netiquette" and standards of professional conduct.

Website Compliance with Ethical Guidelines / Truth in Advertising / Conflict of Interest Issues

Practitioner has:

☐ reviewed the website for compliance with all aspects of the Ethical Intent Checklist (Shaw and Shaw, 2006).

☐ ensured the accuracy of advertising /websites and public statements about online services offered

☐ posted clear information about fee structure and procedure for payment for services and has carefully considered billing practices (ethical billing procedures if conducting multiple online sessions during the same time period)

☐ utilized language that is compassionate, respectful, and acknowledges the unique and diverse experiences of all potential consumers

☐ noted any jurisdictional constraints on geographical locations for service provision

☐ carefully considered the implications of advertisements (if any) that are included on websites utilized for service provision

REFERENCES

Barnett, J. E., & Scheetz, K. (2003). Technological advances and telehealth: Ethics, law, and the practice of psychotherapy. *Psychotherapy: Theory, Research, Practice, and Training, 40*(1/2), 86–93.

Barros-Bailey, M., & Saunders, J. L. (2010). Ethics and the use of technology in rehabilitation counseling. *Journal of Applied Rehabilitation Counseling, 41*(2), 60–64.

Bradley, L. J., Hendricks, B., Lock, R., Whiting, P. P., & Parr, G. (2011). E-mail communication: Issues for mental health counselors. *Journal of Mental Health Counseling, 33*(1), 67–79.

Centore, A. J., & Millaci, F. (2008). A study of mental helath counselors' use of and perspectives on distance counseling. *Journal of Mental Health Counseling, 30*(3), 267–282.

Finn, J., & Barak, A. (2010). A descriptive study of e-counsellor attitudes, ethics, and practice. *Counseling and Psychotherapy Research, 10*(4), 268–277.

Fisher, C. B., & Fried, A. L. (2003). Internet-mediated psychological services and the American Psychological Association Ethics Code. *Psychology: Theory, Research, Practice, Training, 40*(1/2), 103–111.

Heinlen, K. T., Welfel, E. R., Richmond, E. N., & O'Donnell, M. S. (2003). The nature, scope, and ethics of psychologists' e-therapy web sites: What consumers find when surfing the web. *Psychotherapy: Theory, Research, Practice, Training, 40*(1/2), 112–124.

Koocher, G. P., & Keith-Spiegel, P. (2008). *Ethics in psychology and the mental health professions: Standards and cases* (2nd ed.). New York, NY: Oxford University Press.

Lehavot, K., Barnett, J. E., & Powers, D. (2010). Psychotherapy, professional relationships, and ethical considerations in the MySpace Generation. *Professional Psychology: Research and Practice, 41*(2), 160–166.

Mallen, M. J., Vogel, D. L., & Rochlen, A. B. (2005). The practical aspects of online counseling: Ethics, training, technology, and competency. *Counseling Psychologist, 33*(6), 776–818.

Meshriy, N. (2009). Technology in counseling. *Career Planning and Adult Development Journal, 25*(3), 82–88.

Ragusea, A. S., & VandeCreek, L. (2003). Suggestions for the ethical practice of online psychotherapy. *Psychotherapy: Theory, Research, Practice, Training, 40*(1), 94–102.

Ross, W. (2011). Ethical issues involved in online counseling. *Journal of Psychological Issues in Organizational Culture, 2*(1), 54–66.

Rummell, C. M., & Joyce, M. R. (2010). "So wat do u want to wrk on 2day?": The ethical implications of online counseling. *Ethics and Behavior, 20*(6), 482–496.

Shaw, H. E., & Shaw, S. F. (2006). Critical ethical issues in online counseling: Assessing current practices with an ethical intent checklist. *Journal of Counseling and Development, 84*(1), 41–53.

Taylor, L., McMinn, M. R., Bufford, R. K., & Chang, K. B. T. (2010). Psychologists' attitudes and ethical concerns regarding the use of social networking web sites. *Professional Psychology: Research and Practice, 41*(2), 153–159.

Index